M000311192

Social History of Canada

Craig Heron and Franca Iacovetta, general editors

The Patriots and the People: The Rebellion of 1837 in Rural Lower Canada

The Lower Canadian Rebellion of 1837 has been called the most important event in pre-Confederation history. Previously, it has been explained as a response to economic distress or as the result of manipulation by middle-class politicians. Lord Durham believed it was an expression of racial conflict.

The Patriots and the People is a fundamental reinterpretation of the Rebellion. Allan Greer argues that far from being passive victims of events, the habitants were actively responding to democratic appeals because the language of popular sovereignty was in harmony with their experience and outlook. He finds that a certain form of popular republicanism, with roots deep in the French-Canadian past, drove the anti-government campaign. Institutions such as the militia and the parish played an important part in giving shape to the movement, and the customs of the maypole and charivari provided models for collective action against local representatives of the colonial regime.

In looking closely into the actions, motives, and mentality of the rural plebeians who formed a majority of those involved in the insurrection, Allan Greer brings to light new causes for the revolutionary role of the normally peaceful French-Canadian peasant. By doing so he provides a social history with new dimensions.

ALLAN GREER is Associate Professor, Department of History, University of Toronto. His book *Peasant, Lord, and Merchant: Rural Society in Three Quebec Parishes, 1740–1840* won the Sir John A. Macdonald Prize for the best book in Canadian history in 1985.

ALLAN GREER

The Patriots and the People
The Rebellion of 1837 in Rural Lower Canada

UNIVERSITY OF TORONTO PRESS
Toronto Buffalo London

© University of Toronto Press Incorporated 1993
Toronto Buffalo London
Printed in Canada

ISBN: 0-8020-2792-X (cloth)
ISBN: 0-8020-6930-4 (paper)

Printed on acid-free paper

Canadian Cataloguing in Publication Data

Greer, Allan
The patriots and the people : the rebellion
of 1837 in rural Lower Canada

(The Social history of Canada : 49)
Includes index.
ISBN 0-8020-2792-X (bound) ISBN 0-8020-6930-4 (pbk.)

1. Canada – History – Rebellion, 1837–1838.
2. Habitants – Quebec (Province) – Political
activity.* I. Title. II. Series

CF452.G74 1993   971.03'8   C93-094402-X
F1032.G74 1993

Social History of Canada 49

This book has been published with the help of a grant from the
Social Science Federation of Canada, using funds provided by the
Social Sciences and Humanities Research Council of Canada.

To my parents

Contents

List of abbreviations

ACESH	Archives de la chancellerie de l'évêché de St-Hyacinthe
ACESJQ	Archives de la chancellerie de l'évêché de St-Jean-de-Québec
ANQ	Archives nationales du Québec, centre de Québec
ANQ, 1837	ANQ, Documents relatifs aux événements de 1837–1838
ANQM	Archives nationales du Québec, centre de Montréal
ANQM, gr.	notarial files (*greffes*)
BPP	Irish University Press Series, *British Parliamentary Papers*, Colonies, Canada
BRH	*Bulletin des recherches historiques*
CHA, *HP*	Canadian Historical Association, *Historical Papers*
CHR	*Canadian Historical Review*
DCB	*Dictionary of Canadian Biography*, 12 vols (Toronto: UTP 1966–)
JHALC	*Journals of the House of Assembly of Lower Canada*
NA	National Archives of Canada
PACR	Public Archives of Canada, *Report*
RAPQ	*Rapport de l'archiviste de la province de Québec*
RHAF	*Revue d'histoire de l'Amérique française*
UP	University Press
UTP	University of Toronto Press

Preface

I had in mind a much smaller book when I started out. Beginning with an interest in French-Canadian rural society, I thought that the rich documentation on the habitants who were swept up in the turmoil of revolution might shed light on long-standing social tensions and lines of solidarity in the Laurentian countryside. There was also the hope of some reciprocal effect: by looking into rural community life in the pre-Rebellion period, I might be able to contribute to a better understanding of the insurrection itself. In pursuing these modest aims, however, I gradually became aware that the 'masses' played a much more important role in the events of 1837–8 than historians had hitherto been prepared to admit. Further, it became apparent that this 'bottom-up' perspective on the Rebellion did not fit comfortably with the existing literature on the subject; rather, it indicated a need for extensive reconceptualizing of the historical phenomenon as a whole.

In practical terms, my research consisted of two stages. First, I looked for information on Rebellion-related events in the countryside, particularly in the District of Montreal, where most of the disturbances occurred. This was followed by a probe backwards into the cultural and political traditions of rural French Canada before 1837. Sources dealing with habitant actions during the crisis are abundant. They include literally thousands of depositions containing the testimony of witnesses and political prisoners. Many of these accounts have been examined by other researchers, though I did come across major deposits in previously unexploited collections such as the militia records and the correspondence of the civil secretary. This documentation required more than the usual care and critical scrutiny, since so much of the testimony came from individuals anxious to avoid severe punishment and through the medium of examining magistrates with their own particular outlook and agenda.

Even so, it did prove possible to reconstruct with some degree of certainty a number of incidents out of the turmoil of the summer and fall of 1837. It became clear that there was a certain form of popular republicanism, with roots deep in the French-Canadian past, that drove the anti-government campaign. Institutions like the militia and the parish played an important part in shaping the movement, and customs surrounding the charivari and the maypole provided models for collective action against local representatives of the colonial regime. My task was to survey the scattered and fragmentary evidence in an effort to learn more about these customs and institutions in earlier times. Through newspapers, government records, judicial archives, ecclesiastical correspondence, and private diaries, I managed to find out enough about these aspects of rural popular culture to make the behaviour of the rebels of 1837 somewhat less mysterious.

The approach outlined here is not the research strategy favoured by most students of popular participation in the Lower Canadian revolt. In so far as they wanted to know about the peasantry's role in 1837, historians have concentrated on the material circumstances of rural life. The impressive pioneering work of Fernand Ouellet is particularly noteworthy in this regard, but others, including those staunchly opposed to Ouellet's anti-patriot interpretation, have followed his lead in focusing on fluctuations in the agricultural economy, rural occupational structures, patterns of land-holding, and similar topics. The fruits of this approach have been abundant and valuable, but as a vehicle for understanding habitant politics, it is quite inadequate. There is a mechanical and deterministic quality to so much that is written in the socio-economic genre. Analysis seems to be based on the assumption that political attitudes and behaviour, in revolutionary periods as well as in 'normal' times, are the unmediated expression of class interests. Since wheat prices and property distribution are regarded as the keys to the kingdom, little attention is paid to what actually happened in 1837 and to the culture and experience through which the habitants made sense of, and took part in, the political crisis. Given the prevalence of this outlook, a seemingly self-evident point has to be made: to understand the habitants in the Rebellion, we must look at the habitants.

Of course, the peasantry was never a completely independent political force. Its intervention in 1837 took place mainly through a patriot movement that was dominated by a corps of politicians and journalists drawn primarily from the liberal professions. (I follow established convention in referring to this elite and to their parliamentary party as the 'Patriots' with a capital P; the rank and file and the larger movement are designated with the lower case.) Though they were not my main interest, I did have to come to terms with these middle-class radicals in the pages that follow. Inevitably, then, this book frequently ventures beyond the fields and villages of Lower Canada, and yet it makes no pretence of having dealt exhaustively with the events of 1837–8. Other researchers will have to tell us how things look from the perspective of the urban population, of the English speakers, of the aboriginal people, and of others.

Readers will note that I refer, in some places, to the 'events of 1837–8' and elsewhere to '1837.' The ambiguity stems from the fact that my coverage of the period is intentionally uneven. Lower Canada was in political crisis from the spring of 1837 until the winter of 1838–9, and there was fighting in November 1838 as well as in November–December 1837; although I give some attention to the entire period, the summer and autumn months of 1837 receive the lion's share of space. This is simply because they constitute, as far as the political engagement of the habitants is concerned, the most important, and most interesting, episode of the Rebellion period.

The organization of the book represents a compromise between the requirements of chronological order and those of thematic unity; like any compromise, it is less than perfect. The second half of the work is constructed as a narrative of sorts, with episodes from 1837 appearing more or less in chronological order; long digressions bring in any pre-Rebellion evidence that might shed light on the events under discussion. Chapter 6 discusses the issue of French-English conflict with particular reference to a July 1837 incident in which ethnic strife featured prominently. Misogynist outbursts connected with celebrations in August of Queen Victoria's coronation prompt a discussion in chapter 7 of the gender dimension of the Rebellion. Chapter 8 is about the revolutionary reconstitution of local communities in the autumn months. Anti-feudal tendencies began coming to the fore at this time; chapter 9 highlights these trends and traces their connection to pre-Rebellion debates about seigneurial tenure. In the tenth chapter we finally reach the armed encounters of November and December 1837, and chapter 11 takes the account through the repression and renewed insurrection of 1838.

Preceding this modified narrative are five chapters that might be considered 'background' material or, more precisely, subjects that seemed essential to an understanding of the peasants' role in the revolt but did not fit comfortably in any narrative framework. After an introduction, which places the Lower Canadian Rebellion in an international setting, chapter 2 surveys the social structure and agrarian economy of the countryside in the early nineteenth century. It is followed by two chapters devoted to the French-Canadian rural community, its customs, institutions, and local politics in the same period. Chapter 5 looks at the rise of the Patriot party and movement and examines the part it played in the political breakdown that plunged the province into a revolutionary crisis.

Acknowledgments

Parts of this book appeared in different form in three articles: 'La république des hommes: les Patriotes de 1837 face aux femmes,' *Revue d'histoire de l'Amérique française* 44 (Spring 1991): 507–28; 'From Folklore to Revolution: Charivaris and the Lower Canadian Rebellion of 1837,' *Social History* 15 (January 1990): 25–43; 'La rébellion de 1837–1838: une approche géographique,' *Cahiers de géographie du Québec* 33 (December 1989): 345–77 (co-authored with Léon Robichaud). Generous financial assistance came from the Social Sciences and Humanities Research Council, as well as the University of Toronto and the University of British Columbia. I was also lucky enough to be aided at various times by some exceptionally capable research assistants: Irshad Manji, Ed Montigny, Léon Robichaud, and Carolyn Podruchny. My research was facilitated also by the staff of the National Archives in Ottawa; Jim Burant did a great job locating pictorial materials. I am grateful to the Archives Nationales du Québec for making available microfilm copies of their rich collection of Rebellion documents. Special thanks also to the helpful archivists and chancellors of three Catholic diocesan archives: Maurice Demers of St-Jean-sur-Richelieu, Rachel Ayotte of St Jérôme, and Jean-Roch Choinière of St Hyacinthe.

Jean-Paul Bernard generously shared his extensive knowledge of the Rebellion with me. He also brought sources to my attention, as did Colin Coates, Louise Dechêne, Jean-Marie Fecteau,

Serge Gagnon, Peter Moogk, Sylvia Van Kirk, John Willis, and the late Elinor Senior. I am indebted to Bruce Curtis, Franca Iacovetta, Cecilia Morgan, Mariana Valverde, and Tom Wien for reading and commenting on various portions of the manuscript. Thanks also to Gerry Hallowell and Agnes Ambrus of the University of Toronto Press, who guided the work through the stages of publication, to Jerry Bannister, who prepared the index, and to Carolyn Podruchny, who took great pains in preparing the maps.

Finally, let me enter an affectionate word of appreciation to my family: my parents, Ralph and Ethel Greer, to whom this book is dedicated, my wife, Brenda Gainer, and my daughter, Eleanor Greer. Their support has made a difference to every page, every sentence, every word.

THE PATRIOTS AND THE PEOPLE

1

Introduction

The discontented intellectual with his soul searchings has attracted attention wholly out of proportion to his political importance, partly because these searchings leave behind them written records and also because those who write history are themselves intellectuals. It is a particularly misleading trick to deny that a revolution stems from peasant grievances because its leaders happen to be professional men or intellectuals.

Barrington Moore[1]

In 1837–8 Canada came as close to revolution as it ever would. The parliamentary régime had ceased to function in Lower Canada as a movement (the 'patriots') pushing in the direction of democracy and independence ran into a stone wall of British intransigence. Protest provoked repression which in turn led to deeper popular alienation. After assembling military forces from across British North America, the colonial government moved in November to arrest all the leading patriot agitators. The troops met resistance from local militias, and in small but sharply contested battles at St Denis, St Charles, and St Eustache, the patriots were defeated with the loss of about 250 lives. In the wake of this military action the constitution was suspended, as were most

1 Barrington Moore, *Social Origins of Dictatorship and Democracy: Lord and Peasant in the Making of the Modern World* (Boston: Beacon Press 1966), 480

civil liberties; villages were burned; hundreds of men were imprisoned and hundreds more driven into exile. Meanwhile, there were secondary risings in Upper Canada, though the government had little difficulty mastering them. Tensions remained high through 1838, and in November of that year, armed revolt broke out once again in Lower Canada. It was quickly crushed and the punishment that followed was even more severe than that meted out the previous year. By 1839 the province was again firmly under British control.

REBELLION OR REVOLUTION?

Because the colonial régime survived this ordeal and emerged triumphant at the end, English-Canadian historians feel justified in referring to this episode as the 'Rebellion(s).' The term, with its connotations of disobedience justly chastised, drips condescension. For the loyal Whigs and Tories who long dominated English accounts of the Canadian past, the patriots were nothing more than deluded troublemakers, and their revolt was simply an unfortunate diversion from the business of nation-making. Even the liberal minority report could muster sympathy for the patriots only by confusing their political program with that of the Upper Canadian Reformers and portraying the Rebellion as some sort of wake-up call to those in authority, alerting them to the need to grant responsible government to the Canadas and to be more patient with the French Canadians. Historians writing in French have been far less glib: many of them refer to the events of 1837–8 in vaguer, more neutral terms, such as 'les troubles.'[2]

2   The extensive literature on 1837–8 is surveyed in Jean-Paul Bernard's excellent historiographical essay, 'L'évolution de l'historiographie depuis les événements (1837–1982),' in *Les rébellions de 1837–1838: Les patriotes du Bas-Canada dans la mémoire collective et chez les historiens*, ed. Jean-Paul Bernard (Montreal: Boréal 1983), 11–61. See also, in the same collection, Jean-Paul Bernard: 'La mémoire actuelle des Patriotes,' 11–16; and Fernande Roy, '1837 dans l'oeuvre historique de trois contemporains des événements: Bibaud, Christie et Garneau,' 63–89.

Terminology is not really the issue (I shall bow to conventional 'Rebellion' usage), but I would like to suggest that Lower Canada experienced a classic revolutionary crisis.

This was, after all, the Euro-Atlantic world's 'Age of Revolution,' and no one in Lower Canada who could read a newspaper would have been unaware of this fact. The great American and French revolutions were still within living memory, and in the more recent past there had been major upheavals in France, Belgium, Poland, and other parts of Europe, as well as in almost all the countries of Latin America. Even Britain, whose politics were followed closely in the colony, had passed a Reform Bill in 1832 that according to early reports marked the dawn of a new era. Whereas contemporaries were highly conscious of the international context of Lower Canada's political turmoil, later historians have adopted a strangely insular approach with separate English-Canadian and French-Canadian versions. Events tend to be analysed in a strictly Quebec or strictly Canadian context, as though they bore no relation to other national-democratic risings of the period.[3]

I realize that the suggestion that the Rebellion of 1837–8 could in any way be compared to the American Revolution, the French Revolution, or even the German, Italian, or Hungarian revolutions of 1848, will provoke derisive laughter in some quarters. But this is not a point about scope or scale; I am not arguing that the Lower Canada's 'time of troubles' was as big, as bloody, as far-reaching in its challenge to the existing order, or as important in its influence on world history as any of these other events. After all, it occurred in a small (in population terms) and rather out-of-the-way colony, and it was crushed by a powerful opponent before the revolutionary process had gone very far. The significant parallels are of a different order. The economic circumstances of 1837, the social dynamics, and the political principles invoked all invite comparisons with other revolutions in

---

3 Allan Greer, 'Rebels and Prisoners: The Canadian Insurrections of 1837–38,' *Acadiensis* 14 (Autumn 1984): 137–45. Cf. E.J. Hobsbawm, *The Age of Revolution 1789–1848* (New York: Signet 1962).

the 'Atlantic world.' More to the point, events actually unfolded in Lower Canada according to a dialectical logic familiar to students of revolution.

A revolution is fundamentally a political phenomenon, one involving the breakdown of an existing régime, the mobilization of previously passive elements of the population, and widespread and rapid change in political attitudes and behaviour. Central to the whole process is the old order's loss of legitimacy and the attempt on the part of others to reconstitute legitimate rule on new foundations. As long as people consent to be governed by a given state – that is, as long as they accept the basic framework of government, though they may well detest the incumbents currently in office – one cannot really speak of a revolutionary situation. But if that assent is lost, and if new centres staking a serious claim to sovereign authority begin to emerge, then a revolutionary crisis is truly under way. Violent conflict is often a part of this process, but I would not consider it a defining feature of revolution. Consequently, we should avoid the tendency, common in the Canadian literature, to abstract episodes of fighting ('the rebellion') from the larger contest to recast the state; this approach downgrades everything but the clash of arms to the status of 'background.'

In the literature on 1837–8, voluntarist, indeed conspiratorial, approaches have proliferated, as if the object was to discover who decided to stage a rebellion and when they hatched their plot. But a revolution, even a short-lived and abortive one, is not the same as a coup d'état. It is not simply an attempt to change governments by extra-legal means, a singular act with an instigator, an objective, a strategic plan, and a win-or-lose outcome. Revolutionary crises are always more complex than that. Which is not to say that intentions, plans, even conspiracies, are not part of the revolutionary process. Nor is it to deny that attempts are made to unseat governments suddenly and by force; William Lyon Mackenzie led an attempted coup against Toronto in 1837, and the Lower Canadian patriots tried to seize power in November 1838. The point is that these episodes were not revolutions, but *parts* of a revolution. The actors involved were responding to an exceptional situation and their actions naturally provoked reactions on the part of opponents. No one decides to have a revolution. It is something that happens, independent of any individual will, as a result of the clash of various groups with different outlooks and changing assessments of a rapidly evolving situation.

To take seriously this concept of revolutionary crisis, we must look closely at the detailed succession of events in 1837. Historians preoccupied with the blood-and-gunpowder chapters of the story as well as those who focus primarily on the social, economic, and political antecedents of revolt generally gloss over the period of 'turmoil' that immediately preceded the recourse to arms.[4] Reference is sometimes made to the months of unrest that disturbed the Lower Canadian countryside in the summer and autumn of 1837, but the treatment is casual, schematic, and anecdotal, with incidents torn from any context that would make them comprehensible. The accent is on themes of 'anarchy' and 'confusion.' Unconsciously adopting the perspective of the military officer and the colonial official, historians imply that the situation was 'out of hand' and self-evidently needed to be brought under control. Such an account is partial in two senses of the word: not only does it take sides in the conflict, but it glosses over a crucial part of the drama of 1837. The aim in the chapters that follow will be to concentrate on the troubled months before the Battle of St Denis in order to sort out the moves and counter-moves, the actions, reactions, and interactions of the various groups and individuals involved.[5] This sort of narrative reconstruction, which tries to make sense out of the

---

4 This criticism would apply to two of the best books on the Rebellion: Fernand Ouellet, *Lower Canada 1791–1840: Social Change and Nationalism,* trans. Patricia Claxton (Toronto: McClelland and Stewart 1980); Elinor Senior, *Redcoats and Patriotes: The Rebellions in Lower Canada 1837–38* (Ottawa: Canada's Wings 1985).

5 This is the approach recommended by Jean-Marie Fecteau in an incisive, though unpublished paper, 'La mémoire d'un échec: sur l'analyse des Rébellions de 1837–38 au Bas-Canada,' presented to the annual meeting of the Institut d'histoire de l'Amérique française, 1987.

apparently meaningless jumble of evidence and events, is, after all, the basic task of historical interpretation.

Politics and events are of central importance – a proposition the historiography of an earlier generation never doubted for a moment – but this does not mean that the history of the Rebellion can be reduced to the history of politicians. Louis-Joseph Papineau, the Patriot orator, and other leaders of the educated middle class certainly receive in what follows the attention they deserve, but no more than that. The remarkable feature of a revolutionary situation is the sudden intrusion of 'the masses' into the political arena. Previously inarticulate and almost inert subordinate classes become politically active in new ways and in unprecedented numbers. (Not everyone joins the fray: even at the height of the French or the American revolutions most people seem, as far as possible, to have gone about their private business.[6]) Accordingly, the main focus of this study is the 'habitants,' the French-Canadian peasantry which, along with the associated classes of rural labourers and artisans, constituted the overwhelming majority of patriot insurgents in 1837–8.

The habitants were only peripherally involved at the beginning of the revolutionary period, but their importance increased as the crisis deepened. They acted, to a greater or lesser degree, under the tutelage of the bourgeois leaders who had always dominated the patriot movement; at no point did they constitute a fully independent political force. This low profile might have been grounds at one time for banishing them to the wings of the Rebellion drama. Since the writings of Antonio Gramsci have become available to English and French readers, however, there is little justification for such dismissive treatment of the 'subaltern classes.'[7] Gramsci insists that the ascendancy of one class over another – 'hegemony,' as he terms it – is always a reciprocal

6 A point emphasized in Richard Cobb, *Reactions to the French Revolution* (London: Oxford UP 1972).
7 *Selections from the Prison Notebooks of Antonio Gramsci*, ed. and trans. Quintin Hoare and Geoffrey Nowell Smith (New York: International Publishers 1971)

relationship. In plain words, although leaders may have the initiative, followers can decide how, or indeed whether, to follow; the leaders' awareness of the need to secure the voluntary cooperation of underlings tends to affect the style and direction of leadership. Hegemony has a cognitive dimension as well. A group such as the Lower Canadian habitants might well receive their news and information about the wider world from doctors and notaries, and in the process they might imbibe the political doctrines of the latter. Nevertheless, they will inevitably tend to transform these facts and theories as they integrate them with their own distinctive outlook and experience. Thus, when country folk seem to be parroting the views and doing the political bidding of their more educated 'betters,' we must be alert to the possibility that, at least to some degree, they are making sense of the world in their own way and acting in their own interests.

How do we then gain access to the motives and consciousness of lower-class rebels when they so seldom leave the diaries and letters that help historians chart the participation of elite figures? Poorly documented, rank-and-file insurgents are also simply too numerous to be dealt with easily by traditional methods. Statistics from arrest records, censuses, and other quantifiable sources can be helpful, as long as statistical abstractions do not cause us to lose sight of the human complexity of the situation. There is always the danger, in this sort of approach, of ignoring or slighting what is not measurable. Certainly it is valuable to know something about the profile, in terms of wealth, sex, age, and language, of arrested rebels and active loyalists. But what constitutes a 'rebel' or a 'loyalist' in a given time or place? Once again, it is only through close attention to *what actually happened* over the course of the crisis that we can make any sense of the contingent and ideologically charged categories into which numerical data have been placed.

The habitants of Lower Canada are not the only tillers of the soil ever to play a part in a revolutionary upheaval. Before turning to the Rebellion and to their role in it, we might usefully sample the rich international literature on revolution and the peasantry.[8] Such an exercise helps to put things in perspective and suggest avenues of enquiry.

PEASANTS IN REVOLUTION

Agrarian risings have been a part, frequently the crucial part, in most revolutions known to history. In pre-industrial settings peasants typically form the majority of the population, and so in

---

8 One of the most influential works in this connection was Moore, *Social Origins of Dictatorship and Democracy.* Other important syntheses that adopt an ambitious global perspective are Eric Wolf, *Peasant Wars of the Twentieth Century* (New York: Harper & Row 1969); E.J. Hobsbawm, 'Peasants and Politics,' *Journal of Peasant Studies* 1 (October 1973): 3–22; and Theda Skocpol, *States and Social Revolutions: A Comparative Analysis of France, Russia, and China* (Cambridge: Cambridge UP 1979). More specialized monographs and collections that I have found particularly useful: Georges Lefebvre, *Les paysans du Nord pendant la Révolution Française* (Paris: Armand Colin 1924); Georges Lefebvre, 'The French Revolution and the Peasants,' in *The Economic Origins of the French Revolution*, ed. R.W. Greenlaw (Boston: Beacon 1958); Boris Porchnev, *Les soulèvements populaires en France de 1623 à 1648* (Paris: SEVPEN 1963); Charles Tilly, *The Vendée* (Cambridge, Mass: Harvard UP 1964); John Womack, *Zapata and the Mexican Revolution* (New York: Harper & Row 1968); Roland Mousnier, *Peasant Uprisings in Seventeenth-Century France, Russia, and China*, trans. Brian Pearce (New York: Harper & Row 1970); Teodor Shanin, *The Awkward Class: Political Sociology of Peasantry in a Developing Society: Russia 1910–1925* (Oxford: Oxford UP 1972); Rodney Hilton, *Bond Men made Free: Medieval Peasant Movements and the English Rising of 1381* (London: Temple Smith 1973); Henry A. Landsberger, ed., *Rural Protest: Peasant Movements and Social Change* (London: Macmillan 1974); Jean Chesneaux, *Peasant Revolts in China 1840-1949*, trans. C.A. Curwen (New York: Norton 1973); James C. Scott, *The Moral Economy of the Peasant: Rebellion and Subsistence in Southeast Asia* (New Haven: Yale UP 1976); Maurice Agulhon, *The Republic in the village: The People of the Var from the French Revolution to the Second Republic*, trans. Janet Lloyd (Cambridge: Cambridge UP 1982); Samuel Clark and James S. Donnelly, ed., *Irish Peasants: Violence and Political Unrest 1780-1914* (Madison: University of Wisconsin Press 1983); Robert P. Weller and Scott E. Guggenheim, ed., *Power and Protest in the Countryside: Studies of Rural Unrest in Asia, Europe, and Latin America* (Durham: Duke UP 1983); Alan Knight, *The Mexican Revolution*, 2 vols (Cambridge: Cambridge UP 1986)

times of emergency and political breakdown their potential power becomes a factor of real significance. But why do peasantries revolt in some places and at some times, while in others they remain docile? One might think that hunger and deprivation would be the trigger setting off an explosion of desperate violence. The fact is, however, that rural insurrections rarely occur in times of famine; despondency and migration seem to be the more common responses to severe economic distress. Is it oppression, then, that drives cultivators to resist their rulers? Certainly this can be a factor. But some degree of oppression and exploitation is the common experience of all peasantries; it is indeed part of the definition of the word peasant. Besides, for every peasant group that rose in revolt, one could always point to another, even more ground down, that remained quiet. Obviously people get used to long-standing inequities, even if they do not actually approve of them. There are likely to be social tensions in any rural society where the primary producers (i.e., the peasantry) have to turn over some of the fruits of their labour to a superior class, but only under very special conditions will this relationship produce any sort of revolutionary eruption.

Commonly rural folk are roused by some external stimulus: a breakdown of constituted authority or an even more subtle change in the atmosphere. Rumours may reach the countryside of impending land reform; there may be a change in government; or an army may unexpectedly appear on the horizon. In a context of pre-existing social tensions and imperfect information, local peasants would typically experience great hopes and intense fears, making them more prone than usual to undertake collective action. Any weakness or division among the rulers who normally dominate them would favour insurrection. Something more is needed. Whether it is to petition the king, to sue the landlord, or to take up the sword of civil war, concerted action requires some sort of collectivity, and this cannot be conjured out of nothing on the spur of the moment. Groups that have not acquired some sort of 'culture of solidarity,' that is, habits, attitudes, traditions, and institutions of cooperation, are normally doomed to political impotence.

The circumstances of rural life do not always foster such unity. Unlike sailors on a ship or workers in a factory, peasants do not usually work closely with their fellows. Karl Marx remarked on the lack of cohesion of the French peasantry in the mid-nineteenth century in a well-known but frequently misunderstood passage:

The small-holding peasants form a vast mass, the members of which live in similar conditions but without entering into manifold relations with one another. Their mode of production isolates them from one another instead of bringing them into mutual intercourse ... Each individual peasant family is almost self-sufficient; it itself directly produces the major part of its consumption and thus acquires its means of life more through exchange with nature than in intercourse with society. A small holding, a peasant and his family; alongside them another small holding, another peasant and another family. A few score of these make up a village, and a few score of villages make up a Department. In this way, the great mass of the French nation is formed by simple addition of homologous magnitudes, much as potatoes in a sack form a sack of potatoes.[9]

Hostile commentators have tried to make of this last sentence a contemptuous put-down of all peasants, but it is nothing of the sort. On the very next page of *The Eighteenth Brumaire*, Marx goes on to draw a distinction between the passive, conservative peasantry of 1851 and the active, revolutionary peasantry of other periods of French history; he refers to 'the peasant that strikes out beyond the condition of his social existence, the small holding' and to 'the country folk who, linked up with the towns, want to overthrow the old order through their own energies.'[10] Marx does not go into the question of what accounts for the very different political stances of the incoherent peasant aggregate of

9 Karl Marx, *The Eighteenth Brumaire of Louis Bonaparte* (Moscow: Progress 1934), 105–6
10 Ibid., 107

1851 and the anti-seigneurial insurgents of 1789. Indeed, he is probably guilty of considerable oversimplification in his treatment of the country folk of mid-nineteenth century France. Yet he does point the way to a fruitful line of enquiry. What makes some peasantries into potent political and even revolutionary forces? How do rustic people ever overcome the tendency to familial isolation inherent in agrarian life and fight together in a common cause?

Historians and social scientists who have looked more closely at agrarian revolts have generally found that they were the work of peasants who had close ties with their neighbours. James Scott argues, on the basis of research on the peasantries of modern southeast Asia, that cultivators were much less atomized than they seemed: 'A host of informal connections, including local markets, kinship ties, communal rights, religious sects, and pilgrimages, and patterns of petty trading and labor migration have typically provided the social grid for mutual action.'[11] Research on western peasants often emphasizes the way agricultural production was organized so as to require a degree of collective management. In some areas institutions of local self-government gave villagers experience in community affairs. Finally, in Europe and America as well as in Asia the informal sociability that is sometimes called 'popular culture' brought peasants together in festivals, dances, and sports. It is quite dangerous to suggest any strict and direct connection between the institutions of agrarian life and the revolutionary potential of a particular peasantry, but it is worth looking more closely at these cultural traditions that brought some peasants together and helped to equip them for political action.

Regimes of open-field agriculture like those prevalent in the northern half of France and through much of western Europe in the medieval and early modern period certainly fostered habits

11 James Scott, 'Hegemony and the Peasantry,' *Politics and Society* 7 (1977): 270. See also David Sabean, 'The Communal Basis of Pre-1800 Peasant Uprisings in Western Europe,' *Comparative Politics* 8 (April 1976): 355–64.

of joint action at a local level.[12] Under this system the lands belonging to an entire village were divided into three giant fields for purposes of crop rotation. Everyone's cows and sheep were tended by the local herdsman who set them to graze on the fallow or on the stubble of recently harvested grain fields. Thus a limited territory could be made to grow as much grain as possible while still supporting large numbers of domestic animals. The open-field system did not imply communal ownership of land or animals. Although there were no fences within each field, wooden stakes divided each field into narrow strips which were the property of individual peasant families. Yet it did require collective management of agriculture. Villagers had to agree, for example, on when to plough and when to reap; they also had to make arrangements for the pasturing of animals. No doubt there were often disagreements and bickering, especially since most communities were home to landless cottagers as well as to rich and poor peasants. Still, the people of a village did have to work out practical means of settling their differences in the common interest, and such experience could have been only an asset when they were faced with a crisis in relations with external powers.

Throughout its history Russia has been rocked by recurrent peasant insurrections, and these experiences played an important part in the revolutions of 1905 and 1917. Historians have suggested a connection between this turbulence and an agricultural and land-holding pattern that demanded a very close association of villagers. The *mir*, found in large areas of Russia, was an ancient institution of community self-management, which had as its function the periodic redistribution of peasant holdings in such a way as to equalize property to some degree. Villagers met from time to time, discussed issues, came to decisions by consensus, and enforced the will of the *mir*. This was a form of organization that could be and was employed for revolutionary action

12 Marc Bloch, *French Rural History: An Essay on Its Basic Characteristics*, trans. Janet Sondheimer (Berkeley: University of California Press, 1966), 167–89

under certain circumstances. Indeed some argue that the rural soviets of 1917 were simply the *mir* operating under a different name.[13]

In the very different rural society of colonial New England there were also institutions of local self-management, notably the township. A place of religious worship, an agency for distributing land, and a unit of local government, the town administered its affairs through meetings of the inhabitants and elected officers.[14] Modern historians hesitate to call the township a democratic institution, since it was so often dominated by a small section of the community. Nevertheless, it did provide a forum for agitation and a framework for organizing political action at the time of the American Revolution and during earlier crises.

India, by way of contrast, has long had a highly segmented rural society with a peasantry divided by religion and caste. Accordingly, agrarian revolts, though by no means absent from Indian history, have been less significant than they have in China, Russia, or early modern Europe.[15] This is true in spite of the fact that the rural people of the subcontinent have suffered poverty, exploitation, and oppression that could be considered ample motives for revolt.

Around the world country folk have frequently been known to

13 Wolf, *Peasant Wars*, 89
14 There are many good monographs on New England townships; three of the most important are Sumner Chilton Powell, *Puritan Village: The Formation of a New England Town* (New York: Anchor Books 1965); Kenneth A. Lockridge, *A New England Town: The First Hundred Years: Dedham, Massachusetts, 1636–1736* (New York: Norton 1970); Robert A. Gross, *The Minutemen and their World* (New York: Hill and Wang 1976).
15 Eric Stokes, *The Peasant and the Raj: Studies in Agrarian Society and Peasant Rebellion in Colonial India* (Cambridge: Cambridge UP 1978); idem, *The Peasant Armed: The Indian Revolt of 1857* (Oxford: Clarendon Press 1986); A.R. Desai, ed., *Peasant Struggles in India* (Delhi: Oxford UP 1979). Joseph Tharamangalam has challenged the widely held view that the Indian peasantry was less rebellious than many others; he insists that, in the twentieth century at least, agrarian risings have been numerous and significant. See 'Review Article: Indian Peasant Uprisings: Myth and Reality,' *Journal of Peasant Studies* 13 (April 1986): 116–34.

take up arms on their own and for strictly agrarian motives, in which case the resulting clash is often called a 'jacquerie.' Usually these outbursts are localized and short-lived unless, for example, in the case of the German Peasant War of 1525, townspeople and disaffected members of the aristocratic class join the insurrection.[16] More relevant to our purposes are the instances where peasants become involved in revolutionary conflagrations originating outside their immediate world. Teodor Shanin, a Russian specialist, puts it this way: 'When non-peasant social forces clash, when rulers are divided or foreign powers attack, the peasantry's attitude and action may well prove decisive. Whether this potential is realized is mainly dependent upon the peasants' ability to act in unison, with or without formal organization.'[17]

THE HABITANTS AND THE REBELLION

The French-Canadian habitants thus seem unlikely rebels. Next to the rural societies mentioned above, the peasantry of Lower Canada seems at first glance singularly bereft of everything that binds communities together and gives them a basis for political action. Habitant agriculture had nothing of the ingrained collectivism embodied in the open-field system; every farm, with its grain fields, pastures, and meadows, was self-contained and surrounded by fences. There were common pastures in a few places, but they were not widely used. Much more than in most contemporary agrarian societies, the farm work force and the family coincided. Furthermore, there are few traces of anything resembling the 'bees' that brought neighbours together for big jobs in the frontier settlements of nineteenth-century English America. If habitants needed help to raise a barn, they apparently called on relatives or hired help. Neither did Lower Canadians

---

16 Frederick Engels, *The Peasant War in Germany* (New York: International 1926); Peter Blickle, *The Revolution of 1525: The German Peasants' War from a New Perspective*, trans. T.A. Brady and H.C.E. Midelfort (Baltimore: Johns Hopkins UP 1981)
17 Teodor Shanin, as quoted in Skocpol, *States and Social Revolutions*, 112

live huddled together in villages; they built their dwellings out in the 'rangs' (rows of farms), each on its own farmstead. On the other hand, because the lots were long and narrow, houses were not very far from their neighbours. Still, it must be said that the geography of settlement and the organization of agriculture in rural French Canada was individualistic rather than integrative.

An examination of institutional life suggests similar conclusions. Aside from the parish, there were no units of local administration in the Lower Canadian countryside, nothing resembling even the French commune, much less the Russian *mir* or the New England township. This situation existed partly because neither the French nor the British government attempted to impose direct taxes on the Canadian peasantry; there was no need, therefore, for the local administrations required elsewhere for fiscal purposes. The absence of municipal institutions (in the cities as well as the country until about the time of the Rebellion) was in fact part of a deliberate policy of preventing the development of centres of power that might rival the central colonial administration. This policy began under the centralizing monarchy of Louis XIV, and later British governors found no reason to abandon it. French and British rulers certainly did not present the habitants of Canada with much in the way of community institutions that they might use for their own purposes. In so far as they provided any administration in the countryside, it was through agents like militia captains, who were supposed to be servants of the crown, not of the population.

Indeed the French-Canadian peasantry resembled nothing so much as 'potatoes in a sack,' living and working in self-contained family units and enjoying few community institutions. They had never been known for anti-government militancy or violent collective action. 'They are quiet and obedient subjects,' wrote a smug British visitor in 1810, 'because they feel the value and benefit of the government under which they live.'[18] Even on the

18 John Lambert, *Travels through Lower Canada, and the United States of North America, in the years 1806, 1807, and 1808* (1810), as quoted in Yves Zoltvany, ed., *The French Tradition in North America* (Vancouver: Fitzhenry & Whiteside 1969), 224

very eve of the Rebellion, the colony's governor took a similar line in reassuring his superiors: 'Indeed where there is a population so disposed to habits of peace & industry, we have the strongest assurance that order & tranquility will be maintained.'[19]

It is true that in the eighteenth century under the French régime, as well as after the British conquest, there had been demonstrations, petitions, riots, and incidents of passive resistance. By such means the supposedly humble subjects of the king, who had few authorized outlets to express disapproval of their rulers, were able to assert their rights and oppose unpopular measures like food rationing and forced contributions for road-building. The most serious incidents occurred in 1775–6 during the American War of Independence, when the continental army invaded and occupied most of the colony outside the walls of Quebec City. From the outset the habitants resisted the militia call-up that would have forced them to fight the invaders, and after the partial defeat of the British forces, there were risings in many rural communities against the exactions of government, clergy, seigneurs, and merchants.[20] Yet while it is important to take note of this record of popular mobilization and direct action, it is equally vital not to exaggerate its scale. By the standards of early modern Europe and America, French Canada in the two centuries preceding the outbreak of the Rebellion was a remark

19 Gosford to Colonial Secretary, 26 December 1836, as quoted in S.D. Clark, *Movements of Political Protest in Canada 1640–1840* (Toronto: UTP 1959), 288
20 Terence Crowley, ' "Thunder Gusts": Popular Disturbances in Early French Canada,' CHA, HP, 1979, 11–31; Abbé H.-A. Verreau, *Invasion du Canada par les américains* (Montreal: Eusèbe Sénécal 1873); Clark, *Movements of Political Protest*, 75–102; Gustave Lanctot, *Canada and the American Revolution 1774–1783*, trans. Margaret Cameron (Toronto: Clarke, Irwin 1967), 108–23; John E. Hare, 'Le comportement de la paysannerie rurale et urbaine de la région de Québec pendant l'occupation américaine 1775–1776: note de recherche,' in *Mélanges d'histoire du Canada français offerts au professeur Marcel Trudel* (Ottawa: Editions de l'Université d'Ottawa 1978), 145–50

ably quiet place with only a few comparatively minor riots and revolts troubling its internal peace.[21]

Thus it was a great surprise to many when the habitants came bursting onto the scene with such force in 1837. They found themselves thrust to the fore in the course of a political crisis they themselves did not intiate (see below, chap. 5). In view of what has just been said, the really interesting and challenging question is not *why*, but *how*, the habitants managed to break out of their atomized isolation and become a significant political force. There must have been some basis for concerted action, and it could not have grown up overnight. Perhaps the quiet and uneventful record of civil peace in the countryside before that date was evidence not of habitant weakness and passivity, as colonial officials told themselves, but of strength that had never really been put to the test. As part of an attempt to address this issue, chapters 3 and 4, below, will examine habitant popular culture, the Lower Canadian rural community, and its 'small-p political' life. The aim will be to discover whether there was anything more than an old burlap sack holding these potatoes together.

Before proceeding to these subjects, we first need to attend to more down-to-earth matters. The next chapter will therefore examine the social and economic contours of the Lower Canadian countryside in an effort to appreciate the material circumstances of habitant life. It will also provide an occasion to test the validity of the economic interpretation of the Rebellion.

21 Cf. George Rudé, *The Crowd in History: A Study of Popular Disturbances in France and England, 1730-1848* (London: John Wiley and Sons 1964); Pauline Maier, 'Popular Uprisings and Civil Authority in Eighteenth-Century America,' in *Colonial America: Essays in Politics and Social Development*, ed. Stanley N. Katz, 2nd edn (Boston: Little, Brown 1971), 423–52.

2

Rural society and the agrarian economy

Eighteen thirty-seven was not a good year for the Lower Canadian peasantry; times had been hard for several years, but in the previous autumn grain harvests collapsed totally in many parts of the province. The new year had scarcely begun when word reached Quebec City of the 'frightening misery' prevailing in communities such as Trois-Pistoles in the lower St Lawrence: 'It is so bad that several farmers are eating their horses. There have been no crops for four years and many people haven't even a potato. The most well-off barely have enough for themselves and their families, even living very sparingly. What will become of all these poor unfortunates between now and May? It is torture to think about it. It is certain that many of them will die of hunger, unless aid comes at once.'[1] Desperate parishes, where fall frost had destroyed wheat crops, besieged the government with petitions for assistance to allow families to purchase seed for the following year. From Les Eboulements came the report that many families had left their homes to beg for bread, while those who remained, 'threatened with the horrors of the most frightful famine ever to afflict Les Eboulements,' faced 'certain death' if

---

1 *Le Canadien*, 9 January 1837, as quoted in Fernand Ouellet, *Economic and Social History of Quebec, 1760–1850: Structures and Conjonctures* (Toronto: Macmillan 1980), 426

they received no aid.[2] Is this the key to understanding the habitants' insurrection? Did famine and economic disaster force a
peaceable peasantry to abandon reason and habitual docility,
leaving it half-crazed and utterly lacking defences against the
siren song of revolution?

Apparently the Canadian Rebellion took place, as did the great
European revolutionary waves of 1789, 1830, and 1848, at a time
of acute economic distress. Not only was there disarray in the
colony's agriculture, but a financial collapse originating in the
United States plunged the province's business community into
chaos. Montreal and Quebec banks suspended payments in May
1837.[3] Merchants and labourers, farmers and doctors all must
have felt the pinch of depression in 1837, and no doubt the effect
was to accentuate class strife and place severe burdens on the
state and other institutions designed to contain conflict. Such
circumstances certainly go a long way towards explaining the
timing of the political crisis. But do economic factors account for
the participation of the habitants and for the forms that participation took?

Among those who have examined the economic background
of rural revolt in Lower Canada, two major schools of thought
have emerged. The first was sketched out by the geographer,
W.H. Parker.[4] Parker argued that the failure of Lower Canadian
wheat harvests, beginning only a few years before the insurrection, constituted an 'agricultural revolution,' which somehow
(and here the argument gets murky) underlay political disaffec-

---

2 NA, LC Civil Secretary, 523: 13, petition of 139 residents of Les Eboulements,
  2 November 1837 (author's translation). Cf. ibid., 528: 88, Ste Agnès (Saguenay); ibid., 528: 125, Malbaie, 26 December 1837; ibid., 532: 128, Les Eboulements, 23 March 1838.
3 Ouellet, *Economic and Social History*, 422–4
4 W.H. Parker, 'A Revolution in the Agricultural Geography of Lower
  Canada 1833–1838,' *Revue canadienne de géographie* 11 (1957): 189–94; idem,
  'A New Look at Unrest in Lower Canada in the 1830's,' *CHR* 40 (September
  1959), reprinted in, *Constitutionalism and Nationalism in Lower Canada*, ed.
  Ramsay Cook (Toronto: UTP 1969), 58–66

tion. The fact that, according to Parker, the French-Canadian habitants had previously known 'ease and abundance' only accentuated the politically explosive impact of the distress of the mid-1830s. A second position, based on a much more thorough examination of the Lower Canadian economy, has since been proposed by Fernand Ouellet.[5] For Ouellet, the bad harvests of the 1830s represented, not a sudden reverse, but rather the culmination of several decades of economic decline for a peasantry that had stubbornly refused all opportunities to modernize. (Curiously, Ouellet refers to this long-drawn-out disaster as an 'agricultural crisis,' whereas that term seems more suited to Parker's interpretation.) His is a more ambitious attempt to subordinate political unrest to economic failure; step by step, he charts the parallel progress from 1805 onwards of political mobilization and deepening agrarian malaise.

For all their differences, Ouellet and Parker share a common view of the causes of rural insurrection. Both scholars see deprivation, if not necessarily hunger in the literal sense, as the fundamental factor activating the peasant rebels of 1837. Before accepting this economic pathology of rebellion, we must look once more at the issues involved. Was the rural rising of 1837 in any sense the product of material deprivation? If so, how and why exactly did distress translate into revolt? Had the rural masses been ground down by economic difficulties that spanned an entire generation, or was the sudden crisis of the 1830s an unprecedented affliction? Did the agrarian misery – whether acute or long-term – affect the entire Lower Canadian peasantry uniformly? If not, was it the most distressed who took up arms? To answer these questions we shall have to begin with a brief sketch of the enduring features of rural French Canada's social and

---

5 See, especially, Ouellet, *Economic and Social History*. Further developments of Ouellet's thesis can be found in his *Eléments d'histoire sociale du Bas-Canada* (Montreal: Hurtubise 1972) and *Lower Canada 1791–1840: Social Change and Nationalism*, trans. Patricia Claxton (Toronto: McClelland and Stewart 1980).

economic structures. Later we can examine the changes, stresses, and strains that emerged during the decades leading up to the Rebellion. Within this general context it will then be possible to begin differentiating to see whether the economic problems of individuals and regions most closely implicated in the insurrection were particularly severe.

SOCIAL AND ECONOMIC CONDITIONS

Lower Canada might be characterized as a 'pre-industrial society,' which is merely to say that in its essential features it resembled other societies of the period (not including the hunting and gathering peoples and the industrializing regions of Great Britain). Accordingly, most people (89 per cent in 1831) lived in the countryside, and agriculture was by far the most important productive activity. Patterns were set in the seventeenth century, when French settlers carved family farms out of the forests of the St Lawrence valley and emerged as a peasantry not unlike that of old-régime Europe.[6] By the early nineteenth century there was a well-established rural society, numerically dominated by peasants (or 'habitants,' as they were called). Habitants lived upon their own self-contained farms, working as a family labour force to maintain themselves by raising the grains and vegetables, the cattle and pigs they needed for family consumption. To speak of the peasant family household as though it was an indivisible atomic particle is rather misleading when we know that it was made up of men, women, and children with divergent responsibilities, interests, and powers, and yet this was the fundamental productive unit. The habitant economy tended to be organized primarily around the principle of household self-sufficiency, although it was far from a self-contained régime of autarchy. Usually there was a surplus for sale and to acquit obligations to superior classes.

6 Louise Dechêne, *Habitants et marchands de Montréal au XVIIe siècle* (Paris and Montreal: Plon 1974)

Indeed, the habitants still had to contend with the feudal exactions of seigneurs and priests. Most of the agricultural areas of Lower Canada, that is, virtually all the territories settled by the French Canadians, had been granted as seigneuries before the conquest. All habitant farms thus were subject to a variety of dues and restrictions, most notably the 'cens et rentes' (an annual rent in money, produce, and/or labour), the 'lods et ventes' (mutation fine, one-twelfth of the purchase price of lands and improvements), and 'banalité' (seigneurial mill monopoly). As residents of a Catholic parish, cultivators were also required to pay a tithe amounting to the twenty-sixth part of their harvests. The economic weight of these seigneurial and ecclesiastical dues may not have been as great as those that ground down the peasantries of many parts of old-régime Europe, but they were still onerous. Certainly the habitants took them seriously when the Rebellion presented them with an opportunity to call for their elimination.

Stable in some of its essential characteristics, it was by no means a stagnant society. If we turn now to the dynamic features of the rural landscape, the patterns of social and economic change in the half-century or so leading up to the Rebellion, we enter troubled historiographical waters. Perhaps because of its bearing on explanations of political conflict, the evolution of French-Canadian rural society from about the 1790s to the 1830s has been the subject of extensive research and acrimonious debate in the years since Parker and Ouellet first set out their respective positions.[7] While some historians have portrayed the

---

7 In addition to the works by Ouellet and Parker cited above, see Maurice Séguin, *La Nation 'canadienne' et l'agriculture (1760–1850): essai d'histoire économique* (Trois-Rivières: Boréal 1973); Gilles Paquet and Jean-Pierre Wallot, 'Le Bas-Canada au début du XIXe siècle: une hypothèse,' *RHAF* 25 (1971): 39–61; idem, 'Crise agricole et tensions socio-ethniques dans le Bas-Canada 1802–1812: éléments pour une réinterprétation,' *RHAF* 26 (1972): 185–207; idem, 'Sur quelques discontinuités dans l'expérience socio-économique du Québec: une hypothèse,' *RHAF* 35 (1982): 483–521; T.J.A. LeGoff, 'The Agricultural Crisis in Lower Canada, 1802–12: A Review of a Controversy,' *CHR* 55 (March 1974): 1–31; R.C. Harris and John Warkentin, *Canada Before Con-*

Lower Canadian countryside in nothing but the sombrest hues, others paint a bright tableau of prosperity and progress. It seems to me that both pictures are based on considerable oversimplification. Sorting through the conflicting evidence, one can discern various themes, some of them suggesting 'development,' others tension and difficulty. It depends on where one stands, where one looks, and what one means by 'development,' and 'crisis.'

There is no question that powerful forces – above all, demographic growth and commercial expansion – were at work in Lower Canada at this time. The province's population rose from 161,000 in 1790 to over 500,000 by 1831; only a small portion of this growth took place in the cities. Rural French Canada continued, as always, to be a burgeoning, literally expansive society. Along with the demographic growth, therefore, went a tremendous campaign of assarting that transformed the forests into new farms. Where agrarian Canada once consisted of a narrow strip of territory along the banks of the St Lawrence and a few of its tributaries, by about 1830 the good lands of the St Lawrence

federation: a Study in Historical Geography (New York: Oxford UP 1974), 65–109; R.M. McInnis, 'A Reconsideration of the State of Agriculture in Lower Canada in the First Half of the Nineteenth Century,' Canadian Papers in Rural History 3 (1982): 9–49; Allan Greer, Peasant, Lord, and Merchant: Rural Society in Three Quebec Parishes, 1740–1840 (Toronto: UTP 1985); Louise Dechêne, 'Observations sur l'agriculture du Bas-Canada au début du XIXe siècle,' in Evolution et éclatement du monde rural, France-Québec, XVIIe–XXe siècles, ed. Joseph Goy and Jean-Pierre Wallot (Montreal: Presses de l'Université de Montréal 1986), 289-302; Serge Courville, 'La crise agricole du Bas-Canada, éléments d'une réflexion géographique,' Cahiers de géographie du Québec 24 (September 1980): 193–224 and 24 (December 1980): 385–428; idem., 'Le marché des 'subsistances.' L'exemple de la plaine de Montréal au début des années 1830: une perspective géographique,' RHAF 42 (1988): 193–239; Serge Courville and Normand Séguin, Rural Life in Nineteenth-Century Quebec, CHA booklet (Ottawa: CHA 1989); Christian Dessureault, 'Crise ou modernisation? La société maskoutaine durant le premier tiers du XIXe siècle,' RHAF 42 (Winter 1989): 359–87; Fernand Ouellet, 'Ruralization, Regional Development, and Industrial Growth before 1850,' in Economy, Class, & Nation in Quebec: Interpretive Essays, trans. Jacques Barbier (Toronto: Copp Clark 1991), 124–60.

valley and the 'plain of Montreal' were largely occupied. Population densities were still quite low by European standards, but they were sufficiently high to make the Laurentian heartland a mature and fully settled rural society rather than a series of frontier settlements.

Adding to this natural population growth was a stream of immigration that entered the province, first from the United States and then, after the end of the War of 1812 and in more substantial volumes, from the British Isles. Many of the immigrants were poor and unhealthy, particularly the Irish who arrived in the 1830s, and accommodating them placed severe short-term strains on the province's resources. At the same time, their arrival began to have a significant effect on Lower Canada's ethno-linguistic balance. Once an essentially French colony ruled by a handful of anglophones, Lower Canada was about 16 per cent English speaking in 1827; by 1844, 25 per cent of the population was not of French origin.[8] Because most of the old seigneurial areas were already well settled, however, they remained overwhelmingly French Canadian, while the newcomers tended to gravitate towards peripheral parts of Lower Canada and to Montreal and Quebec. Many of these areas – notably the Eastern Townships – were subject to the English tenure of 'free and common soccage.' By the 1830s the English had achieved rough parity with the French in the cities, and in Montreal they actually outnumbered francophones by a small margin.[9]

Even as the number of people – both French and English – grew and as more and more new farms were established, a less obvious but hardly less significant development occurred: the expanding influence of the mercantile economy. Since before the conquest merchants were proliferating, and increasing numbers of them began to set up shop in the countryside. They helped to make imported goods more available to the rural folk, while the

8 Ronald Rudin, *The Forgotten Quebeckers: a History of English-Speaking Quebec 1759–1980* (Quebec: Institut Québécois de recherche sur la culture 1985), 28
9 Ouellet, *Eléments d'histoire sociale*, 181

latter made room for exotic products in their basically self-sufficient household economy. Habitant estate inventories of the
period show how eagerly country people embraced the metal
harrows, the liquor, the tea and coffee, and the various cloths
sold at the merchant's store. 'The silent and insensible operation
of foreign commerce and manufactures' certainly had the effect
of spreading material comforts in the countryside.[10] It also
tended to encourage cultivators to grow larger grain surpluses to
the degree that this was possible. Finally, since harvests varied
from one year to the next and some habitants had trouble growing a surplus even at the best of times, it had the effect of increasing the peasantry's debt load.[11]

Both demographic growth and commercial expansion helped
to foster a measure of 'urban' and 'industrial' development in
rural Lower Canada. As the landscape filled with farming families, many of them prospering in the grain trade, opportunities
for artisans and professional men appeared; masons, shoemakers,
potters, doctors, and notaries began to set up shop in the rural
communities, whereas once the habitants had had to go to the
towns to secure their services. Non-agricultural production
became more common; and it was the work not only of individ-

10 Louis Michel, 'Le livre de compte (1784–1797) du marchand général Joseph
   Cartier: premiers résultats d'un traitement informatisé,' *Histoire sociale –
   Social History* 13 (November 1980): 369–98; Claude Desrosiers, 'Un aperçu
   des habitudes de consommation de la clientèle de Joseph Cartier, marchand
   général à Saint-Hyacinthe à la fin du XVIIIe siècle,' CHA, *HP*, 1984, 91–110;
   Gilles Desroches, 'Les niveaux de fortune de quelques groupes socio-profes-
   sionnels dans la région de Chambly de 1815 à 1835' (mémoire de maîtrise,
   Université de Montréal, 1979), 91–2; Greer, *Peasant, Lord, and Merchant*,
   140–231. The quotation is from Adam Smith, *An Inquiry into the Nature and
   Causes of the Wealth of Nations* (New York: Modern Library 1937), 388.
11 Lise Pilon-Lê, 'L'Endettement des cultivateurs québécois: une analyse socio-
   historique de la rente foncière (1670–1904)' (PH D thesis, Université de
   Montréal, 1978); Jérome C. Denys, 'L'Habitant de Laprairie, de 1790 à 1835,
   et la crise agricole' (mémoire de maîtrise, Université de Montréal, 1980),
   87–8; Greer, *Peasant, Lord, and Merchant*, 173–4, 185–7, 241–4; Dessureault,
   'Crise ou modernisation,' 381

ual artisans but also of substantial manufacturing establishments. Sawmills, distilleries, fulling mills, and similar enterprises requiring several employees were increasingly in evidence, much to the delight of the Patriot press.[12] Some scholars have even flirted with the notion that Lower Canada was passing through a 'proto-industrial stage' at this time.[13] I find it hard to accept this hypothesis given the fact that 'pre-industrial industry' of this sort could be found almost anywhere in Europe and North America long before the age of the Industrial Revolution. Moreover, whereas proto-industrial development usually caters to distant markets,[14] these crafts and 'manufactures' were mostly import-substitution enterprises oriented towards a domestic, if not a regional or local, market. Nevertheless, though Lower Canada was scarcely a world leader in rural industry, this development should definitely be seen as a sign of economic maturity within the pre-industrial context.

A form of urbanization accompanied this industrial development. The artisans and professionals as well as some landless labourers, perhaps a seigneur and various others who did not farm, tended to cluster around the churches that had always been at the centre of every French-Canadian parish. Serge Courville has called the resulting concentrated settlements 'urban villages,'

12 Lucie Blanchette-Lessard and Nicole Daigneault-Saint-Denis, 'Groupes sociaux patriotes et les rébellions de 1837-1838: idéologies et participation' (MA thesis, Université du Québec à Montréal, 1975), 73-81; Serge Courville, 'Croissance villageoise et industries rurales dans les seigneuries du Québec, 1815-1851,' in Sociétés villageoises et rapports villes-campagnes au Québec et dans la France de l'Ouest, XVIIe-XXe siècles, ed. François Lebrun and Normand Séguin (Trois-Rivières: Centre de recherches en études québécoises 1987), 205-19

13 Courville, 'Le marché des "subsistances,"' 231-6

14 Franklin Mendels, 'Proto-Industrialization: the First Phase of the Industrialization Process,' Journal of Economic History 32 (1972): 241-61; Franklin Mendels, 'Agriculture and Peasant Industry in Eighteenth Century Flanders,' in European Peasants and their Markets, ed. William N. Parker and Eric L. Jones (Princeton: Princeton UP 1975), 179-204

and the term is a good one.[15] They were urban in the sense that they were not inhabited by cultivators, as were most European and Latin American villages, but rather by people who lived on rents or on the proceeds of trade or craftwork. On the other hand, they were hardly towns, with their tiny populations (a few hundred at most) and their intimate dependence on the agrarian world that surrounded them. Semi-urban islands in an agricultural sea, the urban villages were still another symptom of the growing complexity of the Laurentian countryside. Whereas at the time of the conquest there were only twenty-four such 'nuclei' in the colony, the census of 1831 identifies 208 with a total population of 40,644 in the area under seigneurial tenure alone.[16]

Along with these rather positive indications of 'development,' one can also detect several symptoms of tension and distress, and these signs too seem connected to the fundamental thrusts of demographic growth and commercial penetration. With every generation in the early nineteenth century, it became more difficult to find farms for all. Not that it had ever been easy for habitants to 'establish' their numerous offspring. Whenever possible, young people secured grants of undeveloped land close to home so that they could clear the trees and erect buildings with the help of family labour and draught animals.[17] Even before the conquest, some of the oldest settlements near Quebec City had

15 Serge Courville, 'Esquisse du développement villageois au Québec: le cas de l'aire seigneuriale entre 1760 et 1854,' *Cahiers de géographie du Québec* 28 (1984): 9–46; idem, 'Villages and Agriculture in the Seigneuries of Lower Canada: Conditions of a Comprehensive Study of Rural Quebec in the First Half of the Nineteenth Century,' *Canadian Papers in Rural History* 5 (1986): 121–49; idem, *Entre ville et campagne: L'essor du village dans les seigneuries du Bas-Canada* (Quebec: Presses de l'Université Laval 1990). It should be noted that, although Courville has examined the phenomenon with unprecedented thoroughness, the growth of villages in Lower Canada did not escape the notice of earlier scholars. See Harris and Warkentin, *Canada Before Confederation*, 73–7.

16 Courville, 'Villages and Agriculture,' 125, 132

17 Greer, *Peasant, Lord, and Merchant*, 84–8

been fully occupied in this way, and young people then had to go up the river to less congested regions. In the nineteenth century, however, there were few convenient outlets for such pioneering ventures. French Canada had always been a river-front civilization, and the river banks were now definitely occupied. In many areas settlement extended to the edge of the barren Shield country. Where lands appropriate for agrarian colonization did remain (e.g., in the Eastern Townships), they were often hard to reach, subject to unfamiliar English civil law, and, because of the effects of speculation, expensive. Certainly there was no absolute barrier to French-Canadian expansion into these territories – in fact it occurred on a massive scale in the mid-nineteenth century – but circumstances did not favour it in the pre-Rebellion period.

We can hardly speak of the Lower Canadian countryside as 'overcrowded' in an absolute sense, even by 1837. Yet it is fair to say that the habitants' traditional system of economic reproduction, the process by which new households were set up for succeeding generations of peasants, was in crisis. Even well-off parents must then have worried about the prospects for their children. Apprenticeship in a craft or work in one of the new manufacturing establishments offered alternative means of making a living, but only to a very small proportion of the supernumerary habitants. Some emigrated to the United States, but this recourse would become a massive phenomenon only in later decades, when the industrialization of New England was well under way and railways made travel much easier. A more common fate for young habitants who did not inherit a farm was to become a landless peasant.

Families of journaliers can be found in substantial numbers in the 1831 census of Lower Canada, ranging from 12 per cent of household heads in the District of Quebec to 24 per cent in the Lower Richelieu near Montreal.[18] Day labourers – or cottagers,

18 Fernand Ouellet, 'La Sauvegarde des patrimoines dans le district de Québec durant la première moitié du XIXe siècle,' RHAF 26 (December 1972): 322; Monique Benoit, 'La formation d'une région: la marche du peuplement de

to use a British term that best fits the case – usually had a small plot of land on which they could raise some vegetables and perhaps keep a cow and a hog. Many found employment in the stores and workshops of the urban villages and performed various odd jobs. For example, Toussaint Langlois dit Latraverse, who happened to be arrested at St Eustache in the wake of the insurrection, mentioned in the course of interrogation that he acted as the village auctioneer, in addition to working on the Ottawa River timber rafts. Most journaliers lived out in the farming rangs, however, suggesting that they were mainly agricultural labourers.[19] Rural workers of this sort – poor, lacking farms, but not entirely destitute – seem to have been more numerous on the eve of the Rebellion than in earlier centuries, and their presence signalled the end of an era when the independence that comes with possession of a farm had been a near-universal rural experience.

Were farms being subdivided to accommodate the burgeoning population? To some limited extent they were, but this was not a result – as historiographical mythology would have it – of the operation of French-Canadian inheritance law. The Custom of Paris gave all legitimate offspring an equal share of their parents' property, but it did not require them to divide a viable family farm into a dozen tiny patches; there were various means by which an heir who received the land could compensate brothers and sisters who did without. All indications are, in fact, that in good grain-growing areas the average size of farms remained remarkably stable through the generations. This is the case in the seigneurie of St Hyacinthe, to take one example; examining landholdings in the 1830s, Christian Dessureault found that farms were largest precisely in those sections of the seigneurie that had

St-Eustache à St-Jérôme et le problème des subsistances' (MA thesis, University of Ottawa, 1980), 119; Greer, *Peasant, Lord, and Merchant*, 197; Dessureault, 'Crise ou modernisation,' 380

19 ANQ, 1837, no. 712, examen volontaire de Toussaint Paul Langlois dit Latraverse, 1 February 1838; Dessureault, 'Crise ou modernisation,' 368

been settled the longest, that is, where property had presumably passed through the greatest number of inheritance settlements. Another researcher, taking a different approach to the same issue, carefully reconstructed land transactions (including transmission from one generation to another) in a prime wheat-growing section of Verchères; she turned up no lasting fragmentation at all between 1730 and 1975.[20] On the other hand, studies of land holdings in regions with poorer soils, places where habitants had had to turn to part-time waged work, show a shrinkage in farm size between the late eighteenth century and the decade of the Rebellion. Sorel and La Prairie are cases in point; both were prime recruiting grounds for seasonal engagés for the Northwest Company fur trade. Far to the northeast, Malbaie was a centre of lumbering and ship-building, and its large farms were also subdivided to some extent.[21] It appears that the subdivision of land holdings was limited to places where natural conditions were unfavourable to farming and where non-agricultural income was an important supplement to the subsistence derived from small plots. In places where agriculture prospered, peasants did their best to preserve intact farms that were a source of profit as well as food for their families. In other words, the forces of commercialization and demographic expansion had opposite effects in different parts of the province.

But was agriculture truly prospering anywhere in Lower Canada? Obviously not at the time of the crop failures of 1834–7, but not in earlier years either, according to Fernand Ouellet. His

20 Dessureault, 'Crise ou modernisation,' 373–7; Pauline Desjardins, 'La Coutume de Paris et la transmission des terres: le rang de la Beauce à Calixa-Lavallèe de 1730 à 1975,' *RHAF* 34 (December 1980): 339. In agriculturally rich St Denis, average farm size was smaller in 1831 than in 1765, but only, it seems, because the seigneur granted smaller lots after 1765 than before. Greer, *Peasant, Lord, and Merchant*, 190
21 Ouellet, *Eléments d'histoire sociale*, 124–5; Denys, 'L'Habitant de Laprairie,' 28; Greer, *Peasant, Lord, and Merchant*, 189–90; Mario Lalancette, 'Essai sur la répartition de la propriété foncière à la Malbaie, au pays de Charlevoix,' in *Sociétés villageoises*, ed. Lebrun and Séguin, 63–77

figures on the grain trade suggest that from about 1800 onwards decreasing quantities of grain, relative to the province's population, were shipped from the port of Quebec.[22] One of the 'bread baskets' of the British empire in the late eighteenth century, French Canada was increasingly unable to compete with the young settlements of Upper Canada on international markets; in many years there was indeed a dependence on breadstuffs shipped from the upper province. What Ouellet fails to note is the fact that these figures on the grain trade reflect not simply the performance of Lower Canadian agriculture, but also changes in the colony's social structure. As the number of cottagers, villagers, artisans, and proletarians grew, the proportion of food consumers to food producers naturally increased. Even if genuine farming families maintained their production levels – and research on one parish indicates that more grain was harvested by the average household in 1831 than in 1765[23] – per capita surpluses for export would have to decline. Western competition is another factor that should be taken into consideration when Lower Canada's agricultural economy is being assessed. John McCallum has shown that the province's fate was bound up in larger North American developments.[24] Just as Lower Canada could not compete with Upper Canada, the cereal agriculture of neighbouring New England was also defeated in the early nineteenth century by the virgin and naturally more fertile lands of the Great Lakes basin.

Many contemporaries saw the decline of the Lower Canadian wheat staple in an altogether different light. Travellers, merchants, journalists, and officials, particularly those of British origin, generally believed that the habitants were simply bad farmers who, encouraged by the province's archaic civil laws and tenure system, stubbornly resisted agricultural improvements of

22 Ouellet, *Economic and Social History*
23 Greer, *Peasant, Lord, and Merchant*, 212
24 John McCallum, *Unequal Beginnings: Agriculture and Economic Development in Quebec and Ontario until 1870* (Toronto: UTP 1980), 35–8

all sorts.[25] This bleak judgment is not confirmed by recent research, which suggests that French-Canadian agriculture was in fact changing in the early decades of the nineteenth century with the adoption of better ploughs and harrows and more careful treatment of the soil.[26] Nevertheless it remained basically a peasant agriculture, and as such was bound to raise the ire of bourgeois commentators, especially those who came from the British Isles, then in the forefront of agricultural 'improvement.' The critique of habitant agriculture was not based primarily on technical considerations. 'Enlightened' observers of peasant agriculture throughout the western world tended to be appalled by what they saw, not only in Lower Canada, but also in France, Russia, Scotland, and elsewhere.[27] Behind their criticisms of this or that method of ploughing or stock-breeding lay a basic opposition to the peasantry as such. The 'improved' agriculture that commanded expert approval was, by and large, capitalist agriculture, carried out with waged labour. In fact, it was not necessarily more 'efficient' agriculture – for equal economic input, small-scale cultivators often get more from the soil than do large operators – though it would certainly have been a better way of making farming a profitable operation for agrarian entrepreneurs. More to the point, the 'merchants' program' implied the liquidation of the peasants as a class and their degradation to the

25 Their views are summarized and quoted extensively in R.L. Jones, 'Agriculture in Lower Canada, 1792–1815,' CHR (March 1946): 33–51.
26 Greer, Peasant, Lord, and Merchant, 210–11; Corinne Beutler, 'L'outillage agricole dans les inventaires paysans de la région de Montréal reflète-t-il une transformation de l'agriculture entre 1792 et 1835?' in Sociétés villageoises, ed. Lebrun and Séguin, 121–30; Dessureault, 'Crise ou modernisation?' 381
27 See, for example, Arthur Young, Travels During the Years 1787, 1788, & 1789; Undertaken more particularly with a View to Ascertaining the Cultivation, Wealth, Resources, and National Prosperity of the Kingdom of France, 2 vols (London: W. Richardson 1794), esp. 1: 408; E.J. Hobsbawm, 'Scottish Reformers of the Eighteenth Century and Capitalist Agriculture,' in Peasants in History: Essays in Honour of Daniel Thorner, ed. Eric J. Hobsbawm (Calcutta: Oxford UP 1981), 3–29.

position of 'servants,' a change with enormous implications for anyone concerned with questions of 'independence' and 'citizenship' in an age when political rights were closely connected to property ownership. Such a wholesale transformation remained a utopian vision, however, and the mass of the population, in so far as they retained their agrarian vocation, kept control of their own lands and labour.

Habitants remained masters of their property only within the limitations imposed by seigneurial tenure. Furthermore, it does appear that seigneurial exactions, never a trivial burden at any time, were tending to weigh more heavily in the decades prior to the Rebellion.[28] Rental rates and other terms of tenure were set once and for all time at the moment a seigneur first granted a given lot to a settler; what could change – and did – was the rent to be charged on new grants of land. Initially, in the seventeenth century, prospective settlers were rare, land was plentiful, and seigneurs were anxious to encourage the development of their estates; annual dues accordingly had been quite moderate. By the late eighteenth / early nineteenth century, however, land had become scarce, pressure from habitants in search of farms was intense, and seigneurs could then be more demanding. They could not raise the rent on lots granted by their predecessors to an earlier generation of habitants, because censitaires enjoyed security of tenure (at least in theory). The result of the process of progressive colonization and seigneurial grants under changing conditions was that by the 1830s seigneurial exactions varied greatly from region to region, from seigneurie to seigneurie, and even within a single fief. Furthermore, various seigneurial monopolies and reserves, as well as other conditions of tenure, were generally more burdensome for habitants holding recently granted lands. The fact that these disparities were widely known only intensified the impression that there was something arbitrary and unfair about the whole business.

28 Fernand Ouellet, 'Le régime seigneurial dans le Québec (1760–1854),' in *Eléments d'histoire sociale*, 91–110; Ouellet, *Economic and Social History*, 359–64

Quite apart from the burdensome conditions being imposed on new grants of land, there seems to have been a general drift towards increasingly hard-nosed styles of estate management. Indulgent and paternalistic seigneurs could still be found who would let back rents accumulate when habitants were in difficulty, but many seigneurs (or their agents) were inclined to take censitaires to court over debts, with the result that the latter were often driven from their farms. Other sharp practices arose that were widely regarded as contrary to custom and law. Some seigneurs exacted a sale price for grants of wild land, while others simply refused to grant lands to settlers, even though in the past they had been required to grant lots to all applicants in return for an annual rent only.

One area where the seigneurial burden weighed particularly heavily on the peasantry was L'Acadie county, west of the Richelieu River and south of Montreal. Not coincidentally, this was one of the main centres of radicalism during the Rebellion. It was also a territory under the control of an unusually grasping set of seigneurs. Much of L'Acadie belonged to a bloc of five seigneuries assembled shortly after the conquest (when they were still largely unsettled and therefore a cheap investment) by Gabriel Christie, a British army officer.[29] By 1835 the Christie estate had passed into the hands of William Plenderleath Christie, a military gentleman like his ancestor, but one who left the management of his fiefs to an agent, William McGinnis. Through his position McGinnis quickly established himself as a powerful figure in the region. Beyond the Christie domain at the western end of L'Acadie lay a bewildering collection of small properties once known as the 'Township of Sherrington.' Initial surveying here had been utterly defective, with the result that the seigneur of Lasalle, to the north, had mistakenly granted farms to habitants outside his seigneurie in a territory that was supposed to be under the English tenure of 'free and common soccage.'

29 Françoise Noel, *The Christie Seigneuries: Estate Management and Settlement in the Upper Richelieu Valley, 1760–1854* (Montreal: McGill-Queen's UP 1992)

Confusion and lawsuits ensued until the government finally sorted out matters in the 1820s by creating four new seigneuries, each made up of a few dozen farms, while leaving part of the township under non-seigneurial English tenure. By the 1830s a Montreal lawyer named John Boston had acquired two of the seigneuries, and the others were owned by John McCallum and François Languedoc.[30]

Conditions in L'Acadie did not favour warm relations between seigneur and censitaire. The area was settled in the late eighteenth/early nineteenth century when terms of tenure worked increasingly to the peasant's disadvantage. Most of the region's seigneurs were English or English Canadian, and anglophones were generally regarded in Lower Canada as hard-hearted landlords. In so far as this reputation was justified – and it was not entirely, since many French-Canadian seigneurs were no better than their English counterparts – it can be explained by the fact that the British tradition of land law and estate management allowed landlords much greater freedom to maximize their returns than did the French. Moreover, the seigneurs of British origin were, for the most part, newcomers and parvenus, lacking any background for the paternalistic attitudes more likely to be found among the clerical orders and the old Canadian seigneurial noblesse.[31] There were indeed no genuinely paternalistic seigneurs in L'Acadie; for none of them, French or English, resided in the region even for part of the year.

Accordingly, the managers of the Christie estates did not hesitate to exact rents of more than £2 a year for an average farm lot, the highest levels of cens et rentes to be found in all of Lower

---

30 Mario Gendron, 'Tenure seigneuriale et mouvement patriote: le cas du comté de l'Acadie' (mémoire de maîtrise, Université du Québec à Montréal, 1986), 42–65

31 For examples of paternalistic leniency in estate management, see Sylvie Dépatie, Mario Lalancette, and Christian Dessureault, *Contributions à l'étude du régime seigneurial canadien* (Montreal: Hurtubise 1987), 79; Greer, *Peasant, Lord, and Merchant*, 12.

Canada in the 1830s.[32] Rents were not as steep in the small fiefs of Sherrington, though they were still much higher than the provincial average. Here, as in the Christie estates, habitants were subject to other sorts of exaction. All the seigneurs of L'Acadie were forcing would-be censitaires to pay substantial entry fees – sums ranging from 12 shillings to £37 are recorded – in return for grants of uncleared land.[33] There were, in addition, the usual mill monopolies, mutation fines, and so on. Inevitably, the habitants of L'Acadie tended to fall behind in their payments, and most were indebted to their seigneur for substantial sums. To keep up the pressure on indebted censitaires, seigneurs and their agents occasionally made an example of one by taking him to court; the invariable result, with accumulated back rents added to crushing legal costs, was a sheriff's sale and the destitution of the habitant family. Little wonder that anti-seigneurial sentiment was a major force in 1837–8, particularly in L'Acadie, but also more generally among the habitants of Lower Canada.

With the wheat staple trade declining, with land more difficult to procure, and with seigneurs reaching ever further into the pockets of the peasantry, one would expect to find that the habitants' standard of living suffered a decline in the pre-Rebellion decades. Indeed, some sectors of the Lower Canadian peasantry were clearly worse off in the 1830s than their parents had been in the 1790s. The average moveable wealth (i.e., excluding land that was not assigned a monetary value) recorded in habitant estate inventories from the parish of Sorel fell from 1,358 livres in the 1790s to 403 livres in the 1830s. Another sample of peasant inventories, this one covering the parish of La Prairie, shows a similar pattern: mean moveable wealth was 838 livres in 1790–5, rising to 1,717 livres in 1810–15 before crashing to 478 livres in

32 Serge Courville, 'Rente déclarée payée sur la censive de 90 arpents au recensement nominatif de 1831: méthodologie d'une recherche,' *Cahiers de géographie du Québec* 27 (April 1983): 45–50
33 Gendron, 'Tenure seigneurial et mouvement patriote,' 74–5

1830–5.[34] Sorel and La Prairie were communities in which the combination of poor soils and employment in the fur trade fostered a pattern of overpopulation, subdivision of holdings, and dependence on seasonal waged work, resulting in an impoverished peasantry unable to support itself from the produce of its own farms. Other localities had a very different experience. Where the land was at all suitable for grain growing, habitants prospered, even well into the 1830s. Several studies based on evidence from estate inventories indicate that average wealth actually *increased* over the first four decades of the nineteenth century. The figures for St Denis and St Ours habitants are 427 livres in 1790–99 and 1,300 livres in 1830–9. There was also an increase, albeit a less dramatic one, for the habitants of the huge seigneurie of St Hyacinthe. Its average moveable wealth rose from 1,296 livres in 1795–1814 to 1,485 livres in 1825–34.[35] Of course, in both the prosperous and the poor parishes average figures hide a variety of individual experiences. Look in almost any French-Canadian community at any time before 1837 and you are sure to find the semi-indigent alongside prosperous peasants like the rebel leader Lucien Gagnon with his five horses, twenty-five head of cattle, and large quantities of grain.[36]

It is difficult to sum up the rather contradictory social and economic changes in rural French Canada from the late eighteenth century to the 1830s except to say that diversity increased. Where once the landscape had featured nothing but subsistence farms occupied by an undifferentiated mass of settler-peasants (to simplify slightly for heuristic purposes), now there were urban settlements, non-agricultural enterprises, landless

---

34 Greer, *Peasant, Lord, and Merchant*, 186; Denys, 'L'Habitant de Laprairie,' 71. Note that only the Sorel figures have been corrected to offset the effects of inflation.

35 Greer, *Peasant, Lord, and Merchant*, 186; Dessureault, 'Crise ou modernisation,' 380

36 NA, Lucien Gagnon Papers, 'Inventory of the Lands, Effects and Moveables of Julian Gagnon now confiscated to our Sovereign Lady the Queen Victoria,' 4 January 1838

labourers, and a growing gap between richer and poorer habitants. This differentiation occurred at more than one level, simultaneously distinguishing region from region, parish from parish, and family from neighbouring family. Does this mean that a once-homogeneous agrarian class was now utterly fragmented into distinct social classes? No; the situation had not changed to that extent. The process was still quite limited in comparison with truly mature rural societies like those existing at the time in Europe. What struck Lord Durham about French-Canadian society was the lack of the extremes of wealth and poverty that he was used to in England, where labour was much more thoroughly subordinated to capital.

The circumstances of a new and unsettled country, the operation of the French laws of inheritance, and the absence of any means of accumulation, by commerce or manufactures, have produced a remarkable equality of properties and conditions. A few seignorial families possess large, though not often very valuable properties; the class entirely dependent on wages is very small; the bulk of the population is composed of the hard-working yeomanry of the country districts, commonly called *habitans*, and their connexions engaged in other occupations.[37]

Though it seems to fly in the face of much of the research outlined above, Durham's description contains an essential truth. Independent habitants were still the majority in the 1830s, and though some were better off than others, none was truly an agricultural entrepreneur. At the other end of the scale, the poorest peasants and the day labourers/cottagers lived lives that were, in many respects, similar to those of their more fortunate neighbours, even if they were much less comfortable and secure. Journaliers, like the village artisans, for the most part seem to have been born into habitant families (this is my impression, at any rate, pending further research) and to have maintained close

---

37 C.P. Lucas, ed., *Lord Durham's Report on the Affairs of British North America*, 3 vols (Oxford: Clarendon Press 1912), 2: 31

ties through marriage and friendship. Moreover, because many craftsmen and labourers had land and grew crops, they are hard to distinguish from the poorer elements of the peasantry proper. For these reasons I believe it is fair to see the rural population as forming one class with several segments and appendages, rather than several distinct social units with clearly differing interests.[38]

The behaviour of French-Canadian rural folk during the Rebellion seems to bear out this social observation. Certainly there is little to indicate that the more destitute elements of the peasantry were particularly active in the anti-government cause. Some research has been done at the local level that attempts to link individuals arrested for treason or otherwise implicated in the insurrection with entries in the 1831 census giving figures on land holdings and agricultural production.[39] For all their appearance of precision, the resulting data are of course the product of a number of factors, including the unpredictable vagaries of repression (which determined for the researcher who was and who was not a 'patriot'); nevertheless, they provide a rough

38 In 'L'égalitarisme paysan dans l'ancienne société rurale de la vallée du Saint-Laurent: éléments pour une ré-interprétation,' *RHAF* 40 (Winter 1987): 373–407, Christian Dessureault points out and attaches great importance to the disparities of wealth within the Lower Canadian peasantry. His research is admirably rigorous but somewhat beside the point, since it refutes a position – all habitants were at exactly the same economic level – that no one could seriously maintain. If Dessureault's figures were placed next to data from European or Asian rural societies, I think that the rough equality of fortunes within agrarian Lower Canada would be more apparent. See also Catherine Desbarats, 'Agriculture within the Seigneurial Régime of Eighteenth-Century Canada: Some Thoughts on the Recent Literature,' *CHR* 73 (March 1992): 21–8.

39 Francine Parent, 'Les patriotes de Châteauguay (1838)' (MA thesis, Université de Montréal, 1984); Lucie Blanchette-Lessard and Nicole Daigneault-Saint-Denis, 'La participation des groupes sociaux aux rébellions dans les comtés de Laprairie et de Deux-Montagnes,' in *Les Rébellions de 1837–1838: les patriotes du Bas-Canada dans la mémoire collective et chez les historiens*, ed. Jean-Paul Bernard (Montreal: Boréal 1983), 327–37

Table 1
Hypothetical agricultural revenues (1831) of habitants of the counties of La Prairie
and Two Mountains implicated in the Rebellions

Income (pounds)	County		Rebels		Difference
	no.	%	no.	%	%
La Prairie					
0–35	118	25	15	27	2
35–79	118	25	15	27	2
79–128	118	25	7	13	−12
Over 128	117	25	18	33	8
Total	471		55		
Two Mountains					
0–23	71	25	2	10	−15
23–60	70	25	5	24	−1
60–107	70	25	3	14	−11
Over 107	70	25	11	52	27
Total	281		21		

SOURCE: Lucie Blanchette-Lessard and Nicole Daigneault-Saint-Denis, 'La participation des groupes sociaux aux rébellions dans les comtés de Laprairie et de
Deux-Montagnes,' in *Les Rébellions de 1837–1838: les patriotes du Bas-Canada dans
la mémoire collective et chez les historiens*, ed. Jean-Paul Bernard (Montreal: Boréal
1983), 335–6

indication of how the economic position of active insurgents
compared with the local average. My reading of the figures in
table 1 is that the patriots represented an economic cross-section
of the rural community; if anything, they were slightly more
prosperous than the average. This confirms the impression provided by qualitative sources that in many parts of Lower Canada
whole communities, rather than isolated individuals, were
involved in the Rebellion.

THE PECULIARITIES OF THE DISTRICT OF MONTREAL

From an economic point of view, was there something special
that distinguished the communities or regions that took up the

patriot cause from those that did not?[40] As it happens, the Rebellion of 1837–8 lends itself nicely to a regional analysis; for virtually all the action took place in the District of Montreal, one of the four sections into which Lower Canada was divided. This is not to say that the patriot movement commanded only limited support. On the contrary, local authorities across the province warned of the basic disloyalty of the habitants. There were some worrying incidents in the District of Three Rivers in 1837, and a British spy who made his way south from Quebec City in February 1838 reported that, if Papineau were to lead an invasion into the Beauce, 'every man would I am certain avail himself of such an opportunity to shew hostility against the British Government.'[41] Revolutionary upheavals, even when they turn out to be national in scope, do not as a rule begin everywhere at once across an entire country. Commonly one or two regions – for example, Massachusetts in the American Revolution or the Caracas area and the Rio de la Plata in the South American wars of liberation – take the lead, while other areas are drawn into the struggle only at a later stage. So it was in the Lower Canadian Rebellion: one sector, the District of Montreal, was clearly at the centre of agitation and military conflict, though here, unlike the situations in the United States and South America, the armed independence movement was crushed before other regions were seriously affected. Without making the mistake of assuming that other parts of the province were *against* the patriots, we do have the opportunity of examining the social and economic peculiarities of the actively rebellious western district to see whether they help to account for the insurrection.

I have therefore assembled figures for the rural sections of the Districts of Montreal, Three Rivers, and Quebec (leaving aside

---

40 This topic is dealt with more fully in Allan Greer and Léon Robichaud, 'La Rébellion de 1837–1838 au Bas-Canada: une approche géographique,' *Cahiers de géographie du Québec* 33 (December 1989): 345–77.

41 NA, LC Civil Secretary, 525: 206, Matthew Bell to Civil Secretary, 29 November 1837; ANQ, 1837, no. 3210, 'Confidential report of Sergeant James McDermott,' 3 February 1838

both the isolated and marginal District of Gaspé and the cities that gave their names to the three major districts) in 1831 and 1844 (tables 2 and 3). The first feature that distinguishes the District of Montreal is its massive demographic preponderance; not only was its population larger than that of the other regions, but one could actually combine the populations, urban as well as rural, of all the other districts of Lower Canada and throw in the city of Montreal for good measure, and there were still more people living in the country parishes of the western region! It might be noted in passing that a revolt based in this section of the province was therefore hardly a minor affair. Since the seventeenth century habitants on the move had always tended to gravitate from the east to the west.[42] This is largely a reflection of geography: the 'plain of Montreal,' with its comparatively mild climate and good soils, presented a wide territory for agrarian colonization, whereas further to the east the mountains tended to confine settlement to a narrower, riverside band. The Montreal district was thus heavily, but also widely, populated compared with the others. Nevertheless, it could not be considered overcrowded; the census figures indicate clearly that the country people of the western region had no less land under the plough than their counterparts in other sections of the province. Indeed, there was slightly more cleared land per capita than in the District of Quebec and about the same as in the District of Three Rivers.

Largely because of the blessings of nature, the District of Montreal had long been the agricultural centre of the St Lawrence valley. Meticulous studies by R.C. Harris and Thomas Wien of the agrarian geography of eighteenth-century Canada show a consistent pattern in 1739 and in 1787–90: substantial surpluses of wheat in the parishes around Montreal contrasting

42 See Serge Courville, Jean-Claude Robert and Normand Séguin, 'Population et espace rural au Bas-Canada: l'exemple de l'axe laurentien dans la première moitié du XIXe siècle,' RHAF 44 (Fall 1990): 243–62.

Table 2
Socio-economic characteristics of the rural sections of the Districts of Montreal, Three Rivers, and Quebec, 1831

	Montreal	Three Rivers	Quebec
Population	258,267	52,598	129,728
Urban villages (seigneurial area only)	109	20	79
Village population (seigneurial area only)	12%	8%	10%
Manufacturing est. (per 100,000)	447	515	430
Immigrants, 1825–31 (per 100,000)	5178	878	2805
Improved land (arpents per capita)	4.7	4.8	4.3
Wheat harvested (minots per capita)	8.1	7.3	7.0
Peas harvested (minots per capita)	3.1	1.1	1.0
Oats harvested (minots per capita)	7.4	8.1	6.1
Potatoes harvested (minots per capita)	16.3	17.3	13.3
Horses (per 100,000)	28,676	25,233	19,539
Beggars (per 100,000)	184	150	477
Average seigneurial rent (*livres* per 90 arpents)	23.0	11.1	9.4

SOURCES: 1831 census returns in *JHALC*, 1831–2, app. OO; Serge Courville, 'Esquisse du développement villageois au Québec: le cas de l'aire seigneuriale entre 1760 et 1854,' *Cahiers de géographie du Québec* 28 (April–September 1984): 31; idem, 'Rente déclarée payée sur la censive de 90 arpents au recensement nominatif de 1831: méthodologie d'une recherche,' *Cahiers de géographie du Québec* 27 (April 1983): 45–50

Table 3
Socio-economic characteristics of the rural sections of the Districts of Montreal, Three Rivers, and Quebec, 1844

	Montreal	Three Rivers	Quebec
Population	324,558	65,580	172,551
French Canadians (%)	78.1	93.9	89.4
Born outside L.C. (%)	10.2	3.2	5.8
Manufacturing est. (per 100,000)	481	500	622
Improved land (arpents per capita)	4.9	4.1	4.3
Wheat harvested (bushels per capita)	1.7	1.8	0.9
Oats harvested (bushels per capita)	12.8	14.0	10.7
Horses (per 100,000)	27,865	20,910	18,542
Beggars and paupers (per 100,000)	316	195	1595

SOURCE: Census tables of 1844, *JLAC*, 1846, app. D

with the mediocre performances recorded downriver.[43] In 1831 and 1844 the District of Montreal still had the edge in wheat production. In fact, the contrast with the other regions is greater than the per capita figures suggest, since a larger proportion of the Montreal rural population was engaged in non-agricultural pursuits. Wheat apart, the farmers of the Three Rivers area seem

43 It should be added, by way of qualification, that there were many highly productive areas within the District of Quebec, as well as some poor parishes in the Montreal region; nevertheless, overall far more surplus grain came from the western part of Lower Canada. Harris and Warkentin, *Canada Before Confederation*, 53; Tom Wien, 'Visites paroissiales et production agricole au Canada vers la fin du XVIIIe siècle,' in *Sociétés villageoises*, ed. LeBrun and Séguin, 183–94. See also Louise Dechêne's map, based on parish priests' reports on harvests in 1815; here too the communities boasting 'abundant harvests' were mostly in the District of Montreal. Louise Dechêne, 'Observations sur l'agriculture du Bas-Canada au début du XIXe siècle,' in *Evolution et éclatement*, ed. Goy and Wallot, 193

to have been as productive as their western counterparts. Indeed, generally there is little in the agricultural statistics to indicate dramatic differences marking off the Montreal region from the other districts.

If any district appears unique, it is the poor Quebec District. This is particularly apparent when one looks at the figures indicating not so much strictly agricultural performance as overall wealth and poverty. There were substantially more beggars and fewer horses in the eastern countryside. Conditions varied greatly within the region, and certainly there were pockets of prosperity as well as areas of dearth in this part of Lower Canada. Yet the overall impression conveyed by the census figures and confirmed by an analysis of habitant estate inventories[44] is of a District of Quebec whose agrarian economy was in much worse shape than that of other parts of the province.

The rural District of Montreal, judged by the same indicators, stood in a comparatively favourable situation. But how did it fare during the acute agrarian distress that gripped Lower Canada about the time of the Rebellion? The census figures show clearly that across Lower Canada wheat production fell dramatically between 1831 and 1844. Some have argued that the setback was most severe in the Montreal region, and indeed the data indicate that the decline of wheat was more pronounced there.[45] However, this is largely a reflection of the relative strength of western agriculture before the collapse. Note that per capita wheat production in the District of Montreal was still double that of Quebec in 1844. It seems to me that in fact the agricultural difficulties of eastern and western Lower Canada in the mid-1830s were of rather a different order. In the Quebec district there was real famine; starvation was averted, contemporaries reported, only by the intervention of the state and private charities. From 1830 to

44 Gilles Paquet and Jean-Pierre Wallot, 'Les Habitants de Montréal et de Québec (1790–1835): contextes géo-économiques différents, même stratégie foncière,' in Sociétés villageoises, ed. LeBrun and Séguin, 101–12
45 W.H. Parker, 'A Revolution in the Agricultural Geography of Lower Canada 1833–1838,' Revue canadienne de géographie 11 (1957): 189–94; Ouellet, Lower Canada, 281

1835 the *Journals of the House of Assembly* list thirty-six petitions from various parishes and counties for famine relief.[46] The regional distribution of the petitions is most instructive. Out of the total of thirty-six, thirty-four came from the District of Quebec and *not one* was from the Montreal district! Not that the collapse of wheat did not have serious consequences for western peasants. The failure of this money-producing crop surely plunged many deeper into debt with the seigneur and the merchant; the problem of securing land for children would have been all the more daunting; people probably had to do without supplies they were accustomed to. But there is no indication that hunger became widespread. As grain crops faltered, families seem to have eked out a living that relied more on poultry and dairy products as well as garden produce,[47] although it is hard to gain precise information on this point from documents that neglect such fruits of the labour of farm women and concentrate on the field crops raised by men. In the household economy of any peasantry there is always some combination of 'subsistence agriculture' and 'market involvement.' The tragedy of the hard years of the 1830s in the District of Quebec is that they apparently hit the habitants at both levels, affecting not simply their purses but their bellies as well. In the western region of Lower Canada, on the other hand, distress was serious but less fundamental, since it involved mainly the sphere of buying, selling, and owing rather than that of simple physical survival.

Outside the strictly agricultural sphere the District of Montreal also had its peculiarities. To begin with, there were far more urban villages here, and together they accounted for a larger proportion of the rural population than did those of the other

46 *JHALC*, vols 39–45, passim. Note that the journals of the Assembly become thin in 1836 and disappear altogether with the political crisis of 1837. This is why the figure cited here covers only the period 1830 to 1835. I did encounter several petitions from 'parishes in distress' dating from the time of the Rebellion in the correspondence of the Civil Secretary (NA, LC Civil Secretary, passim); all these too came from the eastern half of the province, but my browsing was too casual to justify any statistical claims.

47 See Greer, *Peasant, Lord, and Merchant*, 215.

districts. Moreover, some of the western 'villages' were fairly substantial towns. After Quebec, Montreal, and Three Rivers, the eight largest concentrated settlements in Lower Canada in 1831 were located in the western district.[48] This suggests a higher level of development and maturity in the rural society of the west. On the other hand, the data on 'manufacturing establishments' seem to indicate greater industrial development in the District of Quebec. In any case, the relatively advanced 'urbanization' of the Montreal countryside helps to explain, in a more direct way, the regional incidence of rebellion; for, as we shall see, the village centres played an important role in the insurrection.

The District of Montreal was distinguished also by its ethnic composition. Proportionally many more immigrants (almost all would have come from the British Isles) settled here in the six years preceding the 1831 census. As a result, there was a sizeable English-speaking element in the region, while the Three Rivers and Quebec countryside remained overwhelmingly French Canadian. Obviously, the fact that French and English speakers shared this territory had much to do with the ethnic conflict that featured so prominently in the events of 1837–8 (more on this subject in chap. 6).

Finally, there are the figures on seigneurial rents, and here the contrast between Montreal and the other districts is dramatic; on average, annual dues were more than double the rates that prevailed to the east. This disparity occurred partly because the permanently established rates of cens et rentes on new land grants tended to increase over the centuries, and much of the land in the western district had been granted by seigneurs in relatively recent times. The higher rates are also a reflection of the traditionally rich agriculture of the Montreal region. The situation in the county of L'Acadie appears then to have been archetypical of that prevailing in the larger district.

A heavy feudal burden and a substantial anglophone majority:

48 Jean-Claude Robert, 'Montréal 1821–1871: aspects de l'urbanisation' (doctoral dissertation, Ecole des hautes études en sciences sociales, 1977), 102

these, and decidedly not poverty, are the outstanding characteristics that most clearly separated the rebellious part of the province from other rural regions in the period preceding the insurrection. In revealing these peculiarities, the census points in the direction of two important themes – nationality and seigneurial relations – which were to play an important role in 1837. It also suggests parallels between the nationalist movement of Lower Canada and those movements that developed in the small nations of eastern and central Europe. The Czech historian Miroslav Hroch noted a common tendency for nineteenth-century 'national revivals' to be strongest in one particular region, often an area in close proximity to alien linguistic groups. The 'patriotic' heartlands were also characterized by higher population densities, more fertile grain-growing soils, and greater integration into market relations and 'the cultural transformations characteristic of the emerging capitalist society' than other parts of countries such as Bohemia, Norway, and Lithuania.[49]

Unquestionably, material circumstances formed a basic condition for the Rebellion of 1837–38. The general economic crisis must have affected the timing of the outbreak as well as the bitterness of the resulting conflict. Yet the risings cannot be attributed to any chronic agrarian poverty. After all, in the affected areas the relatively rich as well as the poor took part. Moreover, the rebellious District of Montreal was, on the whole, rather more prosperous and developed than the quiet District of Quebec. Indeed, contemporaries were struck by the regional incidence of revolt: 'The theatre is in the centre of the richest, most populous, most flourishing district in all Lower Canada,' wrote a Montreal diarist.[50] For Tories, firmly convinced that the lower classes ought to be content when their bellies were full, the insurgency of the relatively privileged simply demonstrated once again the base

49 Miroslav Hroch, *Social Preconditions of National Revival in Europe: A Comparative Analysis of the Social Composition of Patriotic Groups among the Smaller European Nations* (New York: Oxford UP 1985), 173–4
50 Bibliothèque nationale du Québec, Romuald Trudeau journal, 12: 70

ingratitude of the French Canadians. Of course, the situation of the western habitants was not entirely rosy. As was the case in other parts of Lower Canada, the long-term growth of population and commerce had brought indebtedness as well as improved living standards; above all, it was becoming ever harder to 'establish' sons and daughters on farms of their own. The exactions of seigneurs were becoming increasingly vexatious. Finally, the collapse of wheat in the mid-1830s constituted a real economic hardship for the habitants of the District of Montreal. Thus it was a relatively prosperous peasantry, but one suffering from recent setbacks and worried about the future, that would find itself at the storm centre when revolution broke out in 1837. Would it be equipped to deal with the stresses and political challenges that crisis would bring?

3

Potatoes in a sack? Rural community life

Were the habitants of Lower Canada nothing more than 'potatoes in a sack,' isolated, disconnected, self-absorbed? Was theirs an atomized existence with each little agrarian family turned inward upon itself, unconcerned with any larger collectivity and incapable of joining others in concerted action for the good of all? As we have seen, the circumstances of rural life in French Canada – the absence of collective practices in agriculture, the weakness of local government – all seemed to conspire to make this peasantry even more fragmented than most. And yet we know that the habitants did act with some degree of unity in 1837. It seems necessary therefore to look more closely at the community life of the habitants, such as it was, and see whether there was anything more than a sack holding these potatoes together.

HABITANT CONVIVIALITY

The 'individualism' of rural society certainly did not preclude a rich social life of celebration and entertainment in the Lower Canadian countryside. Foreign visitors almost always remarked, usually in condescending tones, on the politeness and kind hospitality of the habitants: 'It adds greatly to the comfort of travelling in Canada, that you are every where treated with the greatest politeness and attention ... Indeed, you need never be at a loss for a house to stop at. There is not a farmer, shopkeeper, nay, nor even a seigneur, or country gentleman, who, on being civilly applied to for accommodation, will not give you the best bed in the house, and every accommodation in his power.'[1] Even the rather grumpy, though well-travelled, Governor Dalhousie could not help noticing how well travellers were received when they stopped at any farmhouse for a meal: 'I do the Canadians only justice in acknowledging their superiority in these little manners to all peasantry of any other country.'[2] Such testimony is not to be dismissed. Unlike the judgments one often encounters on the 'moral qualities' of the French Canadians ('vain,' 'unenterprising' and so on) which tend to reveal more about the commentator than the subject, these remarks stem from the actual experiences of even the most superficial observer. There was, however, one writer – and this a native Canadian who knew his subject more thoroughly than the others – who rejected the consensus view on habitant manners. Nicolas-Gaspard Boisseau, a country notary writing early in the nineteenth century, found his neighbours 'very rude: they come right into your house, caps on their heads ... pipes in their mouth, and they seat themselves on a chair.'[3] But then Boisseau was in the position of host, whereas our travellers were always guests. Apparently the Canadian peasantry, always ready to offer hospitality to others, also took it for granted when they themselves went calling.

Visiting was indeed a favourite occupation, in the country as well as in the cities of Lower Canada. Distance was no object, since only the poorest habitant families lacked a horse or two, as well as a calèche (carriage) and a cariole (sleigh) for friendly expeditions. Communications were quite good along the St Lawrence valley, especially when winter snows provided a smooth

1 Hugh Gray, *Letters from Canada, written during a Residence there in the years 1806, 1807, and 1808* (London: Longman, Hurst, Rees, and Orme 1809), 126–7
2 Scottish Record Office, Dalhousie Papers, sec. III, no. 543, Lord Dalhousie's diary, 1 October 1822 (NA microfilm)
3 'Mémoires de Nicolas-Gaspard Boisseau,' in *La famille Boisseau*, ed. P.-G. Roy, (Lévis, Quebec: n.p. 1907), 61 (author's translation)

roadway. 'By means of their carioles or sledges, the Canadians transport themselves over the snow, from place to place, in the most agreeable manner, and with a degree of swiftness that appears almost incredible; for with the same horse it is possible to go eighty miles in a day,' wrote one English tourist, adding that pleasure jaunts were a favourite winter pastime.[4] A British officer was similarly impressed with the carioles: 'The inhabitants think nothing of a journey of forty or fifty miles to see a friend, and returning the same day.'[5] Of course one did not have to journey far from home to enjoy the company of friends and relatives. Winter was nevertheless the season for visits near and far; aside from the fact that it was a time of plenty when animals were slaughtered, it was the period of the year when agricultural labours were least pressing.

Parties where large numbers assembled in a private home for dinner and dancing seem to have been common in the winter, particularly on certain holidays, such as Christmas, Epiphany, and Mardi Gras. John Lambert claims to have seen fifty to a hundred revellers sitting down to a rustic Mardi Gras banquet of meat, pies, and soup, together with rum 'by the half-pint': 'The tables groan with their load, and the room resounds with jollity and merriment.' The meal ended, dancing began: 'minuets, and a sort of reels or jigs, rudely performed to the discordant scrapings of a couple of vile fidlers.' Parish priests were naturally concerned about such gatherings. Of the Christmas season one wrote, 'This is the time of year when there is the greatest dissipation, the most amusements and the greatest disorder.'[6]

4 Isaac Weld, *Travels through the States of North America, and the Provinces of Upper and Lower Canada, during the Years 1795, 1796, and 1797,* 4th ed., 2 vols (London: John Stockdale 1807), 1: 276
5 [Thomas Anbury], *Travels through the Interior Parts of America: in a Series of Letters,* 2 vols (London: W. Lane 1789), 1: 142
6 John Lambert, *Travels through Canada and the United States of America, in the years 1806, 1807, & 1808,* 2 vols, 2nd ed. (London: C. Cradock and W. Joy 1814) 1: 177–8; Hébert to bishop, 10 March 1824, quoted in [Azarie Couillard-Després], *Histoire de la seigneurie de St-Ours,* 2 vols (Montreal: Imprimerie de l'institution des sourds-muets 1915–17) 2: 199 (author's translation); ACESJQ, 9A/114, Chabot to bishop, 26 January 1841

What bothered the clergy most was the fact that parties were almost always held on Sundays and holidays. Sunday mass was in fact the occasion when the dispersed residents of a parish would gather together, not only for worship, but 'for purposes of business, love, and pleasure.' 'In short,' continues Pierre de Sales Laterrière, 'Sunday is the grand fête, it forms the most pleasurable part of the habitant's life.' Holidays served similar secular purposes. The annual festival of a parish's patron saint was usually the occasion of particularly lively local celebrations, which often attracted revellers from surrounding communities. Such 'debauchery' was the object, in Lower Canada and in other Catholic countries, of recurrent clerical campaigns aimed at making the holy days truly holy. When threats and exhortations did not work, bishops often decided that no holiday was better than a profaned holiday, and over the years the Church gradually eliminated many fêtes d'obligation and ordered others celebrated on the nearest Sunday.[7]

One variety of celebration that the clergy rarely attempted to suppress was the wedding feast. Since January and February were the favourite months for marriages, weddings tended to fit into the seasonal pattern of holiday festivities: 'At their weddings the same custom is prevalent; a dance and a feasting always succeed this happy event; and not only one dance and one feasting, but, most probably, a dozen. The whole bridal cortège in a long string of calèches if in summer, of carioles in winter, passing from house to house; and each night, for, perhaps, a fortnight, renewing, with unabated vigour, both the eating and the dancing.' A fortnight? Well, perhaps three or four days. But the eating, drinking, and dancing, the procession of carriages through the community were certainly universal. Frequently the

7 Pierre de Sales Laterrière, *A Political and Historical Account of Lower Canada with Remarks on the Present Situation of the People, as Regards Their Manners, Characters, Religion etc. etc.* (Quebec: Fréchette 1831), 121; Henri Têtu and C.-O. Gagnon, ed., *Mandements, lettres pastorales, circulaires des évêques de Québec* (Quebec: A. Côté 1888), 3: 55–9; ACESH, C66, Kelly to Mgr Plessis, 19 June 1821; ACESJQ, 6A/21, Duburon to bishop, 1 July 1795

bride, then the groom, and each of the guests in turn would be called upon to sing a song. And the weddings could be quite substantial affairs; it was the custom, after the invited guests had dined, to admit 'survenants,' that is, young people, even strangers from distant parishes, who had come to join in the dancing.[8]

Music, drinking, and socializing were not limited to private homes. Every community had its tavern and most had several; in the parish of La Prairie there were thirty about the time of the Rebellion. In theory, these establishments were licensed and regulated by the government, but supervision was notoriously lax: 'The Tavern keepers throughout this part of the country have long set the laws regulating taverns at defiance, more particularly those which require their bar rooms to be closed on Sundays.' Of course bars stayed open on Sundays; since many were located near churches, this was the day they would be most likely to attract rural customers emerging from mass. And in the uncommon event that an innkeeper was prosecuted for Sunday sales, he could always persuade his customers to testify that they had not paid for the liquor they drank: they merely had accepted refreshment offered in the spirit of hospitality! The sources tell us little about who frequented taverns and what they did there, although it is apparent that around the time of the insurrections the authorities were convinced that, as places where habitants assembled, they were surely 'hotbeds of disaffection.'[9]

THE PARISH

There was more to habitant collective life than fun and frolics; in addition to informal conviviality, the rural communities of

8 Laterrière, *A Political and Historical Account*, 134; 'Mémoires de Nicolas-Gaspard Boisseau,' 56–9
9 ANQ, 1837, no. 3737, C. Weatherall to Civil Secretary, 18 March 1840; ibid., no. 3716, Edward Bowen to Civil Secretary, 7 February 1839; Archives judiciaires de Sorel, Cour des juges de paix, 7 February 1835; NA, LC Stipendiary Magistrates, Gugy to Murdoch, 4 November 1839

French Canada were bound together by some rudimentary institutions. First among them was the parish, the fundamental framework of community in the Lower Canadian countryside. Like its old-world counterpart, it was initially instituted to serve as what Sidney and Beatrice Webb called a 'unit of obligation' rather than a unit of self-government.[10] Devised by Church and state authorities in the seventeenth century to rationalize and regularize the administration of the countryside, the parish was supposed to be dominated by a curé (priest) who was answerable to a bishop, backed by the secular officials of Quebec City. Lay parishioners were regarded primarily as the objects of pastoral care by those who instituted the colony's parochial framework. They were supposed to give material support to the curé and the church that were provided for the good of their souls, but they themselves were not to run the church. The Church clung to this authoritarian ideal over the centuries, even as it did battle with parishioners who consistently failed to play the role assigned them.

But if the parish was nothing more than a 'unit of obligation,' imposed on a passive populace, why were so many rural parishes originally established on the initiative of the residents themselves?[11] Why did the habitants make such a fuss every time a bishop ordered a church rebuilt in a new location or the boundaries of a parish altered? In a rapidly expanding colonial society adjustments were inevitable, but in a great many cases they met with staunch resistance from people who clearly had their own ideas about the proper contours of the local community. To take one early example from the island of Montreal, an area called the côte Saint-Léonard was to be attached in 1714 to Rivière-des-Prairies instead of the parish of Pointe-aux-Trembles to which it had previously belonged.

---

10 Sidney and Beatrice Webb, *The Parish and the County*, vol. 1 of *English Local Government* (London: Longmans, Green 1906), 40–1
11 Louise Dechêne, *Habitants et marchands de Montréal au XVIIe siècle* (Paris: Plon 1974), 461

The people of Saint Léonard refused and petitioned the bishop. On learning that the latter would not change his mind they became angry and seized the consecrated bread that one of their number, more submissive than the rest, was taking to the new church. The bailiff sent to serve a writ on these rebels reported that all the women of the place were waiting for him, 'with rocks and sticks in their hands in order to murder me'; they chased after him, swearing and saying, 'Stop thief, we want to kill you and throw your body in the swamp.'[12]

Occasionally conflict arose in a parish because the growth of settlement and the consequent shift in the demographic centre of gravity led to calls for a change in the location of the church. Those who lived near the old church were generally opposed to any change, and they could be quite stubborn even when the ecclesiastical authorities ordered a move. This is what happened in Yamachiche in the 1780s.[13] Settlement in this parish had a rather unusual bifocal pattern; most people lived along either the Grande Rivière Machiche or the Petite Rivière Machiche. The church was in the older Grande Rivière section, but it was struck by lightning and burned down in 1780. With the approval of the seigneur, arrangements were soon made to rebuild the church close to its original site and the bishop granted the required authorization. By this time, however, the younger settlement on the Petite Rivière Machiche had grown more populous than the Grande Rivière and the people there chose trustees to press their claim to have the church built in their part of the parish. The case was taken to court and the decision favoured the Grande Rivière, but an appeal to the colony's legislative council reversed the decision (1785). Meanwhile, the deaths of two bishops in succession left the episcopal position on the Yamachiche church uncertain. Construction in fact proceeded on two churches, one

12 Ibid., 464 (author's translation). Cf. Louis Lemoine, 'Une chicane de curés au XVIIIe siècle,' Société canadienne d'histoire de l'église catholique, *Session d'Etudes 1984*, 53–66
13 J.-Alide Pellerin, *Yamachiche et son histoire (1672–1978)* (Trois-Rivières: Editions du Bien Public 1980), 185–95

in each section of the parish. Finally, Bishop Hubert, adding his voice to that of the government in 1788, ordered that the unchristian strife should end and that the church should be built at the Petite Rivière, with all parishioners paying their share of the costs. But the people of Grande Rivière would not give up easily. Armed with clubs and axes, a party eighty strong went to the Petite Rivière, broke up the interior of the chapel, and seized the sacred vases and the bell that had hung from the steeple of the old church, 'their church,' and took them back to their settlement. The outraged bishop ordered that the sacraments be refused to anyone who failed to accept his decision about the site of the church. The stolen property was returned, and eventually, after several years, most of the parishioners of the Grande Rivière were persuaded to contribute their share towards the new church.

The 'great discord,' as this incident is called in the annals of Yamachiche, was not unique, although it was unusual for conflict to reach such a high pitch. Another serious incident occurred when class conflict overlapped with sectional rivalries at St-Pierre-les-Becquets in 1836. Here the residents of the 'front' section along the St Lawrence, led by the seigneur and several men of property, secured the bishop's approval and began work on a church in their part of the parish. They were soon chased from the site by 100 armed men from the rear concessions who had wanted the church built further back from the river.[14] Here, as in the case of Yamachiche, there were peculiar circumstances arising from the geography of settlement.

These parochial dramas do illustrate some points of general significance concerning the French-Canadian parish. They emphasize, paradoxically perhaps, both the sectional tensions that were part of parish life and the great importance attached to the parish as a community unit and to the church as its concrete embodiment. Parishioners fought over the location of a church partly

---

14 NA, Jacques Paquin, 'Mémoires sur l'Eglise au Canada,' 1100-3; NA, LC
Adjutant General, vol. 46, T. Fortier to L.T. Duchesnay, 22 December 1836

because it was a matter of great practical consequence. It determined how far one would have to journey for weekly mass and periodic holiday celebrations. Moreover, since merchants, artisans, doctors, and notaries generally set up shop near the church, habitants who lived in remote parts of the parish were doubly inconvenienced; their property values probably suffered accordingly. These disputes over building sites and parochial boundaries thus did not stem from a purely sentimental attachment to the old village steeple.

The Yamachiche and St-Pierre-les-Becquets incidents also indicate how great a part was played by habitant initiative in directing parish development. Bishops and secular courts might well issue orders about where a church should be built; the habitants of the Grande Rivière Yamachiche or the rear of St-Pierre would make their own decisions on these weighty matters and they would act accordingly. On the other hand, the limits of lay control must also be recognized. The civil courts and the episcopacy were in some disarray in the 1780s, but they still had a hand in regulating the Yamachiche dispute. In St-Pierre the rebels were eventually brought to reason and the church was built in the authorized location. As long as the habitants kept trying to make the parish and the church an expression of the local community they had created, they would find themselves in conflict with a Catholic clergy for whom these were institutions *given* to the people by the Church.

As far as the curés and bishops were concerned, the church was a building belonging to God and therefore entrusted to the care of His clergy. The habitants, for their part, did not question the special religious function of the church, but they do not seem to have found this incompatible with a secular role as a centre of community life. Priests often complained of 'indecent' behaviour in the 'temple of God.' There were often loud conversations during services, men brought their dogs to mass, there was a constant movement to and fro as people retired to the porch for a smoke. Horseplay was not uncommon. In Sorel a favorite local sport in the early nineteenth century consisted of tripping the beadle as he climbed the stairs to distribute consecrated bread in the balcony. The poorer parishioners who could not afford their own pews and who therefore lounged on the staircase seem to have been the culprits in this case. When the exasperated curé stopped the service one Sunday and ordered a man to move away from the stairs, he received a shocking response: 'The man immediately came down and advanced several steps making an insulting gesture with his hand. He began to shout, Do your service, this does not concern you, you are an opulent man and further words to that effect.'[15] In the decades following 1800 'constables' were appointed in many parishes to keep order in church. The 'disorder' that laypeople as well as priests deplored did not necessarily betoken alienation from the religion and the clergy. (Did the man who gave the curé of Sorel so much trouble oppose him as a man of the cloth or as a man of wealth? And if he was simply irreligious, what was he doing in church in the first place?) It was with the concept of the church as a social gathering place as well as a place of worship that the priests of rural Lower Canada had to do battle.

In other words, the parishioners seemed to think the church was theirs; what is more they also believed the rectory belonged to them, even if it was the curé's residence. The fact that they always paid for the construction and upkeep of these two build-ings – often providing materials and labour as well as money – seemed to justify their possessive attitudes. Yet the clergy's offi-cial position was that a church and rectory – a big and solidly built one at that – were the minimum that a parochial flock owed (along with the tithe of course) to its pastor; control of both buildings therefore belonged rightfully to the priest and his bishop. But the habitants apparently saw the rectory as a com-munity edifice in which they allowed the curé to live. In 1826

15 ACESH, C66, Joyer to Plessis, 18 April 1816 (author's translation); Henri Têtu and C.-O. Gagnon, ed., *Mandements et lettres pastorales des évêques de Québec*, 8 vols (Quebec: A. Côté 1887), 1: 540; Ivanhoe Caron, 'Inventaire de docu-ments concernant l'Eglise du Canada sous le régime français,' *RAPQ*, 1941–2, 212; idem, 'Inventaire de la correspondance de Mgr. Jean-Olivier Briand, évêque de Québec,' *RAPQ*, 1929–30, 121

one layman involved in an argument with the curé of Sorel stormed into the rectory: 'Swearing and blaspheming, he said that he was as much the master as any person in the house.'[16]

A rectory in rural French Canada was truly a community hall as well as home to the parish priest. In almost every case it contained an 'habitants' room' or 'public room,' which was used for formal vestry meetings as well as for ordinary socializing, especially before and after mass on winter Sundays. In some places the 'salle des habitants' filled some of the functions of a tavern; men met there for a smoke, a chat, and perhaps a drink. There were complaints, at least in the early eighteenth century, of quarrels and even brawls. The habitants' room was not a male preserve. One Sunday in 1838 Sophie Carignant got embroiled in a political argument with a man she met in the public room of the St Hyacinthe rectory. In some parishes attempts were made to provide separate rooms for men and women.[17]

It was in the public room of the rectory that vestry meetings usually were held. The vestry was the parish community in its financial guise. Its affairs were managed by a board of three or four churchwardens, the senior of whom was the 'churchwarden in charge,' who had to keep the accounts and guard the parish coffers. Vestry revenue came from pew rents, voluntary contributions, a portion of the fees for weddings and funerals, and fines. From this fund were paid the wages of the beadle and the costs

16 NA, Sorel seigneurie, vol. 7, deposition of Sophie Kelly veuve Mignault, 14 September 1826, quoted in Allan Greer, *Peasant, Lord, and Merchant: Rural Society in Three Quebec Parishes, 1740–1840* (Toronto: UTP 1985), 118 (author's translation)

17 'Ordonnance qui fait défense aux habitants qui s'assemblent dans les presbytères avant ou après le service divin de s'y quereller, de s'y battre ou d'y proférer des paroles indécentes ou injurieuses,' 10 February 1723, quoted in Caron, 'Inventaire de documents,' 219; ANQ, 1837, no. 1546, déposition de Sophie Carignant, 5 January 1838; Abbé Félix Gatien and Abbé David Gosselin, *Histoire du Cap-Santé depuis la fondation de cette paroisse jusqu'à 1830* (Quebec: Imprimerie franciscaine missionnaire, 1899), 78; Serge Gagnon, *Plaisir d'amour et crainte de Dieu: sexualité et confession au Bas-Canada* (Quebec: Presses de l'Université Laval 1990), 71–2

of building maintenance, furnishings for the church, the wine, candles, and other necessary supplies. The churchwardens' duties were demanding, but the office conferred prestige and respect. It also brought many churchwardens into conflict with their curés. Particularly in the eighteenth century, priests wishing to purchase oil for altar lamps or to have the rectory roof patched were often vexed when faced with the stubborn opposition of a churchwarden who clearly viewed the matter from the vantage point of the paying parishioners rather than that of the spending priest. Bishop Briand was always fulminating against the 'reign of the churchwardens'; he tried to make rural Catholics believe that churchwardens were, 'people who represent us and who are charged partly in our name to take care of monies belonging to the church and for the use of which they are required to report to us.'[18] But it was of no use; two generations later, in 1838, the curé of St Antoine was telling his bishop about the vestry's refusal to cooperate in legal measures to recover money: 'Your Eminence will perhaps be surprised on seeing that I have so little influence over my parishioners; for my part, I am not at all surprised ever since I was told at a meeting, "these funds belong to us and the bishop has nothing to do with it." '[19]

One major issue dividing the clergy and the lay vestry was the renting of pews in the parish church. Pews were assigned to male heads of property-owning households on lifetime leases that specified an initial entry fee and an annual rent. Since every family had a pew, there was some honour in possessing one, particularly in a choice location near the front of the church. Civil legislation from the French régime specified that vacant pews were to be awarded at an auction to the parishioner offering the highest rent. This rule, if followed, would have ensured that vestry revenues were as high as possible and that the richest families always occupied the most prestigious positions in the church. This sort of practice occurred in old-régime France and

18 ACESH, XVII, C39, Mgr Briand to the inhabitants of St Ours, 1779
19 ACESH, 'Histoire de la paroisse de St Marc,' by Abbé Isidore Desnoyers, 84–5

in the towns of Canada, but not in the French-Canadian country-side. Early nineteenth-century charts of pew locations from the parish archives of the Richelieu show a preponderance of habitants paying modest rents filling the forward ranks, with merchants, professionals, and gentlemen paying much higher dues seated far behind them. Nothing could display more clearly the ascendancy of the habitants in vestry affairs.[20]

Why did the geography of pews in rural churches not reflect the social order more exactly? In St Ours it was because the parishioners ignored the law and set pew rentals at a uniform rate of 3 livres; they did hold competitive auctions, but only for the entry fee. In 1789 a reforming curé attempted to change the system, insisting that the annual dues be set by competitive bid. His efforts were fruitless, and the custom remained unchanged until 1804, when rents were first auctioned. Even then all the winning bids were at the traditional rate of 3 livres, indicating collusion among the bidders. As another means of combating any tendency to competition, the lay people of St Ours took steps to keep pews out of circulation by voting to make them hereditary. The bishop overruled this resolution, but on other occasions he was persuaded to allow inheritance to one generation only when that was what it took to get parishioners to build a new church.[21] The various concessions secured by the vestries had the effect of favouring the claims of long-established property-owning families – that is, of the habitants – at the expense of the very poor, who could not afford the fees, and of the village bourgeoisie, generally newcomers in the early nineteenth century and therefore unlikely to get the chance to bid on a good pew. This situation seems to have changed quite drastically in the early

20 Aurore Dupuis, 'Les contrats de bancs d'église à Montréal au XVIIIe siècle (1692–1760),' (MA thesis, Université de Sherbrooke, 1978); Greer, *Peasant, Lord, and Merchant*, 115–16; St Ours parish archives, vestry accounts, vol. 2; St Denis parish archives, vestry accounts, 'tableaux des bancs de l'église,' 1774, 1794, 1807, 1819
21 St Ours parish archives, vestry accounts, vol. 1, 11 October 1789; ACESH, XVII, C39, Porlier to Mgr Briand, n.d. [1779]; St Denis parish archives, vestry accounts, 25 December 1796

decades of the nineteenth century as the social structure of the District of Montreal countryside became more complex. Land-owning habitants, while still a majority in most parishes, were no longer the only significant class. This fact no doubt made it easier for clergymen to impose genuine auctions and to eliminate the quasi-hereditary transmission, which kept pews out of circulation.

Change in the respective influence of priests and habitants in vestry affairs was connected with alterations in the procedures for choosing churchwardens, or rather in the rules governing admission to the vestry meetings where these officers were elected. In the cities attendance was always restricted to individuals who had previously served as churchwardens, but in most rural parishes in the eighteenth century, meetings seem to have been open to all property holders. In effect this practice gave the peasantry control of the vestry, although a curé could play a crucial role if he had political skills and a forceful personality. My rather unscientific analysis of the 300 churchwardens elected in the three parishes of Sorel, St Ours, and St Denis from 1740 to 1840 suggests that the habitants monopolized this office. Men's occupations are not stated in the records, but I was unable to find the names of any of the region's merchants, doctors, and notaries. Craftsmen do not seem to have been better represented. Of sixty-five potters known to have lived in the village of St Denis before 1840, only one was ever elected churchwarden.[22] There is little doubt that the corps of churchwardens was the exclusive preserve of the peasantry.

In the early nineteenth century many rural priests seem to have succeeded in imposing the narrower, originally urban, franchise.[23] Doubtless the curé's influence was thereby enhanced,

22 The names of St Denis's potters are listed in Michel Gaumond and Paul-Louis Martin, *Les maîtres-potiers du bourg Saint-Denis, 1785–1888* (Quebec: Ministère des affaires culturelles 1978), 157–9. The churchwardens are recorded in the parish archives of St Denis.

23 Allan Greer, 'L'habitant, la paroisse rurale et la politique locale au XVIIIe siècle: Quelques cas dans la Vallée du Richelieu,' Société canadienne d'histoire de l'église catholique, *Sessions d'études* 47 (1980): 30–1

since this system made the churchwardens a self-coopting body largely independent of the parish rank and file. Complaints from priests and bishops about uncooperative churchwardens do indeed become less numerous after about 1800. By the 1820s and 1830s it was mainly in the Montreal district, and particularly the Richelieu region, that the old system of choosing churchwardens remained; here 'notables' were still invited to vestry meetings, which in effect opened elections to all habitant men, since no one wanted to tell a neighbour he was not a notable. At this time Bishop Lartigue of Montreal launched a campaign to rid his diocese of democratic vestries, and the records of his pastoral visits are punctuated with ordinances decreeing that only the 'old and new churchwardens' could attend vestry meetings. The region's laymen resisted this clerical assault with vigour, and they appealed for outside assistance in their struggle.

In January 1831 the provincial Assembly received a petition from two Richelieu parishes complaining of the exclusion of most property-holders from vestry meetings. According to the petitioners, this was contrary to earlier local usage and to the French civil laws supposedly still in force in Canada. The Patriot-dominated colonial Assembly set about gathering information on the subject and later that year passed the 'Fabrique Bill,' which would open meetings to parish 'notables.' Middle-class politicians like Louis-Joseph Papineau defended this position both by appealing to historical precedent and by insisting on the rights of property owners and ratepayers to control community funds. Papineau clearly had in mind a parish constitution that would enfranchise only the relatively wealthy and educated, as a secular opposition that would resist excessive clerical encroachment. Ordinary rural parishioners do not seem to have shared this bourgeois concept; curés complained that all kinds of people attended vestry meetings claiming the status of 'notables' if they owned any little patch of ground. The incipient conflict between the more democratic approach of the habitants and the relatively exclusivist position of the parliamentarians never rose to the surface. The problem of defining the qualifications of a 'notable' would have to wait until the clerical assault on lay participation of almost any sort had been defeated.[24]

Certainly the Catholic clergy was not going to stand by idly and see the Vestry Bill (that 'horribly deformed abortion,' in the words of Bishop Lartigue) become the law of the land. The debates of 1831 galvanized them into political action and a flood of pamphlets, letters to the editor, and private representations to powerful men issued forth and set out the Church's position on the subject. Vestry meetings had always been limited to church-wardens only, it was claimed; more open proceedings would simply cause dissension; in addition, this was an ecclesiastical matter with which the state had no right to interfere.[25] In the end, the clerical campaign was successful and the bill was defeated in the Legislative Council; ironically, the latter was a Protestant-dominated body, though one that had no more use for democracy than did the Catholic hierarchy. From this date until after the Rebellion, relations between the clergy and the Patriot party were utterly poisoned.

The campaign for a constitutional vestry did not die. In many Richelieu valley parishes war continued to rage between laity and clergy. The radical party attempted legal action in St

24 JHALC, 1831–32, 29 Jan 1831; ibid., app. QQ, 'Réponses des curés aux questions d'un comité spécial de la Chambre d'assemblée relativement aux affaires de fabrique, 1831,' letter of M. Blanchet, St Charles; Richard Chabot, Le curé de campagne et la contestation locale au Québec (de 1791 aux troubles de 1837–38) (Montreal: Hurtubise 1975), 76

25 Others have studied this dimension of the subject, but they all tend to accept the clerical version of the story and portray the conflict as one arising from the aggressive anti-clerical impulses of middle-class liberals. My view is that the Church's propaganda was designed to conceal its assault on traditional lay rights. See Fernand Ouellet, 'Nationalisme canadien-français et laïcisme au XIXe siècle,' Recherches Sociographiques 4 (1963): 47–70; Chabot, Le curé de campagne, 75–98; Gilles Chaussé, 'L'attitude de l'épiscopat envers le laïcat vers 1830,' in Le laïc dans l'Eglise canadienne-française de 1830 à nos jours, ed. Pierre Hurtubise (Montreal: Fides 1972), 103–11; Lucien Lemieux, Les années difficiles (1760-1839), vol. 1 of Histoire du Catholicisme québécois: les XVIIIe et XIXe siècles, ed. Nive Voisine (Montreal: Boréal 1989), 153–60.

Antoine; in Chambly they held their own unauthorized vestry meetings and set down rules to govern the selection of church-wardens and the procedures for settling annual accounts.[26] By now the context of debate had changed. The debate over the Vestry Bill and the general political polarization of the mid-1830s tended to lift the struggle out of its purely local framework and harden the lines of conflict. At the same time the leading role of the genuine village 'notables' – notaries, doctors, and merchants – became more pronounced in the liberal offensive. These bourgeois elements had certainly come to the fore in previous parochial tempests, over matters such as pews and church repairs. Naturally enough, habitants would enlist the aid of educated co-parishioners when petitions had to be drawn up or the lay position otherwise articulated. Yet the idea of the parish as an institution of local self-management was not the invention of the professional men, shopkeepers, and politicians of the Patriot movement; this was a cause that the French-Canadian peasantry had championed since the beginning of parochial government in Canada. In so far as the masses followed the lead of the educated bourgeoisie, they 'followed' along a path they themselves had blazed long before.

The French-Canadian rural parish began life as an administrative unit, and it always remained that in the minds of priests, bishops, and government officials. It also functioned to some degree as a unit of self-government, however, and, in so far as it did so, it was largely through the efforts of the peasantry. As they built churches and rectories, as they wrangled over parochial boundaries and pew rentals, the habitants made the parish their own. Their loyalties were particularistic and local and this placed them at a disadvantage when they had to deal with institutions, such as the Church and the state, that were organized on a larger scale. Nevertheless their determination enabled them to gain significant victories in their struggles for lay autonomy.

26 ANQM, gr., Migneault, Protest de Firmin Perrin et autres contre M.M. Cusson, 23 February 1836; ACESJQ, 1A/109, Mignault to Lartigue, 12 February 1834

CHARIVARI

One perennial bone of contention between lay people and clergy was the popular custom of charivari; this is a subject of particular interest to us because of the prominent role it came to play in the events of 1837. Charivari was practised in the towns and villages of Lower Canada, but all our best and fullest accounts of the ritual pertain to urban instances. A British visitor who witnessed a charivari in Quebec City in 1817 wrote of it in a travel book:

Here is a curious custom, which is common through the provinces, of paying a visit to any old gentleman, who marries a young wife. The young men assemble at some friends house, and disguise themselves as satyrs, negroes, sailors, old men, Catholic priests, etc. etc. having provided a coffin, and large paper lanthorns, in the evening they sally out. The coffin is placed on the shoulder of four of the men, and the lanthorns are lighted and placed at the top of poles; followed by a motley group, they proceed towards the dwelling of the new married couple, *performing* discordantly on drums, fifes, horns, and tin pots, amidst the shouts of the populace. When they arrive at the house of the offender against, and hardy invader of, the laws of love and nature, the coffin is placed down, and a mock service is begun to be said over the supposed body. In this stage of the affair, if Benedict invites them into his house and entertains them, he hears no more of it. If he keeps his doors shut, they return night after night, every time with a fresh ludicrous composition, as *his courtship*, or *will*, which is read over with emphasis, by one of the frolicking party, who frequently pauses, whilst they salute the ears of the persecuted mortal with their music and shouting. This course is generally repeated till they tire him out, and he commutes with them by giving, perhaps, five pounds towards the frolic, and five pounds for the poor.[27]

27 John Palmer, *Journal of Travels in the United States of North America and in Lower Canada performed in the year 1817* (London: Sherwood, Neely and Jones 1818), 227–8. On this particular charivari, see also 'Un charivari à Québec,' *BRH* 44 (August 1938): 242–3; *Le Canadien* (Quebec), 10 October 1817. Travel accounts describing other charivaris are cited in Bryan D. Palmer's wide-ranging study, 'Discordant Music: Charivaris and White-Capping in Nineteenth-Century North America,' *Labour – le travail* 3 (1978): 5–62.

Charivari was by this time a well-established custom in French Canada. Bishop Laval had been fulminating against these raucous nocturnal demonstrations as early as 1683; the occasion was a week of 'disorder' aimed against a widow who had remarried three weeks after the death of her first husband. Since the civil authorities seemed powerless to stop the charivari, the bishop intervened with a general prohibition of the practice. His order had little effect apparently; for we learn of another sensational case in Montreal a generation later. A man aged forty-seven had married a woman of twenty-four and the couple was subjected to a charivari. Evidently they refused to 'commute' with the crowd, since the harassment continued for more than a month and ended in violence; criminal proceedings ensued, which is why a record of the incident survives. Other passing references in private correspondence suggest that charivaris were fairly common, even though they do not usually appear in the documents except when something went amiss.[28]

All the earliest and best documented charivaris occurred in the cities, but with the emergence of compact village settlements in the early nineteenth century, we hear of rural charivaris as well. Since the custom requires a crowd, it stands to reason that the ceremony would have appeared somewhat belatedly in the French-Canadian countryside. During the three decades preceding the Rebellion, however, charivari became a common feature of Lower Canadian village life. We have one detailed account, from the pen of a village notary at Terrebonne, of a charivari that took place in January 1833. Rumours that something was afoot were circulating several days before the wedding of Celeste Boileau de Richebourg, a widow of sixty-eight who was to marry young Augustin Malboeuf (age fifty). The tone of public discussion was appropriately jocular. 'The wags are in their

28 Têtu and Gagnon, ed., *Mandements des évêques de Québec*, 1: 114; ANQM, pièces judiciares, requête de Pierre Chartier, 30 December 1717; Marie-Aimée Cliche, *Les Pratiques de dévotion en Nouvelle-France: Comportements populaires et encadrement ecclésial dans le gouvernement de Québec* (Quebec: Presses de l'Université Laval 1988), 221

element,' the notary confided to his diary, 'endlessly joking about what is to come.' Seven or eight revellers wearing masks and disguises began the noisy serenade the very night of the wedding, and they returned on four consecutive nights, their numbers expanding to about fifteen, while the din grew in proportion. Behind them was the inevitable crowd of villagers; more than simple spectators, they obviously played a crucial part in maintaining the atmosphere of festive hostility. The demonstration went on for five days, escalating on each successive night, 'such that, in order to have peace, our young couple were forced to employ a mediator to discuss terms with these gentlemen. After intense negotiations an agreement was finally concluded this morning and it was settled that for three pounds, of which one pound to pay the expenses of the charivari and the rest to be distributed to the local poor, the newlyweds may in future indulge peacefully in all the pleasures of their union.' This was certainly not the first charivari in Terrebonne. In 1832 the same diarist mentioned the death of a cooper nicknamed 'le coq' who was renowned for the 'distinguished part' he had played in more than one charivari.[29]

Charivari was undoubtedly part of the cultural baggage that French settlers brought to Canada from the old country. Analogous practices can be found in England ('rough music'), Germany ('Katzenmusik'), English Canada ('shivaree'), and elsewhere, but the French-Canadian charivari bears – it is hardly surprising – a particularly close resemblance to French models. The mocking, carnavalesque tone of the proceedings, the nocturnal setting, the loud and raucous noise, the masks and costumes of the participants, and the elaborate, insistently public street procession all recall French practices dating back to the Middle Ages.[30] Simi-

29 NA, F.-H. Séguin, diary, 82–3, 71, 24 August 1832, 7 January, 11 January 1833 (author's translation)

30 Among the works dealing with the charivaris of early modern France, see Arnold Van Gennep, *Manuel de folklore français contemporain*, 4 vols (Paris: J. Picard 1937–49), 2: 614–28; Roger Vaultier, *Le folklore pendant la guerre de Cent Ans d'après les lettres de rémission du trésor des chartes* (Paris: Librairie Guénégaud 1965); Natalie Z. Davis, 'The Reasons of Misrule,' in *Society and*

larly, the occasion of charivaris, following a wedding, particularly that of an ill-assorted couple, matches the customs of France.
There were differences: French customs, in this as in other matters, varied greatly from region to region. Moreover, practices
seem to have evolved over the years; by the eighteenth and
nineteenth centuries charivari-type harassment, sometimes associated with other customs, was being directed against all kinds of
unpopular figures, such as corrupt officials, submissive husbands, and promiscuous women. The colonial ritual, by contrast,
seems quite uniform and consistent, from the seventeenth century to the nineteenth and from one end of Lower Canada to the
other. More faithful than their European cousins to early modern
models, the French of Canada always directed charivaris at newly married couples only. This seems to be one of those areas in
which a European overseas settlement functioned as a sort of
'cultural museum' in which customs were distilled, purified, and
preserved, even as they changed drastically or disappeared in the
old country.[31]
    Although the charivari was a custom characteristic of a pre-
industrial society, it would be a mistake, in my view, to regard
it as simply a throwback, an expression of a 'primal ethic,' hostile
to market relations and punitive in its reaction to non-conformist
behaviour.[32] In its Canadian guise at least, the ritual was not

Culture in Early Modern France (Stanford: Stanford UP 1975), 97–123; Claude
Gauvard and Altan Gokalp, 'Les conduites de bruit et leur signification à la
fin du Moyen Age: le charivari,' *Annales: économies, sociétés, civilisations*, 29e
année (May–June 1974): 693–704; *Le Charivari*, ed. Jacques LeGoff and Jean-
Claude Schmitt (Paris: Mouton 1981).

31 Emmanuel Le Roy Ladurie is convinced that French folktales recorded in
   contemporary Quebec display archaic characteristics not present in European versions since the eighteenth century. See *Love, Death and Money in the
   Pays d'Oc*, trans. Alan Sheridan (Harmondsworth: Penguin 1984), 271–2,
   437–9.
32 This phrase comes from Bertram Wyatt-Brown, *Southern Honor: Ethics and
   Behavior in the Old South* (New York: Oxford UP 1982), 435–61. More subtle
   versions of the same view can be found in Edward Shorter, *The Making of the
   Modern Family* (New York: Basic Books 1975), 46–7; and Peter Burke, *Popular
   Culture in Early Modern Europe* (New York: Harper & Row 1978), 200.

part of any larger pattern of collective regulation of marriage and domestic life through public demonstrations. There was no French-Canadian equivalent of the 'azouade' ('donkey-ride') or 'skimmington,' humiliating punishments inflicted in early modern France and England on submissive husbands, scolding wives, and other deviants.[33] Neither did drunks and women accused of premarital sex have reason to fear a charivari, as was the case in some areas of Germany and the U.S. south. Here it was the marital match itself that was at issue, not the content of domestic life. Prior to 1837 Lower Canadian charivaris always followed a wedding, and in every case I have examined, the marriage was a 'mismatch': either the groom was much older than the bride or vice versa, or else one of the partners previously had been married. Several accounts also mention a social mismatch accompanying the disparity in age or marital status. There was, for example, Monsieur Bellet, the target of the Quebec City charivari described above. A prominent merchant of the town, this sixty-seven-year-old widower had married his young servant girl. Just as typical was the charivari directed against a 'widow lady of considerable fortune' who wed 'a young gentleman of the Commissariat Department.'[34]

Widowers marrying again were never the exclusive, or even the primary target of Canadian charivaris. Indeed, weddings joining widows and bachelors were far more likely to trigger a demonstration than the remarriage of men. Moreover, people of all ages and both sexes took part in the festivities, though men appropriated the starring roles. A bishop's ordinance condemn-

---

33 In addition to the works cited in the previous note, see E.P. Thompson, ' "Rough Music": le charivari anglais,' *Annales: économies, sociétés, civilisations* 27e année (March-April 1972): 285–312; Martin Ingram, 'Ridings, Rough Music and the "Reform of Popular Culture" in Early Modern England,' *Past and Present* no. 105 (November 1984): 79–113; Christian Desplat, *Charivaris en Gascogne: la 'morale des peuples' du XVIe au XXe siècle* (Paris: Berger-Levrault 1982).

34 Edward Allen Talbot, *Five Years' Residence in the Canadas: including a Tour through part of the United States of America, in the year 1823* (London: Longman, Hurst, Rees, Orme, Brown, and Green 1824), 300

ing a Quebec charivari in 1683 makes explicit reference to the participation of 'a large number of persons of both sexes.'[35] In Renaissance France, by way of contrast, charivaris were commonly the work of village youth societies, and they were directed against mature widowers or outsiders who deprived local young men of a potential mate. These features have led some anthropologically minded scholars to analyse the ritual and the payment exacted from the victim in terms of a specifically male intervention in the 'marriage market,' but in French Canada charivari does not seem to have arisen from any protectionist impulses of bachelordom.

Why then, if it was not to regulate the local supply of brides, were ill-assorted marriages singled out for persecution? Writing of old-régime France, André Burgière suggests that charivaris directed at widows and widowers stemmed from ancient Catholic misgivings about remarriage. The traditionalist crowd thus took it upon itself to enforce restrictions long abandoned by the clergy. As a result, the Church emerged as the earliest and most consistent opponent of charivari, since the ritual represented a clear assault on its current marital regulations.[36] In seeking links between the mentality underlying charivari and the outlook of the official Church, Burgière opens a promising line of inquiry. Yet it seems to me that the connections may have been much closer than he realizes – at least they were in French Canada. Priests and bishops had reservations, not only about remarriages, but also about the other mismatches that provoked charivaris. Moreover, these were not ancient objections discarded by the clergy centuries before they were taken up by the mob; they were concerns that found expression even in the nineteenth century. The marital ideology of the charivari, I would argue,

35 *Rituel du diocèse de Québec, publié par l'ordre de Monseigneur l'évêque de Québec* (Paris: Simon Langlois 1703), 363 (author's translation)
36 André Burgière, 'Pratique du charivari et répression religieuse dans la France d'ancien régime,' in *Le charivari*, ed. LeGoff and Schmitt, 190–1. See also André Burgière, 'Le rituel du mariage en France: pratiques ecclésiastiques et pratiques populaires (XVIe–XVIIIe siècle),' *Annales: économies, sociétés, civilisations* 33e année (May–June 1978): 637–49.

was not an anachronism and it was not essentially contradictory to clerical views.

As far as the Church was concerned, the wedding ceremony was a sacrament, and therefore it could be approached only in a special spiritual state. The *Rituel* of the diocese of Quebec, a sort of priests' manual published in 1703 but still widely used more than a century later, insisted that prospective brides and grooms must 'have a genuinely pure intent, looking to marriage only for the glory of God and their own sanctification, and not for the satisfaction of their cupidity, their ambition, their greed and their shameful passions.' The fiancés of course had to take confession before the nuptials, and curés were expected to impress upon them the true nature of marriage:

Curés will inform the faithful that the purpose of this sacrament is to give to married persons the grace which they require to help and comfort one another, to live together in sanctity, and to contribute to the edification of the Church, not only by bringing forth legitimate children, but also by taking care to provide for their spiritual regeneration and a truly Christian education. *They will above all point out to those who wish to marry that persons who wed out of sensuality, seeking in marriage only sensual pleasure, or out of avarice, endeavouring only to establish a temporal fortune, commit a great sin, because they profane this sacrament,* and, in using something holy to satisfy their passions, they offend against the grace that Our Lord has attached to it.[37]

To marry for money or out of mere sexual appetite was not just morally reprehensible: it was sacrilegious.

These strictures were all very well at the theoretical level, but how was a priest to detect impure motives and prevent them from profaning the wedding rite? Unless candidates for matrimony made a direct confession of greed or lust, he could never

---

37 *Rituel du diocèse de Québec*, 347, 329 (author's translation and emphasis). Cf. Jean-Louis Flandrin, *Families in Former Times: Kinship, Household and Sexuality*, trans. Richard Southern (Cambridge: Cambridge UP 1979), 161–4.

be sure about their spiritual state. To refuse to marry anyone about whom he harboured suspicions would be to court disasters of all sorts (lay hostility, unsanctioned cohabitation, recourse to Protestant ministers ...); furthermore, secular law would not allow refusal without good cause. In practice, then, the effort to ensure the purity of marriage consisted mainly of general exhortations to this effect and personal discussions, in the confessional and elsewhere, with candidates for wedlock.

Naturally, a curé would give particular attention to couples whose external circumstances seemed suspicious. When a young woman married an old widower, it might just be that she was after his money and that he, for his part, had more than a moderate share of lust in his heart. Thus we find a conscientious Canadian priest writing to his bishop for advice in the case of a rich widow of his parish who wished to marry a bachelor half her age. Legally, 'you may not refuse to celebrate an ill-assorted marriage,' answered the bishop, but 'in your capacity as confessor, you should refuse absolution to anyone who wishes to marry only in order to get rich.'[38] Disparities of age and wealth were not objectionable in themselves, but they did alert vigilant clergymen to the possibility of sinful motives. By the same token, the determination of a widow or widower to remarry, while perfectly acceptable in itself, could also raise questions. Here was someone who had already established a family and who perhaps had children. Were they marrying again for the right reasons or were they simply looking for a new sex partner? Just to be on the safe side, the manual cited above therefore specified a supplement to the wedding ceremony for second marriages that consisted mainly of Psalms 127 and 128, with their heavy empha-

---

38 Serge Gagnon, 'Amours interdites et misères conjugales dans le Québec rural de la fin du XVIIIe siècle jusque vers 1830 (l'arbitrage des prêtres),' in *Sociétés villageoises et rapports villes-campagnes au Québec et dans la France de l'ouest, XVIIe–XXe siècles,* ed. François Lebrun and Normand Séguin (Trois-Rivières: Centre de recherche en Etudes Québécoises 1987), 323 (author's translation). This case occurred in 1810.

sis on wives like fruitful vines and husbands with quivers full of children.

A priest had to marry an 'ill-assorted' couple even if he harboured doubts about the purity of their intentions, but the crowd in the street might react differently to the outward signals of impurity, giving loud and dramatic voice to widely held suspicions. The charivari might then be seen as a symbolic accusation of defiling a sacred rite, which surely is why a wink-and-nudge sexual jocularity, not to say downright obscenity, formed a central theme of most charivaris. Admittedly, sexual allusions were a feature of other carnival-type festivities, but it seems to me that beyond the general cheekiness there was a specific and personal charge of illicit lust implied in the charivari. It is important to emphasize, however, that it was not 'immorality' as such that was being chastised. Recall that in French Canada charivaris were not directed against adulterers, spouse-beaters, and the like. Nor, as far as I can tell, were couples of roughly the same age ever persecuted by crowds who cited other grounds for believing they were marrying out of sensuality or avarice. The immediate purpose of charivari was not to correct immorality or even to guard the sanctity of marriage against 'real' impurity. Rather, it amounted to a ritualistic response to the *signs* of desecration, a public rebuke filled with accusations of lasciviousness, which aired suspicions shared by clergy and laity alike.

More was involved than a simple clearing of the air; charivari was also, as many commentators have pointed out, a punitive procedure. Victims were punished through both humiliation and monetary exaction, two penal techniques favoured by the Church and the criminal courts of the period. Public shaming was of course a central feature of any charivari, inseparable from the noisy charge of desecration. It recalled the 'amende honorable,' a practice common under the French régime, which forced criminals to walk through the town wearing only a shirt, stopping at specified locations to beg God's forgiveness. The ecclesiastical version of the amende honorable, much milder than that prescribed by the judiciary, involved a public confession of sin, for example, by couples who had engaged in premarital sex.[39] Like these practices of Church and state, charivari penalized people by making a public spectacle of their faults. The amende honorable was more than simply a penal technique. In the forms deployed by both priests and judges the wayward subject had to become a penitent, confessing his sin and participating in his own correction. The charivari too, as I shall argue below, involved an important penitential element. But before leaving the subject of the punitive aspects of charivari, let us look at the monetary penalties, which, along with public shaming, were designed to make the ceremony an unpleasant experience for its victims.

Lower Canadian crowds laid great emphasis on the payment of what amounted to a charivari fine. The sums involved were often quite substantial – £50, in one example from Montreal[40] – though the exact amount varied from case to case, depending, it seems, on the subjects' ability to pay. The level of the fine was indeed the subject of elaborate and prolonged negotiation. Usually some respected local figure was employed as a mediator during the daytime intervals between the noisy visitations, and he would try to establish the terms of peace; later he might see that the funds were disposed of according to the agreement. Meanwhile, as negotiations proceeded by day, at night the air still rang with increasingly annoying demonstrations calculated to break down the resistance and loosen the purse-strings of the unfortunate victims. The proceeds of a charivari were normally divided fifty-fifty, with half the fine going to the participants to pay for their 'expenses' (i.e., celebratory drinks in the tavern) while the other half was contributed to an organized charity or distributed directly to the local poor.

This use of fines was another way in which a charivari insisted on its own legitimacy by aping the methods of constituted au-

39 André Lachance, *La justice criminelle du roi au Canada au XVIIIe siècle: tribunaux et officiers* (Quebec: Presses de l'Université Laval 1978), 113–15; Gagnon, 'Amours interdites,' 324
40 Talbot, *Five Years' Residence*, 303

thority. Under the British régime as well as the French, magistrates generally kept a specified share of any fines and ordered the balance to be turned over to a parish vestry, a hospital, or government coffers. The Church also collected monetary penalties, notably from couples seeking permission to marry in spite of the impediment of consanguinity. A bishop usually issued a dispensation only on payment of a substantial fee, set, it appears, according to the petitioners' financial resources as reported by the parish priest. By the early nineteenth century money from this source had come to constitute a major element in the revenues of the diocese of Quebec. Even though the funds were applied to good Catholic charities, the practice aroused serious concerns in the Vatican.[41] Like the clergy, the charivari crowds were probably actuated to some degree by purely economic considerations; all indications are that merchants and other relatively wealthy individuals were singled out for persecution.

Besides functioning as a penalty and as a means of soaking the rich, the charivari fine played a third and equally important role: it acted as a token of agreement signifying the re-establishment of peace between the targets and the perpetrators of ritual attack. In offering money, the newly married couple signified, however reluctantly, their submission to the judgment of their neighbours. Moreover, this forced gift implied a recognition – purely at the level of outward acts, of course – of the legitimacy of the charivari itself. The subjects were needled, nagged, annoyed, and threatened until they made a gesture signifying acceptance of the charivari, until they themselves became participants in the proceedings. When victims treated the ceremony with disdain, when they refused to sue for peace, or, worse still, when they called on the 'forces of order' to stop the demonstration, the invariable result was that the charivari intensified. From the crowd's point of view the offence was then compounded, since, in addition to soiling the wedding rites, the subjects had also challenged its authority to right the wrong. This is why charivaris could go on

41 Gagnon, 'Amours interdites,' 317

and on – sometimes for three weeks or a month – and with escalating intensity; when couples were stubborn in their refusal to pay, the custom itself became the issue and the struggle raged all the more fiercely.

As soon as a fine had changed hands, the harassment stopped. The money served as a token for the crowd as well as for the victim, and it placed the former under an obligation to drop hostilities. There may have been some hard feelings in the wake of a charivari, but there is no indication that under normal circumstances they would have been lasting. On the contrary, we hear of a young man of Montreal who married a widow in 1833 and received a full-scale charivari as a result; within a year, however, he was elected as local representative to the colonial Assembly. Certainly there is no reason to think that Canadian charivari victims were 'permanently marked' as were, according to E.P. Thompson, the targets of the less restrained sort of 'rough music' dished up in the English-speaking world.[42] But accusation and punishment were only part of the ritual of charivari, mere preliminaries to the treaty of peace, marked by the presentation of expiatory coin.

In discussing the charivari fine, we have moved from the area of punishment to the realm of reconciliation. Except where the crowd was defeated or thwarted in its aims, the thrust of its actions seems to have been to bring about, willy-nilly, the reintegration into the community of wayward members suspected of desecration. Nowhere in the French-Canadian record prior to 1837 does one find relentless persecution or any apparent desire to expel or eliminate a 'cancerous element' by means of charivari. This was hardly a lay version of excommunication; the more apt analogy would be to less absolute ecclesiastical sanctions, corrective measures like the fine or the amende honorable that required sinners to make their submission to a higher authority in order to gain readmittance to the fold.

---

42 Robert-Lionel Séguin, *Les divertissements en Nouvelle-France* (Ottawa: Musée nationale de l'homme 1968), 73; Thompson, ' "Rough Music," ' 290

Aiming as it did to reintegrate 'deviants' rather than to expel them, the charivari was not the expression of pure hostility; on the other hand, it was hardly a friendly and anodyne operation. It took resistance for granted and was designed to overcome that resistance. And when opposition, from the charivari subject or from a third party, was serious, ugly scenes could ensue. There were violent riots in Montreal in 1821 and again in 1823 when attempts were made to suppress charivaris.[43] Yet it is important to note that, for all their bluffs and symbolic threats, charivari crowds were normally quite restrained. They did respond to any challenge, however, by insisting on their own authority and on their right – indeed their duty – to carry out their mandate.

An 1807 charivari in the village of La Prairie, one in which no blood was spilt, illustrates this point.[44] A rural parish boasting 'a flourishing, handsome village of 100 well-built houses,' La Prairie was just south of Montreal at a point where travellers from the Upper Richelieu and Lake Champlain boarded ferries to cross to the city.[45] For eight consecutive nights beginning 17 November the streets of this urban village were filled with the sounds of a charivari. The participants wore masks and young men appeared in women's clothes; there were songs and speeches and a parody of the Catholic funeral service, complete with coffin. Almost everyone in the village took part, male and female, young and old, but parishioners in the agrarian rangs of La Prairie were not initially involved. The object of this ritual aggression was a mismatched pair of newlyweds, Joseph Bourdeaux, a young butcher, and Marie-Salomé Samson, an older

43 Talbot, *Five Years' Residence*, 302–3; Palmer, 'Discordant Music,' 28–9; ANQM, P1000/49-1102, émeute de juin 1823 à Montréal; Bibliothèque nationale, Montreal, journal of Romuald Trudeau, 1 June 1823

44 ACESJQ, 2A/17-22; Jean-Baptiste Boucher to bishop, 24 November 1807, 17 December 1807, 7 January 1808, 2 February 1808, 16 March 1808, 11 April 1808. All quotations in what follows are translated by the author.

45 Joseph Bouchette, *A Topographical Description of the Province of Lower Canada, with remarks upon Upper Canada, and on the Relative Connexion of both Provinces with the United States of America* (London: W. Faden 1815), 129

widow. To make matters worse, the bride's previous husband, a Protestant innkeeper, had died only a few months earlier.[46] Prime candidates for a charivari, Marie-Salomé and Joseph were running the village tavern she had inherited from the lately departed husband. Eventually the charivari came to a close when the victims agreed to pay $7 under the usual arrangements with part of the money to be turned over to the poor and the rest to cover 'expenses.'

This was not the end of the matter. The charivari was five days old when the people of La Prairie assembled for Sunday mass and discovered what their priest, Jean-Baptiste Boucher, thought of their activities. From the pulpit came a scorching blast of denunciation. No one involved in the charivari, the curé announced, would be admitted to the sacrament including 'girls and women who had been so immoral as to lend their clothes for that purpose.' Further, Boucher cancelled a novena and promised there would be no midnight mass if the charivari did not end before Christmas. It was a lonely battle for the priest. The secular arm provided no support; indeed, as the disgusted Boucher reported to his bishop, the local magistrates were prominent participants in the charivari and one justice of the peace even took charge of the 'fine' that was to be distributed to the poor. The Church had always been the most determined enemy of charivaris, in early modern France as well as in Canada. It objected to the 'disorder' just as it tended to be hostile to most exuberant exhibitions of popular culture. But charivaris were particularly abhorrent to the clergy because the persecution of couples whose union had been sanctified by the Church implied a challenge to the Catholic clergy's authority to regulate marriage. In the words of a French-régime bishop, 'We desire that priests inform the people of the horror in which the Church holds charivari, a practice very much opposed to the dignity and

---

46 ANQM, parish registers, La Prairie, 17 November 1807; ibid., gr., E. Henry, testament de John Philip Lessert, 21 March 1807

holiness of marriage.'[47] At the same time, it must be noted that J.-B. Boucher was unique among French-Canadian priests in his zeal to stamp out this particular evil; a history of conflict with the parishioners of La Prairie probably explains the curé's extreme reaction.

The villagers were sufficiently pious to suspend the charivari on Sunday night, but on Monday it began again with greater fervour than ever. And now the themes were distinctly anti-clerical. A surplice and cape made their appearance in the mock funeral procession, and 'the words "curé" and "sermon" resounded last night, along with the atrocities addressed to the couple.' Such insults made Boucher all the less willing to let the affair drop once the charivari came to a conclusion. Exasperated that he could get no one to acknowledge that any wrong had been committed – on the contrary, people carefully stored their masks for future use – he insisted that the money 'extorted' from Bourdeaux and Samson be returned, as well as an additional sum of 36 livres to compensate them for loss of business during the demonstrations. Here was the parish priest making himself the advocate of a tavern-keeper once married to a Protestant. Chari-varis made strange bedfellows!

The parishioners remained totally unrepentant, and they answered his charges, not with sullen silence, but with an articu-late defence of the legitimacy of popular customs. They spoke of 'the laws of charivari,' and when Curé Boucher cited Bishop Laval's 1683 prohibition of charivaris along with a similar order from the current bishop, they replied that such documents proved only that the charivari was a universal custom practised everywhere and in all epochs. Over the course of December the habitants of the rural sections of La Prairie joined in the dis-cussions, provoked by Boucher's overreaction to the charivari. Other grievances relating to vestry funds quickly surfaced. On New Years Day the laymen convoked an assembly of parishion-

---

47 *Rituel du diocèse de Québec*, quoted in Séguin, *Les divertissements en Nouvelle-France*, 71 (author's translation)

ers; a great crowd showed up and the priest soon found himself more or less on trial: 'For almost an hour, I found myself surrounded by them (not wishing to glorify myself by the comparison) like Louis XVI in the midst of the people of the faubourgs of Paris.' Furious charges came from all sides, with financial matters and charivari forming one great 'pot pourri' as Boucher put it. The curé did not admit defeat at the time, but all indications are that he relented in his hard line against the charivari. Despairing of collecting the 'fine' he had imposed on the villagers, he eventually paid Bourdeaux and Samson out of his own pocket.

Meanwhile Curé Boucher had fallen behind in his annual parish visitations. Normally a country priest would spend the weeks around Christmas calling at every home in the parish, collecting money, grain, meat, and other produce in what was known in rural French Canada as the 'quête de l'enfant-Jésus.' A season of plenty, when livestock had been slaughtered and wheat was newly threshed, midwinter was the ideal time to ask families to make a contribution to the local church. But Christmas 1807, when the charivari issue was still on the boil, was no time to tax the generosity of the angry parishioners of La Prairie. Eventually the controversy died down, and towards the end of January Boucher judged that the time was right for an attempt. A seasoned priest who had been in the parish for fifteen years by then, he generally knew how to measure the mood of his community (though there were some disastrous lapses!); sure enough, as he proudly reported to the bishop, only two families refused to give something for the vestry.[48] In the sides of beef and sacks of grain, freely offered for the profit of the vestry, Boucher quite justifiably saw signs of acceptance; the battle was over and his flock had acknowledged his position as pastor and their own duty to support the Church. Yet there must have been cold comfort in this restoration, because it had been purchased at the cost of a defeat in the matter of the charivari fine. Clerical authority had been affirmed, but on terms laid down by the subjects. Two

48 ACESJQ, 2A/20, Boucher to bishop, 2 February 1808

years later there was another charivari in La Prairie, but an older and wiser Jean-Baptiste Boucher made no attempt to oppose it.[49]

The pre-1837 charivari was not in any clear and overt sense oppositional. Whereas themes of social and political criticism were very much a part of charivari and carnavalesque entertainments in Renaissance Europe,[50] in French Canada, despite anti-clerical overtones and 'ritual inversion' symbolism like cross-dressing, subversive messages were quite muted. Indeed, one might well consider the charivari a 'conservative' ceremony (in so far as the vocabulary of political doctrine has any meaning in this context). Not only did it ape the procedures of priests and magistrates, it functioned as a complementary form of social control, helping to chasten deviants of a very particular sort in strictly limited circumstances. Its ultimate point of reference, moreover, was the orthodox teachings of Catholicism. Intervening when the purity of the marital sacrament was in jeopardy, the charivari crowd acted to restore harmony and equilibrium in the relationship between individuals and the community, as well as in that linking God and humanity.

Thus, even though many authorities – and in particular the clergy – objected to the tumultuous street demonstrations, charivaris must be recognized as indicative of a hegemonic relationship. People staging a charivari were giving proof of their active attachment to ideological principles justifying a social order in which, for the most part, they occupied subordinate positions. At the same time, they were insisting on their own right to regulate certain specific aspects of the life of the community. This was scarcely a revolutionary position totally at odds with ruling-class precepts; neither bishops nor governors valued passive obedience. The ideal of the 'loyal subject' or of the 'faithful Catholic'

49 Ibid., 2A/23, Boucher to bishop, 26 February 1810
50 Davis, 'Reasons of Misrule'; Burke, *Popular Culture*, 199–204; Emmanuel Le Roy Ladurie, *Carnival in Romans*, trans. Mary Feeney (New York: George Braziller 1979), esp. 301-2, 316; Yves Bercé, *Fête et révolte: des mentalités populaires du XVIe au XVIIIe siècle: essai* (Paris: Hachette 1976), passim

implied a positive commitment and allowed for a good deal of direct popular initiative. Nevertheless, in spite of consensus at the level of general principles, there was conflict when magistrates and priests tried to suppress this particular form of public demonstration. This was not simply a struggle between 'order' and popular 'anarchy,' however much the enemies of the charivari might portray it as such. Clergymen, officials, and charivariers all purported to regulate individual conduct, each in his/her own way. The 'law of the charivari,' as one La Prairie resident called it, was neither all embracing in its demands nor subversive of all authority. It could coexist with the law of the state and the law of the Church. Yet it did demand obedience and respect; it did embody the popular classes' aspirations to self-government, which would not be denied.

4

The habitant and the state

Beyond the walls of Quebec, all regular administration of the country appeared to cease; and there literally was hardly a single public officer of the civil government, except in Montreal and Three Rivers, to whom any order could be directed ... In the rest of the Province there is no Sheriff, no Mayor, no constable, no superior administrative officer of any kind. There are no county, no municipal, no parochial officers, either named by the Crown, or elected by the people.

Lord Durham[1]

The British colonial state in Lower Canada was rather a primitive entity, certainly by today's standards, but even by the standards of the Atlantic world of the early nineteenth century.[2] Its laws were a confused amalgam of English and French, its finances were in chaos, owing to bickering among the different branches of government. Before 1836 there were no recognizably modern

1 C.P. Lucas, ed., *Lord Durham's Report on the Affairs of British North America*, 3 vols (Oxford: Clarendon Press 1912), 2: 112
2 The work of Bruce Curtis, though focused primarily on the post-Rebellion period of Upper, rather than Lower, Canadian history, provides crucial insights into issues surrounding the state and the process of rule in Lower Canada. See, especially, 'Representation and State Formation in the Canadas, 1790–1850,' *Studies in Political Economy* 28 (Spring 1989): 65–8.

institutions of local government even in the cities, much less in the countryside. Routine administration by salaried officials was limited entirely to urban districts, while in the countryside, where the vast majority of the population dwelt, there were virtually no full-time agents of government. The crown did dispose of a network of commissioned delegates – militia officers and magistrates primarily – who, in theory, represented the sovereign authority in every community across the province. As we shall see, however, these 'officials' were firmly rooted in their local milieus and only tenuously connected to the capital. When colonial reformers denounced 'tyranny' in Lower Canada and elsewhere in British North America, they were objecting, not to some sort of pervasive control over the life of society, but rather to the inconsistent, inequitable, and capricious exercise of government power. The administration, they charged, interfered in unpredictable ways in the business of the colonial assemblies; it awarded lucrative offices and contracts to sycophants and well-connected favourites newly arrived from Britain; it generally undermined the régime's own efforts to create prosperous, law-abiding, and loyal colonial societies. Thus the reform critique focused on the basic inefficiency of government.

Many of the state institutions of Lower Canada were modelled on those of the mother country, but as contemporaries frequently pointed out, they did not operate here as they did in the social context of Great Britain. There, unofficial connections of patronage and economic influence tended to parallel and reinforce the official lines of government administration. Rural folk in England might, for example, be doubly or triply subject to the authority of a local squire who, in the context of the state, was their local justice of the peace but who was also their employer or landlord. At the same time, the squire, though largely independent of government supervision in his capacity as magistrate, would typically be caught up in a patron-client web that brought him under the influence of the central government. Parliament and its factions were central to this network; the voters of many House of Commons constituencies were controlled by a few local notables usually affiliated with national 'parties.' Though hardly a model of efficiency and harmonious administration, this system, known to radical critics as 'Old Corruption,' managed to preserve the rule of a small class throughout the eighteenth century and well into the Victorian era. It did so essentially by combining a rather ramshackle state apparatus with a diffuse but highly effective network of social and economic subordination.[3]

Lower Canadian society did not lend itself to such a system of rule. Colonial officials had hoped in the eighteenth century that members of the seigneurial aristocracy would play the role of political managers on the model of an English squirearchy. Some did so, but there were never enough of them to constitute a 'system.' Seigneuries were so large and so many of them were owned by Church bodies and other urban dwellers that seigneurs were not at all thick on the ground in rural French Canada. Furthermore, they had far less power over their censitaires than an English country gentleman had over his tenants. Habitants enjoyed considerable security of tenure, largely freeing them from the threat of eviction. Moreover, few of them were dependent on wages, and within that minority of rural labourers only a handful worked for a seigneur or for anyone else likely to assume the political attributes of an old-country squire.

Another factor worked against the emergence of any Lower Canadian version of 'Old Corruption': the province's status as a colony. While the English system of rural administration and social deference operated as a mode of class rule, in Lower Canada ultimate political power resided in the imperial government, which lay quite outside the indigenous class structure. The fact that the provincial administration and the local elites contained English- as well as French-Canadian elements complicated matters further, but this is not the central point. The social hierarchy and the state structure could never be integrated because the latter was controlled and, at its highest levels, staffed from overseas. Until the 1840s, when the colonial régime was thor-

---

3 See Philip Corrigan and Derek Sayer, *The Great Arch: English State Formation as Cultural Revolution* (Oxford: Basil Blackwell 1985).

oughly revamped,[4] government administration, particularly in the countryside, was bound to be weak and problematic.

Still, the British régime in Lower Canada was by no means impotent. The colony's rulers did dispose of one well-organized and highly effective state agency, namely, the army. The British army had captured Canada from the French in 1759–60 and it ensured that Canada remained British for more than a century. Military garrisons were a major presence in Quebec and Montreal, and even though their main purpose was to defend against any threat of invasion, they undoubtedly conditioned colonial politics in decisive ways. Unlike the colonial forces posted to Canada under the French régime, these were completely metropolitan units, the men, the finances and many of the commands emanating from the mother country. The governor-general of Lower Canada was normally the commander-in-chief of military forces, but in his military capacity he was not answerable to the people of the province or to their representatives in the Assembly. He had at his disposal the weapon of ultimate recourse; once unsheathed, it clearly determined the outcome of the crisis of 1837–8. Apart from discharging some policing duties in the cities, however, British soldiers were not equipped to assist in the mundane business of government.

Consequently, although one might say that the British régime 'worked' in Lower Canada prior to 1837, in that both imperial rule and civil peace were indeed preserved, it remained a government with strictly limited capacity to control and modify civil society. This was a source of immense frustration to people with any sort of activist agenda for the state. Lower Canada's most famous governor, Lord Durham, was one of them; liberal rhetoric of laisser-faire notwithstanding, 'Radical Jack' yearned for a government that would vault Lower Canadian society into the capitalist fast track and was dismayed to discover that the instruments of transformation were not equal to the task. Pre-rebellion

4 See Allan Greer and Ian Radforth, eds, *Colonial Leviathan: State Formation in Mid-Nineteenth-Century Canada* (Toronto: UTP 1992).

governors had similar complaints, as did their allies in the business community, who wanted the state to change property laws, build canals, and promote enterprise. On the opposite side of the partisan divide the nationalist democrats of the Patriot party had a different reform agenda, but they too criticized the existing order as passive and ineffectual. Among the vocal and influential men of Lower Canada there was a high degree of consensus on this fundamental point, but there is no indication that the habitants worried greatly about the weakness of the state.

THE LAW

Law courts in Lower Canada were urban institutions. They sat at Quebec, Three Rivers, and Montreal, and they dealt with suits and criminal prosecutions, which involved mainly townspeople. The same situation had prevailed under the French régime; one study of the Prévoté of Quebec, for example, shows that city dwellers constituted the majority of litigants, even though the district subject to that court's jurisdiction had a population that was 80 per cent rural.[5] Of course this disproportion stems partly from the fact that a city, especially a busy port, tends to generate more litigation per capita than an agrarian region. Practical problems connected with distance from the courts also played a role, as evidenced by the fact that country people living within forty kilometres of Quebec frequented the court much more often than those located further from the city. Did people in the remote settlements have no disagreements over land boundaries and servants' wages, or did they simply find ways of settling disputes without undertaking the long journey to Quebec? In some communities there were seigneurial courts in the seventeenth century, but they rapidly died out, and certainly none was left by the time of the conquest.

5 John A. Dickinson, *Justice et justiciables: la procédure civile à la prévôté de Québec, 1667–1759* (Quebec: Presses de l'Université Laval 1982), 138–55. New France criminal court records indicate a similar urban preponderance. André Lachance, *Crimes et criminels en Nouvelle-France* (Montreal: Boréal 1984), 78

With the advent of British rule, justice was thrown into some turmoil by the superimposition of English legal systems upon the existing French ones. Yet many traditions established under French rule were allowed to continue, among them the urban locale of the courts and the tendency for country folk to stay away from the apparatus of formal justice.[6] Eventually this situation gave rise to vociferous complaint in the radical press:

We have no County courts. Our overpaid Judges sit in the cities, and the people must come up to *them* for judgment, where, responsible to nobody, they dispense law, and sometimes what *they* think *ought to be law*. The district of Montreal extends 50 miles in every direction except the west, where it is settled for 150 miles, and there being no County Courts, if a rogue steals a plug of tobacco, at the farthest extremity he must be brought to the city with the witnesses or escape punishment. Consequently small crimes may be committed with impunity. Civil matters are in the same state, which amounts to a complete denial of justice to a majority of the population. I have known men of small means but determined character, come with their witnesses 50 miles three times before they could obtain a hearing.[7]

Although essentially accurate, this writer does simplify matters for rhetorical effect. There were actually two county courts, one at St Hyacinthe and one at Napierville, established just before this report was written in 1837. And elsewhere the countryside was not without a resident judiciary, as it had been fifty years earlier. Almost every parish had at least one justice of the peace.

The office of justice of the peace was introduced to Canada shortly after the conquest, in the cities at first; magistrates would assemble for periodic 'sessions of the peace' to try offences and to pass local regulations regarding drainage, markets, prices, and so on. At the beginning of the nineteenth century magistrates

---

6 Jean-Marie Fecteau, *Un nouvel ordre des choses: la pauvreté, le crime, l'Etat au Québec, de la fin du XVIIIe siècle à 1840* (Montreal: VLB 1989), 125
7 *The Vindicator*, 2 June 1837

were appointed in the country in increasing numbers, so that by the 1820s most rural parishes had one or more JP. The office was established and grew in an ad hoc way, but, assuming colonial authorities gave much thought to the subject, they presumably intended to duplicate the rural judiciary of England, which was based on unpaid and largely independent magistrates appointed mainly from among the rural gentry. It is ironic that just at this time the whole institution of justice of the peace was falling into disrepute in the mother country. Lord Durham was appalled:

I cannot but express my regret, that among the few institutions for the administration of justice throughout the country, which have been adopted in Lower Canada from those of England, should be that of unpaid Justices of the Peace ... The warmest admirer of that institution must admit that its benefits result entirely from the peculiar character of the class from which our magistracy is selected ... The body of Justices of the Peace scattered over the whole of Lower Canada, are named by the Governor, on no very accurate local information, there being no lieutenants or similar officers of counties in this, as in the Upper Province. The real property qualification required for the magistracy is so low, that in the country parts almost every one possesses it; and it only excludes some of the most respectable persons in the cities. In the rural districts the magistrates have no clerks. The institution has become unpopular among the Canadians, owing to their general belief that the appointments have been made with a party and national bias ... Instances of indiscretion, of ignorance, and of party feeling, and accusations of venality, have been often adduced by each party.[8]

---

8 Lucas, ed., *Lord Durham's Report*, 2: 130–1. Though it is unlikely that he ever read Lord Durham, another astute political thinker, Antonio Gramsci, had a similar view of the social and cultural underpinnings required for the decentralized local administration he refers to as 'self-government': 'Self-government is an institution or a political and administrative usage which presupposes quite specific conditions: the existence of a social stratum which lives off rent, which by tradition is experienced in public affairs, and enjoys a certain prestige among the popular masses for its rectitude and impartiality ... It is thus understandable that self-government has only been

It is difficult to determine exactly what Lower Canadian justices of the peace did, since there was never any legislation setting out their duties, and apparently none of them left detailed records of his proceedings. They seem to have had authority to judge minor criminal offences, to take down affidavits, and to record other sorts of evidence to be used in the regular urban courts; they also played a part in regulating some local matters, such as the issue of tavern licences. In the small town of William Henry (Sorel), in the 1830s there were enough JPs to assemble something resembling a quarter-sessions court. The register of this court indicates that it dealt mainly with cases involving stray animals, disorderly behaviour in church, and public drunkenness.[9]

From the point of view of observers like Lord Durham, concerned about securing obedience to government on the part of the rural population, the problem with the JPs was that they were too independent of the state and insufficiently independent of the people among whom they lived. A rural justice was not a salaried servant of the crown; he derived some revenue from fees charged for his services, but he was not subject to routine supervision and had little economic reason to fear dismissal. At most times state authorities in the capital had no idea what the country magistrates were up to and could hardly use them to implement policy. The Rebellion brought this fact forcefully to the attention of government, and arrangements were quickly made to appoint 'stipendiary magistrates' who had some legal qualifications and, more importantly, who were under the direct and routine control of the state (see below, 354). Before 1839 and the establishment of the stipendiary magistrates, the people of the

possible in England, where the class of landowners, in addition to its condition of economic independence, had never been in savage conflict with the population.' *Selections from the Prison Notebooks of Antonio Gramsci*, ed. and trans. Quintin Hoare and Geoffrey Nowell Smith (New York: International 1971), 186

9 Archives Judiciaires de Sorel, Cour des juges de paix, 1834–9

French-Canadian countryside almost never confronted anyone who was truly and unambiguously an agent of the government.

A justice of the peace in Lower Canada played a role that primarily reflected his position in the local community. Some JPs were seigneurs who could bolster their judicial powers somewhat with the economic ascendancy derived from their command of land and rents. Most seem to have been merchants and professional men. Since a magistrate was supposed to have some education and wide experience, the office was essentially out of the reach of habitants. Moreover, a disproportionate number of magistrates' commissions was awarded to English speakers. Nevertheless, JPs were usually well-established members of their local communities, and even though they enjoyed positions of prestige and influence, they were frequently dependent on the goodwill of their neighbours as customers and clients. Another post-Rebellion commentator justified the appointment of stipendiary magistrates on these grounds:

In a country like Canada it is impossible that an unpaid magistracy will ever fulfil the object for which they were appointed. They in common with the rest of the Inhabitants are possessed of small means in trade, many of them selling spirits and groceries and consequently their livelihood depends greatly on their popularity. In the early stage of the colony when the population were thinly scattered and crime not open to the public view, it might have been sufficient that the magistrates, winking at smuggling and other frauds upon the revenue, arrested the murderer and housebreaker, but now that there are many duties expected from a magistrate it is impossible that a person can give up trade and lend his services gratis, to administer justice to the public, particularly if he is obliged to declare his political creed.[10]

The regulation of taverns was one area where the JPs were notoriously slaves to public opinion. They seldom refused applicants for a liquor licence the required certificate and they generally

10 NA, Colborne Papers, 8236, anonymous memo [1839]

turned a blind eye to infractions of the laws governing public houses.

Some magistrates were known more for capriciousness and corruption than laxity. J.A. Mathison, for example, was accused of petty tyranny in the parish of Vaudreuil. One of his tricks was to find winter sleighing paths that strayed from the proper roadway into the edge of a field; he would then fine all the passing travellers for trespass. He managed to extract 11 shillings each from thirty-two habitants in this way. Justices of the peace were supposed to keep account of fines and forward a portion to the district clerk of the peace, but few did so, since the clerks had no power to enforce this rule. An inquiry by the House of Assembly in 1833 revealed that the clerks of the peace had received payments from only twelve magistrates for fines levied in the previous year; sixty-six justices of the peace had levied fines that had not been accounted for, and 142 magistrates reported no fines at all. The majority of justices of the peace seem to have been either corrupt or inactive.[11] It is hard for the historian to decide which, since the government of the day clearly had no idea what the magistrates were up to!

Justices of the peace were competent only in criminal law. With the exception of disputes over small sums, civil suits had to be settled in the city courts. Legislation passed in 1821 provided for 'courts for the trial of small causes' presided over by commissioners (often called 'cours des commissaires') in rural communities. These courts were established on the initiative of local inhabitants as expressed in a petition, and the commissioners were normally men nominated also by petition. There was a property qualification established by law, but otherwise these courts were essentially community institutions. Unfortunately, records of the 'commissioners' courts' are no more plenti-

11 ANQ, 1837, no. 1064, R. Harwood to Civil Secretary, 4 September 1838; *JHALC*, 1832–3, app. HH. Numerous complaints about venal practices by JPs and about political favouritism in the appointment of new magistrates can be found in the Patriot press: for example, *L'Echo du pays*, 18 July 1833; *La Minerve*, 28 March 1833.

ful than those of the justices of the peace, and it is impossible to know just how busy they were, what sort of cases they handled, and how they made decisions.

But courts of law, whether operated by the 'professional' judiciary of the city or the 'amateur' magistrates and commissioners of the country, were not the only facilities to which rural people could turn to settle disputes or punish criminality. Consider the case of Charles Larivière and Etienne Papillon of St Ours. In 1791 these two habitants had a falling out over the sale of a piece of land, one of them asserting that he was owed damages. They agreed to name arbitrators to settle the affair and had the local notary draw up a 'deed of compromise' so that they could 'terminate their differences and avoid the costs of a trial and live in harmony.'[12] Each of the parties named an arbitrator – Larivière chose a surgeon and Papillon selected a man who, judging by his name, was probably a peasant or an artisan – and the two arbitrators were authorized to name a third arbitrator if they could not agree on a settlement. Larivière and Papillon pledged in advance to accept the arbitrators' sentence and to pay £10 for any contravention. The two judges did turn to a third party, a local seigneur, and the three of them seem to have examined the property and called on witnesses to testify, before rendering judgment. The notarial archives of Lower Canada contain hundreds of 'compromises' or 'accords' of this sort, suggesting that unofficial justice was fairly common. It is impossible to be more precise, since we do not know whether such arbitration arrangements were always set out in notarized agreements. In the case of Larivière and Papillon it is important to notice that this is not an entirely extra-legal procedure. All indications are that the arbitrators would try to apply the law of the land as they understood it; moreover, the whole point of the notarized deed and the provision for a penalty for non-compliance was to make the agreement enforceable in a regular law court. This approach was, none the less, do-it-yourself local justice.

12 ANQM, gr., Bonnet, compromis fait entre Charles Larivière et Etienne
   Papillon, 28 June 1791

Several historians have noted the customs of community regulation, which were a feature of rural life in French Canada from earliest times. It certainly made good practical sense under the French régime, when the expense of trips to the city and the waste of time, not to mention court fees, made litigation a losing proposition for many habitants.[13] In the years following the conquest lawsuits would have been even less attractive, in view of the confusion and unfamiliarity accompanying the introduction of English judicial institutions.[14] In later years, even when the 'king's justice' was more accessible to country folk, the custom of settling matters outside the courtroom endured.

Criminal matters also were handled largely within the rural community itself, as the Quebec journalist John Neilson observed in an interview with Alexis de Tocqueville: 'Public opinion is incredibly powerful here. Even though there is no authority in the villages, public order is better maintained than in any other country in the world. If a man commits an offence, people avoid him and he has to leave the village. If a theft is committed, no charges are laid, but the guilty party is dishonoured and forced to flee. We have seen no capital executions in Canada for ten years.'[15] Specific instances of this sort of trial by 'public opinion' are difficult to document, but cases do occasionally come to light. In the transcript of a court martial of rebels in 1839, for example, there was an exchange in which the accused tried to undermine the credibility of a prosecution witness, Ignace Trahen, a labourer from St Césaire, by proving that he was known in the region as a dishonest man. A farmer was called by the defence to testify about Trahen's character: 'He was my tenant for a year ... He

13 This was not only a rural practice; city merchants often tried to stay out of court by turning to arbitrators. See Jacques Mathieu, 'La vie à Québec au milieu du xviie siècle: étude des sources,' RHAF 23 (December 1969): 420.
14 Douglas Hay, 'The Meanings of the Criminal Law in Quebec, 1764–1774,' in Crime and Criminal Justice in Europe and Canada, ed. Louis A. Knafla (Waterloo: Wilfrid Laurier UP 1981), 88–9
15 Jacques Vallée, ed., Tocqueville au Bas-Canada (Montreal: Editions du Jour 1973), 95 (author's translation)

took away part of the fence from my premises. Q. – by the Judge Advocate – Did you get him punished for taking away your fence? A. – No; he is a poor man; I turned him out of my house at the end of the year.' A butcher was then called to the stand; he declared, 'Twelve years ago, he lived with me for a month, and stole a sheep for his wedding.' He admitted under cross-examination that he had never prosecuted the thief.[16] Yet it does seem that Ignace Trahen was well known in three parishes as a petty thief (how else would the political prisoners have known whom to call in as negative character witnesses?). Such a reputation probably constituted genuine punishment; it cannot have made his life easier. Another case, this one recorded in the notarial archives, concerns a sixteen-year-old boy, Joseph Chayé, who apparently committed several minor thefts in St Denis around 1794. The victims were indemnified by the culprit's brother-in-law, and two uncles promised (hence the notarized deed) that Joseph would reimburse this money when he came of age.[17]

This folk law, civil and criminal, should not be seen as something unique to rural French Canada; Jean-Marie Fecteau remarks that such extra-judicial regulation is common under régimes that he calls 'feudal' (meaning prior to the development of the modern bourgeois state in the mid-nineteenth century). 'The repressive system set up and controlled by the feudal state *is not* the crucial mechanism for reducing various illegalities,' Fecteau writes, 'Most of the tensions generated by the breaking of community rules are resolved within the community itself by procedures of arbitration or conciliation in which the literate petty

16 *Report of the State Trials Before a General Court Martial Held at Montreal in 1838-1839: Exhibiting a Complete History of the Late Rebellion in Lower Canada*, 2 vols (Montreal: Armour and Ramsay 1839), 2: 315–16

17 ANQM, gr., L. Bonnet, déclaration par Toussaint Thibault et Jacques Coder en faveur d'Athanase Frédet, 23 March 1794. On the prevalence of such out-of-court arbitration in eighteenth-century Languedoc, see Nicole Castan, *Justice et Répression en Languedoc à l'époque des lumières* (Paris: Flammarion 1980), 10–47.

bourgeoisie (notary, curé) plays an instrumental role.'[18] Nevertheless, such local 'auto-régulation' must have been particularly important in a place where the institutions of the law were as impoverished as they were in the Lower Canadian countryside.

THE MILITIA

The provincial militia was another agency of the state that had direct dealings with the peasantry. First established under the French régime, when war was a central feature of colonial life, the militia system was revived in a modified form by the British in the late eighteenth century. Almost every male between eighteen and sixty years of age was enrolled. While there were no real wars to fight after 1814, the militia remained an important institution in the Lower Canadian countryside. In fact, it provided one of the few channels through which the government asserted its right to command the obedience of the king's subjects. The basic units of the militia were the company, organized at the level of the parish, and the battalion, composed of several companies within a given county. Since efforts were made to keep companies and battalions at roughly uniform sizes, there were usually several companies in each parish, more or less depending on the population, and several battalions per county. A captain was in charge of each company, assisted by an ensign and a lieutenant. Following traditions established under French rule in the seventeenth century, the captain alone was a prominent local chief. Lieutenant-colonels in charge of battalions, on the other hand, had hardly any civil responsibilities; rather, they served as the link between company officers and the deputy adjutant-general in Quebec City, the only salaried official in the entire colonial militia. Like a JP (and many men held both positions), a militia officer enjoyed the authority conferred by a royal commission without becoming in any sense an employee of the government.

18 Fecteau, *Un nouvel ordre*, 77 (author's translation)

In wartime, militia companies gathered periodically for basic training, but[19] by the 1830s there was only one annual muster, held on 29 June, usually in front of the parish church, and every militiaman was required to attend. There was not much to this exercise, beyond lining up so that the officers could count those present and fill in their reports for the adjutant-general. 'There are no exercises, no guard duties, no fatigues and no distribution of arms. Perhaps 25,000 militiamen possess guns, but these are for hunting.'[20] The muster ended with three cheers for the king, and the militiamen adjourned to the tavern. In 1837 there were still middle-aged veterans of the War of 1812 with practical experience to contribute to the rebel cause, but the younger generation had scarcely been formed into soldiers. Nevertheless, the militia did accustom men to the discipline of a formal command structure.

Besides having to show up for the yearly muster, habitants could be called on at any time to escort prisoners on their way across the parish to a city jail. This could be an annoying burden, particularly for those who lived along a major thoroughfare. It led to some difficulties in the parish of St Eustache: because they lived near the terminus of a major ferry crossing, the militiamen of St Eustache had to handle prisoners from all over northwestern Lower Canada. Their solution was to report for escort duty on foot, stubbornly refusing to obey orders to provide the vehicles needed for the operation.[21] There was no question of blind obedience to military authority. French-Canadian habitants accepted the duty of militia service and recognized the need for discipline and subordination, but they do not seem to have recognized all commands as fair and legitimate.

19 *Rules and Regulations for the Formation, Exercise and Movements of the Militia of Lower-Canada* (Quebec: New Printing Office 1812)
20 Isidore Lebrun, *Tableau Statistique et politique des deux Canadas* (Paris: Treuttel et Wintz 1833), 457 (author's translation)
21 NA, LC Adjutant General, vol. 26, Dumont to Vassal de Monviel, 23 October 1822

At the local level it was the captain who personified militia authority. Captains had a number of administrative and policing responsibilities in addition to their strictly military duties. Besides arranging for the transportation of prisoners, they were supposed to apprehend army deserters, vagabonds, and 'disorderly persons' found in the parish and take them before a magistrate. Indeed, captains were called upon to arrest all sorts of malefactors. Along with local justices of the peace, they provided the certificates required by applicants for a liquor licence. Theoretically, they also enforced the laws regulating taverns. Finally, they were expected to organize elections for local offices such as fence inspector.[22]

There was more to the captain's position than the rather limited powers bequeathed by legislative enactment. The office had deep historical roots in rural French Canada; it had a mystique and was surrounded with rituals that made the captain a genuine community leader as well as a delegate of the king. There was, for example, the maypole ceremony described below, as well as the 'banc du roi,' a special pew at the front of each church reserved for the senior captain of the parish. Like the honorific pews set aside for the seigneur and the churchwarden, the captain's pew was supposed to be rent free; the attempt by one parish vestry to impose an annual fee on the 'king's pew' led to a great commotion and to appeals all the way to the governor of Lower Canada. Clearly, the position of militia captain had a significance for rural people that was quite out of proportion to the rather minor military and policing duties specified by the law. How else can one account for the tremendous indignation that followed a politically motivated purge of radical officers in 1827? There is a report of one man weeping openly on hearing that his commission as captain had been revoked.[23]

22 Lower Canada, *Provincial Statutes*, 3: 146–88, 43 Geo III, ch 1; NA, LC Adjutant General, vol. 46, requête des notables habitants de St David (1835)
23 NA, LC Adjutant General, vol. 34, Buckinghamshire, 1828–30; ibid., Dumont to Vassal de Monviel, 20 July 1827

I have no statistical data about the social class of militia captains, but my strong impression is that the majority were habitants.[24] In the villages of Lower Canada the officers were mainly merchants and professional men; companies drawn from the fully rural rangs, however, could be commanded only by peasants, for hardly anyone else lived there. Generally, men were awarded captains' commissions on the basis of seniority only after years of service as a subaltern. Most captains must therefore have been mature individuals. How did one become an officer and what determined promotions? Officially, it was the governor who issued commissions on behalf of the king and on the advice of the adjutant-general. Since he stayed in Quebec City, the adjutant-general could have had little direct knowledge of most parts of the province; he had to rely, therefore, almost entirely on the battalion commanders for information and advice – hence the crucial role of the lieutenant-colonels as arbiters of the fate of candidates for militia commissions.

The position of lieutenant-colonel of rural battalions seems normally to have been reserved for aristocrats.[25] In correspondence relating to the appointment of a new lieutenant-colonel, it is always taken for granted that a local seigneur should have preference. John Pangman ought to have the command of the La Chenaye battalion, the governor was informed, since it was composed 'wholly of his Censitaires.'[26] Jean-Baptiste-René Hertel de Rouville, seigneur and lieutenant-colonel of Rouville county, wrote to the adjutant-general to urge that another aristocrat, Melchior-Alphonse de Salaberry, be made lieutenant-colonel in neighbouring Chambly. A rival claimant, de Rouville explained,

24 Fernand Ouellet's study, 'Militia Officers and Social Structure, 1660–1815,' in *Economy, Class, and Nation in Quebec: Interpretive Essays*, trans. Jacques A. Barbier (Toronto: Copp Clark 1991), 87–120, is unhelpful on this point, since the figures mix together high- and low-ranking officers, in command of rural and urban militias; moreover, they relate to an exceptional period, the War of 1812.
25 See Ouellet, 'Militia Officers,' 106, 109.
26 NA, LC Adjutant General, vol. 39, McKenzie to Governor, 6 July 1830

'was not born to be at the head of a militia battalion; he was not even born to enter polite society.'[27] The petitioner was clearly on intimate terms with the adjutant-general, L.-J. Juchereau Duchesnay, himself a member of the old Canadian nobility, and so the suggestion was followed. Yet there was no hard and fast rule on appointments of this sort. When Louis Dumont, one of the local seigneurs and long-time commander of the first battalion of Two Mountains county, died in 1835, his son applied for the vacancy. 'It is difficult for me as I am now the primary seigneur of Mille Iles to find myself in a battalion under the command of my censitaires,' he explained. (His younger brother, who possessed a smaller share of the seigneurie, later requested promotion on the grounds that 'It is beneath my rank [in society] to be commanded by my censitaires.') There were rival claimants, however, who pointed to their war records and long service; one was also a co-seigneur of Mille Iles. Perhaps because Two Mountains had been a disturbed county and the elder Dumont a very controversial lieutenant-colonel, the government decided to award the command to a J.-B. Laviolette, an old major and store clerk.[28] Elsewhere, particularly where there was no resident male seigneur, merchants and professional men might be given battalion commands; I know of no habitants who attained this rank. The bias in favour of seigneurs can be explained partly by the aristocratic outlook of the officials who controlled the province's militia. They were not prepared, in the absence of compelling reasons, to subvert the rural social order by setting up a contradictory military hierarchy. At a more functional level, there must have been a recognition of the value of allying the seigneur's local knowledge and influence to the militia commander's authority.

Certainly patronage was what the lieutenant-colonel disposed of. The Terrebonne notary, F.-H. Séguin, knew whom to thank

27 Ibid., vol. 46, Hertel de Rouville to Duchesnay, 27 July 1835 (author's translation)
28 Ibid., vol. 45, C.-L. Dumont to Vassal de Monviel, 30 April 1835; ibid., vol. 47, S.-L. Dumont to Duchesnay, 2 March 1837 (author's translation)

for his promotion: 'The Hon. Rod. MacKenzie [the local lieutenant-colonel] ... seems to have looked out for me,' he confided to his diary, 'for I learn today of my nomination as captain for the Terrebonne division ... one more token of the kindness with which this gentleman has not ceased to favour me up to the present.'[29] Lieutenant-colonels did not have complete carte-blanche in these matters. The adjutant-general constantly urged them to follow the rule of seniority in recommending, for example, which lieutenant should be promoted to captain. Yet a lieutenant-colonel could always find a reason to favour a junior candidate if he wished; this man knew how to read and write, he would report, or his father had been a captain, or his residence was more conveniently located. One did not have to be literate or the son of a captain or a lieutenant of long standing to become a militia captain, but these factors helped, particularly if one's lieutenant-colonel wished to lend his support. Many lieutenant-colonels stuck quite closely to the rule of seniority, knowing that to pass by the senior candidate would be considered an 'injustice' by the adjutant and the men alike.

From time to time the militia came into the limelight as the object of political debate. This was the case under Governor Dalhousie in 1827–28 when many officers were dismissed in a crude attempt to influence assembly elections. In the county of Two Mountains the seigneur and lieutenant-colonel, Louis Dumont, was a government candidate in the election of 1827. He did not hesitate to purge radical supporters from the officer corps of his battalion; some of those who were not dismissed resigned in protest.[30] Later, a more conciliatory governor reinstated most of those who had lost their commissions. The House of Assembly also launched an inquiry and passed a Militia Act in 1830, which required that officers must live in the territory under their command and, for the first time, specified a property

29 NA, F.-H. Séguin diary, 17 March 1831 (author's translation)
30 *Report of the Special Committee, to whom was referred that Part of His Excellency's Speech which referred to the Organization of the Militia* (Quebec: Neilson and Cowan 1829)

qualification for militia officers (£25 annual revenue for captains and subalterns, £50 for higher ranks).[31] This hardly seems a democratizing measure; if enforced, it would have deprived many habitant-captains of their command. However, it was not and could not be enforced systematically in the absence of any mechanism for checking the wealth of candidates. Indeed, this aspect of the law seems to have had the effect mainly of giving militiamen one more pretext for opposing unpopular officers; rightly or wrongly, they could always claim the captain they disliked lacked the property qualification and hope that no one noticed that the man they proposed as his replacement was no richer. The property restriction was perfectly in keeping with the liberal philosophy subscribed to by the middle-class politicians of the Patriot party; they saw substantial property as an essential guarantee of the independence of individuals holding public office. They also wished to regulate, in some measure, the distribution of militia patronage and thus to protect themselves from executive interference in Assembly elections. A 'democratic' militia, then, was not in the gift of the provincial legislature.

The drive to make company officers true representatives of the local community came primarily from the mass of the rural population itself. Even though they had no official say in the choice of company officers, the rank and file found ways of influencing the selection. A lieutenant-colonel would often be guided by representations from the militiamen of a community, but not in all cases. For example, in the 1830s the people of the newly formed parish of St Dominique assembled and, in effect, elected their own captain. He was a conservative, however, and the Patriot lieutenant-colonel refused to put his name forward to the adjutant-general.[32] Even if the party-political configuration of this incident presents a paradox (one best explained, incidentally, by the tension between town and hinterland), it is important to take note of the independent community initiative,

31 Lower Canada, *Provincial Statutes*, 13: 554–62, 10–11 Geo IV, ch 3
32 NA, LC Adjutant General, vol. 48, Brunelle to Gosford, 23 August 1837

the democratic effort to secure popular leaders, that it represents. This impulse was more often exercised negatively by militiamen attempting to remove unpopular officers. There are cases of men simply refusing, en masse, to follow orders on the parade ground, a form of protest requiring advance organization. More commonly, militiamen addressed petitions to the governor, requesting the removal of a captain on the grounds of drunkenness, favouritism, or religious prejudice. One frequent cause of complaint was the attempt by lieutenant-colonels to appoint a captain who lived in a different part of the parish than the men of his company. The commander might argue that he could find 'qualified' men only in the village or river-front section, but militiamen in the rear concessions were determined to have an officer who lived among them and was truly their own leader.[33] Often, of course, the appointment of company officers was completely uncontroversial, colonel and habitants having no particular reason to disagree on the choice.

MAYPOLES

Besides striving to secure the appointment of acceptable captains, rural folk also developed their own ritual of investiture: the maypole ceremony. Every militia officer required a commission, signed by the colony's governor on behalf of the king, but captains normally had another, more imposing, symbol of office that no superior authority could provide. A late-eighteenth-century visitor from Massachusetts could not help noticing the maypoles that punctuated the Richelieu valley landscape: 'The militia are officered by men elected from among themselves, and their respective companies have alarm posts assigned, and the officer's residence is marked by a pole with an evergreen top. In this mode, in all cases of distress and danger, a resort is immediately

33 Ibid., vol. 40, petition of inhabitants of St Vallier, 8 March 1831

pointed out, for the inhabitant and stranger.'[34] Of course, officers were not elected – though the American's mistake is revealing – but they did usually have maypoles outside their houses (at least the captains did). These served the practical purpose mentioned above, but they also had a symbolic role, which is why the planting of a maypole for a newly appointed militia captain was surrounded by so much pomp and circumstance in rural Lower Canada.

A country notary, Nicolas-Gaspard Boisseau, who practised in the Quebec area in the early nineteenth century, has left the best description of this ritual.

The May Pole Ceremony in the Countryside
On the last day of April every year, four heads of household go to the home of the parish militia captain to ask his permission to plant a may pole (that is an evergreen tree sixty feet high and decorated at the top with a weather vane) in front of his door; the captain always agrees to this for it is a mark of distinction for him. Following this permission, the same four family heads can be observed arriving at his house the next day, early in the morning; they are followed by a dozen young men, armed with guns and escorting the may pole pulled by two horses hitched to two pairs of small wheels, twenty feet apart, upon which the may pole rests. As soon as they arrive at the spot indicated by the captain, they dig a hole four feet deep and raise the pole in the following manner. One strong man positions himself at the base and places a board in the hole for the pole to lean against. While some of the men lift it with pieces of wood twelve feet long, the others steady it with grappling hooks, working their way towards the base as the may pole rises. Once it is erect and they have made sure that it is straight, a strong and

---

34 J.G. Ogden, *A Tour through Upper and Lower Canada by a Citizen of the United States* (Litchfield, Conn.: n.p. 1799), 35. Cf. Adam Fergusson, *Practical Notes made during a Tour in Canada and a Portion of the United States, in MDCCCXXXI* (London: T. Cadell 1833), 58; Frederick DeRoos, *Personal Narrative of Travels in the United States and Canada in 1826* (London 1827), 116.

lively young man quickly seizes a hoe and fills in the hole around the pole. Next, while some continue to hold the pole steady, the others drive in stakes all around it with great blows from a sledge-hammer until there are enough stakes to hold it up. They then place six supporting pieces around the may pole. These supports are five feet long. With the may pole thus installed, the young men fire off a volley to salute the captain, to which he replies by firing a shot as well. The leader of the party immediately pulls out a bottle of brandy that he has hidden in the hood of his coat and offers a drink to the captain and then to all the others present, as they stand around the may pole.

On the completion of this ceremony, the captain begs them to enter his house where they find the table set with quantities of pancakes, sprinkled with molasses or maple sugar, together with some meats, but mainly lots of brandy. Every time a drink is taken, three young men jump up from the table, go out and discharge their guns against the may pole. They do this to make powder stains for the greatest mark of honour consists in blackening the entire pole with gun shots. The rest of the day is spent dancing.

And it is the may pole ceremony which is done not only for captains of militia but for all the other officers as well.[35]

It is important to emphasize that the maypole ceremony was entirely a popular ritual. For this reason, and because it was practised only in rural parishes, it seldom attracted the attention of the government officials and journalists who provide most of our historical sources. Only when an accident occurred (e.g., when a man was killed by a piece that fell from a maypole in 1831) or when, as in 1837–8, the maypole became the symbolic focus of political struggle did it enter the written record. The evidence suggests that rituals like the one described above were performed in all the rural communities of French Canada in the first four decades of the nineteenth century (and earlier, no

---

35 'Mémoires de Nicolas-Gaspard Boisseau,' 85–6. Cf. Philip Stansbury, *A Pedestrian Tour of two thousand three hundred miles in North America* (New York 1822), 217.

doubt). Although Boisseau states that militia officers of all ranks were presented with maypoles, the instances I encountered concerned captains only. Apparently not every captain received this honour. Our Terrebonne diarist, F.-H. Séguin, wrote of a captain that 'his militiamen distinguished him from those of his rank by the presentation of a mast [i.e., a maypole].'[36]

If anything, the maypole ceremonies of the District of Montreal in the 1830s were more elaborate than the ones Boisseau observed in eastern Lower Canada. Instead of a meal of pancakes and brandy, we read of great banquets, where guests dined on fourteen roast turkeys and 'all sorts of cakes'; formal toasts were offered to the captain, the governor, the king, and so on. The maypole itself always seems to have been a substantial tree, apparently with all the branches removed, except the very top ones. It was generally decorated, often with a flag of some sort. After the militiamen of Varennes had set up a maypole for J. Lemoine de Martigny, the senior captain of the parish in 1836, they hoisted on it 'a magnificent flag on which was set out in brilliant letters the name of Mr. de Martigny.' A conservative Montreal paper reported this act of deference towards a well-known anti-patriot, but often maypoles were decorated with liberal or even republican motifs. The mast set up for Captain Joseph Roy of Beauharnois in 1830 was decorated with a tricolour sewn for the occasion by the wives of the men of his company.[37]

Like most aspects of French-Canadian folklore, the maypole ceremony had European roots. The practice of setting up bushes, trees, or poles on the first of May was common in various parts of France and western Europe many centuries before the French came to North America. In some regions a young man would set up a 'mai' in front of the house of the girl he loved; elsewhere

---

36 E.-Z. Massicotte, 'La plantation du mai autrefois,' BRH 29 (May 1923): 151–2; NA, F.-H. Séguin diary, 8 January 1832 (author's translation)
37 L'Ami du Peuple, 11 May 1836; ANQ, 1837, no. 2209, déposition de Josephte Merleau et Catherine Roy, 3 January 1839. Cf. La Minerve, 12 May 1828.

priests or seigneurs might be honoured in this way; there were also places in France where a 'mai' was set up to commemorate the election of a mayor or alderman. There was more to this than simply bestowing honour on an individual. One French folklorist argues that the ritual of planting the maypole and accepting food from the person so honoured implied a reciprocal exchange that discharged both parties of their obligations. For example, harvest labourers would sometimes erect a maypole for their employer after their work was done and they had received their wages; he would then provide a banquet, all in recognition of the fact that the duties of servants and master had been completed.[38]

The earliest maypoles we hear of in Canada were those set up in front of seigneurial manors. It is difficult to know when the custom began and how widespread it was. We do know that censitaires were not always willing to honour their landlords in this way. By the eighteenth century some seigneurs began inserting clauses in the deeds by which they granted land to settlers requiring the grantee to help provide a maypole; some even specified the height of the pole. Habitants in the seigneurie of Varennes were offered exemption from the banal mill monopoly as well as from the duty of planting the maypole in return for an annual payment of wheat. In 1793 one seigneur was apparently prepared to sue censitaires who did not participate in the ritual.[39] With censitaires paying homage to their betters under threat of legal action, one can imagine the jolly scene in front of many a manor house on the first of May! I found no references to seigneurial maypoles after 1800, and it may be that the recal-

38 Arnold Van Gennep, *Le Folklore du Dauphiné (Isère): Etude descriptive et comparée de psychologie populaire*, 2 vols (Paris: Librairie Orientale et Américaine 1932), 1: 300–1; idem, *Manuel de folklore français contemporain*, 4 vols (Paris: J. Picard 1937–49), tome I, partie IV, 1516–75; Mona Ozouf, *La fête révolutionnaire 1789–1799* (Paris: Gallimard 1976), 293

39 Louis Lemoine, 'Une chicane de curés,' 54; E.-Z. Massicotte, 'La plantation du mai dans le bon vieux temps,' *BRH* 26 (May 1920): 155; Allan Greer, *Peasant, Lord, and Merchant: Rural Society in Three Quebec Parishes, 1740–1840* (Toronto: UTP 1985), 100

citrant censitaires prevailed, or that the seigneurs simply lost interest in such unspontaneous demonstrations of respect. In the nineteenth century masts do not seem to have been used to cement relations *between* the major agrarian classes. The instances I have encountered suggest a more 'democratic' object: either to mark unusual events (late spring thaws led to the erection of maypoles on the St Lawrence ice at Montreal in 1817 and at Quebec in 1836)[40] or to symbolize a relationship *within* a class, between a militia captain and his men.

How then should we make sense of the maypole ceremony as it concerns the militia captains of rural Lower Canada? The response of parlour psychoanalysis would no doubt be to regard the pole as a phallic symbol meant to honour a powerful father-figure. There is certainly something to this interpretation, as far as it goes; for indeed the militiamen were giving a token of their submission to a superior officer. On the other hand, it must be remembered that the presentation of the maypole was always followed by a feast. Reciprocity was never absent from the proceedings; the men presented their captain with a symbol of his authority, while he for his part had to make a gesture of repayment. In accepting the symbol of power, the captain also accepted the responsibility it implied, responsibility, that is, towards the men under his command, rather than towards his superiors.

There is another layer of meaning in the maypole ceremony, one derived from its simple existence rather than from its particular form. The ritual should be seen as constituting popular ratification of an appointment. Militiamen did not normally choose their officers – they were appointed from on high – but they did choose whether or not to recognize a captain as such. Since it was customary to identify a captain by the mast that stood in front of his house, a man who lacked one would not be seen as a captain in the full sense of the term, even if he did

40 E.-Z. Massicotte, 'La plantation du mai autrefois,' *BRH* 29 (May 1923): 151–2; *L'Ami du Peuple*, 4 May 1836

have a parchment commission from the king and his name appeared in the official gazette. Yet the maypole ceremony was voluntary and depended on popular initiative. Admittedly, captains had sufficient power that their men would be foolish to insult them by refusing the normal initiation rite, but they did not have the legal right claimed by some eighteenth-century seigneurs of ordering underlings to give them a maypole. By making the maypole an essential token of office, the habitants reserved to themselves the power to invest a militia captain and by so doing to transform him from the appointee of a distant capital into the leader of a local community.

THE HOUSE OF ASSEMBLY

Elections and a representative assembly were introduced to French Canada for the first time in the wake of the Constitutional Act of 1791. The British parliament took this step, partly in response to the demands of colonial subjects, but also as a means of imposing additional taxes on Canadians without violating cherished constitutional principles. The framers of the Constitutional Act, heeding the lessons they thought they had learned from the American Revolution, took care to counterbalance this 'democratic' element of the colonial state with other agencies embodying 'aristocratic' and 'monarchical' principles. Thus, the Assembly shared legislative power with a Legislative Council whose members were appointed for life by the crown. A governor, sent by Westminster, headed the colonial executive and was largely independent of Assembly control; Canadian governors had sole control over considerable revenues, which made them even less dependent on the goodwill of elected politicians than were the governors of other British colonies. The House of Assembly therefore began life in a rather beleaguered situation, with powers that were not clearly defined and that had to be shared with another quite separate body.

It did live up to its billing as the 'democratic' component of government. By the international standards of the time, Lower Canada had an exceptionally broad franchise. Actually the Act of

1791 had simply applied the 40 shillings property qualification used in many British constituencies, but the effect in the Canadian context, where property was so much more widely distributed than in Britain, was to give a vote to almost every family.[41] Women, natives, and urban workers were sometimes allowed to vote, but their participation was uncertain and contested. However, a substantial majority of adult males (exact figures are unavailable) could vote, and this fact implies a degree of masculine democracy that would have been unheard of in Britain, in most of the United States, and even in revolutionary France, where universal manhood suffrage was proclaimed but never practised. It also meant that the habitants, because they outnumbered all other classes combined, held the key to every election.

Initially they took full advantage of the powers conferred on them, electing several peasants and tradesmen to the House of Assembly. After a brief transitional phase, however, a new political elite of merchants and professional men established a monopoly that effectively excluded plebeian elements from the legislature. Rural counties typically returned a doctor, a lawyer, or a notary, usually a local resident, though sometimes a city dweller, and usually, though not always, a French Canadian. The majority of these deputies, along with a number of urban representatives, formed a loosely organized opposition faction known as the 'Canadian' or 'Patriot' party. The electoral prospects of these politicians were excellent, thanks to their close relations with the peasantry, which, in Lower Canada, controlled a clear majority of votes. By the first decade of the nineteenth century there was at least one notary, and very often a doctor as well, in every rural parish in the province. No other local figure was likely to have the writing skills and knowledge of the wider world needed to operate effectively on the colony's political stage, except for the priest, the seigneur (if there was one resident), and the merchant. But the curé was subject to the supervision of a

41 John Garner, *The Franchise and Politics in British North America* (Toronto: UTP 1969), 74–5

conservative hierarchy, and, like the seigneur, his relationship with the habitants was likely to be tense and problematic. The political orientation of country shopkeepers varied, but many of the larger merchants tended to identify with the British empire, whose imperial trading system helped to guarantee their prosperity. Legal and medical practitioners, on the other hand, dealt with habitants on a daily basis and depended for their livelihood on the goodwill of the latter.

Besides capturing the votes of the majority of the peasantry, the men of the liberal professions exercised a more wide-ranging political leadership in the Lower Canadian countryside. They communicated news from the colonial capital and from overseas. Often they organized public meetings and they drew up and circulated petitions asking the government to authorize a new road, establish a 'commissioners court' or provide relief from seigneurial exactions. The decades leading up to the Rebellion saw the hegemony of the professional bourgeoisie grow in strength. The habitants were increasingly drawn into the parliamentary political process under the leadership of the Canadian/ Patriot party (see below, chapter 5). Riots, demonstrations, and other forms of direct action became even rarer than they had been in the eighteenth century as country people transmitted their grievances through the legislature and channelled their political energies into electoral contests.

'Domesticated' in a sense by their involvement in a parliamentary process that had no room for them at the most prominent levels of public life, the peasants and artisans of Lower Canada should not be regarded as politically passive. Politics in the early nineteenth century had not yet developed into the sort of ritual confrontation of public relations specialists familiar to us today, one in which the electorate plays the role of somewhat alienated spectators periodically exercising a consumer's choice at the ballot box. At that time it was common for the 'yeomanry' of a given community to assemble in order to deliberate on some matter of public concern, whether the repair of a local bridge or the state of the constitution, and to vote on resolutions. Assembly elections, with the rival candidates present on the hustings, crowds of supporters, speeches, and open public voting were, in a sense, simply a local meeting of a special sort in which candidates, rather than propositions, were examined and a representative was selected, instead of a resolution. Even with a broad franchise, the small population of each constituency ensured that a significant proportion of voters would be personally acquainted with the candidates.

Electoral contests could be quite tumultuous affairs in these years before the adoption of the secret ballot. There was an advantage to any party that could gain physical control of the polling place; consequently riots and pitched battles were not unheard of. Even reforming spirits could not conceive of the elimination of violence; they urged only that it be moderated. 'The people ought not to be encouraged to use so fatal a weapon as a club,' wrote a Quebec City editor. 'As long as men merely use their fists, much injury cannot be done.'[42] Trouble of this sort was more common in the urban constituencies of pre-Rebellion Lower Canada, but it sometimes occurred in agrarian districts as well. On the other hand, in many cases candidates were elected by acclamation.

Uncontested elections, violence at the polls, a franchise that was still far from universal: all this suggests an electoral process that falls far short of modern standards of procedural rectitude (however well Lower Canada may have borne comparison to other jurisdictions of the period). Yet it is also important to note the degree to which this process depended on the active involvement of habitant men. Even as they deferred to politicians of the professional middle class, the plebeian voters of rural French Canada, far from being alienated, were intimately implicated in the political process. They were, in fact, well integrated into the affairs of one branch, the House of Assembly, of the Lower Canadian state system. But the Assembly itself was so detached from the colonial régime as a whole that this peasant participation can

42 *The Liberal*, 5 July 1837

hardly be seen as advancing the cause of government administration in the countryside.

The evidence presented in this and the previous chapter makes it clear, I hope, that there was more to the Lower Canadian rural community than initially meets the eye. What seems at first an atomized collection of self-contained agrarian families held together by nothing more than the authoritarian bonds of institutions imposed from above, turns out to have unsuspected cohesiveness. Mid-winter parties, church construction projects, and May-day celebrations – activities reflecting basic human gregariousness – helped to bring people together. And regulatory practices, such as informal justice and charivari, helped to keep them together by containing conflict within certain limits. The circumstances of pre-industrial life in rural North America, particularly in institutionally poor French Canada, conspired to keep households isolated from one another; to counteract their effects, to make a life of security and cultural richness, required real creative effort on the part of the habitants and other rural plebeians. This impulse to create a collective life found outlets not only in purely 'popular' customs, but also in the parish and the militia, institutions set up and directed by external authorities. In the eyes of clergy and civil officials, these were primarily mechanisms to supervise a subject population, but the rural masses, with their maypoles and their vestry meetings, found ways of appropriating them and making them to some degree expressions of their own local community.

Only rarely did the habitants directly challenge the leadership of their 'betters' or the complex of tithes, rents, and interest through which they supported the latter. On the whole, they genuinely believed in the social order that placed them in an inferior position. Their intense interest in parish and militia affairs not only testifies to popular civic mindedness and political strength, but also indicates real allegiance to external authorities. The maypole ceremony, for example, was an equivocal rite, expressive of both habitant self-assertion and habitant subjection.

The campaigns against clerical 'interference' in vestry affairs took for granted the right of priests and bishops to rule on religious and moral questions. In the informal legal procedures that settled many disputes without recourse to the courts, one also sees the ideological subjection of the populace who apply the basic principles of the aristocratic Custom of Paris, even as they more or less unconsciously modify them to suit their needs. Generally the habitants seemed prepared to obey legitimate authority, but their actions in innumerable local squabbles indicate that they reserved to themselves the right to decide which authorities were legitimate and how far their powers could rightfully extend. Consequently, the status quo they accepted was, to a considerable extent, of their own making. Superficial observers at the time did not usually understand this; for them the country folk of Lower Canada constituted the most docile of lower classes: 'The great mass of the people are quiet and inoffensive,' wrote a typical English traveller of the early nineteenth century.[43] Those who knew them best, however – the curés above all – never ceased to complain of their anti-authoritarian combativeness. Without ever having launched a major agrarian revolt before 1837, the peasants of Lower Canada certainly had lengthy experience with forging the bonds of community and fighting to preserve them.

People of this sort, for all their history of assertiveness, could not be expected to bring down a government through their own unaided efforts. Potentially powerful, if only by virtue of their numbers, the habitants had the political weaknesses typical of peasantries the world over. Before they could act as a potent force on the provincial stage, they would need allies from other classes better placed to appreciate the broader political picture and to help them to transcend the narrow limits of rural life. It was the doctors, journalists, and notaries of the 'Patriot party' who provided this leadership in the pre-Rebellion decades, and their radical rhetoric of 'liberty,' 'independence,' and the 'rights

43 Hugh Gray, *Letters from Canada, written during a Residence there in the years 1806, 1807, and 1808* (London: Longman, Hurst, Rees, and Orme 1809), 334

of the people' had a tremendous impact in the country parishes of French Canada. It is hardly surprising that language of this sort would resonate with the habitants. Even if they knew nothing of the classic works of western liberalism, opposition to dictation from above was something with which they had more than a passing acquaintance.

5

The Patriot movement and the crisis of the colonial régime

Their avowed object now is to alter the whole frame of the Constitution, & Government of the colony – to render the former purely Democratic, & the latter purely Elective.

Lord Aylmer (governor), 1833[1]

Acute partisan strife was a feature of Lower Canadian political life from about 1805 until the Rebellion brought the parliamentary system to a close. Throughout this period the initiative belonged to a circle of like-minded Assembly politicians variously known as the 'popular party,' the 'Canadian party,' and the 'Patriot party.' Like other democratic opposition parties of the day, this group was composed mainly of doctors, lawyers, and notaries, along with a sprinkling of small merchants and landlords. Educated and articulate, yet not well integrated into the existing régime, the men of the liberal professions were perfectly suited to lead a democratic movement. Their youth and their ambition were great assets, fortified as they were with a sense of being on the right side of inexorable historical forces. Just as important were the warm relations they enjoyed with Lower Canada's peasantry. Thanks to the consistent support of the

1 Aylmer to Secretary of State, 28 February 1833, quoted in S.D. Clark, *Movements of Political Protest in Canada 1640–1840* (Toronto: UTP 1959), 272

French-Canadian habitants, the politicians of the Canadian/ Patriot party were almost always assured of a majority in the House of Assembly. For all that, their real power remained limited, their enemies numerous and formidable.

THE CANADIAN PARTY

Party divisions began to appear in the first decade of the nineteenth century, when the political neophytes of the French professional class started coming into conflict with the colonial executive and its supporters within the Assembly. This clash drove them to undertake an intensive self-education campaign in order to master the wonders of British constitutional law, the better to understand the representative system that had been installed in 1791. They founded a newspaper, Le Canadien, to complement their efforts in the parliamentary arena; they crammed its pages with quotations from Blackstone and DeLolme and ransacked the records of other British colonies for useful precedents. By 1805, if not earlier, these young politicians had assimilated the language of English constitutional law and made it their own; even on the eve of the Rebellion they continued to express themselves in this idiom, although by then they had given it a strongly republican accent. 'Political language,' as J.G.A. Pocock insists, 'is by its nature ambivalent,'[2] and so the Canadien group was eventually able (and with no hypocrisy) to express and justify its opposition to the government in terms of theories framed to demonstrate the perfection of Great Britain's 'balanced constitution.' Whether they knew it or not, these 'new subjects' of his Britannic majesty were recapitulating the intellectual voyage of English radicals and American colonists of the eighteenth century, who had also developed a 'country ideology' of opposition from the malleable materials of ruling-class thought.[3]

2 J.G.A. Pocock, Virtue, Commerce, and History: Essays on Political Thought and History, Chiefly in the Eighteenth Century (Cambridge: Cambridge UP 1985), 8
3 See Bernard Bailyn, The Ideological Origins of the American Revolution (Cambridge, Mass.: Harvard UP 1967); Pocock, Virtue, Commerce, and History, 78.

Taking to heart the proclaimed wish of the mother country's parliament to shape the colonial state in the image of Britain's, the professional men of the Canadian party concentrated on guaranteeing the rights and privileges of the House of Assembly, their own power base and the one constituent of government under the control of the colonial electorate. This focus led, among other things, to bitter struggles over control of the provincial purse strings. The Canadian party also became embroiled in a number of disputes where they felt the central issue was the 'independence' of the Assembly. Always wary of the governor's power to influence the composition and proceedings of that body through the use of patronage and restrictions on freedom of debate, they fought, for example, to keep judges from taking seats in the Assembly. The invasive tendencies of power, such as that enjoyed by colonial officials who were not subject to electoral control, constituted a deadly danger to the delicate balance of the constitution; the colonial opposition therefore combated 'corruption' of this sort just as vigorously as the English and American quasi-republicans of an earlier generation had done.[4] The point of view of the Canadian party was also quite similar in its essentials to that of 'reform' movements in the other colonies of British North America.

The Canadian party was not simply one more incarnation of colonial opposition. From the beginning it had a special vocation as the champion of a non-British linguistic group occupying a precarious position within the British empire. 'Notre langue, nos institutions et nos lois' was the phrase eventually adopted as the masthead slogan of *Le Canadien*, expressing in unambiguous terms that publication's commitment to the preservation of French-Canadian nationality. The party and its newspaper were born during the Napoleonic wars, when a francophobic spirit

---

4 On the 'civic humanism' of Canadian party discourse, see Louis-Georges Harvey, 'Locke, American Revolutionary Ideology and the Rise of French-Canadian Republicanism, 1815–1837,' paper presented to the annual meeting of the Canadian Historical Association, 1988.

seemed to pervade ruling circles in Britain and its empire: 'This province is already too much a French province for an English colony,' read a letter to the editor of another paper. 'To *unfrench-ify* it, as much as possible ... should be a primary object, particularly in these times, when our arch-enemy is straining every nerve to Frenchify the universe.'[5] This wartime intolerance of the language and supposed foreign allegiance of the French Canadians was linked to a socio-economic critique of their laws and customs. Anglo-Canadian merchants in the early nineteenth century were growing loudly impatient with the inheritance laws, land tenure system, and business practices of 'the conquered,' which they regarded as inimical to the spirit of enterprise and development. It required no exceptional degree of paranoia in such an atmosphere to imagine that Canada's established 'language, institutions and laws' were in peril. The response of the 'canadien' politicians was to enunciate a defensive proto-nationalism, insisting on the fundamental loyalty of the French Canadians to Britain's empire. A middle-class ethnic and broadly democratic alignment, the Canadian party carried on the struggle against anglicization and 'executive interference,' accumulating parliamentary experience with the passing years and contributing to the political education of the habitants and other voters.

Arrayed against it in the Assembly was a collection of members, sometimes called the 'English party,' whose orientation was urban and mercantile and who tended to be critical of French-Canadian culture and nationality. Some conservative francophones also were involved, but the English party was dominated by the British merchants of Montreal and Quebec and by a small circle of colonial officials. Because its electoral base was narrow, the party was never strongly represented in the Assembly. To offset the parliamentary ascendancy of the Canadian party, the

5 *Quebec Mercury*, 27 October 1806, as quoted in Jean-Pierre Wallot, *Un Québec qui bougeait: trame socio-politique du Québec au tournant du XIXe siècle* (Sillery: Boréal Express 1973), 78

government therefore appointed 'English party' adherents in increasing numbers to the non-elective branches of government, notably the legislative and executive councils. From the canadien point of view, their opponents were simply 'bureaucrats,' minions of the executive who had no claim to the independence that was absolutely necessary to any honest representative of the people.

A number of political collisions punctuated the political history of Lower Canada.[6] One dramatic confrontation occurred in 1810, when a cantankerous governor, James Craig (1807–10), threw his support behind an English party campaign to anglicize the French-Canadian majority over the long run and to curtail their political influence in the immediate future. A military man like most of the governors of Lower Canada and an appointee from Britain as all of them were, Craig lost patience with the 'democrats' and 'demagogues' of the Canadian party. He closed down its newspaper, jailed some of its prominent leaders and urged the imperial government to revoke the franchise of the majority of voters. The ensuing tumult was short lived and did not greatly involve the mass of the population, but it nevertheless convinced the British government to recall Craig and appoint in his place a more conciliatory figure, who was able to restore political peace by the time the War of 1812 broke out. Another major controversy erupted in 1822 over a scheme to unite the governments of Upper and Lower Canada as a means of bringing the French-Canadian politicians to heel. The union bill raised a storm of protest which brought together middle-class canadien politicians and seigneurial aristocrats in a successful campaign to preserve the existing political map.

6 The classic work on the subject is Helen Taft Manning, *The Revolt of French Canada 1800–1835: A Chapter in the History of the British Commonwealth* (Toronto: Macmillan 1962). Also important are Mason Wade, *The French Canadians 1760–1945* (Toronto: Macmillan 1955); Ramsay Cook, ed., *Constitutionalism and Nationalism in Lower Canada* (Toronto: UTP 1969); Wallot, *Un Québec qui bougeait*; Fernand Ouellet, *Lower Canada 1791–1840: Social Change and Nationalism*, trans. Patricia Claxton (Toronto: McClelland and Stewart 1980).

Through the 1820s and 1830s colonial finances were a perennial bone of contention.[7] A series of governors, together with their 'bureaucrat' supporters, controlled some revenues themselves but wished the Assembly to vote additional funds to pay the 'civil list' of salaries and pensions. The canadien-dominated Assembly, for its part, claimed control over all state revenues and insisted on the right to approve or reject every detail of government expenditures, rather than voting on the civil list as a package. Events came to a head in 1827–28, when another uncompromising governor, Lord Dalhousie, became embroiled in partisan politics and made use of his control over the militia and other mechanisms of coercion to punish the canadien opposition. A vigorous campaign of protest led the British House of Commons to conduct a full-scale inquiry; the resulting report of the Canada Committee (1828) implicitly condemned Dalhousie's authoritarian measures and enhanced the Assembly's financial powers.

THE PATRIOT PARTY

The struggle against Dalhousie tended to radicalize the anti-government forces; the most uncompromising politicians of the Canadian party now began to call themselves 'patriotes' and to think of themselves, not simply as defenders of the rights and privileges of the House of Assembly, but as spokesmen for a nation. In adopting the title 'Patriots,' the Lower Canadian radicals associated themselves with dozens of national-democratic movements of the day, as well as with the American, Dutch, and French revolutionaries of the previous century.[8] In most respects,

7 See D.G. Creighton, 'The Struggle for Financial Control in Lower Canada, 1818–1831,' in *Constitutionalism and Nationalism*, ed. Cook, 33–57.
8 Among the many relevant works, see R.R. Palmer, *The Age of the Democratic Revolution: A Political History of Europe and America, 1760–1800* (Princeton: Princeton UP 1959); E.J. Hobsbawm, *The Age of Revolution 1789–1848* (New York: New American Library 1962); George Rudé, *Revolutionary Europe 1783–1815* (New York: Harper & Row 1964); Georges Lefebvre, *The Coming of the French Revolution*, trans. R.R. Palmer (Princeton: Princeton UP 1947);

their social composition and ideology resembled those of patriotic groupings in other parts of the Atlantic world. Even more than most of their overseas counterparts, however, the Lower Canadian Patriots stood at the head of a mass movement. Not only did this support guarantee the electoral success of the Assembly majority, it legitimized, in Patriot eyes, their pursuit of power.

By the end of the 1820s the Patriots, especially the most prominent among them, Louis-Joseph Papineau, a Montreal lawyer and speaker of the House of Assembly, seemed to be riding high. Their control of the Lower Canadian Assembly was unassailable, they had secured the removal of two hostile governors, they had blocked attempts to alter the constitution, and they had, at least to some extent, won their point on the financial question. Indeed, hostile voices complained loudly of a 'French ascendancy,' which supposedly put British immigrants in the position of an oppressed minority in this conquered land. Yet the power of the Patriot faction extended only as far as the Assembly itself. Other elements of the colonial régime – notably the executive, the judiciary, the army, and the upper house of the legislature – were not only independent of the House of Assembly, they were staffed and run largely in defiance of the wishes of the Patriots and the electors they represented. The state was admittedly a small and comparatively toothless institution by modern standards, but it included a number of bodies appointed from on high and crammed with opponents of the Patriot movement, many of them natives of the mother country. Other forces counteracting Patriot influence came from within French Canada itself. As the movement became more radical over the course of the 1830s, the old Canadian nobility – still influential, though clearly

idem, *La Révolution Française* (Paris: PUF 1963); Pauline Maier, *From Resistance to Revolution: Colonial Radicals and the Development of American Opposition to Britain, 1765–1776* (New York: Random House 1972); William L. Langer, *Political and Social Upheaval 1832–1852* (New York: Harper & Row 1969).

on the wane – and the increasingly powerful Catholic clergy began to range themselves on the side of its enemies.

In so far as the Patriots did dispose of significant powers, they naturally used them to further their own partisan fortunes and to advance the cause of 'liberty' and of 'the nation.' Their political principles were, in the context of the time, typical of middle-class democratic thought and in line with the traditions of liberalism. Like the bourgeois reformers of the day in other western countries, the Patriots defended freedom of the press and other civil liberties (though they were not above prosecuting editors who libelled the Assembly itself). They were staunchly secularist and tended over the years to take increasingly anti-clerical positions. Their view of government was essentially negative, and they endeavoured to protect individual citizens from the authority of state officials and other holders of 'irresponsible' authority. One means of guaranteeing such individual liberty was to make public authority subject to the populace, directly or by way of its elected representatives. Hence the Patriots formulated laws designed to introduce electoral practices in areas such as parochial government. On the question of who should vote, however, views were divided. Religion, the Patriots believed, should have nothing to do with the franchise, and so they granted the vote to Lower Canada's Jewish population in 1831.[9] On the other hand, they did see sex as providing valid grounds for discrimination and took steps to ensure that women could not vote (see below, chap. 7). Property too was a requirement of active political life, as far as they were concerned, and their reforming legislation always included property qualifications as part and parcel of any extension of electoralism. The linkage of property and active citizenship was not as irretrievably conservative as it seems; one implication that could be (and was) drawn from it was that widespread property ownership was essential to the health of the body politic.

9 John Garner, *The Franchise and Politics in British North America* (Toronto: UTP 1969), 150

This point brings us to the area of political economy, a subject on which the Patriots have been consistently misinterpreted. A substantial body of historical opinion, from Lord Durham's time down to the present, has portrayed the Lower Canadian radicals as implacably hostile to Progress, Development, Free Enterprise, and all the central tenets of liberal economics; what they yearned for, it has been seriously argued, was a static, agrarian economy, preferably one in the mould of the feudal ancien régime.[10] This is certainly not the message of pronouncements in the Patriot press on general economic principles: 'We should wish to see every man in the Colony, no matter in what situation in life he may be placed, reaping the benefits of his industry in a manner profitable to himself and advantageous to the community at large, protected by a just government whose anxious care would

10 C.P. Lucas, ed., *Lord Durham's Report on the Affairs of British North America*, 3 vols (Oxford: Clarendon Press 1912), 2: 48–50. Durham's condemnation of Patriot political economy is actually more qualified and subtle than the versions put forward by twentieth-century historians. For Donald Creighton, political strife in Lower Canada was, at root, 'a battle between commercialism and the stiffened feudalism of the St. Lawrence.' *The Empire of the St. Lawrence* (Toronto: Macmillan 1956), 161. Fernand Ouellet writes that the professional men of the canadien party dreamed of 'a sort of withdrawal into the past, into a tradition essentially rural and agricultural ... a society centred around the St. Lawrence Lowlands, devoted to agriculture, enclosed by the seigneury and by the *Coutume de Paris*, and directed by them.' *Economic and Social History of Quebec, 1760–1850: Structures and Conjonctures* (Ottawa: Gage 1980), 212. Cf. ibid., 375–81, 433–5. For the textbook version of this interpretation, see Edgar McInnis, *Canada: A Political and Social History* (Toronto: Holt, Rinehart and Winston 1982), 245.

Scholars sympathetic to Quebec nationalism have challenged this view. See, for example, Gérald Bernier, 'Le parti patriote (1827–1838),' in *Personnel et partis politiques au Québec: Aspects historiques* (Montreal: Boréal 1982), 221–4. I agree with Bernier's critique of the Durham interpretation in its essential features, but I believe he goes too far in eradicating distinctions between the republican political economy of the Patriots and the business-oriented liberalism of Durham and the Lower Canadian merchant community.

be further to develop the natural resources of the country.'[11] On more specific points as well, Patriot positions reflected nineteenth-century liberal orthodoxy: they proclaimed the sanctity of private property, they favoured free trade, and they disapproved generally of government 'interference' in the economy. Trade and industry, properly conducted under private enterprise, were for the Patriots a Good Thing. 'Commerce,' opined the radical paper, *La Minerve*, 'is in fact the most reliable evidence that a country is civilized. The more widely trade extends, the more the civilization of a people advances.'[12] This approval was not unqualified; the sentence from *La Minerve* continues, 'if this trade does not take place exclusively among very few.' The Patriots found some of their more ferocious enemies within the province's business community, and they attacked their enemies, not as merchants per se, but as monopolists. It should be noted that in their hostility to the latter they had on their side the weight of classical economic opinion, which tended to be quite severe on the issue of conspiracies to eliminate competition.[13]

Patriot opposition to 'monopoly' was based more on political than on purely economic considerations however. Under its slogan, 'Justice to all Classes – Monopolies and Special Privileges to None,' the *Vindicator* (the main English-language Patriot organ) reminisced about the Northwest Company, already in 1837 a landmark of Canadian business history. Of these 'fur skin potentates' the editor wrote, 'a more thorough paced set of ruffians never infested a country ... They were to the poor Indians with whom they dealt, savage taskmasters ... Rum and gunpowder were the grand instruments by which these cruel traders

---

11 *Le Libéral* (Quebec), 17 June 1837
12 *La Minerve*, 6 June 1837, quoted in Lucie Blanchette-Lessard and Nicole Daigneault-Saint-Denis, 'Groupes sociaux patriotes et les rébellions de 1837–1838: idéologies et participation' (MA thesis, Université du Québec à Montréal, 1975), 74
13 Adam Smith himself worried about the deplorable tendency of merchants to evade the laws of the marketplace. *An Inquiry into the Nature and Causes of the Wealth of Nations* (New York: Modern Library 1937), 429

reduced the poor savages to their will.'[14] Large-scale enterprises of the day, such as the British American Land Company and, above all, the chartered banks, aroused intense Patriot ire. The Patriots objected to chartered banks on the same grounds as the American Jacksonians and the Upper Canadian radicals fought them: they were powerful institutions sanctioned by government, and, as such, they threatened the integrity and independence of the legislature and even of the electorate itself. Lower Canadian radicals, in addition, resented the fact that the major banks were entirely anglo-Canadian creatures, which operated on and accentuated national exclusiveness in the province.[15]

Does this mean that the Patriots were basically anti-capitalists? Certainly they were opposed to some capitalists, but capitalism as a social system, one in which entrepreneurs and wage-workers were the basic classes, was not a subject on which they had clear views. This lack is only natural; capitalism in this sense scarcely existed, except in embryo, in 1830s Canada, and no one – radical, conservative, British, American, or European – fully comprehended its nature at that time. Certainly the Patriots were not prophets of a classless society, as their pronouncements about 'Justice to all Classes' make clear. They were quite out of sympathy with Lower Canada's nascent proletariat, and indeed they enacted legislation that made disobedience and 'desertion' among forest-industry workers a criminal offence.[16] Their reaction to destitution was as punitive as that of any Victorian bourgeois; in Lower Canada, as in other western countries, liberal social reformers were insisting that the 'idleness' and 'vagrancy' of the poor were punishable offences. Accordingly, the Patriots out-

14 *Vindicator*, 28 March 1837. Cf. Stanley B. Ryerson, *Unequal Union: Roots of Crisis in the Canadas, 1815–1873* (Toronto: Progress 1975), 60.
15 Ouellet, ed., *Papineau*, 66–8; *Le Libéral*, 5 July 1837. Cf. 1831 remarks by Thomas Hart Benton quoted in Arthur M. Schlesinger, Jr, *The Age of Jackson* (Boston: Little, Brown 1945), 81.
16 Robert Tremblay, 'Un aspect de la consolidation du pouvoir d'Etat de la bourgeoisie coloniale: la législation anti-ouvrière dans le Bas-Canada, 1800–50,' *Labour – le travail* 8/9 (Autumn/Spring 1981/82), 247

lawed begging and Papineau spoke out against government relief efforts to famine-stricken parishes. If public funds were to be spent, the radicals preferred that they be invested in jails and Houses of Industry for the moral regeneration of the poor.[17] The system of state-funded schooling which the Patriot-dominated Assembly did so much to establish was also intended, among other things, to instil discipline in the populace. All in all, a functionalist might reasonably portray the Patriots as busily engaged in laying the cultural foundations of a capitalist order.

Of course, that is not what they thought they were doing. They thought they were promoting the prosperity of Lower Canada and protecting its citizens from abuses of power and from the effects of favouritism and privilege. Rather than trying to categorize the Patriots as simply for or against capitalism, we should try to see them, against the backdrop of their times, as political actors grappling with the dilemmas of liberalism. They cherished the ideal of a community of free (male) citizens enjoying equal political rights, and at the same time they also favoured private property, trade, and economic development. However, the political and the economic programs of liberalism cannot always be reconciled; the Patriots were especially concerned about the threat to equal political rights posed by any concentration of wealth, particularly when economic power was allied to 'irresponsable' government office. There was debate and disagreement within the Patriot movement on these matters, but on the whole the claims of 'liberty' weighed more heavily than the claims of 'prosperity.' This emphasis, rather than any basic philosophical disagreement, is what separated the Patriots from their political opponents within Lower Canada and placed them in a 'democratic' camp along with the Jackson coalition of the United States, the English Chartists, and various republican groups in Europe.

17 Jean-Marie Fecteau, *Un nouvel ordre des choses: la pauvreté, le crime, l'Etat au Québec, de la fin du XVIIIe siècle à 1840* (Montreal: VLB 1989), 231 and passim; Fernand Ouellet, ed., *Papineau: textes choisis* (Quebec: Presses de l'Université Laval 1970), 35

Preoccupied as they were with fostering the solidarity of Lower Canadians and advancing their political interests, the Patriots also need to be considered from the point of view of nationalism. Their nationalism grew out of but was distinct from the earlier posture of ethnic defence of the Canadian party. No longer simply pressing the case of the French Canadians as good British subjects who deserved a secure place in the empire and a fair share of government jobs, the nationalists of the Rebellion decade clearly looked forward to the day Lower Canada would be independent and when the political power of French speakers within the province would be commensurate with their demographic preponderance. This was a more self-confident and aggressive posture, but it went along with a less narrowly ethnic orientation. We can see this development in an editorial from *Le Libéral*,[18] a newspaper established by radical Patriots in Quebec City in 1837 to challenge the moderate *Le Canadien*, still the organ of the older defensive nationalism. 'Nos institutions, notre langue et nos lois,' was the *Canadien*'s slogan, and the new paper poured scorn on the stubborn conservatism these words implied: 'The progress of civilization is everywhere marked by a parallel progression in the reform of "institutions and laws" and, we might even say, in "the language" of a country.' Far from being perfect, argued the editorialist, all our institutions need reforming and the civil law preserved since the French régime has aspects, such as dower rights and secret hypothèques, which cause uncertainty and hamper the free exchange of property. Not every Patriot would have subscribed to the views outlined in the *Libéral*, but this editorial does suggest movement away from any ethnic exclusiveness or uncritical veneration of French-Canadian traditions.

As for language, the editorial continues, French 'belongs to the people by natural right,' but English is nevertheless necessary for commercial transactions with the rest of North America: 'this language will share with French a divided rule over all the

18 *Le Libéral*, 5 July 1837

classes of society.' This was a position very much in line with the mainstream of Patriot thought. In striking contrast with Quebec nationalists of a later age, those of the 1830s did not advocate any use of the power of the state to protect the French language. To the extent that they gave the matter any thought, they seem to have leaned towards what we would call a 'policy of bilingualism.' Education laws passed by the Patriot Assembly in the years preceding the Rebellion made no attempt to eliminate English schools or to prevent anyone who wished to go from attending them. On the other hand, Patriots did their best to limit the size of Lower Canada's anglophone minority by opposing, often in outrageously xenophobic terms, immigration from the British Isles. Yet there was nothing particularly French-Canadian about this opposition; hostility to 'pauper immigration' was just as intense in the maritime provinces and in Upper Canada.

The Patriots professed a passionate commitment to their nation, but as is always the case among nationalists, they never gave that entity a clear and precise definition. Sometimes they seemed to be standing up for colonists of French language and ancestry; in other instances their rhetoric implied solidarity with residents of Lower Canada, regardless of their origins or language. It is little help to examine Patriot vocabulary; the term 'Canadian/*canadien*' embodied this very ambiguity in either language. Depending on the context, it could mean 'native-born French Canadian' or simply citizen/inhabitant of Lower Canada. It even tended to take on a political sense, as a Patriot spokesman explained to a committee of the British House of Commons: 'In written documents, all are called Canadians who are on the Canadian side, and all are called not Canadians who are against the Canadian people.'[19] Of course this is hardly an unambiguous formulation: being a Canadian is a matter of conviction, but the choice required is to side with 'the Canadian people'! There was an effort on the part of the Patriots – and I see no reason to

19 *BPP*, 1: 143, A.-N. Morin, testimony before Select Committee on the Affairs of Lower Canada, 1834

doubt its sincerity – to express their nationalism in ethnically inclusive, territorially based terms, to confine their hostility to the active 'Bureaucrats' within the English-speaking community while cultivating good relations with other anglophones. But the English minority as a whole remained understandably suspicious of a movement that tended to operate as if Lower Canada and French Canada were the same thing.

The nationalism of the Patriots is another aspect of the movement that has been poorly served by the partisan and rather insular perspective of historians. Because it has often been portrayed as a unique phenomenon, the by-product of economic incompetence and social frustration, it is essential to note that this nationalism was in fact altogether typical of middle-class reformers and revolutionaries around the western world at this time. Of course France and England, because they had long been organized as nation-states, produced nothing quite like the nationalism of the French-Canadian professionals, but in central and eastern Europe analogous movements abounded. Ireland provides a particularly striking parallel in many respects, and the Patriots were well aware of the connection; Papineau was proud to be known as 'the O'Connell of Canada.'

Hostile commentators have also presented Patriot nationalism as a retrograde ideological force, a kind of primitivism that was fundamentally at odds with the liberal and democratic principles espoused by the movement. Nothing could be further from the truth. In the generations that followed the French Revolution, nationalism was the democratic and revolutionary ideology par excellence.[20] It was linked to notions of equality and enfran-

---

20 Among the more important works bearing on this subject, see J.P.T. Bury, 'Nationalities and Nationalism,' in *The New Cambridge Modern History*, vol. 10 *The Zenith of European Power, 1830–70* (Cambridge: Cambridge UP 1960), 213–45; Hans Kohn, 'Nationalism,' in *International Encyclopedia of the Social Sciences* (n.p.: Macmillan 1968), 11: 63–70; Hobsbawm, *Age of Revolution*, 163–77; V. Kiernan, 'Nationalist Movements and Social Classes,' in *Nationalist Movements*, ed. A.D. Smith (New York: St Martin's Press 1976), 110–33; Yves Person, 'Luttes nationales et luttes de classe,' *Les temps modernes* 37

chisement as against domestic privilege and 'alien rule.' The drive to independence on the part of Belgians, Poles, and Italians was profoundly threatening to the domestic and international order of post-Napoleonic Europe, as Metternich well understood. Even in the 'Grande Nation' and in England, patriotism was generally the property of the left in the first half of the nineteenth century.[21] It was an inherently populist ideology, embodying as it did a call to 'the people' to take up the rights and responsibilities of active participation in the affairs of the nation. When the alternative to popular national consciousness was, not universal human solidarity, but pure parochialism, nationalism seemed a force clearly on the side of the progress of freedom.

Paradoxical though it may sound, patriotism and the 'national principle' were widely believed to be quite compatible with, indeed the essential prerequisite for, international peace and the 'brotherhood of all mankind.' Eventually it became clear that nationalities were not always easy to sort out and that the overlapping claims of 'oppressed nations' could lead to war and new varieties of national oppression. This realization came as a surprise to nationalists, who had assumed that the old multi-national empires were the source of all evil in this regard. The 'dark side' of nationalism became really apparent in the second half of the nineteenth century when it was harnessed to the chariots of Europe's ruling classes. Patriotic sentiment was focused on existing states (in French Canada the Church, rather than the state, was the main beneficiary of this domesticated nationalism), and

(March 1981): 1555–77; Tom Nairn, *The Break-Up of Britain: Crisis and Neo-Nationalism* (London: NLB 1977), 329–63; Geoff Eley, 'Nationalism and Social History,' *Social History* 6 (January 1981): 83–107; Ernest Gellner, *Nations and Nationalism* (Oxford: Basil Blackwell 1983); Benedict Anderson, *Imagined Communities: Reflections on the Origin and Spread of Nationalism* (London: NLB 1983); Tzvetan Todorov, 'Nation and Nationalism: The French Variant,' *Salmagundi* 84 (Fall 1989): 138–53; E.J. Hobsbawm, *Nations and Nationalism since 1780: Programme, Myth, Reality* (Cambridge: Cambridge UP 1990).

21 Linda Colley, 'Whose Nation? Class and National Consciousness in Britain 1750–1830,' *Past and Present* 113 (November 1986): 97–117

nationalism tended increasingly to reinforce rather than to menace western rulers.[22] In the context of the 1830s, however, the nationalism of the Lower Canadian Patriots was in harmony with, was indeed part and parcel of, their broadly 'democratic' stance.

In attempting to counter some of the historiographical cheap shots of which the Patriots have so frequently been victims, I have no wish to deny that their collective political posture contained contradictory elements, foolish delusions, and rhetorical puffery at odds with their actual practice. There were undeniable tensions between their attachment to private property and free trade and their commitment to 'independence' and political equality. Moreover, universalistic appeals to the 'rule of the people' disguised all sorts of unresolved ambiguities. Who or what was 'the people'? Did it include women? The poor? And how exactly should the people exercise its sovereignty? Directly? Through an elite of elected representatives? In addition to these problems inherent in Patriot ideology, we could cite hundreds of instances (some of which will be dealt with in subsequent chapters) where the requirements of real-world political action led to violations of principled positions. It is not helpful to conclude that the Patriots were simply 'dishonest' or that their 'nationalism' somehow defeated their 'liberalism,' as those who treat descriptive labels as real things might have us believe. To understand the Patriot movement, as opposed simply to dismissing it, we must recognize its leaders as creatures of their age trying to square the same circles as their reform-minded contemporaries in other lands. Fairly typical bourgeois democrats of the 'Age of Revolution,' they can also be seen as people grappling with fundamental and perennial political conundrums. When we ourselves succeed in putting the ideals of democracy into practice, when everyone subject to the power of the state really does partake in equal measure of that power, then perhaps we shall be justified in treating the Patriots with contempt.

22 E.J. Hobsbawm, *The Age of Capital, 1848–1875* (New York: New American Library 1979), 87–105

BUILDING A MASS MOVEMENT

The Patriots grew increasingly radical in the 1830s as it became clear that merely winning elections and dominating the Assembly would not allow them to carry out their programs. Whereas once they had demanded that, in effect, the parliamentary régime of 1791 be allowed to function 'properly,' they now called for constitutional reform to make the framework of government more democratic. Their main target was the Legislative Council, the appointive body whose powers and functions mirrored those of the Patriot-dominated Assembly. The Council had by then become a bastion of the anglophone merchants and officials whom the Patriots called 'bureaucrats,' and it was increasingly using its powers to block bills passed by the lower house. The Patriots' solution was to make positions on the Council elective, and they pressed their point in the famous 'Ninety-Two Resolutions' of 1834 and other representations to the imperial government. Their argument for reform of the Legislative Council rested on sound constitutionalist grounds. According to the Patriots, the Council was not 'independent' but rather a creature of the official clique surrounding the governor; thus the upper house was a subversive instrument that extended executive influence into areas that were supposed to be controlled by the people's representatives.

The Ninety-Two Resolutions, as many critical observers have remarked, form a long-winded and rather disorganized collection of grievances, assertions, and threats.[23] They dwell at length on the iniquities of the Legislative Council (resolutions 9–40), while shorter passages are devoted to financial issues, the privileges of

23 It is nevertheless surprising, in view of the importance of this manifesto, that the text has not been made available to modern readers. Moreover, there are no studies of its contents, origins, and thrust that go much beyond the superficial cataloguing presented in this paragraph. The Ninety-Two Resolutions as originally published can be found in *JHALC*, 1834, 310–35; see also W.P.M. Kennedy, ed., *Documents of the Canadian Constitution 1759–1915* (Toronto: Oxford UP 1918), 366–88.

the House of Assembly, the British parliament's attempts to regulate land tenure in the province, partiality in the administration of justice, and discrimination against French Canadians in the awarding of government appointments. Several resolutions hold up the democratic system of the United States as an example for Lower Canada. The framers clearly took for granted the colony's eventual separation from Great Britain, and at more than one point there were thinly veiled threats to the effect that the split would come all the sooner should the mother country fail to revise Lower Canada's constitution along the lines laid down by the Patriots. Taken as a whole, the Ninety-Two Resolutions had none of the earmarks of an inspiring manifesto. Long, detailed, and legalistic, the document was clearly addressed mainly to colonial officials and parliamentary committees rather than to the Lower Canadian masses. Obviously the situation had not reached the stage in 1834 that the Thirteen Colonies had attained by 4 July 1776 or France on 26 August 1789, when leaders who were determined at last upon a fundamental break with the past would set out their basic principles in simple, elegant, and ringing phrases.

Yet the revolutionary thrust of the Ninety-Two Resolutions was not lost on Lower Canadians of all political persuasions. Debated in the press, discussed in the taverns and on church doorsteps, they served to accelerate the polarization of an already divided province. Anti-Patriots were quick to seize upon all the symptoms of 'disloyalty' and 'French republicanism'; they appropriated for themselves the title of 'Constitutionalists' (though in the radical lexicon they were still 'bureaucrats'). Extremists within the English community of Montreal organized paramilitary units like the 'British Rifle Corps,' which was determined 'to preserve inviolate the connection which exists between Great Britain and Lower Canada, and to maintain unimpaired the rights and privileges confirmed to them by the Constitution.'[24]

24 Robert Christie, *A History of the Late Province of Lower Canada, Parliamentary and Political, From the Commencement to the Close of its Existence as a separate Province*, 2nd ed., 6 vols (Montreal: Richard Worthington 1866), 4: 143

Patriot partisans, on their side, were much slower to gird themselves for physical conflict, but they did organize large public
meetings and circulated petitions that gathered some 80,000
signatures in support of the Ninety-Two Resolutions. Some politicians previously identified with the Patriot party were alarmed
at the radicalism of some of the resolutions, and they went over
to the Constitutionalist side, along with earlier defectors such as
John Neilson, the moderate from Quebec City. Waverers, however, were trounced in the ensuing election campaign. The
Assembly election of 1834 was fought over the Resolutions, and
the result was an unprecedented landslide victory for the radical
Patriots who had approved them.

The agitation surrounding the Ninety-Two Resolutions, as
opposed to their manifest content, highlights the re-emergence of
mass politics in Lower Canada. Having previously domesticated,
so to speak, the dangerous political potential of the plebeian
electors, the middle-class politicians of the Patriot party had
begun a few years before 1834 to push the rank and file into a
more active and prominent role. The mere winning of votes and
securing of Assembly majorities were no longer enough. Now
that the immediate objective was constitutional reform and the
main struggle one pitting the Patriots against opponents in Britain and in the colony who were quite beyond the control of the
electorate, it was obvious that extra-parliamentary pressure was
indispensable. The radicals' growing commitment to the ideals of
democracy and of republican citizenship also drove them in the
direction of mobilizing the people. Accordingly, newspapers
were founded, committees of correspondence were established,
and public meetings large and small succeeded one another at a
rapid pace. None of this activity constituted a break with the
practices of the Canadian party in earlier decades; indeed it built
upon and accelerated the development of a political culture that
had been evolving since the turn of the century.

There were several Patriot newspapers at this time, including
Le Canadien in Quebec, resurrected after its suppression by Governor Craig, and at Montreal *La Minerve* and the English-language *Vindicator*. Most had only a few pages per edition and

were published once or twice a week. Though addressed to rural as well as urban readers across a wide region, they, like all papers of the time, had a very limited press run; there were only 300 subscribers to *La Minerve* near its inception in 1827.[25] Moreover, literacy levels were still very low, particularly in rural French Canada; country schools were beginning to have a major effect on the children of the habitants, but at best only one adult in ten could read in the 1830s.[26] It is clear, however, that the influence of these papers went far beyond the narrow circle of literate subscribers. In country districts the more educated patriots read the papers to their illiterate neighbours. Some villages established public 'reading rooms' where large audiences could assemble to listen to the news from *La Minerve* and other periodicals.[27] These early newspapers were crammed with material from Lower Canada and from around the world. The proceedings of the House of Assembly featured prominently – debates were frequently quoted in extenso – but there were also 'letters to the editor,' usually anonymous and always filled with strong opinions, as well as extensive reports lifted from imported papers on the affairs of the other colonies of British North America, of Britain itself, the United States, and Europe. The subjects were generally serious, and the editors – for example, E.B. O'Callaghan of the *Vindicator* and Ludger Duvernay of *La Minerve* – strove for an elegance of expression that sounds positively pompous to twentieth-century ears. Yet their papers were never dull: the columns were filled with indignation and energy; scorn and ridicule for the enemies of Lower Canada poured forth from every page. Humour abounded, especially in the many satirical songs and poems published in the patriot press; set to familiar tunes and performed at all sorts of congenial gatherings,

25 Claude Galarneau, 'La press périodique au Québec de 1764 à 1859,' *Transactions of the Royal Society of Canada*, 4th series, 22 (1984): 154
26 Allan Greer, 'The Pattern of Literacy in Quebec, 1745–1899,' *Histoire Sociale – Social History* 11 (November 1978): 295–325
27 See, for example, *Vindicator*, 31 October 1837

these works probably played an important part in disseminating the radical message through the populace.[28]

Mass meetings also had a role to play; following patterns established during the campaigns of 1822 and 1827, they were held at ever more frequent intervals after 1832. They took place in both the cities and the rural districts, usually billed as 'an assembly of the freeholders of [such and such] county.' In some cases they were called to protest a specific event, such as the fatal shooting in 1832 of three Patriot supporters by British soldiers during an election riot in Montreal. More common after 1834 were meetings expressing general support for the movement for constitutional reform and denouncing the Colonial Office, the governor, and the Legislative Council. These events were normally held on a Sunday at or near a church, which practically ensured a crowd. Speeches were always presented, as well as a series of indignant resolutions. But the seriousness of the occasion never eclipsed the festive side: banquets, songs, and socializing were very much in evidence. Exactly how many people attended these meetings we cannot be sure; even less exact is our knowledge of what they meant to the peasants and village artisans in the audience. Certainly they fit to some degree into rural political traditions and patterns of popular culture that were much older than the Patriot party. Yet the bourgeois Patriots tended to act as if the political apprenticeship of the masses had barely begun when the crisis came to a head in 1837.

POLITICAL BREAKDOWN

In the three years following the passage of the Ninety-Two Resolutions, political conflict in Lower Canada grew so intense that

---

28 For examples, see 'De c'est la faute à Papineau aux Quatre-Vingt Douze Résolutions' *Revue d'ethnologie du Québec* 5 (1977): 51–112; Emile Dubois, *Le feu de la Rivière-du-Chêne. Etude historique sur le mouvement insurrectionnel de 1837 au nord de Montréal* (Saint-Jérôme: Imprimerie Labelle 1937), 293–302; John Hare, *Les patriotes, 1830–1839: textes* (Ottawa: Edition Libération 1971), passim.

the framework of government could no longer contain it. The growing polarization was not marked by bloodshed and violence, although paramilitary organizations on both sides were adopting warlike postures. The main symptom of breakdown was the progressive inability of the colonial state to function normally. The Patriot-controlled Assembly still refused to approve budgets in the form demanded by the executive. Worse still, there was virtually no effective legislative authority in Lower Canada, since every bill passed by the Assembly was routinely vetoed by the Legislative Council and every measure proposed by the Council, with its Constitutionalist ascendancy, met with a similar fate at the hands of the Assembly. In 1836 the Council quashed the Assembly's education legislation, with the result that government funding to elementary schools throughout the province ended abruptly. Similar squabbling kept the two bodies from renewing the mandate for the recently established municipal governments of Montreal and Quebec, leaving the two cities to be governed once again as overgrown villages.

The situation, obviously unstable and unacceptable to all parties, seemed to require a decisive intervention on the part of the British government. For some time, however, the latter failed to appreciate the depth of the Lower Canadian crisis and the strength of popular support for Papineau and the Patriots.[29] They sought at first to mediate between the contending forces and foster the growth of a moderate party. To this end they dispatched the conciliatory Lord Gosford to Lower Canada as governor and head of a commission of inquiry in 1835. Gosford did succeed in securing some cooperation, particularly among Patriot politicians from the Quebec region, thus creating another of the periodic splits in which the party lost some of its more moderate elements. Most Patriots, particularly those based in the Montreal region, resisted Lord Gosford's charms, and when it

---

29 Phillip Buckner, *The Transition to Responsible Government: British Policy in British North America, 1815–1850* (Westport, Conn.: Greenwood 1985), 176–204

eventually became clear that the governor was not authorized to contemplate the sorts of fundamental reforms demanded in the Ninety-Two Resolutions, the radicals were able to discredit his commission as a hoax and his Lower Canadian friends as treacherous collaborators. In March 1836 they withdrew in protest from the Assembly, and lacking a quorum, that body to all intents and purposes ceased to exist. Tensions mounted to a higher pitch than ever, and after Gosford had submitted his disillusioned reports (he remained governor of Lower Canada until the end of 1837), a change in imperial policy seemed inevitable.

The ten resolutions presented to parliament by Lord John Russell's government in March 1837 set out the cabinet's plans for dealing with the Lower Canadian crisis. From the British point of view they contained real concessions to the colony's Assembly,[30] but they were utterly unacceptable to the Patriots. By the resolutions the metropolitan government finally made it clear that an elective Legislative Council was out of the question. They indicated further that they would deal with the financial deadlock by permitting the colonial executive to draw on funds for certain purposes without the Assembly's approval. There was no mistaking the fact that the mother country intended to bring the Patriot movement to heel. Anticipating resistance, Russell's ministers made arrangements to bolster Lower Canada's garrison of 2,400 British regulars by transferring troops from other parts of British North America.[31] Naturally, trouble erupted – though strictly of a non-violent and rhetorical nature – as soon as the contents of the Russell Resolutions became known in Canada.

The Patriots were furious: not only had their calls for constitutional reform been rebuffed, concessions previously won (on finances) had been rolled back. Such actions, the Patriot press declared, amounted to 'coercion' compounded with larceny.

A combined and dishonorable junction of Whigs and Tories, in a House of Commons 'reformed' but in name, may pass Resolutions to annihilate

30 Buckner, *The Transition to Responsible Government*, 221
31 Ibid., 228

the last remnant of Liberty left in the Colonial Legislatures ... Russell may, therefore order his Deputy, Gosford, to plunder our public chest ... but this will not legalize the plunder. Our rights must not be violated with impunity. A HOWL of indignation must be raised from one extremity of the Province to the other, against the ROBBERS, and against all those WHO PARTAKE OF THE PLUNDER.

HENCEFORTH, THERE MUST BE NO PEACE IN THE PROVINCE – no quarter for the plunderers. Agitate! *Agitate*!! AGITATE!!! Destroy the Revenue; denounce the oppressors. Everything is lawful when the fundamental liberties are in danger. 'The guards die – they never surrender.'[32]

Behind the white-hot rhetoric of the *Vindicator* stood a less fierce strategy of practical resistance. What the Patriot leaders apparently envisaged at this early stage of the crisis (April-May) was a series of public meetings of a sort quite familiar to Lower Canadians, combined with a campaign of non-importation of British products. The idea was to choke off government revenues, derived mainly from duties, by turning to homespun textiles and other 'domestic manufactures' and by smuggling goods from the United States. Soon the *Vindicator* was sending out a warning about the dangers of more direct action before conditions were ripe. 'There are some, we are aware, who object to this course, because it is too slow. They would strike at once. We are not of their opinion, just yet. The Americans waged war on the breeches pockets of their enemies, long before they had recourse to the *ultima ratio*. Let us act cautiously, but unanimously, as have done those who preceded us in the holy war for freedom, and we may depend on it, we too shall succeed in obtaining "justice." '[33]

Obviously the situation was delicate for the Patriots; they wanted to mobilize public opinion and send a strong message to Britain, but they knew that premature moves towards an all-out struggle might bring disastrous repression. Besides the strictly

32 *Vindicator*, 21 April 1837, quoted in Christie, *History of the Late Province*, 4: 354
33 *Vindicator*, 5 May 1837

strategic dilemma, there must have been social anxieties as well. If they were anything like middle-class revolutionaries in other countries at this time, the Patriots had misgivings about letting the genie of popular revolt out of the bottle. Who could be sure, after all, that the privileges of the educated and the form of civilization they cherished would be spared once the ploughman and the tinker had taken up arms? Louis-Joseph Papineau has sometimes been portrayed as a 'divided soul' with psychological problems that prevented him from acting with consistency and determination,[34] but his situation was hardly unique. Most of his colleagues must have been torn by the same contradictory impulses – to encourage popular resistance and at the same time to restrain it – and the resulting uncertainty and vacillation seems, if not particularly heroic, quite understandable. Faced with agonizing dilemmas, the Patriot leaders for a time found reassurance in what they took to be the lessons of history.

Writings and speeches from the spring and summer of 1837 are studded with references to the American Revolution. Just as generals are notorious for preparing to fight the last war, revolutionaries tend to be guided by the experience of previous revolutions. Throughout nineteenth-century Europe the dramas of the French Revolution were re-enacted time and again, and in the non-western world of the twentieth century communist insurgents in moments of crisis wondered whether they had arrived at their own 1917 or merely a 1905-style rehearsal. So it was in Lower Canada, where the struggle for independence on the part of Britain's older North American colonies seemed to offer an obvious precedent. In the months following the announcement of the Russell Resolutions Patriot publications drew attention to the similarities between the current situation and the events that led to the breakup of the first British empire, and their analogies were often quite specific. Allusions were not to the skirmish at Lexington or even to the Boston Tea Party, but rather to the

34 Fernand Ouellet, *Louis-Joseph Papineau: A Divided Soul* (Ottawa: CHA booklet 1961)

Stamp Act Crisis of 1765. Clearly the Patriots believed that the Lower Canadian version of the War of Independence was far in the future. Papineau was quite open about this belief in a speech delivered at the beginning of June 1837: 'Let us examine what the Americans did, under similar circumstances. Ten years before they took up arms, they adopted the course which we are now about to recommend to you. They abstained from taxed articles ...'[35]

Apparently in the early summer of 1837 the Patriot leaders still felt that they were just beginning a long process of mobilization; recognizing this position helps us to understand their failure to undertake practical military preparations to match their revolutionary rhetoric. It may have been natural to think along lines suggested by historical analogies and indeed references to the American Revolution were indispensable morale-builders (they did it, why can't we?), but there were pitfalls in this mode of reasoning. The situation in 1837 was quite different from that prevailing in 1765 in a great many ways, not least of which was that now anyone, including the opponents of revolution, could see where such developments were likely to lead. Thus it was that the government and its supporters never gave the Patriots the leisure they had counted on to build an invincible movement but instead acted promptly to suppress the agitation. Such moves precipitated a dialectical process of resistance and counter-resistance which hastened the armed confrontation that Papineau and his colleagues did not initially expect and were completely unprepared to deal with. These events are explored in later chapters; for the present we must return to the protest meetings that captured the attention of Lower Canadians between May and September of 1837.

The first 'anti-coercion assembly' was held at the village of St Ours, where the freeholders of Richelieu county gathered to express their views on the Russell Resolutions and other matters

---

35 *Vindicator*, 6 June 1837. Later in the summer, however, Papineau did begin comparing Lower Canada's situation to that of the old colonies in 1774. Ibid., 4 August 1837

on 7 May. More than 1,200 attended, according to sympathetic accounts, but Governor Gosford was assured that this figure was a gross exaggeration.[36] The resolutions had an unmistakably revolutionary import; for they not only denounced the Russell Resolutions, they denied the imperial government any right to interfere in Canadian affairs. The colonial régime, they asserted, was not a legitimate government. '7. Resolved, That henceforth, considering ourselves attached by force to the British Government, we will be subject thereto only as to a government of force, waiting on God, our right and on circumstances for a more favourable lot ... We regard ourselves bound in duty as in honour to resist a tyrant power, in every way at present at our disposal.' Other resolutions called for a boycott of British goods, the encouragement of smuggling, the establishment of a 'patriotic association,' and the raising of funds through a 'Papineau tribute' modelled on the Irish 'O'Connell tribute.' There was no hint of military preparations, however, and any thought of immediate action to overthrow the government must have been far from the minds of the framers of the twelfth resolution, which called on electors to vote for the Patriots in the next election!

A week later there was a second meeting at St Laurent, near Montreal, and in the months that followed county after county followed suit. The Patriot press, cheering on the faithful, hailed each new assembly under the title 'Progress of the Movement.' Messages of support came from Britain and the United States, and the editors eagerly published them as evidence of the legitimacy and righteousness of the radical cause. The majority of meetings was concentrated in the District of Montreal, though several took place in the Three Rivers and Quebec regions, as well as in the English-dominated Eastern Townships.[37]

36 *BPP*, 9: 28–9, Gosford to Glenelg, 25 May 1837
37 Maps plotting the locations of anti-coercion meetings can be found in Allan Greer and Léon Robichaud, 'La Rébellion de 1837–1838: une approche géographique,' *Cahiers de géographie du Québec* 33 (December 1989): 345–77 and in Jean-Paul Bernard, ed., *Assemblées publiques, résolutions et déclarations de 1837–1838* (Montreal: VLB éditeur 1988), 21. These maps differ slightly because the criteria used in the two studies for deciding which meetings to

All the meetings took essentially the same form, their pageantry borrowed from earlier protest campaigns and electoral contests. Papineau and other Montreal leaders frequently attended; their carriage would be escorted to the site by a contingent of local militia or by a cortège of private vehicles, producing a scene very much like an habitant wedding party touring the parish. In a field near the village centre a platform would have been erected and decorated with flags and banners. 'Honor to our Representatives,' 'Fly Tyrants, for the People are Awakening,' 'Death Before Slavery,' 'Papineau, the Man of the People,' read the legends.[38] Sunday, when a crowd of curious church-goers was always on hand, was the favoured day for anti-coercion rallies. Always there would be fiery speeches from local notables and provincial dignitaries, invariably followed by a series of indignant resolutions, 'duly proposed, seconded and unanimously adopted.' According to the published reports, the resolutions were often moved by habitants and other working people, and there is indeed every reason to believe that the 'lower classes' took an active part in preparing the anti-coercion meetings.[39] The wording and the substance of the resolutions, however, suggest a continuing middle-class ascendancy within the Patriot movement. They bristle with historical allusions and specific references to policies, bills, and ministries; throughout they show the marks, not only of formal education, but of legal training and parliamentary experience. One does detect evidence of a peasant social program, especially in the occasional resolution condemn-

---

include did not coincide exactly. Note that the volume edited by Bernard contains a very useful compilation of the resolutions passed at each of the assemblies.

38 *Vindicator*, 6 June 1837

39 According to the *Vindicator* (15 August 1837), leaders from Montreal found one of the resolutions proposed at a meeting at St Constant 'too strong' and they tried to suppress it. The habitants insisted, however, and the resolution passed. I mention this incident for the record, even though one would hesitate to accept at face value this paper's version of events, unsupported as it is by other testimony.

ing seigneurial exactions, but these are muted voices filtered through bourgeois interpreters.

Faced with British intransigence, the Patriot politicians had to mobilize 'the people' of Lower Canada for determined resistance. Some naïve souls apparently hoped that a display of unity and force might pressure the imperial government into conceding an elective Legislative Council. The less optimistic expectation was that conflict would continue, in which case the meetings and agitation would play a useful role in giving the rural masses an enhanced appreciation of their own potential power and in rousing them for anti-colonial action at a later date. Of course one can hardly expect to stimulate political engagement of this sort without provoking some negative reactions.

Certainly the patience of the imperial authorities was not infinite, although their initial attempts to stem the tide of revolution proved ineffectual. Pressed by Constitutionalists to take repressive action, the governor of Lower Canada finally issued a proclamation on 15 June which prohibited meetings 'having for their objects the resistance of the lawful authority of the King and Parliament, and the subversion of the laws.'[40] Even though the patriots had as yet done little to translate into action all the rhetoric about smuggling and resistance, this extraordinary edict appeared to the otherwise conciliatory Lord Gosford justified by the revolutionary implications of some of the resolutions passed at the county 'anti-coercion meetings.' The governor could not afford to appear passive, and so he took the initiative and jettisoned the troublesome principle of free speech in an attempt to put a stop to the agitation.

The June edict turned out to be a symbolic response to theoretical revolt, because the government lacked the means to enforce the governor's order. Constitutionalist justices of the peace posted printed copies in various public places, only to find them torn to bits the next day; they read out the proclamation at the church door, and their words were drowned in a chorus of whis-

40 *PACR*, 1923, 270–1

tling habitants.[41] Finally, someone in Quebec City hit on the idea of making use of the annual militia review, held every year on 29 June, to communicate the ban to a captive audience made up of all the men in Lower Canada. The problem with this device was that it depended on the goodwill of local militia officers, which the government could not count on as it turned out. While some captains and lieutenants willingly cooperated, many firmly refused to read the proclamation; in other cases officers followed the letter of their orders and then told the militiamen how much they disagreed with the governor's policies. Tumultuous scenes occurred on several parade grounds where the document was read out. At Baie du Febvre, for example, Amable Lacerte, famed for his ability to imitate the bleating of a sheep, managed to get every dog in the village barking while the lieutenant-colonel struggled to make himself heard. The moment Ensign John Fraser began reading the proclamation at Terrebonne, the rank and file simply dismissed themselves, shouting the traditional three cheers for the king before walking away.[42]

The anti-coercion meetings succeeded one another without a pause, only now the patriots had a new grievance to protest. The 'phoney war' of defiant resolutions and official proclamations continued. Even as he built up British military strength in Lower Canada, the governor seemed determined to master the situation through the normal channels of the civil administration. The proclamation of 15 June was not wasted effort, since it did help to clarify the situation, especially as far as magistrates and militia officers were concerned. These nominal agents of the crown were explicitly directed to make every effort to prevent 'seditious assemblies,' but it soon became clear that, far from enforcing the prohibition, many of them were active in promoting the banned meetings. Pressed by increasingly angry and nervous Constitu-

41 NA, LC Civil Secretary, 513: 236, James Cuthbert to S. Walcott, 19 June 1837; ibid., 514: 42, A. Pinet to S. Walcott, 3 July 1837; ibid., 519: 158, Johnson Perez et al. to Gosford, 20 September 1837
42 NA, LC Adjutant General, vol. 48, petition of several inhabitants of Baie du Febvre, 30 December 1837; ibid., F. Dugal to R. Mackenzie, 5 July 1837

tionalists, the governor therefore instituted a purge of the province's judiciary and officer corps. His civil secretary had only to examine the accounts of meetings published in the radical press to find lists of speakers and movers and seconders of resolutions. Those who held royal commissions were then dismissed if they could not prove their innocence. His program was reminiscent of Governor Dalhousie's campaign ten years earlier, except that the number affected was far greater. By early September Gosford had revoked the commissions of eighteen magistrates and thirty-five militia officers.[43] This was no trifling punishment: as we have seen, these positions were highly prized in Lower Canada. None the less, the Patriots called upon to account for their conduct generally replied defiantly, striking noble poses as willing martyrs in their country's cause. Their correspondence of course made marvellous copy when published in the columns of the *Vindicator* or *La Minerve* under a suitable title like 'The Reign of Terror.'

The importance of the purge is that it tended to bring the crisis in relations between Lower Canada and Great Britain down to the level of local authority in the countryside. As public sympathy and admiration for the 'persecuted' officers and magistrates grew, good Patriots who had been overlooked by the government began voluntarily resigning their commissions. They did so, some explained, not simply as a gesture of solidarity with their dismissed colleagues, but in order to dissociate themselves from a corrupt and tyrannical régime. Rural patriots in the District of Montreal began to regard as an enemy any JP or militia officer who kept a commission from the government, and, as we shall see presently, this attitude eventually led to a major upheaval in local governance. Thus ensued a dialectical process, typical of revolutionary situations, in which measures designed to end the crisis only provoked countermeasures that deepened it. The prospect of a return to business-as-usual politics seemed increasingly remote by the summer of 1837. Attempts were made

43 *PACR*, 1923, 305, Gosford to Glenelg, 9 September 1837

to resolve matters by calling the Assembly into session in August, but they proved fruitless. Nothing could be accomplished, it seemed, unless either the government or the Patriots capitulated. Violence was what all responsible citizens dreaded in such tense circumstances, and they began to receive disturbing reports as early as the beginning of July.

6

Two nations warring

I expected to find a contest between a government and a people: I found two nations warring in the bosom of a single state: I found a struggle, not of principles, but of races; and I perceived that it would be idle to attempt any amelioration of laws or institutions until we could first succeed in terminating the deadly animosity that now separates the inhabitants of Lower Canada into the hostile divisions of French and English.

Lord Durham[1]

Robert Hall was a farmer of British origin who lived in the predominantly French-Canadian parish of Ste Scholastique, north of Montreal. In late June and early July of 1837 he and other English speakers in the county of Two Mountains began to suffer various forms of ill treatment at the hands of their francophone neighbours. Several families fled to the city, Hall's among them, and there he found a magistrate and swore out the following deposition.

I have lived with my family in the said parish of Ste Scholastique for two years past. I have always lived on the best terms with my neigh-

---

1 C.P. Lucas, ed., *Lord Durham's Report on the Affairs of British North America*, 3 vols (Oxford: Clarendon 1912), 2: 16

bours the Canadians but since political meetings have been held in that, and the adjoining parishes of St Benoit and others the Canadians have ceased to have any communication with the inhabitants of English extraction.

After certain committees were organized and appointed in his parish depredations were committed almost nightly on the said English inhabitants as also some Scotch inhabitants and on the Canadians who do not belong to the patriote party. On the night of the twenty eighth June last the door of his house was broken open by that party and one of the windows of his house smashed to pieces with stones. One of the stones about five pounds in weight fell very near to some of my infant children who slept on a bunk on the floor. Part of my fences were thrown down and destroyed and my corn field laid open to the cattle in which I found several heads of cattle the ensuing morning. My horses manes and tails were shaved and so disfigured as to be almost unfit for use, so much so that when I travel with them I am universally laughed at.[2]

The English minority of the region was boycotted quite thoroughly. A St Benoit blacksmith, Donald McColl, suddenly found he had no more customers; only two French Canadians patronized him in a month and both found their horses minus mane and tail the next day. He hired a local carter to drive him to the next village and the poor carter's horse was similarly shaved. McColl's father was a small-scale entrepreneur, but after June no French Canadians could work for him or sell him ashes for his potash works without suffering threats and vandalism.[3] To all appearances the campaign to defend the liberty of Lower Canada had already degenerated into a series of ugly attacks on members of a cultural minority.

Was the conflict in Lower Canada fundamentally ethnic (or, to follow nineteenth-century usage, 'racial'), as Lord Durham and a host of commentators before and after him have argued? Was a fight that seemed to be over democracy and national independ-

2 ANQ, 1837, no. 607, deposition of Robert Hall, 15 July 1837
3 Ibid., no. 836, deposition of Duncan McCall, 11 July 1837

ence actually a tribal conflict of English and French in which the two sides took up contradictory political positions as a means of justifying more primitive impulses to strife? Difficulties arise the moment one begins considering these questions seriously, since Lord Durham's catchy formula is based on a series of false dichotomies. Why must a conflict be *either* 'of principles' *or* 'of races'? Can it not be both? And if a government is of one nationality and the bulk of the people it rules of another, as was the case in Lower Canada, surely any contest between the two will inevitably take on a 'racial' coloration. Lord Durham's reductionist analysis is based on the assumption that different nations cannot live peacefully 'in the bosom of a single state,' and so any confrontation pitting English against French would have to arise from their cultural differences. This was a comforting doctrine for a liberal representative of the crown who might have had some qualms about reimposing imperial rule on a defeated population had he not been assured that popular opposition was based on mere national prejudice. Canadian historians have also tended to find this interpretation congenial, since it lends credence to the view that 1837–8 saw no revolutionary crisis with fundamental political issues at stake; the Rebellion was simply one more instance, like the imperial wars of the seventeenth and eighteenth centuries or the conscription crises of the twentieth century, when relations between English and French took a violent turn.

One response to the Durham interpretation is to deny the reality of French-English conflict in the Rebellion by pointing to the many anglophones, including prominent leaders like O'Callaghan and the Nelson brothers, who rallied to the Patriot cause, and to the francophones who supported the government. The insurrection was 'really' a class struggle, say some, not an ethnic conflict.[4] This is just another false dichotomy and one that flies

4 Daniel Salée, 'Les insurrections de 1837–1838 au Québec: remarques critiques et théoriques en marge de l'historiographie,' *Canadian Review of Studies in Nationalism* 13 (Spring 1986): 13–29

in the face of the empirical evidence. The ethnic polarization was by no means perfect, but French and English speakers certainly did tend to line up on opposite sides in 1837. One needs only to glance at the lists of rebel prisoners and 'Loyal Volunteers' to notice the overwhelming prevalence of French names on the first and of British names on the second. Moreover, the geography of rebellion seems to support the notion that the mutual irritation of the two linguistic groups played a part in the conflict; as we have seen (see above, 49), most of the action occurred in the section of the province (cities excepted) where the French and the English had the greatest contact. One might go further and note that, even within the turbulent District of Montreal, in localities where immigrant settlements adjoined French-Canadian communities, such as Beauharnois, L'Acadie, and Two Mountains counties, some of the most serious fighting in 1837–8 took place. Indeed, Robert Hall's county of Two Mountains was the area where the revolutionary process developed most rapidly and went the furthest; surely this precocity was connected, in some measure, to the local pattern of ethnic duality.

THE COUNTY OF TWO MOUNTAINS

Though it contained some excellent agricultural lands and was located not far from a major city, the county of Two Mountains was settled later than other parts of the St Lawrence valley.[5] The rock-studded Rivière des Mille-Iles presented an obstacle to both land and water transportation. Thus it was only at the end of the French régime that settlers came from the Ile Jésus and the island of Montreal to clear farms in the seigneuries of Deux Montagnes

5 Serge Courville, 'Origine et évolution des campagnes dans le comté des Deux-Montagnes 1755–1971,' (MA thesis, Université de Montréal, 1973); Christian Dessureault, 'La seigneurie du Lac des Deux-Montagnes de 1780 à 1825' (MA thesis, Université de Montréal, 1979); Monique Benoit, 'La formation d'une région: la marche du peuplement de St-Eustache à St-Jérôme et le problème des subsistances' (MA thesis, University of Ottawa, 1980)

and Rivière des Mille-Iles. These communities prospered and grew in the second half of the eighteenth century as succeeding generations pushed into the interior, especially up the fertile valley of the Rivière du Chêne. The parish of St Eustache was formed here in 1769, and in later years its territory was divided to create daughter parishes – St Benoit in 1799 and Ste Scholastique in 1825 – with little regard for the seigneurial geography of the region. An urban village took shape around St Eustache church at the ferrying point, the region's only link to Montreal until a bridge was built at Ste Thérèse in 1832. By 1830 the village, with about 150 houses and a population of some 1,000 souls, was known as 'one of the handsomest and most populous in the province.'[6]

While French Canadians were thus occupying Two Mountains from the south, English-speaking settlers, mainly from the United States, around 1800 began to enter the county through its 'back door.' A small stream of immigration occupied the banks of the Ottawa River at this time, and a few of the newcomers ascended the Rivière du Nord to settle at Lachute and St Andrews. Only years later were trails blazed and was contact established between these 'English' communities in the north and the French parishes in lower Two Mountains. The county remained overwhelmingly French Canadian until the late 1820s and the early 1830s, however, when the local English-speaking population was bolstered by the great wave of immigration from the British Isles. The Irish played a prominent part in this movement; a contingent of Catholics settled en bloc in an area organized in 1837 as the parish of St Columban, while Protestants – most of them Orangemen – from Ulster occupied the nearby township of Gore. In 1844 (the first time a census recorded national origin), about one-third of the county's population was not French Canadian. Clearly by the mid-1830s the English-speaking element, though still a

6 Joseph Bouchette, 'St Eustache,' *A Topographical Dictionary of the Province of Lower Canada* (London: Longman, Rees, Orme, Brown, Green, and Longman 1832), (unpaginated)

minority, was a substantial component of the population of Two Mountains. At the same time, the expansion of settlement had brought French and English into closer contact; in fact, anglophones could be found scattered throughout the county, though members of the two national groups tended to remain in distinct territories.

On the whole there was remarkably little friction between the French Canadians and the English-speaking newcomers in Two Mountains and elsewhere in the province. There were indeed some ugly battles in the Ottawa valley, where axe-swinging Irish loggers (the 'Shiners') attacked French Canadians in the lumber camps and ambushed their rafts on the way down river. Though it inevitably provoked Canadian counter measures, the 'Shiners' War' scarcely arose out of any nativist tendencies. Since it was the Shiners who opened hostilities and pursued their opponents relentlessly, this incident must be understood in terms of the brutal strategies worked out by Irish immigrants to secure employment in a rather inhospitable New World. Lower Canada was only one of many places where Irishmen relied on ethnic solidarity and violence to gain a foothold, and the French Canadians were not their only victims.[7] Behaviour of this sort (though it was certainly not the only cause of anti-Irish prejudice) helped to fuel violent nativist reactions in New England, the Maritimes, and Upper Canada.[8] Hostility to Irish immigrants was comparatively mild in Lower Canada. Outside the marginal districts dominated by the forest industry, the French and the Irish seem to have got along fairly well, and though Patriot newspapers and

7 H.C. Pentland, *Labour and Capital in Canada, 1650–1860* (Toronto: Lorimer 1981), 96–129; Michael Cross, 'The Shiners' War: Social Violence in the Ottawa Valley in the 1830s,' *CHR* 59 (1973): 1–26; Ruth Bleasdale, 'Class Conflict on the Canals of Upper Canada in the 1840s,' *Labour – le travail* 7 (1981): 9–89

8 Ray Billington, *The Protestant Crusade 1800–1860: A Study of the Origins of American Nativism* (New York: Quadrangle 1938); Scott W. See, 'The Orange Order and Social Violence in Mid-Nineteenth Century Saint John,' *Acadiensis* 13 (Autumn 1983): 68–92

politicians fulminated against 'pauper immigration,' one looks in vain for riots such as those which rocked the towns of Saint John and Woodstock, New Brunswick. Of course in New Brunswick and Massachusetts xenophobia was reinforced by religious prejudice, whereas the French and Irish of Lower Canada, though hardly united by a common Catholicism, were at least not separated by religion.

At the same time, there is little evidence of conflict on religious grounds between the French Canadians and the Protestant English-speakers of the province. Visitors, particularly those with Irish experience, were struck by the absence of sectarian feuding between groups divided by religion as well as by language: 'There is a deep sentiment of religion spread, we believe, over the whole population of the country, and we are happy to bear testimony so cordially as we can do, that it is accompanied with fewer feelings of acerbity of the followers of one creed towards another, and particularly of Protestants towards Catholics and Catholics towards Protestants, than perhaps in any country where distinctions so marked and so numerous exist.'[9] Indeed, in so far as there were quarrels over religion, they were limited mainly to the Irish community of Two Mountains. The Catholic militiamen of St Columban who, 'came over to this country to avoid the persecution which awaited them at home on account of their religion,' complained of a Protestant major who 'insulted and abused them on account of their religion.'[10]

---

9 Lord Gosford, quoted in Lucas, ed., *Durham Report*, 2: 39n
10 NA, LC Adjutant General, vol. 45, petition of many inhabitants of North River, Ste Scholastique, n.d. [1834]. There was one case of anti-Protestant sentiment on the part of the French-Canadian habitants in the years before the Rebellion. This was in the St Jean area of the Upper Richelieu where a group of Swiss Protestants had established a mission. Popular hostility seems to have been aroused by the missionaries' aggressive proselytism and by their connections with the highly unpopular seigneur, William Plenderleath Christie. See René Hardy, 'La rébellion de 1837–1838 et l'essor du protestantisme canadien-français,' *RHAF* 29 (September 1975): 180–1; Françoise Noel, *The Christie Seigneuries: Estate Management and Settlement in the Upper Richelieu Valley, 1760–1854* (Montreal: McGill-Queen's UP 1992), 79.

This is not to say there was no conflict in Two Mountains. On the contrary: as early as the 1790s, there were extended disputes in St Eustache over questions about where bridges should be built and who should pay for them.[11] The seigneur of Mille-Iles, Louis-Eustache Lambert Dumont, wanted the Rivière du Chêne traversed at its mouth, where his manor house, seigneurial mill, and other assets were located. Since the village of St Eustache was located at this spot, he had no difficulty securing the support of the settlement's merchants and artisans. The farming habitants of the parish, on the other hand, wanted a crossing further upstream, because it would be cheaper to build and would give them better access to Montreal. The issue may sound trivial, but it mattered deeply to the people involved. Led by their militia captain, Joseph Ethier, the habitants conducted a determined campaign of protest featuring petitions to the government, litigation in the courts, and various forms of civil disobedience (refusal to provide the money, materials, and labour required by law). After nine years of angry meetings, manoeuvres, and counter-manoeuvres, two bridges were finally built in a compromise that satisfied no one. The bitter campaign apparently left the St Eustache region more deeply divided, town from country and seigneur from censitaire, than most parts of Lower Canada. It also provided the habitants of Two Mountains with valuable political experience. It even propelled Joseph Ethier onto the provincial stage; though a genuine peasant, unable to read and write, he was elected to the Lower Canadian House of Assembly.

The seigneur Dumont also became more active in electoral politics. A member of the pre-conquest nobility and a lieutenant-colonel of militia, he had the benefits of social prestige and powerful connections outside the region. Within Two Mountains county he stood at the centre of a group of small-town notables – merchants, professional men, and co-seigneurs – interconnected to a large extent through blood and marriage. This little 'Family Compact,' based in the village of St Eustache, did its best to secure a dominant position in the region's public affairs. When

11 Léon Robichaud, 'Le pouvoir, les paysans et la voirie au Bas-Canada à la fin du XVIIIe siècle' (MA thesis, McGill University, 1989), 115–27

Lower Canada was rocked by political conflict, as it was in 1810 and 1827, the Dumont clique always threw its support behind the governmental and Tory forces, since they offered the best bulwark against the troublesome forces of peasant democracy represented by Joseph Ethier. It had some success over the years, but the provincial electoral campaign of 1827 dealt it a severe blow. During that year there had been protests across Lower Canada against the arbitrary and authoritarian measures of Governor Dalhousie. The St Eustache Compact sided with the unpopular governor, however, while, just as predictably, the county's anti-Dumont forces took the lead in the campaign against Dalhousie. The 'patriots,' as they were now beginning to call themselves, were no longer a strictly peasant faction: they included merchants and professional men from the settlements that had recently grown up north of St Eustache. The village of St Benoit was their headquarters, but their support came primarily from the region's peasantry, which had by then been doing battle with the seigneur's clique for at least a generation. With petitions, protest rallies, and finally an electoral campaign, the Two Mountains Patriots aroused the habitants and succeeded in linking the Dalhousie régime with the local 'tyranny' of the Dumont faction. The latter responded to this activity with traditional techniques of political management. For example, they purged Patriot activists from the officer corps of the militia and gave commissions to men who would support them; in this way Eustache Cheval, a staunch loyalist who would play a prominent role in 1837, first became an officer. But this anachronistic strategy, particularly when it was applied in so crude a manner, was no match for the more modern techniques of political mobilization employed by the Patriots. The reformers won Two Mountains in 1827 and kept it until the insurrection.[12]

12 Emile Dubois, *Le feu de la Rivière-du-Chêne: étude historique sur le mouvement insurrectionnel de 1837 au nord de Montréal* (St Jérôme: Imprimerie Labelle 1937), 50–3; *Report of the Special Committee, to whom was referred that Part of His Excellency's Speech which referred to the Organization of the Militia* (Quebec 1829), 55. Even after 1827, however, the Dumont group still enjoyed considerable influence within the parish of St Eustache. For example, it completely dominated the local school board elected in 1831. ANQM, gr., J.A.

French-English conflict seems to have played little part in the Two Mountains election battle of 1827, which is not surprising given the small English population at the time. The confrontation must be seen in a different light; in fact, it reflected several connected and mutually reinforcing lines of division. To some degree it was a sectional struggle between a recently settled 'frontier' and an older parent community. There was also a related rural-urban axis of conflict, with an agricultural district emancipating itself from the domination of the miniature metropolis of St Eustache. Then there was the clash of agrarian classes: peasants, supported by a rural bourgeoisie, rising up against the rule of the seigneurial clan. Finally, there was the clash of conservative and populist/democratic political philosophies. All these levels of contention could be traced back to the 1790s in Two Mountains county, and together they imparted a special local sharpness to the political dissensions then disturbing Lower Canada as a whole.

The region came into the provincial limelight once again during the election of 1834, the last one before the Rebellion.[13] In many respects the election campaign of 1834 was similar to that of 1827. Colonial autonomy and the power of the elective Assembly were still the questions of the day. Across Lower Canada the great issue of the 1834 election was the Ninety-Two Resolutions, recently passed by the Assembly with the enthusiastic support of the Patriot members for Two Mountains, Jean-Joseph Girouard and William Henry Scott. Scott and Girouard, like the reformers of 1827, gained the bulk of their support from the inland parishes of St Benoit, Ste Scholastique, and St Columban. They were opposed, as in the past, by the town of St Eustache and its vicin-

Berthelot, 'Election de syndics d'école, paroisse St Eustache,' 30 October 1831

13 Accounts of this electoral contest are of course partisan and contradictory. The Patriot view can be found in *Relation historique des événements de l'élection du comté du Lac des Deux Montagnes, en 1834* (Montreal: n.p. 1835), while the Constitutionalist version of events appears in *L'Ami du Peuple*, 19 and 29 November 1834. I have also consulted articles on the leading personalities in the *DCB*.

ity, still dominated by the Dumont faction of seigneurs and office-holders; indeed one of the Constitutionalist candidates was F.-E. Globensky, a francophone of Polish origin who was related to the Dumonts, administrator of their seigneurie, and a major local money-lender. A new figure in the St Eustache Constitutionalist camp was the parish priest, Jacques Paquin, who, like many clergymen, became an active opponent of the Patriots in the 1830s.[14]

If the electoral campaign had been, like those of the 1820s, essentially a matter of middle-class radicals vying for habitant votes with a seigneurial/office-holding elite, then the Patriots would have had an easy victory. But the composition of the Two Mountains electorate had changed between 1827 and 1834. Now there was a sizeable English-speaking population in the northern sections of the county. Moreover, over the course of the 1830s Lower Canadian anglophones rallied increasingly to the Constitutionalist cause, making it in some measure an ethnic party. Just after their defeat in the election of 1834, immigrant settlers in Two Mountains formed a 'Constitutional Association,' whose first object was 'To obtain for persons of British and Irish origin, and others His Majesty's subjects, labouring under the same privation of common rights, a fair and reasonable proportion of the Representation in the Provincial Assembly.'[15] The association's rules were printed only in English, its membership list had no French names, and it met at St Andrews, in the heart of the county's anglophone district.

For all its 'national exclusiveness' this was certainly a popular movement, rallying 'public opinion' in a thoroughly modern way quite distinct from the traditional election management practised by the St Eustache conservatives. No one can understand the

14 W.S. Reid, 'The Habitant's Standard of Living on the Seigneurie des Milles Isles, 1820–50,' *CHR* 28 (September 1947): 277; Richard Chabot, *Le curé de campagne et la contestation locale au Québec de 1791 aux troubles de 1837–38* (Montreal: Hurtubise 1975), 179–81
15 NA, Barron Papers, vol. 1, 'Rules and Regulations for the Government of the Constitutional Association of the County of the Two Mountains ... '

Rebellion or the developments leading to it without taking account of Constitutionalism as a militant mass movement among Lower Canada's English-speaking population. Patriot leaders always tended to assume that their opponents were 'bureaucrats,' that is, the officials and merchants who were in some sense creatures of the colonial government and who opposed the popular movement because their privileged position in the province depended on keeping the French Canadians in subjection. They were therefore at a loss when dealing with the rank-and-file anglophone settlers, whose anti-Patriot sentiment had little to do with the privileges of the conqueror. Just as we must distinguish between bourgeois and popular French-Canadian nationalism, we must also differentiate the Toryism of the anglophone oligarchy from the counter-nationalism of the English-Canadian mass.

The bulk of the Scottish, Irish, and American immigrants who came to Lower Canada in the forty years preceding the Rebellion – their numbers reaching significant proportions only after 1828 – were agricultural settlers, artisans, and urban workers.[16] They were hardly pensioners of the colonial state; in fact their social profile resembled nothing so much as the French-Canadian base of the Patriot movement. One might have expected that a population composed of these classes would have constituted a sympathetic audience for a political program, such as that proposed by the Patriots, that was hostile to privilege and friendly to the aspirations of small proprietors. Indeed, many anglophones in Two Mountains, and even more in the Eastern Townships, did throw in their lot with the patriot cause. Yet the bulk of the English-speaking population became politicized in the opposite direction, in part no doubt as a reaction by immigrants, still attached to the mother country, against a Patriot party that seemed bent on independence. Their Toryism would thus have

16 Ronald Rudin, *The Forgotten Quebeckers: A History of English-Speaking Quebec 1759–1980* (Quebec: Institut québécois de recherche sur la culture 1985), 69–93

similar roots to those of the British immigrants who were settling on the other side of the Ottawa River. In Upper Canada, as in Lower Canada, the Rebellion tended to pit recent immigrants against long-established residents, whether born in Canada or the United States.[17]

But there was much more to popular Constitutionalism than sentimental ties to the old country, which explains why so many Lower Canadians of American origin were attracted to it. Quite apart from the fact that they spoke the language of the British empire, the English Lower Canadians constituted a cultural minority, and, as such, they tended to be unresponsive to the nationalist appeals of the Patriots. It did not matter to them that the Patriots of the 1830s no longer stood for the simple defence of ethnic distinctiveness, that they now espoused a nationalism linked to universally applicable democratic and egalitarian principles. For many anglophones the movement was too strongly marked by its French-Canadian origins. So much about the Lower Canadian radical movement – the specific issues it espoused, its language, its symbolism, its historical memories – reflected the French-Canadian experience out of which it grew. Small wonder then that it had difficulty securing the allegiance of immigrants from the British Isles. But the anglophone community did not simply remain ignorant and indifferent to the patriots; it emerged instead as a fierce antagonist.

The militant Constitutionalism of the English minority should be understood as a direct reaction to the rapid politicization of the majority in the years leading up to the Rebellion. Almost all revolutions – even those without a strong nationalist coloration – tend to stimulate the opposition of ethnic and linguistic minorities. When the Magyars rose against the Hapsburgs in 1848, they naturally provoked the counter-nationalism of the Croatians who

17 Ronald J. Stagg, 'The Yonge Street Rebellion of 1837: An Examination of the Social Background and a Re-assessment of the Events,' (PH D thesis, University of Toronto, 1976), 291; Colin Read, *The Rising in Western Upper Canada, 1837–8: The Duncombe Revolt and After* (Toronto: UTP 1982), 178–204

shared the Hungarian territories with them; 'loyal' Croatian armies therefore fought under the standard of the emperor, since that was the best way to oppose the Magyars.[18] The annals of the revolutions of 1848, particularly where they concern the complicated ethnic geography of central Europe, are filled with similar cases. The American Revolution also generated a contrary movement, though a fragmented and therefore relatively weak one. W.H. Nelson observes that Loyalists were disproportionately numerous among minority groups of various sorts: Germans in South Carolina, Highland Scots in New York, Presbyterians in the South, and Blacks everywhere: 'Taking all the groups and factions, sects, classes, and inhabitants of regions that seem to have been Tory, they have but one thing in common: they represented conscious minorities, people who felt weak and threatened ... Almost all the Loyalists were, in one way or another, more afraid of America than they were of Britain.'[19] Of course the Canadian Tories were far less diverse and therefore not nearly as weak as the American Loyalists (a factor that helps to explain why the two revolutions turned out so differently), but they were still a minority that had reason to feel threatened by the larger national group or, more exactly, by a political movement associated with the majority nation.

It was not simply 'the French' as such that aroused the ire of the English speakers, any more than the Magyars or the 'Americans' automatically and by their simple presence alone frightened the minorities who shared their territories. It was the aggressive mobilization of the population in a revolutionary crisis that provoked alarm. As the demand that power be vested in 'the people' came increasingly to the fore, the question of who or what the people were seemed all the more problematic to those whose

---

18 A.J.P. Taylor, *The Habsburg Monarchy 1809–1918: A History of the Austrian Empire and Austria-Hungary* (New York: Harper & Row 1965), 65; Istvan Deak, *The Lawful Revolution: Louis Kossuth and the Hungarians, 1848–1849* (New York: Columbia UP 1979)

19 William H. Nelson, *The American Tory* (Oxford: Oxford UP 1961), 91

status in the community was rather uncertain. The revolutionary process itself – the intensification of politics, the direct involvement of previously passive people and classes, the displacement of political struggle into novel channels – was bound to distress a minority that felt it had found a niche in the pre-existing order.

It was out of this sort of distress that the plebeian counter-nationalism of English Lower Canada grew and added its weight to the anti-patriot struggle long waged for somewhat different motives by the colonial oligarchy. Popular constitutionalism was a potent force among the settlers of northern Two Mountains, and by 1834 the latter accounted for a substantial minority of the county's electorate. Since support for the Patriots was intense and deeply rooted in the older parts of the county, a close and bitterly fought election campaign was almost inevitable and violence at the polls virtually assured.

Voting took place first at St Andrews, in the midst of the anglophone settlements, from 4 to 10 November, and there was a certain amount of jostling between the rival gangs of 'bullés' ('bullies' or 'goons'). The Constitutionalists, Globensky and James Brown, easily won this poll, but their opponents counted on overtaking them at the St Eustache poll, to be held after three days' interval. The first serious clash occurred after the St Andrews poll closed. That night a group of French Canadians escorting the Patriot candidates home was ambushed by a club-wielding 'bande d'Ecossais' and severely beaten. Rumours then spread that the northern Constitutionalists would descend on St Eustache and take over the polling place. Crowds of patriots therefore ringed the rectory where hustings had been set up and prepared for the expected assault. Sure enough, groups of anglophones from the north began to appear; according to Constitutionalist accounts they had come merely to exercise their franchise, while the patriots insisted they had already voted at St Andrews. Since the patriots were too numerous to be easily dislodged, the Constitutionalists settled into quarters provided for them at St Eustache and awaited reinforcements. The patriots too sent for additional forces. After a few days of stand-off, fighting broke out, not around the polling place, but at various points in and around the town, with night raids on enemy lodgings and attacks on isolated stragglers. The climax was an attempt by mounted Constitutionalists to charge their horses through the crowd. Apparently the patriots held fast and Globensky and Brown eventually conceded defeat.[20] There were broken heads and damaged property in the wake of this unprecedented rioting, but no one was killed. Nevertheless, southern patriots would remember the incident as a terrifying invasion from the north and the memory conditioned the behaviour of both parties during the crisis of 1837.

Certainly the violent election of 1834 had all the appearances of a 'national' conflict. Even the participants spoke openly of their allies and opponents in ethnic terms: the 'Irish' of St Columban, the 'Scots' of St Andrews, the 'Canadians' of St Benoit. Yet if the presence of two substantial linguistic groups in Two Mountains helps to explain the peculiar bitterness of the 1834 election, national dualism did not *create* political conflict. The latter was clearly visible in 1827 before the 'English' presence had become a significant political factor. The immigration of the early 1830s and the mobilization of the anglophones against 'French Republicanism' simply altered the balance of forces in the county and inserted an ethnic movement into a pre-existing conflict. Two Mountains thus appears almost as a microcosm of Lower Canada in the troubled 1830s, and the election of 1834 foreshadows the far more serious dramas of 1837.

THE JULY TROUBLES

The events of 1837 began here on a festive note. The Two Mountains anti-coercion meeting, held at Ste Scholastique on 1

20 The Constitutionalists were still in the lead by a small margin at this point. Patriots, however, claimed – and with considerable plausibility, given the political geography of the county – to have hundreds of votes 'in reserve,' more than enough to carry the election. Globensky and Brown withdrew, according to their own account, to prevent further violence, though their appreciation of the likely outcome of future rioting and voting may have influenced their decision.

June, was a splendid event carefully staged by the middle-class leaders – Scott, Girouard, Dr Luc Masson, Emery Féré, and others – of the county's Patriot movement. 'The Great Meeting of the Men of the North,' as the *Vindicator* called it, followed a format pioneered at St Ours. There was a triumphant procession from St Benoit, through the heart of radical Two Mountains, to the assembly site in front of the rectory at Ste Scholastique. All along the way the houses were decorated with flags and banners and the air rang with 'patriotic national songs, and repeated bursts of fervent cheers for Papineau, the Assembly and the honest Patriots of this and the neighbouring Colonies.'[21] The meeting itself featured a long address delivered by Papineau himself as well as speeches in both French and English by lesser luminaries. Finally a series of resolutions was presented to the acclamation of the crowd. Following the precedent established during protest campaigns earlier in the decade, a 'permanent committee' was set up, with representatives from each parish in the county, to coordinate future activities and to correspond with Patriots in other parts of the province. All these proceedings, exciting as they may have been for one section of the population, were most disturbing to the Constitutionalists of Two Mountains, and when extra-legal actions began a few weeks later, the latter had little doubt that the 1 June meeting and the sinister committee established then were to blame.

It was at this time that the ostracism of the 100 or so English-speaking families of St Eustache, St Benoit, and Ste Scholastique began in earnest. Stones were thrown and fences toppled, and, as Robert Hall reported in his deposition quoted above, manes were shaved and property damaged. These depredations must have been annoying, even terrifying, for the human victims, but it was the horses of Two Mountains that bore the brunt of patriot hostility. A common form of ritual aggression in this county during the troubles of 1837, the cropping of manes and tails was

21 *Vindicator*, 6 June 1837

comparatively rare in other parts of the province.[22] It seems to have been regarded more as an indignity than an injury. Robert Hall says he was 'universally laughed at'; other accounts of Two Mountains tail croppings also convey a sense of the carnavalesque spirit which holds the owner of the damaged animal up to ridicule. In some parts of early modern England cuckolds were humiliated by being paraded through the village atop a mare with its mane and tail shaved.[23] What amused Robert Hall's neighbours was no doubt the symbolic castration suggested by his shorn horse.

There was more to the Two Mountains troubles than mockery and ostracism. Crops were damaged, windows broken. Young men gathered at a country tavern in Ste Scholastique and threw stones at the carriages of passing Constitutionalists.[24] Individuals known to be hostile to the patriots were threatened, most commonly with having their houses and barns burned. Throughout the crisis of 1837–8 there were numerous threats of arson, and they were reported in various parts of Lower Canada. It was the obvious menace, perfectly calculated to chill the hearts of people who lived with their families and all their valuable pos-

22 ANQ, 1837, no. 659, déposition d'Eustache Cheval, 4 July 1837; ibid., no. 3446, W.K. McCord to T.M.C. Murdock, 27 April 1840; Hardy, 'l'essor du protestantisme,' 180; Le Populaire, 29 September 1837. Perhaps animal mutilation was a practice the local habitants picked up from the Irish immigrants who lived in their midst; for we know that the mutilation of livestock, often in quite gruesome forms, was a favoured punishment directed against landlords and others who broke community norms in the Irish countryside. On the other hand, there is evidence of mane and tail cropping in rural French Canada from before the conquest. George Rudé, Protest and Punishment: The Story of the Social and Political Protesters transported to Australia 1788–1868 (Oxford: Oxford UP 1978), 149–52; Louise Dechêne, personal communication

23 Martin Ingram, 'Ridings, Rough Music and the "Reform of Popular Culture" in Early Modern England,' Past and Present, 105 (November 1984): 87

24 NA, LC Civil Secretary, 515: 265, George Gillanders to S. Walcott, 23 July 1837

sessions in wooden houses situated on relatively isolated farm-steads. What could be easier than to put the torch to a barn, and how could even the most vigilant foil a determined incendiary? Fire was indeed a favoured weapon in popular struggles in many other parts of the world, and yet there were very few cases of buildings' actually being burned in Lower Canada; or, to be more exact, there were very few until after the patriots had been defeated and the 'forces of order' had gained the upper hand. The patriots may have been restrained simply because the mere threat of arson was all the terror that was required.

It was certainly enough to keep John Oswald, a St Eustache farmer, up at night. About 11 p.m. on the night of 7 July, he later recounted, 'being then watching his property being kept in continual fear of its being damaged through reports and menaces, heard loud screamings towards Belle rivière occasioned by a mob, and that screaming was used by said mob at every old country man's house and canadian loyalists, hourrahing for Papineau and the Patriots; said mob crossed the river, and directed their steps towards a barn belonging to Messire Paquin curate of St Eustache which barn was that night demolished, the screaming continuing for some time when at that barn.' The destruction on this occasion was not as great as it sounds, because the barn was under construction and only half built. No doubt it presented too tempting a target for the 'mob' to resist. It was unprotected, since the owner lived far away in the village. Moreover, it was likely being built to receive tithe grain, which could hardly have endeared it to these Catholic cultivators. Finally – and this seems to have been decisive – Curé Paquin was a notorious Constitutionalist; recently he had begun using the pulpit, as he had in 1834, to speak out against the patriot movement. 'That was good for a chouayen priest,' one of the party later declared, using a popular term meaning 'traitor' or 'coward' but reserved in 1837 for anti-Patriot French Canadians.[25]

---

25 ANQ, 1837, no. 789, deposition of John Oswald, 15 July 1837; ibid., no. 816, déposition de Toussaint Cheval, 10 July 1837

The destruction of the barn was an isolated event, but the 'screaming mob' that John Oswald heard, seems to have been one of several that disturbed the peace of Two Mountains county about that time. Groups of men up to 100 strong went out at night wearing red toques, their faces blackened, and roamed the villages and the rangs shouting patriot slogans and making as much ruckus as possible. The disguises, the nocturnal setting, and the noise all recall in a vague way the custom of the charivari, and, like a charivari, these demonstrations required some organization. A country store-cum-tavern in Ste Scholastique seems to have been the meeting place. Michel Rochon, a tanner and no friend of Papineau, happened to come there on business one day, and the proprietor asked him if he was a patriot. There were several men present and all of them seemed interested in his response; the tanner gave a prudent, rather than a strictly accurate, answer. 'Good,' replied the merchant, 'I'll show you your night clothes,' and he produced a 'red cap decorated with paper' and carbon to blacken his face. Rochon went with the band that night and shouted himself hoarse, but after that he stayed home. A troop passed his house the next night and he heard someone yell, 'Rochon, you may be sleeping quietly with your wife, but if you were a *chouaguen*, you wouldn't be left in peace.'[26] Clearly the purpose of these midnight expeditions was to intimidate the hostile and the wavering. The actions were scarcely bloody; in fact, except for pulling down the frame of a barn, the 'screaming mob' committed almost no action at all. Yet there was a tangible menace of violence. The charivari form, combining a spectacle of symbolic aggression with actual restraint, was therefore wonderfully appropriate.

The marauders did cross the line dividing ritual violence from the real thing one night when they fired shots through the windows of two houses, one of them belonging to Captain Eustache Cheval of St Eustache. A senior habitant close to sixty years of

---

26 Ibid., no. 815, déposition de Michel Rochon, 8 July 1837 (author's translation)

age, Cheval happened to have conveyed his farm by a notarized deed of gift to one of his sons only a month before the attack, and so we have some record of his material circumstances in 1837.[27] His 117-arpent farm, with house, barn, equipment, and livestock, can be described only as typical of the period. Though he was no longer, strictly speaking, a land-owner as of May, his deed of 'gift' was loaded down with so many restrictions that it made his son a virtual tenant-farmer, if not a hired hand, for the rest of Eustache's life. None of these circumstances would have set Cheval apart economically from most other habitants of his age, but his militia commission and his political leanings did. Cheval had originally gained his militia commission during the elecion campaign of 1827 as a reward for supporting his seigneur and lieutenant-colonel, and he was well known in the area as a creature of the St Eustache Dumont clique.

A decade of standing up for an unpopular cause may have toughened Cheval. Certainly he was not easily intimidated; when he was warned in advance that his property would be a target of patriot ire, he prepared for resistance, gathering four friends to help guard his home. In the middle of the night prowlers were spotted by the stable, but Cheval managed to chase them away. Later, however, a shot crashed through the window and a little girl was cut by the broken glass.[28] Eustache Cheval was sure that the intention was to assassinate him, which is probably what the attackers wished him to think. Actually, this incident seems to be consistent with the larger campaign of restrained terror; it was simply the extreme case where a more dramatic threat seemed necessary to deal with an opponent more determined than most.

What then was the point of these threats and this harassment? Who wished to frighten whom and why? Among those named in the depositions as taking an active role in the July campaigns

27 ANQM, gr., J.-L. de Bellefeuille, donation entre vifs par Eustache Cheval et son épouse à Frs-Xavier Cheval leur fils, 29 May 1837
28 ANQ, 1837, no. 659, déposition d'Eustache Cheval, 4 July 1837

were three 'yeomen' (i.e., habitants), three labourers, and one tanner.[29] There is no mention of the prominent middle-class politicians of the area. Only the Major brothers, small merchants of Ste Scholastique, qualify marginally as bourgeois, and they do seem to have played a leading role. More so than the actions of later stages of the crisis of 1837, this was a wholly plebeian campaign, and one carried out by the peasantry, including a disproportionate number of presumably poor labourers.

But were these people acting under the orders or at the instigation of the Patriot 'high command'? Many victims of the campaign of harassment noted that the troubles began soon after the Ste Scholastique meeting. Papineau and the other speakers certainly used every rhetorical device to rouse the patriotic indignation of their massive audience, but the accounts of the speeches give no indication that they advocated violent measures. Far from fanning the flames of national hostility, the resolutions passed on that June afternoon called for understanding and reconciliation.

We therefore fervently implore all the inhabitants of the Province of every creed, origin and language, to be united for their common defence; to sacrifice their prejudices for the honor and safety of the country, and to help each other, for the purpose of obtaining a wise and protecting Government, which, in re-establishing harmony amongst us, would, at the same time, cause agriculture, commerce, and our national industry to flourish, and we on our part assure of our fraternity and of our confidence our fellow subjects of British origin who superior as well to the cajoleries as to the antipathies of power, have united with us in our just demands, that we never entertained, but on the contrary that we have always reproved, the unfortunate national distinctions which our common enemies have sought, and still wickedly seek, to foment amongst us.[30]

When violence was later reported in Two Mountains, the radical papers of Montreal seemed quite embarrassed by the commotion

29 Ibid., passim.
30 *Vindicator*, 6 June 1837

and did their best to ignore it. Meanwhile, dozens of protest meetings were being held all across Lower Canada, and none of them was followed by disturbances. What was so special about Two Mountains county that political mobilization there should lead to bitter civil conflict?

Surely the peculiar balance of patriot and Constitutionalist forces was what distinguished Two Mountains from other rural counties. A substantial section of the county was hostile to the Patriots and had given proof in 1834 of its willingness to resort to violence. Three years later, by June 1837, it was clear that the province was on the verge of a much more serious crisis. Papineau might talk vaguely of a great revolution in the distant future, but the people of southern Two Mountains must have been more keenly aware of the dangerous reactions such rhetoric was likely to provoke both from the government and from their Constitutionalist neighbours. We cannot hope to understand the actions of these people unless we appreciate the danger to which the anti-colonial mobilization exposed them. Hence the more rapid preparations for action, the noisy bravado to reassure the committed and intimidate the hostile. Hence also the punitive reaction against figures such as Curé Paquin who were identified with the larger threat. If the flags, the slogans, and the speeches of the Ste Scholastique meeting gave voice to the hopes of the patriots of Two Mountains, the attacks on Robert Hall and Eustache Cheval expressed their fears.

Alongside the rather 'paranoid' dimensions of these incidents, there is also a more rational sense to the campaign of 'persecution.' All the testimony indicates that the immediate and expressed purpose of the intimidation and harassment was to force people to change their political allegiance. 'Join the Patriot party,' was the demand put to dissidents; otherwise, 'there will be trouble.'[31] No one seems to have been asked to change his language, religion, or customs: only his politics. In some cases

31 ANQ, 1837, no. 834, deposition of Duncan McColl, 6 July 1837; cf. ibid., no. 833, deposition of Alexander McColl, 6 July 1837; ibid., no. 835, deposition of William Starke, 6 July 1837; NA, LC Civil Secretary, 514: 132, F.E. Globensky to D. Daly, 11 July 1837 (author's translation)

men were asked to sign a free trade petition to the United States Congress that was being circulated throughout Lower Canada. But surely a few additional signatures – which could always be forged in any case – did not justify all the commotion and scare tactics. Clearly the petition itself was less important than the public gesture of support for the patriots implied by the act of signing. The real purpose of intimidation was, first, to get the timid, the wavering, the opportunistic to commit themselves to the patriotic cause. People like Michel Rochon were likely to side with the stronger party at any given time; pressuring him to take part in charivaris made him an accessory and therefore less likely to help the government forces (although Rochon did in fact inform on the patriots). The second purpose of intimidation was to identify the staunch and determined opponents of the movement. When Robert Hall refused, in spite of strong pressure, to make even a symbolic gesture of solidarity, he showed himself to be altogether different from those who held back out of timidity or a lack of civic spirit. He was not a negligent citizen: he was an enemy. There was political logic then to the actions of the marauders; it could in fact be called a terrorist logic, though that seems a rather strong term to attach to such restrained coercion. Both brutal political rationality and fear-inspired outbursts can be discerned in the July troubles, and both can be traced to the special situation in which Two Mountains patriots found themselves in the summer of 1837.

Of course the irony is that the disturbances only hastened the outside reactions that the radicals dreaded. Rumours spread that the tough Orangemen of the Gore had promised to come to the aid of the beleaguered anglophones of the south. And every frightened Constitutionalist who swore out a deposition in the city made armed intervention of the state more likely. As allies and witnesses on the side of the threatening outside forces, anti-patriots in St Eustache, St Benoit, and Ste Scholastique seemed all the more threatening. Toussaint Cheval, a Ste Scholastique labourer and no doubt suspect because he was related to the notorious Eustache, was one of those who fell afoul of his neighbours. On the evening of 10 July four men whom he apparently knew well stormed into his house and began shouting accusations to the effect 'that he had been to the River du Chêne [St Eustache village] to sign up to get troops.' Shaking his fist under poor Toussaint's nose, Isidore Lauzon denounced him for 'swearing a deposition against us.' In fact, since Cheval's name does not appear in the surviving depositions sworn before that date, the specific charge was probably unfounded. But Isidore Lauzon had no access to certain information on that point. All he knew was that a punitive expedition was rumoured to be on its way and that Toussaint Cheval, because of something he said or did, appeared to be blameable. 'You've put our heads in a noose,' he continued, 'you cannot live among us any more. You can pack up and leave right now.' Cheval took seriously this sentence of banishment and the threat that lay behind it; without delay he left for Upper Canada and stayed there for two weeks. Returning at last to the parish, he had to hide out in the woods for a day and a night before he ascertained that the alarm had passed and it was safe to return to his family.[32]

The noisy promenades, the stone-throwing, the shots, the horse mutilation, and the fence-breaking, combined with rumours and threats of much worse horrors, made a vivid impression on the little Constitutionalist contingent of St Eustache, St Benoit, and Ste Scholastique. By mid-July, even though no one had been hurt, these people were well and truly terrified.[33] News of the events was then spreading through the province as the Tory press of Montreal published lurid accounts of the 'anarchy' in the northern countryside. The government, still hoping to defuse the larger political crisis, was placed in a difficult position. Clearly the law had been broken repeatedly, and the local delegates of the state either were themselves involved in the actions or were completely powerless to oppose them. Something had to be done

32 ANQ, 1837, no. 610, déposition de Toussaint Cheval, 6 September 1837 (author's translation)
33 NA, LC Civil Secretary, 514: 90, petition of several inhabitants of St Eustache to Governor Gosford, 9 July 1837

if the government was to appease Constitutionalist extremists and maintain its own sovereignty in the region. The solicitor-general therefore decided to offer a reward for information that would identify those who had shot at Cheval. At the same time, he ordered the arrest of four men already named in the depositions sworn by Robert Hall and the others.

On the morning of 13 July, with the Montreal garrison on the alert, a party led by the high constable left the city on its way to St Eustache. This officer (whose duties normally involved organizing the night watchmen of Montreal) had warrants to arrest four men on charges of 'conspiracy,' and he was accompanied by two bailiffs, a carter, and two other private citizens.[34] They must have formed a curious and highly conspicuous procession, bumping along the dusty roads in their five calèches, looking for all the world like the legal officials who came to serve warrants of execution when a farm was seized for debt.

Another pair of bailiffs had ridden out separately from Montreal charged with distributing posters offering, in the name of the governor, a reward of £100 for information in the Eustache Cheval case.[35] Arriving at the village of St Benoit, they went straight to a tavern owned by a man named Coursolle. When they tried to post the proclamation, however, the innkeeper stopped them, unimpressed by their announcement that they were acting under orders from the attorney-general. Coursolle proclaimed 'that the Attorney-General was filthy damned trash [sacré crasseux] and so is the governor,' before he went to get help. Dr Masson, a local Patriot leader, arrived with other neighbours and took charge. He told the bailiffs their lives would be in danger if they put up their posters in the village and added, in a remark that nicely expressed current local notions of crimi-

34 ANQ, 1837, no. 669, déposition d'André-Henri Baron, 14 July 1837; ibid, no. 837, affidavit de Joseph Aymond et François Poitra, 14 July 1837; ibid., no. 838, affidavit of Benjamin Delisle, 14 July 1837; ibid., no. 839, affidavit d'Amable Loiselle, 14 July 1837
35 Ibid., no. 669, déposition d'André-Henri Baron, 14 July 1837

nality and legitimate authority, that he would like to offer £100 for the governor's head. But the conversation was cut short when a man galloped up to announce the arrival at Côte St Joseph of a larger party that had come to take prisoners. Everyone rushed off in pursuit. One man was heard to suggest that the high constable should be stripped naked and tied up at the top of the mountain and left to be eaten by the mosquitoes.

Meanwhile, the high constable's expedition was also running into difficulty.[36] When it landed at St Eustache, inquiries were made to locate the four men named in the warrants, but of course no one would say where they lived. According to Patriot accounts, the officers attempted to intimidate the population by saying that they were being followed by a force of soldiers and artillery.[37] The scare tactics may have been effective, since they did manage to locate one of the accused, François Labelle, at his farm three leagues back from the river in the parish of St Eustache. Labelle tried to run away, but he was soon captured. As they were securing the prisoner, the captors noticed Labelle's wife running to the neighbours for help. Other residents were going from house to house, and soon a crowd had gathered around, armed with sticks and farm implements. The lawmen brandished guns to keep the people at bay and hurried off towards the ferry almost ten kilometres away. All along the way angry crowds gathered by the roadside, menacing the constables and shouting encouragement to the prisoner.

Hopes were lodged with the party of militia men now speeding to the rescue from St Benoit. The band of would-be rescuers, according to one report, was made up of about fifty men armed with sickles, axes, and pitchforks,[38] but they did not arrive at St Eustache in time to bring this agricultural weaponry into play.

36 Ibid., no. 837, affidavit de Joseph Aymond, 14 July 1837; ibid., no. 838, affidavit of Benjamin Delisle, 14 July 1837; ibid., no. 839, affidavit d'Amable Loiselle, 14 July 1837
37 *La Minerve*, 27 July 1837
38 *Le Populaire*, 14 July 1837

The law officers narrowly beat them to the river crossing and, turning their guns on the ferryman, forced him to take them over to Ile Jésus. The St Benoit contingent came galloping up to the shore just in time to see their quarry in mid-stream, rowing furiously towards the opposite shore in the only available boat. A few pot-shots were fired, but there was no question of pushing the pursuit any further. The urban authorities may have taken one prisoner, but the patriots of Two Mountains had been successful in driving them away, along with the placard-posting bailiffs, before they could accomplish their mission. Now they had every reason to fear retaliation from the military expedition promised by the high constable. Accordingly, the force from St Benoit divided into parties of four or five men each and scattered to hide and ambush any troops that might arrive. They stayed in the woods all night, but no invasion materialized.[39]

The fear of military intervention was vivid in Two Mountains, and with good reason. Under the circumstances, the high constable's threats seemed only too plausible, especially in view of the troop movements currently taking place in the province. The government was moving units from Quebec City up to Montreal, and the first contingents of reinforcements from Nova Scotia began to arrive in the capital on 11 July.[40] Two hundred soldiers had in fact been placed on the alert on the day of the constables' foray, but they were never dispatched to Two Mountains. The authorities were too worried about troubles in Montreal itself, and they kept the troops standing by in case urban patriots tried to force the release of François Labelle.

In the wake of the events of 13 July both parties seemed to draw back from the brink of armed conflict. The government, wishing neither to press matters to a showdown nor to let an open challenge to its authority go unanswered, sent the deputy sheriff to serve the three remaining warrants two days later. This legal officer seems to have travelled north without an armed

---

39 ANQ, 1837, no. 607, deposition of Robert Hall, 15 July 1837
40 Le Populaire, 14 July 1837

escort and to have carried out his mission with considerable tact. Some of the Patriot leaders of St Benoit, including the tavern-keeper Coursolles and the radical priest Etienne Chartier, claimed they cooperated with the deputy sheriff in securing the surrender of one of the delinquents.[41] It might be more correct to say that the deputy sheriff cooperated with the Patriots, because some sort of unofficial peace treaty seems to have been negotiated, the terms of which allowed the official barely to save face while protecting the accused from any serious punishment. In the end, one of the three men named in the warrants was persuaded to appear, but in St Benoit, not in Montreal. Rather than face criminal charges, he had only to post a bond for good behaviour, which he did before a Patriot justice of the peace, effectively ensuring that the bond would remain a dead letter.

Lower Canada's attorney-general, Charles Ogden, came up to Montreal about this time and gave his approval to the policy of conciliation.[42] Without a regular police force, Ogden shrewdly pointed out, the government had few options. It would be very risky to send in a military expedition. Armed resistance seemed likely and, even if the regular soldiers proved stronger, which seemed certain, would they succeed in arresting the men named in the warrants? If it was not entirely successful, said Ogden, an army intervention would have the most disastrous effects. Moreover, even if arrests could be made, would the accused men be convicted in a court of law? This result, too, seemed uncertain given the impossibility of gathering good evidence in such a case. (Of course the attorney-general was quite right on this point: the Montreal grand jury eventually threw out the case against François Labelle in early September.) All he could suggest was that the governor try to enlist the aid of the Catholic clergy. Thus the local crisis of legitimacy was left unresolved. In the five months following the ill-fated expedition of 13 July there

41 Ibid., 19 July 1837; Archives du diocèse de St Jérôme, Chartier to Lartigue, St Benoit, 18 July 1837
42 NA, LC Civil Secretary, 515: 186–9, Ogden to Gosford, 17 July 1837

were no further attempts to assert government authority in the patriot sections of Two Mountains.

And what of the ethnic dimension of Two Mountains' troubled summer? Were the attacks on English-speaking settlers simply the expression of some primitive French-Canadian xenophobia, as the Tory press would have it? The Montreal *Gazette* thundered:

Is it to be permitted for one moment that men of the Old Country shall be insulted and menaced, their properties ruined and destroyed, and themselves and their little ones driven from their homes in this land, to which they are entitled as much as any 'enfant du sol' that vegetates around them, simply because they do not choose to relinquish the laws, the language, and the institutions of their forefathers, or to link themselves to a FRENCH faction, whose sole end and aim is to deprive them of every vestige of nationality – to tinker them into FRENCHMEN?[43]

Suspicion of the 'other' was no doubt a reality on both sides of the linguistic divide in Two Mountains, but it is hardly the key to the aggressive acts of June and July 1837. The persecution of 'men of the Old Country' was not the culmination of years of ethnic hatred; rather it was something quite unprecedented, as the victims themselves recognized. Echoing the words of Robert Hall, Duncan McColl declared that he and his family had lived in St Benoit for eighteen years, 'in the greatest peace and harmony with our Canadian neighbours until the time when a certain political meeting took place at Saint Scholastique ... about a month ago.'[44] Note also that the two most serious attacks were directed against Curé Paquin and Captain Cheval, both French Canadians associated with the Dumont connection of St Eustache. Moreover, several of the region's Patriot leaders were English speakers: William Henry Scott, to take the most prominent example, or, at a second level of leadership, John Hawley, a

43 *Gazette*, 21 September 1837
44 ANQ, 1837, no. 836, deposition of Duncan McColl, 11 July 1837

Yankee wool carder, was most active in the cause. The Irish parish of St Columban was in fact notorious as a hot-bed of radicalism.

The lines of conflict then were fundamentally political and incidentally ethnic. It was those who opted for Britain rather than Canada and who defied the hegemony of the Patriot movement who made themselves the target of popular ire in the southern parishes of Two Mountains. 'Join us or suffer the consequences,' was the brutal message of the stone-throwers and mane-shavers. Certainly this was coercive politics, but it was hardly racist.

FRENCH AND ENGLISH AT WAR

As the struggle between the Patriot movement and the government developed into outright war, the ethnic polarization in Two Mountains and elsewhere in the province became more pronounced and more bitter. The two sides girded for battle, leaving less and less room for polite inquiries. In the confusion and uncertainties of civil strife actors on both the government and the rebel sides had to be able to distinguish enemies – actual and potential – from friends. Lives often depended on a rapid assessment. Experience taught that French Canadians were likely to rally to the patriot colours, while English speakers generally gravitated to the opposite side. It was only natural, therefore, that in emergency situations people acted as though language was a clear boundary between friend and foe. The inevitable injustices that ensued served of course to embitter the atmosphere and deepen the national cleavage.

During the risings of 1837 and 1838 the first act of the insurgents in many parts of Lower Canada was to send expeditions against local anglophones. One of these originated in St Jérôme, a French-Canadian parish situated near the ragged linguistic boundary of the Two Mountains region. When news of the initial skirmishes of November 1837 reached St Jérôme, it seemed clear that the crisis was nearing its long-awaited military climax. That being the case, the attention of local patriots would normally be focused on Montreal, the main enemy stronghold in the western half of Lower Canada. Yet it was not south towards Montreal, but north in the direction of a less distant source of danger that the people of St Jérôme first turned. New Paisley, just up the river from St Jérôme, was settled by Scottish immigrants only in the 1820s; with a population of 191 at the time of the 1831 census, it was numerically much weaker than its neighbour. As far as I can tell, there was no history of conflict between the two communities. St Jérôme and New Paisley seem to have gone their separate ways without paying much attention to one another. Three St Jérôme men who were later arrested and interrogated referred variously to the settlers as 'les irlandais,' 'les anglais,' and 'les habitants d'outre-mer,' indicating how little they knew their Scottish neighbours![45] The question local patriots had to ask themselves as the Lower Canadian crisis came to a head was how would the immigrants behave in the ultimate conflict? A largely unknown but apparently inoffensive settlement, New Paisley nevertheless took on an ominous character for the patriots, because its position to the rear of St Jérôme made it the potential source of a blow from behind.

Accordingly, on 20 November an armed party set off northward from St Jérôme under the leadership of Jérôme Longpré, a thirty-nine-year-old habitant.[46] Previously, a St Jérôme blacksmith had been to New Paisley, ostensibly on business but in fact to find out how many settlers possessed firearms. Meanwhile the St Jérôme militia was ordered to turn out on Monday, 20 November; no doubt the arrangements were made on the day before when everyone had assembled for church services. Pressure was brought to bear on any men who appeared reluctant to participate. A local merchant and innkeeper named William Scott, for example, made himself very unpopular by his staunch refusal to join the expedition. 'Too bad for the English if the Canadians

45 Ibid., no. 572, examen volontaire de Jean Latour, 14 February 1838; ibid., no. 574, déposition de Jean-Baptiste Renaud, 31 January 1838; ibid., no. 577, examen volontaire de François Pillon, 14 February 1838
46 Ibid., no. 643, examen volontaire de Laurent Longpré, 14 February 1838

win,' Longpré warned him, 'and you more than the others.'[47] Most men were glad to take part, however, and some 2–300 congregated on the appointed day with whatever guns they could procure and marched off to New Paisley. As they approached the Scottish settlement, a party of New Paisley men advanced to meet them. James Rennie, a local leader in Paisley, reports that the intruders began by asking what the people of New Paisley intended to do in the current crisis.[48] Remain in peace and quiet was the answer. But that is impossible, retorted the St Jérôme spokesman, for the war has now begun. (This was perfectly true; before long a company of Loyal Volunteers was formed in New Paisley, armed by the government and under the command of James Rennie.) The interpreter from St Jérôme explained to Rennie that 'Most of the Scotch won't go to fight [and so] they must give up their arms – for we mean to go and attack Montreal and we cannot get our people (meaning the Canadians) away leaving you all armed behind their settlements.' The demand then was that New Paisley give up its guns, and since Rennie and his followers were so badly outnumbered, they had no choice but to comply. The announcement of the surrender was greeted with 'great hallooing' from the St Jérôme men. They went from house to house and collected thirty-one firearms.[49] No further aggression was committed against New Paisley, even though the Scottish settlement was now completely at the mercy of the St Jérôme patriots.

Though thirty-one rusty muskets hardly constituted a major addition to the patriot armoury, the expedition was nevertheless deemed a success. It had effectively neutralized a potential opponent and, perhaps more importantly, it had demonstrated that the habitants of St Jérôme were capable of concerted action when required. Returning to St Jérôme, about twenty-five of the militia-

---

47 Ibid., no. 571, deposition of William Scott, 1 February 1838 (author's translation)
48 Ibid., no. 633, deposition of James Rennie, 5 February 1838
49 Ibid., no. 702, examen volontaire de Jérôme Longpré, 14 February 1838

men stopped at William Scott's tavern for a drink to mark their victory. 'Treat us to free drinks, you,' shouted Jérôme Longpré, waving his sword through the air. 'We really won; we have had a good march.' Needless to say, the drinks were on the house. The Constitutionalist innkeeper reported that his unwelcome guests had insulted and abused him for having stayed at home instead of going with them to New Paisley. Victory celebration, punitive visitation, and warning for the future (not to mention armed robbery), this little party served many purposes. And why was William Scott singled out for victimization? In sorting out this question we must consider, not only the hostile talk about 'les anglais,' but also the fact that his neighbours wanted Scott to join them, to accept the responsibilities of a full-fledged resident of the parish of St Jérôme. As far as they were concerned, the community itself was in real danger and therefore refusal to march against New Paisley implied indifference – or something worse – towards St Jérôme as well as 'the nation.'

New Paisley did have its revenge. Thousands of enraged anglo-Canadians rushed to take up arms against the patriots, and although they played only a minor role in the military engagements of the Rebellion, these Volunteers proved to be zealous rebel-hunters in the ensuing pacification campaigns. The 'Loyal Volunteer Corps' quickly became an anglophone preserve. Even though many French Canadians remained attached to the government, an English officer was appalled to find that 'not more than 100 out of the 10,000' provincial Volunteers were French Canadians.[50] Thus the atmosphere was particularly bitter when a second revolt broke out in November 1838 and the national polarization became even more pronounced. Bands of patriots began in most localities by disarming or arresting the English-speaking men in their midst (frequently members of the hated Volunteer Corps). David M'Clennaghan later recalled a conversation with one of his captors: 'I asked him what he meant by

50 Quoted in Elinor Senior, *Redcoats and Patriotes: The Rebellions in Lower Canada 1837–38* (Ottawa: Canada's Wings 1985), 109

taking the arms from the old country people? and he replied, "We want the arms from the old country people, that they may not come behind us when we go to face the soldiers." [51] As in 1837, attacks against immigrants were mainly motivated by elementary considerations of military security, although no doubt revenge also played a part.

The second rising was mastered even more easily than the first, but nevertheless it unleashed a francophobic outburst even more ferocious than those of the past. When Olivier Gagnez of Lacolle went to join the Volunteers preparing to repel a rebel invasion from Vermont, the captain told him (through an interpreter), 'that he would not take those who did not speak English.' Instead, he placed poor Gagnez in jail for two days![52] The military occupation of regions involved in the insurrection gave wide scope for brutal bigots such as a Volunteer sergeant named Harrison, who, without provocation, pistol-whipped an habitant near Napierville. Called to account, he declared that such behaviour was 'not only proper but indispensable in dealing with the French Canadians.' His commander let the matter drop.[53] The Harrison case is extreme, but it does express a view, widely held at the time in 'loyal' anglophone circles, that anyone who spoke French was politically suspect. Even a civilized and humane man like Lieutenant-Colonel W.C. Chandler had difficulty when ordered in 1839 to purge his Nicolet militia battalion of officers whose loyalty might be questioned. 'The local population, comprised, as they are principally of French Canadians; for although there does exist amongst them many well disposed individuals, the question is, how to discriminate, in these times.'[54]

'How to discriminate': that was precisely the problem that

---

51 *Report of the State Trials, Before a General Court Martial Held at Montreal in 1838-1839: Exhibiting a Complete History of the Late Rebellion in Lower Canada,* 2 vols (Montreal: Armour and Ramsay 1839), 2: 162

52 ANQ, 1837, no. 1145, examen volontaire d'Olivier Gagnez, 22 November 1838

53 NA, LC Stipendiary Magistrates, vol. 2, Gugy to Goldie, 25 March 1839

54 NA, LC, Adjutant General, vol. 51, Chandler to Young, 17 June 1839

faced both patriots and Constitutionalists in those troubled times, when political conflict over the shape of the Lower Canadian state reached a revolutionary crisis, and language and national origin often came to serve as rough and ready indicators of political allegiance. The armed conflict served only to accelerate the process of national polarization, so that by the time Lord Durham visited Canada in 1838, hatred between English and French was at an all-time high. Who can blame him for assuming that virulent 'racial' hostility was a fundamental fact of Lower Canadian public life and for concluding, quite erroneously, that the revolutionary upheaval was the product of national animosity?

Rivière-du-Loup (now Louiseville), near Trois-Rivières, ca 1781. Two maypoles are visible in the background; their function is unknown; possibly one stands before the seigneurial manor house, while the other marks the militia captain's dwelling. Detail, pen and ink with watercolour by James Peachey

Wolfred Nelson, physician, politician, and son of a United Empire Loyalist. Nelson led the victorious patriots at the Battle of St Denis, 23 November 1837. Charcoal sketch by Jean-Joseph Girouard

British troops bivouacked at the manor house at St Hilaire de Rouville, 24 November 1837. After partaking of the hospitality of the seigneur, Jean-Baptiste-René Hertel de Rouville, this force went on to attack the patriot stronghold of St Charles the next day. From a sketch by Lord Charles Beauclerk

Battle of St Charles, 25 November 1837. From a sketch by Lord Charles Beauclerk

Village of St Denis and the Richelieu ferry, 1837. Watercolour by Philip Bainbrigge

Bonaventure Viger, the Boucherville habitant who led the militia party that ambushed the Montreal Cavalry at Longueuil and rescued the patriot prisoners on their way to Montreal, 17 November 1837. Charcoal sketch by Jean-Joseph Girouard

Battle of St Eustache, 14 December 1837. From sketches by Lord Charles Beauclerk

Jean-Joseph Girouard, notary public and Patriot leader at St Benoit, county of Two Mountains. Self-portrait

Three of the 851 rebels carried to the Montreal prison in the aftermath of the rising of early November 1838. From a drawing by H.A. Hayes

Louis-Joseph Papineau, from an oil portrait by R.A. Sproule

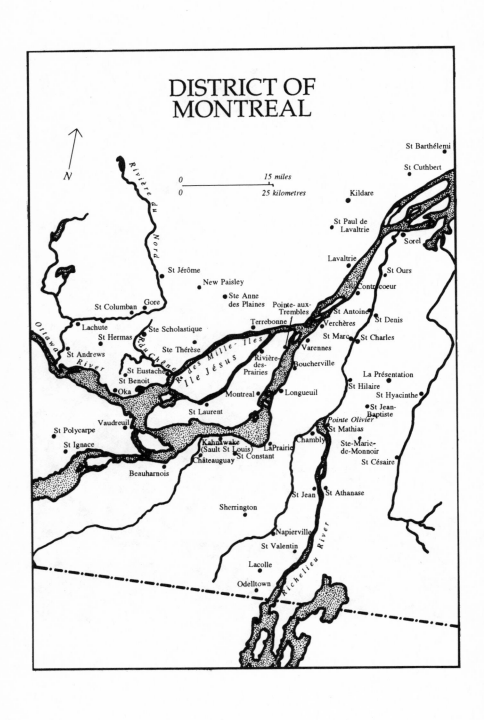

DISTRICT OF
MONTREAL

N

0   15 miles
0   25 kilometres

St Barthélemi

St Cuthbert

Kildare

Riviére du Nord

St Paul de
Lavaltrie

Sorel

Lavaltrie

St Ours

St Jérôme

New Paisley

Contrecoeur

St Columban   Gore

Ste Anne
des Plaines

Pointe-aux-
Trembles

St Antoine

St Denis

Lachute

Ste Scholastique

Terrebonne

Verchères

St Hermas

Ile des Mille- Iles

St Marc

St Charles

St Andrews

Ste Thérèse

Varennes

Ottawa River

St Eustache

Rivière-
des-
Prairies

Boucherville

La Présentation

R. du Chêne

Ile Jésus

St Benoit

St Hilaire

Oka

Montreal

Longueuil

St Hyacinthe

St Laurent

St Jean-
Baptiste

Vaudreuil

Pointe Olivier

St Polycarpe

St Mathias

St Ignace

Kahnawake
(Sault St Louis)

Chambly

Ste-Marie-
de-Monnoir

LaPrairie

St Constant

Châteauguay

St Césaire

Beauharnois

St Jean

St Athanase

Sherrington

Napierville

Richelieu River

St Valentin

Lacolle

Odelltown

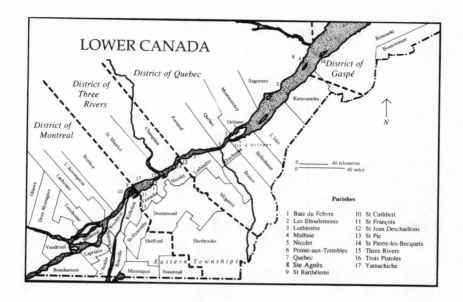

LOWER CANADA

District of Quebec

District of
Three
Rivers

District of
Montreal

Saguenay

Kamouraska

District of
Gaspé

Rimouski

Bonaventure

N

Montmorency

Portneuf

Quebec

Orléans

Île d'Orléans

L'Islet

Bellechasse

Beauce

0 _____ 40 kilometres
0 _____ 40 miles

Champlain

St Maurice

Berthier

L'Assomption

Lachenaie

Ottawa

Deux-Montagnes

Terrebonne

Vaudreuil

Montreal

Laprairie

Beauharnois

Chambly

Verchères

Rouville

L'Acadie

Richelieu

St-Hyacinthe

Yamaska

Missisquoi

Stanstead

Nicolet

Lotbinière

Mégantic

Drummond

Shefford

Sherbrooke

Eastern Townships

Parishes

1	Baie du Febvre	10	St Cuthbert
2	Les Eboulements	11	St François
3	Lotbinière	12	St Jean Deschaillons
4	Malbaie	13	St Pie
5	Nicolet	14	St Pierre-les-Becquets
6	Pointe-aux-Trembles	15	Three Rivers
7	Quebec	16	Trois Pistoles
8	Ste Agnès	17	Yamachiche
9	St Barthélemi		

St Benoit surrendered on 15 December 1837, and even though local patriots
turned in their weapons without a hint of resistance, the village was burned to
the ground. Drawing by Jean-Joseph Girouard

Patriot militiamen after the capture of the seigneurial manor house at
Beauharnois, 4 November 1838. Watercolour by Jane Ellice, daughter-in-law of
the seigneur; she spent a week as a prisoner of the insurgents.

7

The queen is a whore!

Do you want to know men? Study women. This maxim is general, and up to this point everybody will agree with me. But if I add that there are no good morals [manners] for women outside of a withdrawn and domestic life; if I say that the peaceful care of the family and the home are their lot, that the dignity of their sex consists in modesty, that shame and chasteness are inseparable from decency for them, that when they seek for men's looks they are already letting themselves be corrupted by them, and that any woman who shows herself off disgraces herself; I will be immediately attacked by this philosophy of a day which is born and dies in the corner of a big city and wishes to smother the cry of nature and the unanimous voice of humankind.

Jean-Jacques Rousseau[1]

Women's role is not to be found in public life, the life of action and agitation, but truly in the internal life, that of sentiment and of the tranquility of the domestic hearth ...

Pierre-Joseph Proudhon[2]

1 Jean-Jacques Rousseau, *Politics and the Arts: Letter to M. D'Alembert on the Theatre*, trans. Allan Bloom (Glencoe, Ill.: Free Press 1960), 82–3
2 Quoted in Jane Rendall, *The Origins of Modern Feminism: Women in Britain, France and the United States, 1780–1860* (London: Macmillan 1985), 235

I see that this harmful philosophy is infecting everybody and that Rousseau's *Social Contract* makes you forget St Paul's Gospel: 'Wives, be subject to your husbands'.

Louis-Joseph Papineau to his wife, 1830[3]

Queen Victoria ascended the throne of England in August 1837, just as tensions in Lower Canada were reaching a boiling point. There is no indication that the seventeen-year-old monarch gave much immediate thought to the political squabbles wracking her North American possessions, but her coronation provided Canadians with an occasion for further reflections on sovereign authority and state forms. 'Loyal' Montreal managed to mount a parade to celebrate the happy event, and at Sorel the little garrison fired off a salute. A tavern-keeper's wife remarked to onlookers at the latter, 'There you are, celebrations for the coronation of the queen; she had better watch out or she'll be decrowned.'[4] It was the Te Deum ordered for the middle of August by the bishop of Montreal, the usual service on such occasions, that aroused the greatest controversy. At St Polycarpe, where the curé dared to say a few words in praise of the new monarch, local patriots managed to stop the ceremony. 'No sooner did the *Te Deum* commence, than the people quitted the church bodily, leaving the women and *marguilliers* (churchwardens) to keep his Reverence company. The deputy beadle was beginning to ring the bell when the people got out, but the parishioners stopped him, telling him that the bell belonged to them, and not the Queen of England, and that it should not be rung.'[5]

3 Quoted in Micheline Dumont et al., *Quebec Women: A History*, trans. Roger Gannon and Rosalind Gill (Toronto: Women's Press 1987), 122. Papineau appears to have made this observation in jest, playfully inverting his wife's and his habitual roles as pious Christian and Enlightenment sceptic. Nevertheless, this is one of those jokes that reveals much about basic attitudes.

4 Bibliothèque nationale, Montreal, journal of Romuald Trudeau, 12: 25; ANQ, 1837, no. 1698, Welles to Goldie, 19 November 1838 (author's translation)

5 *Vindicator*, 1 September 1837

Note the language used by the *Vindicator* to describe this incident: the counterposing of 'the *people*' and 'the *women*.' Half the population of the province might well have viewed these words as ominous signals, emanating as they did from the presses of a journal dedicated to the principle of popular sovereignty!

That this was no accidental slip is underlined by the sexual references in protests against the coronation Te Deum. In the parish of Contrecoeur a radical merchant led an exodus from the church shouting, 'It is painful to have to sing the Te Deum for the damn queen, damned whore with her legs in the air.' A Patriot orator addressing the people of Nicolet from the church porch was reported to have said, 'As for the king, he is nothing but a big zero to whom Canadians pay a pension ... The proof that kings are nothing but zeros is that we are now governed by a young queen seventeen years of age.' Later, at the time of the battles of November and December, an American patriot sympathizer got into trouble at St Athanase by throwing 'ridicule on the person of the sovereign by saying the loyalists were governed by a little girl, that they were governed by petticoats.'[6] Such language would certainly have shocked English radicals; they were well disposed towards the young queen who seemed to them a much more sympathetic figure than her notorious uncle, William IV.[7] At the same time, it directs our attention to some important characteristics of the Patriot movement as regards both gender and concepts of legitimate political authority.

6 ANQ, 1837, no. 324, déposition du Baron Augustin de Diemar, 21 December 1837 (author's translation); ibid., no. 242, déposition de Joseph-Louis Pinard, 1 February 1838; ibid., deposition of Thomas Casson, 31 December 1838 (cf. ibid., no. 1483, Lacombe to Walcott, 23 August 1837). The loyalists, for their part, struck a chivalrous posture, vowing to 'make any sacrifice in maintaining the legitimate authority of our young and beauteous Queen.' Speech by the Hon. Mr McGill, Montreal, 23 October 1837, in *Assemblées publiques, résolutions et déclarations de 1837-1838*, ed. Jean-Paul Bernard (Montreal: VLB éditeur 1988), 239

7 Dorothy Thompson, personal communication

MONARCHY OR REPUBLIC?

All the abuse of poor Victoria indicates that of course the queen and the monarchy were not 'a zero' in the French Canadian countryside. For all that the habitants took for granted a certain popular sovereignty within the local community, their concept of the state and the empire was highly personalized, focusing on the reigning king or queen. There is nothing peculiar in this attitude; it is common among peasants throughout the western world. Even among the 'educated classes' the notion that a stable political structure needed to be embodied in a royal personage still enjoyed widespread support in the first half of the nineteenth century. Royalist habits of thought may have been somewhat more strongly entrenched in French Canada than in some countries, because there had never been a republican interlude here as there had been in England, the Netherlands, colonial English America, and much of Italy; there was no alternative to monarchy in the Lower Canadian historical memory. On the other hand, the conquest may have made the monarchy seem less sacred by demonstrating its mutability.[8] If so, the resulting uncertainties must have remained largely submerged until 1837. People still expressed themselves in royalist language, government property being 'crown property,' military duties called 'the king's service'; even disaffected militiamen refusing to hear the governor's proclamation shouted 'Vive le roi!'

Canadians of course lived far from any flesh and blood monarch, although governors under the French and British régimes did do their best to put on a display of viceregal pomp and ceremony in the colony. More generally, political authority in our

---

8 Douglas Hay offers speculation along these lines with respect to the law under the early British régime. His point might be extended to cover the state and the monarchy as well, though of course there is no way of proving this. Douglas Hay, 'The Meanings of the Criminal Law in Quebec, 1764–1774,' in *Crime and Criminal Justice in Europe and Canada*, ed. Louis A. Knafla (Waterloo: Wilfrid Laurier UP 1981), 96–100

period did manifest itself in personal terms that reinforced monarchical habits of thought, no doubt accentuated by the strong military presence in Canada. Moreover, the Church did its utmost to impress on the faithful their duty to the king, not only in Te Deum services for coronations and royal births, but also in sermons from the pulpit. Political leaders added their voices in support, including the Patriots, who until the eve of the Rebellion always protested their loyalty to the crown even as they denounced colonial Tories and wicked British ministers.[9]

A basically royalist political vocabulary does not imply a docile acceptance of authority. People who have been taught to regard the distant king as a father-figure who has the best interests of his subjects at heart, often tend to conclude, when things go badly, that exploitive officials, merchants, or aristocrats are the monarch's enemies as well as their own. In this way royalism can become a revolutionary ideology (though one with built-in limitations inhibiting the development of popular democracy), as it was indeed in countless plebeian risings, such as the one that shook rural France in the summer of 1789 when thousands of peasants attacked seigneurial chateaux, acting, so they thought, 'on orders from the king.'[10] It should be noted that the peasant class is not the only one that tends to venerate the king while blaming his advisers. The American and French revolutions were already well under way before their bourgeois leaders began to attack George III, Louis XVI, and the institution of monarchy.[11] (Tom Paine's *Common Sense* caused a sensation early in 1776 when it called for an independent American republic.) Yet the dynamic of the revolutions eventually broke the spell of royalty and led to the full development of a republican political dis-

---

9 See, for example, Papineau's speech on the occasion of the death of George III, in *Papineau: textes choisis*, ed. Fernand Ouellet (Quebec: Presses de l'Université Laval 1970), 21–2.
10 Georges Lefebvre, *The Great Fear: Rural Panic in Revolutionary France*, trans. Joan White (Princeton: Princeton UP 1973)
11 Pauline Maier, *From Resistance to Revolution: Colonial Radicals and the Development of American Opposition to Britain, 1765–1776* (New York: Knopf 1972)

course, one that had often been there all along in embryonic form. So it was in Lower Canada, where the crisis of the 1830s moved the bourgeois Patriots to an entirely republican outlook. Hence their determination to discredit the monarch as the personal symbol of government authority and metropolitan rule.

One can also see signs of this anti-monarchical sentiment at the level of the rural masses. During the November insurrection a Constitutionalist merchant asked Jérôme Longpré, an habitant leader, by what right he presumed to issue orders. 'It is by our own right,' came the reply. 'We couldn't care less about the king or the queen or the clergy.' At Lacolle 'Down with the king!' was the rallying cry of men (obviously not up to date on dynastic affairs!) drilling for the coming struggle. During the second rising in 1838 François Patenaude indicated, in a moment of panic, who he thought the enemy was; rushing into the house he called to his wife for weapons, crying, 'we must defend ourselves against the crown.'[12] Needless to say, there is something very naïve in all this; the kings and queens in question lived thousands of miles away and had only the remotest connection to the Lower Canadian conflagration. On the other hand, such remarks indicate a conception of the conflict that transcended purely local concerns and went to the heart of the question of sovereign power. However crude the formulations, such language suggests a hard-won victory over the intellectual limitations inherent in peasant life.

It was nevertheless a partial victory, for ingrained habits of thought do not die overnight. One man was denounced to the authorities for having sung treasonous songs at a gathering of habitants. Neatly balancing themes of republicanism and constitutional monarchy, the singer began with 'Allons enfants de la patrie, le jour de gloire est arrivé,' then moved on to a second song: 'If our august queen knew of the abuses, she would say

12 ANQ, 1837, no. 641, déposition de Casimir de Montigny, 1 February 1838; ibid., no. 92, deposition of Robert Leeson, 10 February 1838; ibid., no. 1314, déposition de Zoé Dupuis, 30 November 1838 (author's translation)

to all good patriots, crush these ass-lickers' (author's translation).[13] More significant was the tendency of a personal cult to grow up around Louis-Joseph Papineau, a cult that in some respects mirrored the royal mystique. We can see the mental association between monarch and revolutionary leader in the words of another church-door orator, the blacksmith Edouard Moreau dit Duplessis of St Jérôme: 'He sang a revolutionary song and cried Hurrah for Pépère (i.e., Papineau) ... and he spoke in the most uncouth terms against our sovereign the Queen.' Did the patriots then aim to liberate Canada from Britain only to subject it to a new monarchical yoke? This is what historians anxious to portray the movement as wholly retrograde would have us believe. But the role of charismatic leadership in a revolutionary movement is not quite so simple. Listen to the words of a Nicolet shoemaker overheard just before the battles of November 1837: 'L.J. Papineau would come with his people and they would go down to Quebec and capture the city ... He would be happy to see the crown on Mr Papineau's head and if he did not behave properly as king, the patriots would replace him ... We should make ourselves independent like the American government.'[14] Clearly we are dealing here with a man who has not read his Tom Paine; nor has he managed to find any but a royalist vocabulary to give voice to his political views. But just look at the sort of reign the shoemaker envisions for Louis-Joseph I: king as long as the majority approves his conduct! This is admittedly unsophisticated political thinking of a sort that would be vulnerable to Bonapartist demagoguery, but its essential thrust is more republican and democratic than royalist.

The spell of traditional authority, as represented by priest and bishop, governor and queen, was giving way. People of different

13 Ibid., no. 3522, deposition of John Nicholas Demange, 11 December 1838
14 Ibid., no. 1103, déposition de François-Xavier Renaud, 18 December 1838; ibid., no. 226, déposition de Jean Parmentier, 5 February 1838 (author's translation). References to Papineau as king are in fact extremely rare in the sources relating to the Rebellion.

classes and levels of education were considering new ways of constituting a state and governing a human community. Could Canadians rule themselves? Could government derive its legitimacy from the people rather than historic rights of conquest and religious sanction? Patriot leaders answered these questions in the positive, and they drove home the point explicitly in speeches and newspaper articles, while expressing the same message in symbolic forms as well, notably through the use of flags and banners. Long before he began to take the movement seriously as a military threat, the commander of British forces in Lower Canada fretted over the emblems of popular sovereignty sprouting up in the Richelieu valley. 'The tri coloured flag has been displayed at two taverns between St Denis and St Charles,' wrote Sir John Colborne in October 1837. 'Many of the taverns have discontinued their signs and substituted for them an Eagle.'[15]

Flags were an important element in the repertoire of symbols, and they were a favourite device at protest meetings, processions, and later at insurgent camps. Several designs were employed. Most provocative to Tories were the three-coloured banners (the sources do not specify which three colours), with their frankly revolutionary associations. Flags of American inspiration, featuring stars and eagles, were also displayed. Finally, there was at least one wholly original design, conceived apparently by Jean-Joseph Girouard of St Benoit. Girouard's flag, pierced with musket balls at the Battle of St Eustache, still survives. Its rather crowded features include maple leaves, pine cones, a Maskinongé fish, as well as the initials 'C' (for Canada) and 'J-Bte' (for Jean-Baptiste). One might add to the list the various slogan-emblazoned banners flown from may/liberty poles and paraded through country parishes. There was, for example, the one carried to an anti-coercion meeting by a rural militia captain with 'a crown reversed and above it an Eggle [sic]' or the blazing red flag proclaiming the word 'Liberté' that went before

15 NA, British Military Records, C1272: 8, Colborne to Gosford, 6 October 1837

a group of reinforcements headed for the Battle of St Charles.[16] All these different pieces of coloured fabric held aloft on a pole had the effect of expressing and reinforcing a collective spirit. They also asserted, to one degree or another, the ideal of national independence. It is true that, while patriots were determined to rally round the flag, they were not at all sure which flag to gather under. This absence of a single national flag is perhaps a symptom of the movement's immaturity (hardly remarkable: the Americans had no common flag at a comparable stage of their revolution), as well as its vitality. Perhaps the most important feature of all the patriot banners is that none of them was the Union Jack and the message of that negation could not have been clearer.

MASCULINE POLITICS

Granted that the patriots objected to the institution of monarchy and to the fact of British rule; but why did they have to make an issue – and in such a cruel and personal way – of Queen Victoria's sex? Well, certainly their sensitivity was not unique in the international republican community of the period. Recent scholarship has demonstrated that considerations of sexual difference were of central concern to political writers and revolutionaries of the late eighteenth-early nineteenth-century period. To the degree that they challenged existing hierarchies on egalitarian grounds and insisted that 'the people' ought to rule, philosophes, Jaco-

16 *Report of the State Trials Before a General Court Martial Held at Montreal in 1838–1839: Exhibiting a Complete History of the Late Rebellion in Lower Canada*, 2 vols (Montreal: Armour and Ramsay 1839), 1: 157, testimony of Thomas Thompson; *Le Populaire*, 27 September 1837; ANQ, 1837, no. 71, affidavit of Leonard Brown, 15 February 1838; Béatrice Chassé, 'Le notaire Girouard, patriote et rebelle,' (PH D thesis, Université Laval, 1974), 210; Elinor Senior, *Redcoats and Patriotes: The Rebellions in Lower Canada 1837–38* (Ottawa: Canada's Wings 1985), 134; NA, LC Adjutant General, vol. 48. Harwood to Duchesnay, 25 August 1837; ANQ, 1837, no. 398, déposition d'Eloi Roy, 5 December 1837

bins, and American patriots had to grapple with the question of what 'the people' was. It certainly was not all human beings resident in a given territory: not everyone was to participate equally and in the same way in sovereign authority. Women in particular tended to be excluded from direct political participation in the republican city. Pronouncements may have been cryptic and susceptible to multiple interpretations, with much assumed and little expressed; the effect was none the less for sex to become increasingly the primary dividing line between rulers and ruled in the age of the great bourgeois revolutions. Partly this exclusion arose by default, as older conceptions of political privilege based on birth, sacerdotal status, and so on came under attack, but also it derived from a profoundly gendered republican concept of citizenship.

Inspired by a particular reading of the history of ancient Greece and Rome, modern republicans such as Jean-Jacques Rousseau believed that men were uniquely qualified for the responsibilities of citizenship.[17] They were better suited for military combat, and, it was felt, all good citizens had to be prepared to defend their country on the battlefield. More fundamentally, Rousseau thought that males were by nature more apt to subordinate selfish and sectional interests for the good of the whole community. Women, by contrast, were necessarily associated with childbirth and nurturing; consequently, their orientation was to the family, a particularistic allegiance which they could not fully transcend without denying their nature. Thanks to their looser attachment to specific loved ones, men had the potential to develop the civic virtue – the dedication to the common good – required in any healthy republic. It is important to note, however, that Rousseau did not consider women inferior to men. On the contrary, he attached great value to the loving and nurturing

17 This point is made in several studies, but I found particularly useful Joel Schwartz, *The Sexual Politics of Jean-Jacques Rousseau* (Chicago: University of Chicago Press 1984). The basic texts are the *Discourse on the Origins of Inequality*, the *Social Contract*, *Letter to M. d'Alembert*, and *Emile*.

domestic sphere where women found their true calling. His effusions over motherhood and conjugal bliss underline the fact that for Rousseau women's familial role was the essential complement of active male citizenship. Domestic life and public life, he implied, were equally important elements of civilized existence. In order to discharge her duty, the republican woman needed to exercise a special sort of virtue: not public-spirited courage, but 'sexual innocence and chastity' were her distinguishing characteristics, and as an outward guarantee of monogamous behaviour, she had to confine herself to the private realm.[18]

Rousseau was in no simple sense a male-supremacist; indeed his contemporary defenders insist that he accorded a great deal of legitimate power to women, though it was covert power, exercised through their sexual influence over particular men.[19] Moreover, with his emphasis on liberty and on the cultivation of the individual personality, he can plausibly be seen as the intellectual ancestor of modern women's liberation. One need only extend to females the reasoning that the philosopher applies to 'Man' and unsettling conclusions soon follow. (Indeed, the quotation at the head of this chapter shows that at least one Lower Canadian noticed these possibilities in Rousseau!) The fact remains that Rousseau himself did not present a feminist reading of Jean-Jacques. Everywhere one turns in his writings, the needs of men take precedence, and women appear in a positive light to the degree that they are helpful to men.

I have dwelt on Rousseau, not because his works provided an instruction manual for Lower Canadian Patriots, but because he was one of the few writers of the period who gave sustained and explicit attention to the gender dimension of politics. Without denying the originality of his genius, I think it is fair to suggest that many of the essential features of Rousseau's thought in this

18 Joan B. Landes, *Women and the Public Sphere in the Age of the French Revolution* (Ithaca: Cornell UP 1988)
19 Schwartz, *Sexual Politics*

area were characteristic of the international republican movement. Certainly echoes can be detected in the Patriot press of the
notion that men and women possessed complementary but fundamentally different moral natures. An article published in *La
Minerve* under the title 'The Two Republics' makes this point
quite explicitly:

The moral world is a mixture composed of men and women and it owes
to this combination the greatest part of its customs, usages and ceremonies; if there were no more women in the human race, men would be
unrecognizable. It is only in seeking to please the opposite sex that they
manage to refine themselves ... Women, for their part, owe everything
to that other half of the human race, to which they find themselves
joined ... It is to the desire to please him [man] that they owe that gra-
cious air, those eyes which say so many things, that modest blush which
embellishes their complexion, that voice so soft and touching. This
reciprocal desire is indeed a precious instinct in both sexes, one which
tends towards the perfection of each of them. Thus a man with no
interest in women will ordinarily become a savage; by the same token,
a woman, intended by nature to get along with and to appear with man,
can scarcely hate or despise him without becoming a ferocious and
unbearable creature.[20]

Such sentiments were by no means limited to republican
circles. Indeed, the basic notion that women belonged in a
(valorized) domestic setting while men should run the state and
the community became widely prevalent everywhere the bourgeoisie gained the ascendancy throughout the eighteenth century
and well into the nineteenth. During the French Revolution, for
example, there was some initial encouragement for the politicization of women, but it was soon followed by a policy of rigid
exclusion from public life on the grounds that both the polity
and the family suffered when women strayed into the male
realm of active citizenship. Such treatment at the hands of the

20 *La Minerve*, 28 July 1836 (author's translation)

Jacobins led the feminist/royalist Olympe de Gouges to protest that 'Women are now respected and excluded, under the Old Régime they were despised and powerful.'[21] Earlier, American women had been treated similarly during 'their' revolutionary war.[22]

Women were not always 'respected' under the new order: witness the patriots' misogynous and obscene verbal assault on Queen Victoria. In this respect, too, Lower Canadian behaviour seems to reflect widespread attitudes of the period, attitudes particularly characteristic of republicanism. What one might call the 'vulgar Rousseauian' outlook venerated the virtuous woman who kept to the domestic sphere, and was profoundly suspicious of any woman who ventured into the political realm. Quite apart from the fact that women were not by nature equipped to cope with public affairs, their attempts to take part in politics posed a direct danger to the hallowed conjugal family, because public life was conceived of in republican discourse as entailing a literally *public* performance open to the gaze of the community. Whereas for men publicity was the guarantee of virtue, the opposite applied for women. Self-display was repugnant to good women because it signified sexual immorality, just as surely as female confinement to private pursuits indicated chastity. In Rousseau's words, 'A woman's audacity is the sure sign of her shame.' Thus were the two meanings of the phrase 'public

21 Darline Gay Levy, Harriet Branson Applewhite, and Mary Durham Johnson, ed., *Women in Revolutionary Paris, 1789–1795* (Urbana: University of Illinois Press 1979); Sîan Reynolds, 'Marianne's Citizens? Women, the Republic and Universal Suffrage in France,' in *Women, State and Revolution: Essays on Power and Gender in Europe since 1789* (Amherst: University of Massachusetts Press 1987), 101–22; Landes, *Women and the Public Sphere.* The de Gouges quotation is from Dorinda Outram, 'Le langage mâle de la vertu: Women and the Discourse of the French Revolution,' in *The Social History of Language,* ed. Peter Burke and Roy Porter (Cambridge: Cambridge UP 1987), 126.
22 Linda Kerber, *Women of the Republic: Intellect and Ideology in Revolutionary America* (Chapel Hill: University of North Carolina Press 1980)

woman' – that is, politically prominent individual and prostitute – elided in the republican mind of the period.[23]

Sexual disorder on the part of women, as evidenced by political self-assertion, was considered deplorable for all sorts of reasons, but it is important to note that it posed specifically *political* dangers from the republican point of view. When women forsook the family hearth, they could not support their husbands or raise their sons as good future citizens. More fundamentally, they acted against their chaste and modest nature; the result, since women are so important and men so highly dependent on them, was to denature men, to make them effeminate and therefore susceptible to tyranny. Thus it was that republicans tended to associate political corruption among males – and this of course was the primary threat to liberty – with sexual corruption among females.[24] It is when we recognize this linkage between public roles for women, sexual disorder, and political corruption and tyranny that we begin to understand why the patriots could even conceive of accusing Victoria Regina – innocent, young, but undeniably a prominent public figure – of being a 'whore.'

A reader might well protest at this point that neither Rousseau nor the Patriots invented patriarchy. The notion that 'a woman's place is in the home' and under the authority of her husband

---

23 Landes, *Women and the Public Sphere*. Rousseau quotation, 75

24 Outram, 'Le langage mâle.' A wonderful illustration of this outlook can be found in the work of Rousseau's English contemporary and fellow republican, Edward Gibbon. Gibbon devotes several long and salacious pages in chapter 20 of *The Decline and Fall of the Roman Empire* to the misdeeds of the sixth-century empress, Theodora, whose fond husband, Justinian, committed the fundamental error of making his wife not a consort but a co-ruler. Long before she managed to seduce Justinian, Gibbon explains, Theodora was renowned in Constantinople and beyond for her beautiful face and figure: 'But this form was degraded by the facility with which it was exposed to the public eye, and prostituted to licentious desire. Her venal charms were abandoned to a promiscuous crowd of citizens and strangers, of every rank and of every profession: the fortunate lover who had been promised a night of enjoyment was often driven from her bed by a stronger or more wealthy favourite.' And so on.

was of course quite ancient, as Papineau made clear when he quoted Scripture to chastise his wife's 'independence.' What was new in the early nineteenth century was the peculiarly insistent emphasis on the 'cult of female domesticity,' and the concomitant male monopoly over public affairs. Under an earlier tradition (what one might call, in a very loose sense, the 'ancien régime'), matters were less clear-cut, particularly where politics was concerned, and there was no justification for asserting that men should partake of the sovereign power of the state simply because they were men. Most people were regarded as *subjects* and, to that degree, men and women were politically on a par. Conversely, some women – from Madame de Pompadour in France to Madame Péan in Canada – did exercise great influence over affairs of state.[25]

The mass of the population was not supposed to have a political voice, according to the ideologues of absolutism, though in fact they could make their views felt through the threat of demonstration, riot, and insurrection; and women often played a prominent part in these activities. In eighteenth-century French Canada women were at the forefront in several community battles with Church authorities over parish boundaries, and protests over food shortages and rationing during the Seven Years' War were almost entirely the work of women.[26] Later, when rural insurrection broke out during the American occupation of

25 'This social system,' writes Colin Coates, referring to New France and to the tribulations of Madeleine de Verchères, seigneuresse and military heroine, 'though patriarchal, allowed certain women to wield a great deal of power.' He might have added the qualification 'overtly' to distinguish better the eighteenth century from the nineteenth, when men still expected elite women to wield power, but quietly and privately. Colin Coates, 'Authority and Illegitimacy in New France: The Burial of Bishop Saint-Vallier and Madeleine de Verchères vs. the Priest of Batiscan,' *Histoire sociale – Social History* 22 (May 1989): 65–90

26 Louise Dechêne, *Habitants et marchands de Montréal au XVIIe siècle* (Paris and Montreal: Plon 1974), 464; Terence Crowley, ' "Thunder Gusts": Popular Disturbances in Early French Canada,' CHA, *HP*, 1979, 19–22

Canada in 1775, women once again played an important role in many localities. At Pointe-aux-Trembles two women went from door to door blackening the faces of all their neighbours who had cooperated with the British militia call-up. Elsewhere, it was reported: 'The widow Gabourie, nicknamed the queen of Hungary, has done more damage in this parish than anyone else. She often held meetings at her home at which she presided and which tended to excite people against the government and in favour of the rebels.'[27]

For many years Lower Canadian women even enjoyed the suffrage, at least to some extent.[28] The Constitutional Act of 1791 had accorded the vote in Legislative Assembly elections on the basis of a property qualification, with no mention of sex. Accordingly, women possessed of the requisite property (usually this meant widows) often cast their votes. Female suffrage was not universally accepted; evidence from surviving poll books indicates that, depending on the election and on the constituency, substantial numbers of women or none at all might vote.[29] Certainly there were returning officers who turned women away from the hustings 'in consequence of their sex.' In one case, this reaction provoked objections from men whose candidate stood to benefit from a sex-blind franchise. 'Property and not persons,'

27 'Journal ... pour l'examen des personnes qui ont assisté ou aider les rebels ... 1776,' *RAPQ*, 1927–8, 480 (author's translation). See also ibid., 447, 450, 470, 496.

28 W.R. Riddell, 'Woman Franchise in Quebec, a Century Ago,' Royal Society of Canada, *Proceedings and Transactions* 22 (1928), section 2, 85–99; Fernand Ouellet, *Le Bas-Canada, 1791–1840: changements structuraux et crise* (Ottawa: Editions de l'Université d'Ottawa 1976), 42–3, 350; David De Brou, 'Mass Political Behaviour in Upper-Town Quebec, 1792–1836' (PH D thesis, University of Ottawa, 1989), 94–8

29 In addition to the works noted above, see NA, Lower Canada Election Records, vol. 21, poll books for: Quebec county, 1804 (no women voted); Charlesbourg county, 1817 (no women voted); borough of William Henry, 1827 (three women attempted to vote, one rejected). In the Montreal West election of 1832, on the other hand, Ouellet found 199 women among the 1,533 voters.

they insisted, 'is the basis of representation in the English government,' pursuing an argument for female suffrage that in the context can only be called 'conservative.'[30] (We might note in passing a fact that has escaped the attention of nationalist/ feminist historians: this partial and contested female franchise was not unique to Lower Canada. It was not unheard of for women's votes to be accepted in Britain and its colonies in the eighteenth century, and there were French women who helped elect representatives to the Estates-General of 1789.)

The spectacle of women voting appeared increasingly anomalous to Lower Canadian parliamentarians, and in 1834 they passed a bill formally disenfranchising women. It is worth noting that this measure was not controversial, nor did it seem very important to its supporters. The clause in the law regulating elections that disenfranchised women in fact received less attention than matters like the appointment of returning officers and the administration of oaths. It was originally proposed by John Neilson, a moderate from Quebec City who had earlier broken with Papineau and the more radical Patriots. None the less, Papineau threw his full support behind the measure, in spite of his bitter feud with Neilson. Indeed, I have been unable to find a trace of any sort of objection to the exclusion of women from the electoral process. Lower Canadian newspapers of every political stripe (needless to say, all were written by men and for men) either ignored the measure or treated it as a straightforward housekeeping matter.[31] Even in the turbulent and fiercely

30 Petition of divers electors, Upper Town, Quebec, 1828, in *Documents relating to the Constitutional History of Canada, 1819-1828*, ed. A.G. Doughty and N. Story (Ottawa: King's Printer 1935), 520

31 *L'Ami du Peuple*, 27 January 1834; *Montreal Gazette*, 1 February 1834; *La Minerve*, 3 February 1834. *Le Canadien* and *L'Echo du Pays* took no notice of the disenfranchisement of women. It should be noted that the electoral bill of 1834, after sailing through the House of Assembly, was held up at subsequent stages of the legislative process and, for reasons quite unconnected with the clause relating to female voters, it never seems to have been enacted into law. Nevertheless, women do not seem to have been admitted to the hustings after 1834. Just to be sure, the parliament of the province of Canada prohibited women from voting in 1849.

partisan 1830s there were subjects on which the parties could agree!

Louis-Joseph Papineau was the only member of the Assembly to articulate a justification for an exclusion the necessity for which seemed entirely self-evident to his colleagues. Significantly, in framing his argument against females' voting, he did not allude to any sort of defect in judgment or political understanding that ought to disqualify women, although he did take it for granted that married women would vote the same way as their husbands. What concerned Papineau was rather the danger posed to the domestic sexual order by women's participating in the public exercise of the suffrage (recall that this was long before the introduction of the secret ballot). 'It is ridiculous,' he declared, 'it is odious to see women dragged up to the hustings by their husbands, girls by their fathers, often against their will. The public interest, decency and the modesty of the fair sex require that these scandals cease.'[32] Never mind the fact that all this anxiety about fathers and husbands is irrelevant in a situation where almost all the female voters were widows. We might even pass over the irony of this male politician casting himself in the role of gallant protector of frail femininity as he substantially narrows the political rights of women. What seems to me impossible to ignore – and characteristically republican – about Papineau's speech is the way it associates three things: (1) 'the public interest,' (2) feminine chastity and 'modesty,' and (3) the withdrawal of women from the public arena. Such a linkage is of course in line with Rousseau's convictions. Thus it seems entirely fitting that, while male politicians of every persuasion were in basic agreement on gender-political issues, it should be a radical who took the strongest stand.

Yet there were counter-currents, possibilities – however limited – for an alternative construction of the republican discourse on gender and political rights. In Lower Canada, as in Europe and

---

32 *La Minerve*, 3 February 1834 (author's translation). See also *Montreal Gazette*, 1 February 1834.

the United States, the rhetoric of equality, and even the language of 'separate spheres,' could be appropriated to serve proto-feminist purposes. On the eve of the Rebellion, one lonely contributor to *La Minerve* appealed to the nationalism of the patriots, calling on them to recognize sexual equality as a distinguishing feature of the French-Canadian nation.[33] 'Adelaide' (it was customary to use pseudonyms in letters to the editor) began by observing that an insidious English practice was creeping into the old Canadian custom of celebrating the pre-nuptial signing of a marriage contract. When called upon to witness the contract, some married women in Montreal were apparently signing with their own Christian names coupled with their husband's surnames. This abandonment of the established practice whereby women signed with their fathers' family name was disturbing to Adelaide; for it suggested more fundamental shifts in concepts of marriage. The use of the premarital family name was associated with a legal and moral system that allowed a married woman to preserve her property and her identity. Adelaide draws a sharp contrast in this regard between Lower Canada and England where, she believes, wives could not own property and were completely subordinate to their husbands. Among French Canadians the management of family property and the raising of children is by 'mutual collaboration.' 'Our laws, in harmony with our customs [moeurs], make the woman the partner of the man as well as his wife.'

'Adelaide's' propositions on marital law and custom do not exactly represent a bald description of reality. They should instead be read as a programmatic and normative statement, one that puts the accent on French-Canadian tendencies in the direction of sexual equality while conveniently ignoring contrary tendencies. For example, she neglects to mention that, while husbands and wives were accorded equal shares of family property under the Custom of Paris, the law clearly stated that 'the

33 Ibid., 2 February 1837

husband is master of the conjugal community.'[34] It is true that the civil law of Canada protected the property rights of widows and of inheriting offspring of both sexes to a much greater extent than did English law. Accordingly, a French-Canadian pater familias did not dispose of the economic leverage or the threat of disinheritance to bully his 'dependants' after the manner of those domestic tyrants that populate so many English novels of the eighteenth century. However, this does not mean that French Canada was not a patriarchal society; it means simply that male power was based on different mechanisms of control. For example (and this is only one element in a patriarchal complex with too many ramifications to be adequately discussed here), under the French régime disobedience on the part of wives and children might be a punishable criminal offence.[35]

It is nevertheless true that the institution of the conjugal community and the inheritance provisions of the Custom of Paris requiring equal division among sons and daughters did constitute important safeguards for girls and women, subject though the latter were to male ascendancy in other realms of life. Yet in the pre-Rebellion decades these safeguards were eroding. Most contemporaries were probably unaware of it, so gradual was the change, but increasing numbers of habitants were finding ways to bequeath all or most of their property to their sons, leaving their daughters to be beholden to future husbands for whatever wealth they might acquire.[36] Behind this partial abandonment of the rules of French-Canadian civil law lay a number of factors, such as the growing scarcity of land for new settlement. The influence of English legal traditions may also have played a role

---

34 François-Joseph Cugnet, *An Abstract of Those Parts of the Custom of the Viscounty and Provostship of Paris, which Were Received and Practised in the Province of Quebec, in the Time of the French Government* (London: Eyre and Strachan 1772), 56; Allan Greer, *Peasant, Lord, and Merchant: Rural Society in Three Quebec Parishes, 1740–1840* (Toronto: UTP 1985), 53–6

35 John F. Bosher, 'The Family in New France,' in *In Search of the Visible Past,* ed. Barry Gough (Waterloo: Wilfrid Laurier UP 1977), 9

36 Greer, *Peasant, Lord, and Merchant,* 80-1, 223

in encouraging the belief that a man should be able to dispose of 'his' property as he saw fit (with emphasis on the unspoken, but crucial, assumption that family property ought to be vested in the father/husband). Perhaps that is why the writer of the 'Adelaide' letter was so worried about the adoption of English practices in the comparatively insignificant matter of signing marriage contracts.

At any rate, it is clear that Adelaide was presenting what amounted to a plea for greater sexual equality. And she made her case in the only terms that could be expected to appeal to readers of La Minerve: those of nationalist republicanism. Like other early feminists, including Mary Wollstonecraft, she was unable to mount a fundamental challenge to the prevalent concept of female domesticity. Instead, she insisted on the virtues of harmony, mutuality, and equality within the private conjugal sphere. Obviously, this was not an argument for female 'independence' as the late twentieth century would understand the term, but in the real world that 'Adelaide' inhabited much would have had to change if all couples were to live together with genuine cooperation and mutual respect. And was her appeal to the men of the Patriot party successful? Not if one judges by the absence of any response to her letter in subsequent editions of La Minerve. Nor did the behaviour of the radicals during the Rebellion suggest a deep attachment to Adelaide's concept of French-Canadian marital equality. When the conjugal community regime came up as an issue in 1837–8, it did so because patriots were demanding its abolition as an infringement on a man's right freely to control 'his' property![37]

In the context of the 1830s the patriot movement certainly had no monopoly on patriarchy, and their defeat in the course of the Rebellion certainly did not signal the liberation of Lower Canada's women. Indeed, the state structure and political order instituted after 1838 was, if anything, more thoroughly masculine

37 See La Minerve, 14 August 1837.

than anything the patriots seem to have contemplated.[38] The ideology of 'separate spheres' was gaining strength throughout the Euro-Atlantic world at this time, and influential men of virtually all shades on the political spectrum were affected. One can nevertheless see the Patriot party as the Lower Canadian spearhead of this wider shift in the politico-sexual order. It was within its ranks that the democratic conception of a 'public sphere' open to every citizen without privilege or distinction was enunciated most clearly and forcefully. Since the patriots' definition of citizenship excluded women, their discourse of liberation was as much about sex as it was about politics. Accordingly, one might well regard the Rebellion of 1837–8 as constituting, among other things, a significant moment in the process of gender formation in French Canada.

MEN AND WOMEN DURING THE REBELLION

The crisis of the summer of 1837 began, in fact, with a rather awkward attempt on the part of the Patriots to attract the active support of women. It was in the context of the campaign to boycott British imports that radical men turned to their wives and mothers for support. In both the boycott itself and the consequent mobilization of women the Patriots were following the pre-Revolutionary American experience, as Papineau and his associates were well aware.[39] Women were thought to have a critical role to play, in the first instance as consumers. Since textiles accounted for a large part of British exports to Canada, the Patriot press felt called upon to lecture the ladies of the country on the need to forgo foreign finery in favour of plain homespun.

38 See Lykke de la Cour, Cecilia Morgan, and Mariana Valverde, 'Gender and State Formation in Nineteenth-Century Canada,' in Colonial Leviathan: State Formation in Mid-Nineteenth-Century Canada, ed. Allan Greer and Ian Radforth (Toronto: UTP 1992), 163–91.
39 See Papineau's speech as reported in Vindicator, 6 June 1837. Cf. Kerber, Women of the Republic.

Women of Canada! Little as ye think it, it is in your power partly to avert the awful storm now threatening us with such terrific fury ... There is a demon rapidly destroying your country's prosperity, the virtue of your children and the happiness of your own hearts. You feel it not; you know it not; yet is it a thousand times more terrible in its influence than the all-devouring serpent in days of yore ... The demon that I speak of, that hath taken possession of, and sullied, the purity of your minds, *is an inordinate love of dress.*

We may leave to one side the question of how anyone with that kind of writing style could presume to champion the cause of chaste simplicity and simply note the typically republican linkage of national salvation with feminine modesty. The article concludes with a ringing call to the women of Lower Canada: 'Throng not your city's streets clothed in foreign apparel. Let the leading ones among you assume the dress of humble *toile*, and, believe me, by so doing, they will have tended more to the preservation of their country's *rights* and *trade*, than the numberless resolutions of the grey-beards and councillors.'[40]

Who was to spin the yarn and weave it into patriotic toile? Certainly not the greybeards and councillors! The non-importation campaign entailed the mobilization of women above all in the role of domestic producers. In some parts of the province – particularly the Richelieu valley – women did take up the challenge. At St Charles a man later recalled, 'Even the women shared the general enthusiasm ... And they competed with one another to produce the finest cloth.'[41] Previously ignored in Patriot discourse, women began to appear repeatedly in the

40 *Vindicator*, 27 June 1837. Though presented here specifically in relation to the anti-British boycott, the general theme of the moral dangers posed by women's weakness for fancy clothes was a major preoccupation for nineteenth-century bourgeois commentators. See Mariana Valverde, 'The Love of Finery: Fashion and the Fallen Woman in Nineteenth-Century Social Discourse,' *Victorian Studies* 32 (Winter 1989): 169–88.

41 NA, MG24, B82, 'Quelques notes historiques sur les événements politiques de 1837 en Canada,' 9

radical press, though usually in anonymous and stereotyped terms. At a banquet at Contrecoeur, for example, fifty-six men raised their glasses to toast 'Josephte, the wife of Jean-Baptiste, as patriotic as she is beautiful, no less virtuous than she is pleasant, she will make a powerful contribution to the happiness of the country by her industry and by her efforts to encourage domestic manufactures.'[42]

First they take away Josephte's vote, then they ask her to toil at the hand-loom in order to free the country! The temptation is great to treat the Patriot appeal to women with complete cynicism. Yet there was some complexity to the position of the radical men and some hints of movement in the direction of fuller citizenship for women as the crisis of 1837 deepened. A newspaper reprinted extracts from Harriet Martineau's work, 'The Political Non-existence of Women.'[43] It also gave favourable reports of the formation of patriotic women's associations in several rural parishes. Little is known about these organizations themselves, but by September 1837 they seem to have extended their attention to other matters in addition to the boycott.

HONOR TO OUR PATRIOTIC LADIES

A party of two hundred and fifty ladies, belonging to the parish of St. Antoine, celebrated, on Thursday, the 10th inst. their love of country and their patriotism, by a public dinner, from which every *imported* article was rigidly excluded. Various patriotic toasts, appropriate to the spirit of the times, were proposed. A guard of honor, composed of forty men belonging to the parish, was in attendance with their muskets, and occasionally complimented the fair party by firing a *feu de joie* [sic]. So far from being frightened by the smell of powder, or the roar of musketry, many of the ladies, to prove that they can act in case of need, took the muskets and discharged them with the most admirable tact and courage. When the *women* of Canada are displaying such patriotism, it is not very probable the *men* will be backward when the day of trial comes.[44]

42 *La Minerve*, 17 August 1837 (author's translation)
43 *Vindicator*, 4 July 1837
44 Ibid., 22 September 1837

Of course no one really expected women to shoulder arms in the coming struggle. Still, behind the condescending treatment of the 'patriotic ladies' lies a recognition of the reality of feminine patriotism and of the importance of women's contribution to the national mobilization. Like other middle-class radicals in other countries, the Patriots found themselves impelled by the revolutionary situation itself to modify their views somewhat in order to bring women into the movement. Their more democratic approach to poor men was analogous. But where women were concerned, there was perhaps a more deeply felt ambivalence about this widening process, because the relationships involved were more intimate than those of class. Thus, while it tried to stimulate and encourage women's politicization, the radical press constantly betrayed, by repeated reference to the ladies' weakness and beauty, its anxiety about the dangers of subverting the sexual hierarchy. With some misgivings, Patriot men stretched and extended the malleable concept of female domesticity in ways that allowed women to become more directly involved in the national struggle; nevertheless, they emphatically did not abandon the ideology of separate spheres.

The inescapable fact is that the Patriot movement was a fundamentally masculine phenomenon, in its style as well as in its philosophical orientation. Orators at the protest meetings held in the summer of 1837 emphasized themes of independence, honour, and manly valour in appeals clearly addressed to men. Women were certainly a presence at these meetings; in fact, Constitutionalist newspapers liked to declare that the crowds attending anti-coercion rallies were mostly composed of women and children. The response of the Patriot press was revealing: rather than challenging the assumption that a female presence detracted from the seriousness of the proceedings, the *Vindicator* would instead insist that 'the handsome and patriotic ladies' had confined their participation to waving handkerchiefs from the windows of nearby houses.[45]

45 See, for example, the accounts of the meetings at Ste Scholastique and Napierville in *Vindicator*, 6 June 1837 and 25 July 1837.

This approach was not calculated to further the Patriots' attempts to appeal to women, nor, presumably, was the movement's pronounced anti-clericalism. In Lower Canada at this time, as in other parts of the Catholic world, religion was becoming a peculiarly female affair within the family.[46] One finds evidence of this trend in statistics on membership in various devotional sodalities. Whereas men formed an overall majority in the seventeenth century, women became more numerous in the first half of the eighteenth century, and their numerical predominance increased over the years.[47] Though the official Church remained subject to a strictly masculine hierarchy, women of all classes were tending to develop a special relationship with the clergy. For all its authoritarianism, the Church did have a place for women in a way that the republican movement did not.

It is hardly surprising then that women generally did not embrace the patriot cause with great enthusiasm. To say so is not to deny or to belittle the very real suffering of the hundreds of women who found their possessions stolen, their homes in ashes, and their husbands in prison in the wake of the battles of 1837 and 1838. We know, moreover, that in addition to their efforts on behalf of the non-importation campaign, women sewed banners, sheltered fugitives, and otherwise aided the insurgents; one woman even acquired a reputation in the parish of St Benoit by composing satirical songs directed against the 'chouayen' priest of a neighbouring parish.[48] Yet aside from these auxiliary contributions, evidence of active female commitment to the patriot cause is almost non-existent. Among the 1,356 names on the official lists of political prisoners for the Rebellion period, not

46 Jean-Pierre Wallot, *Un Québec qui bougeait: trame socio-politique au tournant du XIXe siècle* (Sillery: Boréal 1973), 203
47 Marie-Aimée Cliche, *Les pratiques de dévotion en Nouvelle-France: comportements populaires et encadrement ecclésial dans le gouvernement de Québec* (Quebec: Presses de l'Université Laval 1988), 181–3, 208, 232
48 Marcelle Reeves-Morache, 'La canadienne pendant les troubles de 1837–1838,' *RHAF* 5 (June 1951): 99–117; Dumont et al., *Quebec Women*, 118–24

one can be identified as a woman.[49] The thousands of depositions and other narrative sources convey a similar impression: nowhere did women play a prominent or even a very active role, either as fighters or as spies, agitators, or journalists.[50] It is true that women have generally been slighted in the records favoured by historians, but it would be a serious mistake to attribute the resounding silence on this score merely to documentary bias.

Women do appear in the sources, but they do so principally in a stance of opposition to the patriots and their insurrection. The testimony of dozens of witnesses and prisoners mentions wives urging their husbands to stay home rather than report to a rebel camp. Of course contemporaries explained this behaviour as nothing more than the weakness of the weaker sex, but one wonders whether the women concerned might not have displayed greater firmness had they found the cause more inspiring. Certainly there is no reason to think that the women of French Canada held back from full support of the Rebellion out of any ingrained timidity or 'conservatism.' Their record of anti-government activism in the eighteenth century is sufficient refutation of that hypothesis. Obviously something had changed between 1775, when the 'Queen of Hungary' had led the peasants of the Ile d'Orléans, and 1837, when the anti-government forces could boast no heroines. One new factor on the scene was the Patriot movement which, in spite of half-hearted attempts to sponsor

49 *BPP* 14: 405–25. Of course a man was more likely to be arrested than a woman, even if each committed the same political offence. Nevertheless, in spite of the obvious bias in arrest figures, the complete and absolute absence of women political prisoners is remarkable.

50 Some have attempted (see works by Reeves-Morache and Dumont et al. cited above) to make Emilie Boileau of Chambly into a patriot Madeleine de Verchères, but their case is quite unconvincing. It seems to rest on a passage in the memoirs of R.S.M. Bouchette, in which Bouchette describes a gathering of patriots at the home of Emilie and her husband, Timothée Kimber, during the crisis of 1837. Bouchette was impressed by the fact that Madame Kimber was holding a pistol. Far from firing this weapon, or even brandishing it in any encounter with anti-patriot forces, there is no indication that she ever carried it outside her own house!

women's organizations, clearly stood for a masculine – indeed a masculinizing – politics in which women were not welcome. And no doubt many women had no desire to be involved in political struggle, for or against the British colonial régime in Lower Canada. After all, the evolving ideology of female domesticity was not the exclusive property of patriots, nor was it limited to men alone. As it gained hegemonic status through the Euro-Atlantic world,[51] women themselves tended increasingly to subscribe to the notion that national affairs should be left to men.

Not every woman, however, was prepared to accept the assigned role. Indeed, in the tense pre-Rebellion period two heroines in the Madeleine de Verchères mould gained province-wide notoriety thanks to their willingness to engage in dangerous armed confrontations. Hortense Globensky, the wife of Guillaume Prévost, a Ste Scholastique notary, was a staunch Constitutionalist who earned the hatred of local patriots during the July troubles in Two Mountains county. Taking up a rifle at the approach of a hostile crowd, which she truly thought was about to ransack her home, she organized the household defences so effectively that the 'mob' went away without pressing the attack. The sister of a central figure in the Dumont clique of St Eustache, Madame Prévost was used to political brawling. Even in the autumn of 1837 she was not afraid to plunge into Patriot meetings denouncing sedition. Her habit of brandishing a loaded pistol on such occasions did get her into some trouble; Ste Scholastique's patriots had her charged with illegal possession of a firearm. Tory Montreal, on the other hand, made a great fuss over her, because she had proved that 'even a woman' could put the cowardly mob to flight. Urban Constitutionalists expressed their appreciation in the form of a silver tea urn, which they presented to Madame

---

51 Among other studies suggesting a parallel tendency in various countries in the nineteenth century for women to withdraw from political activism that seemed normal in the eighteenth century, see Janet L. Polasky, 'Women in Revolutionary Belgium: From Stone Throwers to Hearth Tenders,' *History Workshop* 21 (Spring 1986): 87–104.

Prévost, as the English inscription read, 'in memory of her heroism, greater than that expected of a woman.'[52]

An even more formidable champion of Constitutionalism was Rosalie Cherrier ('Madame St Jacques') of St Denis.[53] Like Hortense Globensky, she was a courageous and outspoken opponent of radicalism right in the heart of patriot country, but no one ever offered Madame St Jacques an engraved teapot; so defiantly unconventional was she in her personal life as well as her politics that heroine status with the respectable Tory press was out of the question. Cherrier's loyalist convictions certainly did not come from her family: she was the sister of a Patriot politician and cousin to Louis-Joseph Papineau. As a matter of fact, Rosalie Cherrier seems to have been completely alienated from her family. Some time before the Rebellion she had separated from her schoolteacher husband, which may have been the origin of the breach with her relations. Living in St Denis with her two teenage daughters, as well as a young American man who lodged with her as a semi-permanent guest, Madame St Jacques was a prime target for sexual slander in a small town. She was known as 'la Poule,' the kept woman of Sabrevois de Bleury, onetime Patriot lately gone over to the government, who herself kept a young man around the house to satisfy her depraved appetites. To make matters worse, the radical press reported, after she had fallen foul of local patriots, that she was known to walk the streets of St Denis at night, dressed in the habit of a Grey Nun, arm in arm with her lover. A deviant in her domestic arrangements as well as in her political allegiance, Rosalie Cherrier was a woman doubly at odds with her family and her community.

Obviously a very strong-willed person, Rosalie seems to have had no fear of confrontations. She made no secret of the fact that

52 *DCB*, 10: 306–7; *Le Populaire*, 12 July 1837; *Montreal Gazette*, 26 October 1837
53 J.-B. Richard, *Les Evénements de 1837 à Saint-Denis-sur-Richelieu* (St Hyacinthe: Société d'histoire régionale de Saint-Hyacinthe 1938), 21–7; *Montreal Gazette*, 30 September 1837; *La Minerve*, 12 October 1837; *Vindicator*, 29 September 1837; *Le Populaire*, 29 September 1837, 2 October 1837, 9 October 1837, 16 October 1837; NA, MG11, Q238-1: 190, Gosford to Glenelg, 12 October 1837; Toronto Public Library, George Nelson journal, 6

she wrote reports on regional affairs for the Constitutionalist paper, *Le Populaire*. When St Denis's patriots staged a demonstration in September 1837 that featured the hanging in effigy of Governor Gosford and several of his Lower Canadian supporters, Cherrier marched out and tore down the signs attached to the effigies; she then proceeded to treat the stunned audience to her own views on the issues of the day. That evening a noisy crowd surrounded her house in the urban village, singing obscene songs and demanding that she leave the parish. Instead of fleeing, she went out and purchased a gun the next day and melted down her spoons for ammunition. An even larger group assembled to resume the charivari the following night, but Madame St Jacques was prepared for them. The crowd grew ever louder and more menacing until suddenly a shot rang out from a window of the house. It was never determined whether Rosalie herself or some other member of the household actually fired the shot. What is clear is that after the dust had settled, two men who had come to enjoy the charivari lay seriously wounded (one almost died), Cherrier and her household had escaped, and her house had been reduced to a pile of rubble by the furious crowd.[54]

In the aftermath, journalists argued about whether this rumpus had been a political charivari or a traditional charivari, one aimed at a marital non-conformist, a partisan opponent, or a woman who had dared to intrude into the public sphere of political debate. Yet surely it was all these things. Feminine chastity and domesticity was the necessary counterpart of masculine civic virtue in the republican discourse of the period, and so, for the villagers of St Denis as well as for the bourgeois Patriots of Montreal, Rosalie Cherrier's 'immodest' political outbursts and her alleged sexual depravity were all of a piece. Her allegiance to the colonial régime simply confirmed both her and its basic corruption.

54 Rosalie Cherrier was captured the following day and taken to Montreal, where she stood trial for attempted murder; apparently she was acquitted. Unfortunately, the relevant judicial records for this period are not open to researchers.

8

Parish republics

What do we mean by the Revolution? The war? That was no part of the Revolution; it was only an effect and consequence of it.

John Adams[1]

Meanwhile, as male republicans continued to insult the queen and revile the monarchy, the colonial government of her majesty suffered attacks of a more practically damaging sort in the parishes of western Lower Canada. The autumn months saw changes, momentous in their implications, in the way sovereign power was actually constituted and exercised at the local level. The 'people' were beginning to rule themselves, and this phenomenon, more than the declarations published earlier in the Patriot press or the blood later spilled on the field of battle, is what made 1837 truly a revolutionary year.

PARISH GOVERNMENT DEMOCRATIZED

Clashes over the allegiance of militia officers and justices of the peace were, by September, developing into something more serious in the rural District of Montreal than mere gestures of

---

1 Quoted in Bernard Bailyn, *The Ideological Origins of the American Revolution* (Cambridge, Mass.: Harvard UP 1967), 1

protest. As the anti-coercion meetings succeeded one another over the course of the summer, the governor's secretary had added more and more names to the list of revoked commissions; all the while sympathetic magistrates and officers who had escaped the purge continued to resign. Now patriot supporters were beginning to wonder about the allegiance of anyone who kept a government commission; indeed the decision to resign or to stay on as militia captain or justice of the peace emerged as the crucial political test for local notables. Only a few months earlier the issues and actors involved in the Lower Canadian crisis were rather remote from the experience of country people, but now the contest within the British empire had come right down to the level of the parish and its little elite. Now there were targets for popular ire closer to home than Governor Gosford in his palace on Cape Diamond. In the county of Richelieu it was reported that 'the people are insisting that all remaining officers of Militia (Magistrates there are none, now) should throw up their Commissions, as they consider it a disgrace to serve under the present Government.'² Initially, recalcitrant officeholders seemed, from the patriot point of view, selfish men who placed personal honours before civic duty, but as the crisis deepened in the fall of 1837, they came to be seen in a more sinister light, as voluntary agents of a hostile power whose pretensions to rule Lower Canada were quite illegitimate. Accordingly, the pressures to resign intensified enormously.

Victims of the government purge were lionized as heroes who had refused to bow down to despotism, and all across the rural District of Montreal honours were heaped upon them. By early September patriots in several parishes were holding public meetings for the purpose of symbolically reinstating dismissed officers, and maypoles played an appropriately prominent role in these grass-roots initiatives. 'The people have elected the dismissed officers of the militia to command them,' wrote the commander of her majesty's forces. 'At St. Ours a pole has been

2 *Vindicator*, 1 September 1837

erected in favor of a dismissed Captain, with this inscription on it – "Elu par le peuple." '[3] This may have seemed at first nothing more than a symbolic gesture of defiance, but in fact something significant was afoot.

Not surprisingly, the troubled county of Two Mountains was at the forefront. A month after the alarms of July most of the justices of the peace and militia officers from the French-Canadian areas of the county had been dismissed; there were no magistrates left in the parishes of St Benoit and St Hermas, and elsewhere the judiciary of this highly polarized region was entirely in the hands of Constitutionalists. These events were of course reminiscent of the tempests under Governor Dalhousie ten years earlier, when the revoking of royal commissions to punish political opponents had been particularly flagrant in Two Mountains. The situation was more serious in 1837, however, and it deteriorated further when the government began naming 'loyal' subjects to replace officers and magistrates who had resigned or been dismissed. Most shocking to patriots was the appointment of a violent Constitutionalist who, as justice of the peace for St Eustache, had led the anti-patriot forces during the election riots of 1834. It was in reaction to these developments that northern radical leaders went beyond simply honouring purged officers and began organizing their own judicial apparatus.

At a meeting of the 'Permanent Committee of the County of Two-Mountains' held at St Benoit on 1 October 1837 a series of resolutions was passed arranging for the establishment of 'Justices of the Peace and Pacificators' (an awkward translation from the French: 'juges de paix amiables compositeurs').[4] Invoking 'the authority invested in it by the people,' the committee recom-

---

3 Colborne to Gosford, 6 October 1837, quoted in Robert Christie, *A History of the Late Province of Lower Canada, Parliamentary and Political, from the Commencement to the Close of its Existence as a Separate Province*, 2nd ed., 6 vols (Montreal: Richard Worthington 1866), 5: 32–3. See also *La Minerve*, 11 September 1837, 19 October 1837; *Vindicator*, 15 September 1837.

4 *Vindicator*, 6 October 1837

mended that the inhabitants of every parish in the county meet
to elect at least three 'pacificators' to adjudicate disputes. Local
'Reformers' (i.e., everyone but government supporters) were to
bring their legal cases to one of these judges, who would listen
to both parties, call in witnesses as required and render his decision 'in conformity with the dictates of his conscience without
being obliged to observe the forms and proceedings of courts.'
Two or more pacificators could preside jointly, and in serious
cases they were to empanel a jury. To ensure the authority of the
new judiciary, the permanent committee ordered that anyone
who defied its rulings or undermined its jurisdiction by taking
cases to the regular courts should be excluded from public office
and rigorously ostracized by all good patriots. There was also
provision in the resolutions of 1 October for a revolutionized
county militia with elected officers, but the main emphasis was
on the new judicial apparatus.

This plan for a system of adjudicating disputes in Two Mountains is an interesting document, and it is worth pausing a
moment to examine its features and their origins and antecedents. Obviously the tribunals were modelled to some degree on
the British judicial system that had taken root in Lower Canada,
with its juries and its justices of the peace, the latter acting uni-
laterally or sitting with colleagues in quarter sessions. The
patriots did not replicate existing institutions exactly. Their program embodied several departures from current practice. For one
thing, it had no room for a rigid separation of civil and criminal
jurisdiction; the pacificators in fact combined the functions of a
justice of the peace and a 'commissioner for the trial of small
causes.' More than was the case under the prevailing judicial
arrangements, the patriot system of Two Mountains provided
convenient local facilities rather than institutional specialization.
It was also intended to be informal, a characteristic generally
prized by popular revolutionary movements intent on making
justice comprehensible and accessible to all. To that end also, no
fees were to be charged. Finally, the judge-pacificators were to be
locally elected rather than appointed by external authority. Simplicity, accessibility, community control: these were the character-

istics that the northern patriots tried to build into their upstart judiciary.

While the plan in its general features bears testimony to the political philosophy that the bourgeois Patriots shared with radicals throughout the western world, clearly many of its details grew out of the institutions and customs of rural French Canada. The procedure for electing local pacificators, for example, is an exact copy of the way in which churchwardens were selected in country parishes. Moreover, as in the case of a vestry board, one year's service was mandatory for anyone elected by his neighbours. Just as striking is the continuity between the new office of 'juge de paix amiable compositeur' and that familiar Lower Canadian figure, the arbitrator. Extra-judicial conciliation, as we saw earlier, was a well-entrenched practice in French Canada long before the conquest. A trusted local resident, or perhaps a committee of three, would try to settle small suits 'à l'amiable' when called upon by parties anxious to avoid the expense of a formal application to the courts. The 'Justice of the Peace and Pacificator' clearly represented an effort to establish this function on a more regular basis while combining it with some of the powers and responsibilities of a JP.

No habitant could have drawn up the St Benoit resolutions instituting a revolutionary judiciary for the county of Two Mountains. Obviously, the initiative was not popular in that sense. Quite likely Jean-Joseph Girouard, together with other local doctors, merchants, and notaries, was the driving force behind this and other actions of the 'Permanent and Central Committee.' Nevertheless, it was scarcely a case of middle-class leaders ramming a doctrinaire program down the throats of passive followers. The institution of the elective judge-pacificator arose, in very large measure, out of the traditions and experience of the people – plebeian as well as professional – of rural Lower Canada. That is what made it 'popular.' Arising in dialectical response to repressive measures by the government, the new judiciary was shaped by the history of French-Canadian community life generally, as well as by the specific conflicts that had troubled Two Mountains over the course of a decade.

Just how the insurgent tribunals operated is impossible to say. If records were kept, the patriots involved must have had the sense to destroy them when Two Mountains was invaded by troops and loyalists. We do know that justices/pacificators were indeed appointed in accordance with the guidelines set down by the Central Committee. At a public meeting held in the middle of October in the parish of St Benoit, featuring speeches by regional Patriot leaders, twenty-two men were elected judges for St Eustache, Ste Scholastique, St Hermas, and St Benoit.[5] Most of those selected were merchants, doctors, and notaries, though there were also rank-and-file patriots like the habitants Pierre Danis and Joseph Robillard. The deference to middle-class candidates is unsurprising – these were the sort of literate and widely respected individuals who, along with priests, would normally be chosen as arbitrators – but it does reflect the continuing bourgeois hegemony within the movement. Since several of the professional men were former justices of the peace lately dismissed by the government, there was also in their election an element of righting wrongs and rewarding virtue.

Middle-class leadership was much less pronounced a month later as Lower Canada girded for war and parishes across the District of Montreal proceeded to elect officers for a revolutionized militia. One meeting in late November – also at St Benoit – was held to name officers 'in opposition to those of the government.'[6] About this time 150 to 200 men met for the same purpose in the rectory of St Eustache, traditional locale for vestry meetings and churchwarden elections. Six officers were elected, only one of whom was a merchant; the rest were all cultivateurs. A government spy who attended the meeting reported that Dr

5 La Minerve, 16 October 1837; ANQ, 1837, no. 808, déposition d'Antoine Danis, 8 January 1838; ibid., no. 824, examen volontaire de Jean-Baptiste Dumouchelle, 3 February 1838; NA, LC Rebellion Records, 1: 359–64, affidavit de Joseph Robillard, 26 December 1837
6 ANQ, 1837, no. 803, déposition de François Groux, 11 February 1838 (author's translation)

Jean-Olivier Chénier gave a speech urging the people 'to attack and destroy Her Majesty's Troops,' but according to François Mallet, one of the habitants elected lieutenant, Chénier was the only 'notable' present.[7] Elections of this sort were by no means limited to the county of Two Mountains. There were several specific reports from other parts of the province of revolutionized militia commands, in addition to the early cases in the Richelieu mentioned above. Even the apparently quiet parishes of the Berthier area were not immune to the contagion of revolt, according to the loyalist seigneur James Cuthbert. 'The parishes of St Cuthbert and St Bartholomew were almost universally impregnated, and large numbers in Berthier; most of the militia officers that were dismissed, and some of those who gave in their resignations, allowed themselves to be reappointed by their former militia men.'[8]

Hesitant and uneven though they were, the steps taken in the fall of 1837 to establish a patriot local administration with elected judges and militia officers were of enormous significance. Rather than complaining about the current government, people were attempting to organize a new one with completely different foundations. This could mean only one thing, concluded the editor of the anti-patriot *Populaire* after reporting the meeting at St Benoit: 'La révolution commence!'[9]

7 Ibid., no. 583, déposition de Joseph St-Aubin, 9 February 1838; no. 682, déposition de Jean-Baptiste Jubenville, 30 December 1837; no. 685, examen volontaire de François Guérin, 29 January 1839; no. 700, examen volontaire de François Mallet, 30 January 1838; no. 721, examen volontaire de Jacques Dubeau, 31 January 1838; no. 769, déposition de Pierre Lamoureux, 18 November 1837

8 NA, LC Civil Secretary, 529: 28, Cuthbert to Walcott, 2 January 1838. See also ANQ, 1837, no. 125, déposition d'Amable Dupuis, 10 January 1838; no. 129, affidavit de Pierre Besse, 25 November 1837; no. 130, affidavit de Luc Bétourné, 2 December 1837; no. 131, déposition de Louis Fréchette, fils, 12 December 1837; *Le Populaire*, 20 November 1837

9 Quoted in Félix Leclerc, '1837–1838, dates et événements,' in *Les rébellions de 1837–1838: Les patriotes du Bas-Canada dans la mémoire collective et chez les historiens*, ed. Jean-Paul Bernard (Montreal: Boréal 1983), 102

THE GRAND MEETING AT ST CHARLES

With a booming cannon shot, the 'Great Meeting of the Five Counties' was called to order at noon on 23 October. Over the course of the previous day and night, some 1,000 to 5,000 people (depending on whether one consults Patriot or Constitutionalist sources) had descended on the village of St Charles, coming from the southern counties of St Hyacinthe, Rouville, Chambly, Verchères, and Richelieu. At the last minute they were joined by a delegation from L'Acadie to form the 'Confederation of the Six Counties.' The delegates and casual spectators assembled in a meadow at the edge of the village where they listened to speeches from all the most renowned Patriot orators; they passed a set of resolutions by acclamation and cheered loudly for their country and its leaders. There were tricolour flags and banners proclaiming 'Fly Gosford, Persecutor of the Canadians,' 'Long live Papineau and the Elective System,' and 'Liberty! We'll Conquer or Die for Her.' In many respects the proceedings resembled those of the county protest meetings that had succeeded one another in the summer of 1837. It was a more elaborate affair, however, extending over two days and involving various rituals not normally associated with a political meeting. Moreover, the St Charles assembly had been convoked, not simply to protest political injuries, but to establish a regional 'federation' and to celebrate the unity and determination of the people. Surely the organizers had in mind the French Revolution and 'those defensive pacts which in the winter of 1790 linked city to city, militia to militia, and which were accompanied by ceremonies which we might call "festivals of federation." '[10] Politics – indeed, collective life in general – seemed to be finding new channels outside the institutional structures of the colonial state, and it was this promise of a new departure that gave St Charles a genuinely revolutionary flavour. No wonder that the enemies of the Patriot

---

10 Mona Ozouf, *La fête révolutionnaire 1789–1799* (Paris: Gallimard 1976), 51 (author's translation)

movement observed preparations for the meeting with the greatest alarm.[11]

It is not clear who conceived the idea of a mass multi-county meeting, but it seems likely that the impulse came from the Patriot leaders of the Richelieu like Doctor Wolfred Nelson of St Denis. The idea of a spectacular demonstration at St Charles would have been particularly appealing in the context of regional politics; for the 'Village Debartzch,' as it was known, was the home of 'that prince of renegades,' Pierre Debartzch, a powerful seigneur and sometime radical, recently named to the Executive Council (see below, 287).[12] Certainly Papineau and the other Montreal leaders approved the project and played a prominent part at the St Charles meeting. They helped to draft the formal resolutions to be put to the meeting and, along with middle-class leaders from the region, they dominated the platform when it came time for speeches. Papineau himself rambled on for two and a half hours.

The content of the speeches and the resolutions, like the men who populated the stage, suggested continuities with the parliamentary wrangles of the past. Four resolutions dealt with the composition of the Legislative and Executive councils, calling for the reform of long-standing 'abuses.' The thrust of most of the motions was much more revolutionary. Beginning with an excerpt from the preamble to the American Declaration of Independence, the resolutions of the Six Counties emphatically denied the legitimacy of the current régime and insisted on the right of the people to govern itself. An 'Address of the Confederation of the Six Counties to the People of Canada' issued an ominous warning. Under conditions of oppression, it declared, 'it becomes the imperative duty of the people to betake themselves to the serious consideration of their unfortunate position – of the dangers by which they are surrounded – and by well-concerted organization, to make such arrangements as may be necessary to

11 *BPP*, 9: 72, Gosford to Glenelg, 12 October 1837
12 *Vindicator*, 27 October 1837

protect, unimpaired, their rights as citizens, and their dignity as freemen.'[13]

But how exactly were the people of Canada to 'protect their rights'? The boycott of British goods had clearly failed to secure concessions, and accordingly there was little talk at St Charles of the non-importation campaign. Indeed, far from retreating in the face of patriot gestures of protest and defiance, the government was bringing in more troops to Lower Canada. The call for 'well-concerted organization' made some sense under the circumstances, but those in charge of the St Charles meeting had precious little to offer in the way of specifics. The resolutions spoke of a 'Convention' of delegates from across the province that would presumably form the basis of an insurgent régime, but the meeting went no further than to call on citizens 'seriously to consider if the time is not at hand when it ought to meet.' Even the Confederation of the Six Counties itself proved to have no lasting existence. No one seems to have thought of giving it institutional form, and so, once the resolutions had been passed and the manifestos published, the participants packed up and departed and the confederation effectively dissolved.

The St Charles meeting was not completely ineffectual. It did urge concrete and immediate action in the area of local administration. Expressing indignation over 'the arbitrary dismissals from office, ordered by the Governor-in-Chief ... against a number of justices of the peace, officers of militia, and commissioners for the summary trial of small causes throughout the parishes,' the resolutions urged the region's patriots to follow the example of the county of Two Mountains.

That it is of urgent necessity, under such lamentable circumstances, to replace the individuals whom an administration inimical to the country will name to those offices, by men worthy of confidence; that all the parishes of the Six Counties are hereby invited simultaneously to elect, between the first day of December and the first day of January next, pacificator justices of the peace and officers of militia; and that the regulations of the county of Two Mountains be provisionally adopted for their direction and jurisdiction.[14]

It was this call for a revolutionized local administration that was the most powerful and controversial of the proceedings at St Charles. Timothée Franchère, the St Mathias merchant who seconded the motion quoted above, had a good deal of explaining to do when he was interrogated four months later in the Montreal prison. According to the prisoner, he had objected to any call for the election of militia officers, since such a move was 'too strong and tended to encroach on the rights of government.'[15] Nevertheless, Papineau persuaded him to set his objections aside. One does not have to accept every detail of Franchère's story to acknowledge that both he and the examining magistrate were aware of the implications of this particular resolution. In the aftermath of the 1837 insurrections several other prisoners and witnesses dwelt on this aspect of the St Charles meeting, either because they found it particularly striking or because their interrogators were preoccupied with the issue of local elections. Joseph-Léon Beauchamps, for example, recalled Papineau's speech in these terms: 'he also recommended to the people to hold elections for officers of militia and *amiables compositeurs* who would judge their affairs.'[16] Such advice must have seemed particularly serious sedition to the magistrates of Montreal, because it did more than call into question the legitimacy of the government, it proposed – admittedly in a hesitant manner – measures to replace it.

But where did the idea of an elective militia and magistracy

14 Ibid., 9: 96
15 ANQ, 1837, no. 49, examen volontaire de Timothée Franchère, 19 February 1838
16 Ibid., no. 42, affidavit de Joseph-Léon Beauchamps, 11 December 1837. Cf. ibid., no. 40, affidavit de Jean-Louis Beauchamp, 6 December 1837; no. 44, affidavit de Joseph Petit, 7 December 1837.

originate? Certainly not at St Charles and not in the mind of Louis-Joseph Papineau. It is essential to recognize that the campaign to revolutionize local government was well under way before 23 October. It had developed primarily in the county of Two Mountains, although it was not entirely limited to the northern region, and it depended heavily on the traditions, the initiative, and the active support of the habitants and artisans of the countryside. In contrast to the revolutionary mimetism of the boycott of British imports, this campaign developed organically out of the Lower Canadian confrontation of 1837. Responding directly to government actions that were generally considered unjust, northern patriots defended traditional rights while laying the foundations of a democratic administration. Certainly there was middle-class leadership from the start, but the campaign drew its potency from the fact that the plebeians of Lower Canada had fought for generations to make institutions like the parish, the militia, and the magistrature into expressions of their communities. The St Charles meeting had the effect of spreading and accelerating the revolution in local government; it did not create it.

Just as important as the manifest content of the speeches and resolutions – probably more significant in its effects – were the festive and symbolic aspects of the assembly of the Six Counties. This was no mere political meeting: it was a celebration of national unity and public determination. Accordingly, it was staged with all the pomp and circumstance that the Richelieu valley could muster. Martial themes were prominent, anticipating the coming military confrontation perhaps, but also reflecting the importance of the militia in rural community life.

During the Meeting, a company of between 60 and 100 Militia Men attended, with arms on the ground, under the command of Capts. Lacaisse and Jalbert. They went through their manoeuvres in very good style; a volley was fired at the passing of every Resolution ...

A very handsome column, surmounted with 'a cap of Liberty,' was erected, on the occasion, in honor of PAPINEAU, on the ground. It bears an inscription: – 'To PAPINEAU, by his grateful brother patriots, 1836

[sic].' After the meeting was over, Mr. PAPINEAU was led to the front of the column, and addressed by one of the gentlemen, to which the Hon. gentleman replied in a suitable manner. The young men who attended the meeting afterwards marched in procession to this pillar, before which they sung a popular hymn, and laying their hands on the column, swore that they would be faithful to their country, and conquer or die for her. This solemn vow was registered in the hearts of all present, amid vollies of musketry and the thunders of artillery. It was a solemn and impressive sight.[17]

Evidently the cult of Papineau was at its height. The irony of course is that the honourable speaker no longer possessed the initiative in Lower Canada; in fact, increasingly after 24 October he would find himself overwhelmed by events. For the time being, however, he played a tremendously important role at St Charles, not only rousing the multitude with his oratory but, above all, serving as the human embodiment of the Patriot cause and the Lower Canadian nation. Still, he was not the object of blind personal devotion. Note that the 'young men' swore allegiance to 'their country' rather than to their leader. Moreover, whereas Papineau's close associate, E.B. O'Callaghan, author of the lines quoted above, emphasized the dedication of the 'Papineau column' to the great man, less eminent spectators viewed the event from a slightly different angle. An habitant from Varennes later remembered 'a column topped with a red bonnet that was called "the liberty pole."' [18] There is no denying the politically primitive nature of hero-worship; yet we do have to recognize symbolic discourse when we see it. The festivities at St Charles tended to identify Papineau, the pillar, liberty, and the nation, but this does not mean that those present took the identification in a literal sense.

The 'message' of these rituals is important, but the 'medium'

17 *Vindicator*, 24 October 1837
18 ANQ, 1837, no. 40, affidavit de Jean-Louis Beauchamp, 6 December 1837 (author's translation)

in which they were expressed is just as significant. The contribution of popular traditions is unmistakable: the 'liberty pole' clearly was a transformed maypole, and its dedication to Papineau recalled, in almost every respect, the popular investiture of a parish militia captain (see above, 107–13). Native traditions like the musket salute blended neatly, with a touch – the red bonnet – linking St Charles with the festivals of the French Revolution. About this time there were similar, though more modest, ceremonies featuring the politicized liberty/maypole in different parts of the District of Montreal. A government report in the wake of the patriot defeats at the end of 1837 referred to a disloyal lieutenant named Jean Villicot dit Latour of Ste Anne des Plaines: 'At the death of Séraphim Bouc his Captain, believing the command had devolved upon himself, his men collected and planted a liberty pole at his door and he entertained them.' Captain Séraphin Robert of St-Jean-Baptiste was denounced for similar reasons. After returning from the St Charles meeting,

The said Séraphin Robert invited the deponent and the militiamen of his company to go to his home and shoot at his maypole or mast [this is, of course, the custom of blackening the pole with gunpowder]; the deponent and part of the company went and passed almost a whole day there. The said Séraphin Robert supplied the powder and had a flag on his maypole for liberty on one side and on the other side in favour of Papineau, and having an inscription at the base to the same effect. The said Robert gave them speeches in favour of liberty.

One deposition refers to 'un mai de liberté,' demonstrating the degree to which the maypole and the liberty pole had come to be identified at a time when the militia officer corps was at the storm centre and when the traditions of community life were helping to sustain the national struggle.[19]

19 NA, LC Civil Secretary, 532: 175, report signed John Fraser on disloyal militia officers, Terrebonne county, 30 March 1838; NA, LC Adjutant General, vol. 52, déposition de Gabriel Sansoucy, 27 September 1839 (author's translation); ANQ, 1837, no. 1114, déposition de Joseph Beauchamp, 15 November

As local contingents made their way home from St Charles in little processions, they took with them flags and paraphernalia that would soon decorate their own villages. At Ste Marie-de-Monnoir, the notary had a picture of the St Charles 'liberty tree' painted on the side of his house.[20] In its festive and symbolic aspects the Six Counties meeting clearly drew upon the long-standing cultural traditions of French Canada, traditions that were already in the process of being forged into a revolutionary weapon. At the same time, the assembly had the effect of stimulating and accelerating the political transformation of popular culture in the southern countryside. Exciting for some, the profusion of eagles, tricolours, and liberty poles was profoundly distressing for other Lower Canadians.

THE BISHOP INTERVENES

Among those alarmed by the drift towards revolt was the Catholic clergy of Lower Canada, particularly the bishop of Montreal, Jean-Jacques Lartigue. Friction between priests and patriots was of course nothing new; they had clashed in the past over matters like education and local government. But now, as the existing government was coming under serious attack, Lartigue felt the time had come to condemn revolution in no uncertain terms. Accordingly, he issued a pastoral letter ('mandement') on the day that the St Charles meeting concluded and ordered that curés read it the following Sunday from the pulpit of every church in the diocese. The burden of the bishop's message is quite simple: no Catholic might join in a 'revolt against the established government.' It consisted largely of passages quoted from Gregory XVI's papal encyclical of 1832 against the Polish revolution, together

1837. Something similar occurred during the American Revolution: see Peter Shaw, *American Patriots and the Rituals of Revolution* (Cambridge, Mass.: Harvard UP 1981), 182.

20 ANQ, 1837, no. 1372, déposition de Louis Ostiguy, 28 February 1838; ibid., no. 110, examen volontaire de François Ranger, 17 February 1838

with quotations from scripture and warnings of the bloodshed and misery that were sure to accompany civil war.[21]

There was nothing remarkable about a nineteenth-century pastor instructing his flock to respect authority and shun violence. Nevertheless, the mandement did represent a significant intervention by a prestigious figure – and at a crucial moment – in the Lower Canadian debate over the proper foundation of legitimate state power. Patriots had to take it seriously, because it was transmitted to the bulk of the population – literate and illiterate alike – and they were, with few exceptions, a population of believing and practising Christians. Middle-class radicals knew that there were flaws in Monseigneur Lartigue's theological reasoning; they also knew that a much more liberal line was conceivable even within the Catholic Church: witness the tolerant position of Belgium's bishops during the recent revolution in that country. But what about the uneducated mass of habitants and craft workers? Would they simply obey the instructions of their spiritual superior? No one familiar with the stormy relations between clergy and laity in the rural parishes of French Canada would have expected blind obedience to episcopal dictate. For over a century and a half settlers had resisted curés and bishops whenever the latter attempted to interfere in community matters that the people considered their own business. At issue in so many parochial struggles had been the question of the proper limits of clerical authority, and of course that was precisely the bone of contention in late October 1837. The peasantry of the diocese of Montreal hardly needed the help of bourgeois Patriots to conclude that in lecturing them on politics

21 BPP, 9: 98–100. An English translation can be found in Christie, A History of the Late Province, 4: 417–21. See also Fernand Ouellet, 'Le Mandement de Mgr Lartigue de 1837 et la réaction libérale,' in Constitutionalism and Nationalism in Lower Canada, ed. Ramsay Cook (Toronto: UTP 1969), 67–74; Gilles Chaussé, Jean-Jacques Lartigue, premier évêque de Montréal (Montreal: Fides 1980), 199–205. For European comparative background, see William L. Langer, Political and Social Upheaval, 1832–1852 (New York: Harper & Row 1969), 519.

Bishop Lartigue had overstepped the narrow bounds of his legitimate authority.

Consequently, the episcopal mandement met with a hostile reception in many rural churches. When the curé of Chambly read the document from the pulpit, a group of parishioners stormed out of the church in protest, while about twenty others who stayed drowned out the reading in shouts of 'Vive Papineau! A bas l'évêque!' Most of the congregation at St Charles also took their leave rather than listen to the bishop's words; here the protesters adjourned to the habitant's room of the rectory and held a critical discussion of the pastoral letter's doctrine. Feeling ran so high against Lartigue's manifesto that many parish priests tried to dissociate themselves from its contents by adopting an ironic tone of voice. The curé of Ste Scholastique was afraid to read the mandement at all; 'Ubi non est auditus, non effundas sermonem,' was his motto. Some parish priests, particularly those of conservative political leanings, read the bishop's message to a hostile audience and added their own personal rebuke to local patriots. 'Imbeciles!' shouted the curé of St Césaire at the parishioners who tried to interrupt him. This was not the end of the matter, of course, since the radicals were in no mood to tolerate insults; soon the priest had, 'recd. notice that if he preaches next Sunday, he will be torn from the pulpit.'[22]

Another overzealous priest, Monsieur Amiot of Napierville, wrote to Bishop Lartigue about the furore that had erupted in his parish:

Since the publication of Your Grace's pastoral letter people have become more and more excited against the clergy, as evidenced by the impious and infamous resolutions passed after services the morning of the very day the *mandement* was read. Since that time, they have declared open

---

22 Chaussé, *Lartigue*, 205; NA, 'Quelques notes historiques sur les événements politiques de 1837 en Canada,' 7–8; *La Minerve*, 13 November 1837, 16 November 1837; Archives du diocèse de St-Jérôme, Bonin to Lartigue, 20 December 1837 (author's translation); ANQ, 1837, no. 3557, Chaffers to Gosford, 9 November 1837

war on the clergy. Everywhere, they spread the word that it is time to demolish the tithes as well as the seigneurial dues; everywhere one hears nothing but impious and irreligious speeches against both religion and its ministers. It has been said that they even plan to come and treat me to a charivari to force me to embrace their cause, or at least to make me evacuate the rectory, taking with me my belongings; as far as the latter are concerned, they have promised them to the poor ...

At the confessional, those who are asked about their loyalty to the king reply dryly: 'Monsieur le curé, I did not come here to talk politics. If you do not want to take my confession, I shall leave.' In vain does one attempt to prove to them that it is not at all a matter of politics but solely a duty of conscience: they do not listen to you and they leave promising never to return.[23]

Echoes can be heard here of the struggle, far less serious and purely local in scope, that had pitted Jean-Baptiste Boucher against the parishioners of La Prairie thirty years earlier (see above, 81–5). Like Boucher, the curé of Napierville was soon the object of an anti-clerical charivari: 'Your Grace has no doubt learned that on the ninth [of November], at 11 o'clock in the evening, they came and sang my *libera* under the window of my bedroom; then at midnight they came back, knocking at my door and making me get up. They ordered me not to preach politics and let me know that they were determined to get along without a curé rather than to allow themselves to be led into error.'[24]

Not every priest suffered this sort of indignity, but then few were as virulently anti-patriot as curé Amiot. Some were indeed quite sympathetic to the popular movement, and one, Abbé Etienne Chartier of St Benoit, was a prominent radical leader. Most were rather more ambivalent, opposed to strife and bloodshed, yet convinced that Britain was not dealing justly with the

23 Amiot to Lartigue, 7 November 1837, reprinted in Richard Chabot, *Le curé de campagne et la contestation locale au Québec (de 1791 aux troubles de 1837–38)* (Montreal: Hurtubise 1975), 213 (author's translation)
24 ACEJQ, Amiot to Lartigue, 16 November 1837 (author's translation)

Canadians. It was one thing for Bishop Lartigue to condemn revolution from his episcopal throne in Montreal, but parish priests had more complicated loyalties. Besides being faithful members of the ecclesiastical corporation, most rural curés were also integrated to some degree into the communities where they served. Many had lived among their parishioners for decades, knew them well, and felt a bond with them, in spite of occasional disputes over vestry finances and other matters. They were also well placed to observe that the pastoral letter of 24 October was powerless to stem the revolutionary movement and succeeded only in turning people against the Church. Accordingly, a group of Richelieu valley priests met at St Hyacinthe on 4 November and drew up a petition to the bishop, asking him to moderate his anti-patriot stand. 'It is clear,' they warned, 'that for some time now the clergy has been losing the attachment and the confidence of the Catholics of this diocese.'[25] By then it was too late. In the political crisis that was moving rapidly towards a military confrontation, the Church had become a marginal force. When the troops moved into the Richelieu in late November, several curés compromised themselves with the authorities by blessing the patriot militiamen as they went off to fight the British,[26] while others scurried to bury the parish silver before fleeing to safer regions.

And what about the layfolk of rural Lower Canada? What did the Rebellion mean for them as far as their relationship with the Church and the clergy is concerned? Well, certainly there was no sudden abandoning of Catholicism. Many patriots seem to have been very glad to avail themselves of the confession and mass offered by sympathetic priests on the eve of engagements with

25 Quoted in Chaussé, *Lartigue*, 213 (author's translation). Bishop Lartigue himself seems to have had little confidence in the efficacy of his pastoral letter, because about this time he was making arrangements to flee to the relative safety of Quebec City. Mason Wade, *The French Canadians 1760–1945*, 2 vols (Toronto: Macmillan 1955), 169
26 Ouellet, *Lower Canada*, 300–1

the enemy. This is hardly surprising: they knew they were about to face death, and even the stray sheep is likely to be susceptible to the appeal of religion in such circumstances. More striking is the case of Bonaventure Viger, the hero of the skirmish at Longueuil that opened the fighting in November 1837. A few days before that action Viger was busy collecting money 'to help pay for a high mass so that the rebels would win out in their cause against the British government.'[27] While some patriots were persecuting priests, others were purchasing masses: this does sound like evidence of a confused and contradictory attitude! Yet both actions accord perfectly with the traditions of the French-Canadian peasantry. Habitants had always taken their religion seriously and accorded their curés respect, but they were never blindly obedient, and they would not brook clerical interference in the secular affairs of the community.

Plebeian patriots were well aware that there were 'good' priests and 'bad' priests and that the clergy did not form an undifferentiated bloc as far as politics was concerned. Nevertheless, it was clear in the wake of the failed insurrection of 1837 that the Church's stance had been, on the whole, a conservative one best epitomized by Lartigue's pastoral letter. This perception surely helped to alienate rural Catholics of the diocese of Montreal from the Church, just as the curés assembled at St Hyacinthe had feared it would. Operating in the same direction was the general tendency, characteristic of a revolutionary situation, for established institutions and relationships of subordination to come into question. Accordingly, there were more open calls for the abolition of the tithe as the crisis deepened. When the habitants rose again in November 1838, many displayed fierce hostility towards the 'black pigs' and seemed intent on taking parish priests prisoner. One country priest was able to find a silver lining in the dark clouds of anti-clericalism: 'These days the burden of work is not crushing here, especially in the

27 ANQ, 1837, no. 62, affidavit de Jean-Marie Morin, 2 December 1837 (author's translation)

last year since these political crises have broken out we have more time to ourselves.' Previously overextended, this curé could now enjoy some leisure because his parishioners were learning to get along with less help from the mother Church. The habitants' disengagement from religion, I would like to emphasize once again, was not simply the product of 'external influences,' whether from reading Voltaire or listening to Papineau (although that was certainly part of it). It should be seen rather as a logical extension, accelerated by revolutionary upheaval, of the age-old spirit of lay autonomy. In 1839 a stipendiary magistrate stationed at La Prairie made the following observation: 'The clergy I believe to be generally loyal, but they possess less influence with the people than the clergy do in any other Catholic country.' By that time, however, the process of secularization was just about to be rolled back. Soon the clergy would take advantage of the disarray of its liberal opponents, capitalize on the credit its loyalty had earned with the government, and, with swelled numbers and a revitalized spirit, go forth to Catholicize French Canada root and branch. It would be an exceedingly long time before anyone could once again speak of Quebec priests lacking 'influence with the people.'[28]

TERRORISM AND MIDNIGHT MARAUDING

One evening in early November, about a week after the St Charles meeting and the bishop's pastoral letter, Captain Louis Bessette, his wife, their son, and their daughter-in-law were sitting down to supper when they heard the sound of a cart pulling up in front of their house in the parish of St Athanase, in the upper Richelieu. They paused, waiting for the visitors to enter, but no one came to the door. Voices could be heard outside, followed by the ringing of an axe as it bit into dry wood.

28 Ibid., no. 1665, déposition d'Agathe Vient, 30 December 1838; Chabot, *Le curé de campagne*, 121; ACESH, XVII, C25, Demers to Lartigue, 5 November 1838 (author's translation); ANQ, 1837, no. 3731, Weatherall to Civil Secretary, 14 November 1839

Bessette must have realized he was in for trouble; the Federation of the Six Counties had called for the resignation of all justices of the peace and militia officers and he still retained the queen's commission. Why he chose to defy the patriot majority is not entirely clear. He does seem to have been an unusually rich habitant, a 'coq de village' who owned, not only a prosperous farm, but even some shares in a steamboat business.[29] Bessette was not a staunch and vocal supporter of the government as Eustache Cheval of St Eustache was. In fact, he had earlier attended a patriot meeting in his parish and voted for a resolution insisting that all local magistrates and officers return their commissions.[30] Yet somehow he could not bring himself to resign. Was he afraid of offending the government, worried about the bishop's condemnation of rebellion, or simply reluctant to give up the coveted office of captain? Or was this old and wealthy farmer coming to a belated realization of just how much he had to lose in any revolutionary upheaval? Whatever his motives, Bessette found himself in a delicate situation: the region he inhabited was quite thoroughly aroused against the government. He would reply evasively when neighbours asked about his intentions respecting the captain's position, but unfortunately for him, the patriots of St Athanase were losing patience. On the day before the strange visitation to the Bessette home, a local habitant named Jacques Hébert had warned him that the time for a decision had come. Turn in your commission today, the captain was told, because 'we will wait no longer.'[31]

Louis Bessette therefore cannot have been surprised when he

29 ANQM, gr., P.-P. Démaray, transport par Louis Bessette à Richard Bowen, 25 March 1837

30 ANQM, Affaires Criminelles, déposition de Jean-Baptiste Arcand, 7 December 1837

31 ANQ, 1837, no. 257, déposition de Louis Bessette, 5 November 1837. Cf. ibid., no. 258, déposition de Louis Bessette, fils, 11 November 1837; no. 259, déposition de Joseph Ouimet, 20 November 1837; no. 260, déposition de Louis Gélinoux, 20 November 1837; no. 261, deposition of Charles Stuart Pierce, 4 November 1837; no. 262, deposition of John Hill Roe, 27 November 1837.

went to the door and discovered a small group of men gathered by the roadside. Two of the band were busy chopping at the base of his captain's maypole, and this desecraton sent Louis into a rage. 'You'll pay for my mast, you cretin, you toad,' he shouted, but he was answered with similar insults, followed by a volley of stones; he quickly retreated into the house. The chopping resumed; soon the mast was crashing to the ground, while the onlookers cheered loudly.

Bessette's was neither the first nor the last maypole to fall victim to patriot axes in the crisis of 1837–8. A colonel of the Rouville county militia reported about this time that 'Capt. Alex. Nadeau and Lieut. A. Julien Piedaleu have tendered me their commissions as officers in the provincial militia in consequence of their Poles having been cut down and graves dug at the foot of them by bands of armed men during the night, and threats held out that unless they resigned in two days their houses and barns would be burned and their lives and that of their families destroyed.' Another captain, named Doucet, had his mast felled, and he himself was forced to run around the prostrate pole crying 'Vive Papineau!' Lieutenant-Colonel Théophile LeMay of Ste-Marie-de-Monnoir, the leading Constitutionalist in the region, was also a victim. His was 'a magnificent maypole, 94 feet tall and decorated with a flag and all its accessories,' but early in November, after the terror-stricken LeMay had fled to Montreal, it too was toppled. Across the upper Richelieu valley the patriot bands took a substantial harvest of militia officers' maypoles in the early part of November 1837; by the sixth of that month a Montreal newspaper reported that over forty masts had already been cut down.[32]

The victims of this form of assault did not take their losses lightly. Some, like Louis Bessette, were indignant; others were

32 NA, LC Adjutant General, vol. 48, McCallum to Duchesnay, 6 November 1837; *Le Populaire*, 6 November 1837, 26 July 1837, 10 November 1837; NA, LC Civil Secretary, 524: 3, Lemay to Walcott, 16 November 1837; *Le Populaire*, 6 November 1837. For other examples, see ANQ, 1837, no. 158, déposition d'Ambroise Bédard, 10 November 1837; ibid., no. 803, déposition de François Groux, 11 February 1838.

terrified. Perhaps the undertones of castration conditioned these responses to some degree, even if the people involved had no consciousness of this aspect of the gesture. At another level, both the choppers and the victims must have been well aware of the symbolic message conveyed by this particular form of vandalism. If the presentation of a maypole signified popular ratification of the appointment of a militia officers, then the destruction of the mast also had a clear meaning. Bessette must have seen that the men of St Athanase were telling him: you are no longer our captain.

The felling of the captain's mast did not bring an end to the disturbance at Louis Bessette's farm; it was only the prelude. Men continued to arrive, until there was a crowd of at least two dozen. They began shouting; stones and lumps of frozen earth were hurled at the house. Half an hour and several smashed window-panes later, there was a great pounding at the door and, rather than wait for the door to be broken in, Mrs Bessette let the men in. As they came into the light, she could see that they were disguised. 'Here is a band of devils,' she announced. 'You may have masks and blackened faces, but I recognize you.' (In fact, Louis Bessette and his son were able to name only six of the attackers, though the whole group seems to have been composed of St Athanase men; the disguises must have been effective). The house filled to overflowing with the noisy intruders, some carrying clubs, others guns, and all of them contributing to the horrendous din. 'We want the commission!' chanted the invaders at the top of their lungs. Captain Bessette tried to explain that his commission was not in the house, but he could hardly make himself heard. The men banged their sticks for emphasis and soon had smashed a table, broken several more windows, and knocked down the stove-pipe. Finally Bessette prevailed on them to stop by promising to deliver his commission the next day. The captain was as good as his word; he went into the village the following afternoon and gave his commission to the local notary public and Patriot leader, Eusèbe Bardy. 'You will not be troubled in the future,' the notary assured him, adding that he himself would stop the group if it tried to resume the charivari.

There were dozens of political charivaris in October and November 1837, mainly in the Richelieu valley and in the county of L'Acadie. We happen to know more about this one and about the individuals involved in it because three of the participants signed full confessions three weeks after the event.[33] What induced them to take this step remains a mystery, but they certainly named names, twenty-eight in all; moreover, the lists coincide almost completely and they include all of the six individuals Louis Bessette was able to identify. Of these twenty-eight, sixteen could be found in the 1831 census rolls for St Athanase parish. This in itself is a significant finding, one that shows that the majority of participants were not only well-established local residents but also local patriarchs, since the census provides the names only of household heads. Those not found in the census may have lived in another parish, they may have moved to St Athanase between 1831 and 1837, or they may not have had the status of household head at the time of the census. Though this source does not give ages, the figures on family size set out in table 4 indicate that even six years before the Rebellion most of these men already had substantial households. The charivari was scarcely the work of youths. Nor did the rootless and landless predominate: every one of those traced to the census was a proprietor and most were habitant-farmers with modest holdings. Of the two 'day labourers' one seems to have been incorrectly labelled, since he had one of the larger agricultural establishments; and we know that the other, François Macé, had set himself up as an innkeeper by 1837, since he was notorious as a patriot leader then. All in all, the profile of the St Athanase charivari crowd resembles that of the larger patriot rank and file, in so far as the latter can be identified from arrest records,[34] and, like that wider group, it seems to have constituted a rough cross-section of the rural population.

33 ANQ, 1837, no. 259, déposition de Joseph Ouimet, 20 November 1837; ibid., no. 260, déposition de Louis Gélinoux, 20 November 1837; ANQM, Affaires Criminelles, déposition de François Ouimet, 20 November 1837
34 Cf. Lucie Blanchette-Lessard and Nicole Daigneault-Saint-Denis, 'La participation des groupes sociaux aux rébellions dans les comtés de Laprairie et de Deux-Montagnes,' in Les rébellions de 1837–1838, ed. Bernard, 327–37.

Table 4
Participants in the charivari against Louis Bessette, 2 November 1837

	Occupation	No. in family	Land (arpents)	Horses
François Macé*	labourer	4	0	0
Jean-Bte Arcand*	butcher	4	6	1
Jacques Hébert*	farmer	8	56	2
Paul Rougier	farmer	8	60	2
Louis Haché	farmer	7	38	1
François Ouimet	farmer	6	36	1
Joseph Ouimet	farmer	11	56	3
Pierre Duclos	blacksmith	5	1	1
Charles Bissonant	farmer	11	56	0
Louis Tremblay	farmer	10	56	1
Joseph Goyette	farmer	7	54	1
Louis Lavallée	farmer	5	92	2
François Plante	farmer	5	54	4
Charles Tremblay	labourer	3	56	4
Dominique Lavallée*	farmer	8	56	2
Isaac Tremblay	farmer	5	112	2
Antoine Robert dit Lafontaine				
François-Xavier Bissonet				
Pierre Bombardier dit Labombarde				
Charles Sabourin père				
Amable Lamare				
Louis Chenville				
A.-Eusèbe Bardy				
Michel Hétier				
Etienne Robert				
Jean-Bte Choinière dit Sabourin				
Vincent Huot dit Duval				
Louis Gélinoux				

*Leader/spokesman
SOURCE: Economic information comes from 1831 census MS, St Athanase parish.

A certain amount of coordination and even a measure of discipline were required to get all these men together to mount an assault on the home of the victim. Our three repentant charivaristes give some idea of the preparations that preceded the descent on Louis Bessette's farm. Bessette had been issued an ultimatum the day before, but it was only on 2 November, the day of the charivari itself, that definite plans were made for action. Some men had gathered at Sancerre's tavern. Among them was an habitant named Joseph Ouimet, who recalled the conversation this way: 'A number of people said, we must go to Louis Bessette's place and make him turn over his commission. They also said that they would take Captain Arcand's company to carry out the action, as well as a part of Vincent Huot's company, and that they would make them march.'[35] Ouimet is rather coy about the identity of the speaker or speakers, but his host, the innkeeper and prominent local patriot François Macé dit Sancerre, likely took a leading part in the discussions. What seems most remarkable about this passage is the fact that the instigators immediately had recourse to the militia as an instrument of organization. The militia had always been one of those ambiguous entities, partly community institution, partly government imposition, but now the two aspects had been sundered, and the people's militia was being turned against the governor's militia.

A party of men set out along the concession roads of St Athanase that afternoon, stopping at each house to summon the male residents to their duty. Their procedure prefigured almost exactly the patriot militia call-ups that were to occur in many parishes a few weeks later when the armed clash with the British broke out. Unlike the later musters, frequently brutal because of the emergency conditions, this one was fairly casual. The band arrived at Louis Gélinoux's house at about 4 p.m. and asked him to join. Gélinoux was busy at the time but promised to meet the men later, and the recruiting party went on to the next farm without him.[36] He caught up with the others two hours later at the assigned rendezvous, Gagnon's tavern; some of his comrades had by then already drunk a good deal of rum. It should be noted that participation in this expedition was not entirely

35 ANQ, 1837, no. 259, déposition de Joseph Ouimet, 20 November 1837
36 Ibid., no. 260, déposition de Louis Gélinoux, 20 November 1837

optional. On the way from the tavern to Bessette's place, the party stopped at the home of a man who had failed to report and tried to induce him to come along; Captain Jean-Baptiste Arcand used the flat side of his sabre in a most persuasive way and in fact broke the weapon over the man's shoulder! Arcand was a fifty-five-year-old butcher from the village centre of St Athanase. He had resigned his commission in October 1837, but he continued to act as militia captain and was indeed the main leader and spokesman during the confrontation at Louis Bessette's house.[37] The captain of the parish's third company was Vincent Huot. He must have resigned his commission, but he showed no willingness to participate in the charivari. His company was therefore led by Dominique Lavallée, who seems to have been an habitant, though I have been unable to identify him with any certainty.

Were these habitants and artisans working entirely on their own? Remember that Louis Bessette turned over his commission, not to Captain Arcand, but to the notary Eusèbe Bardy. Was Bardy then the sinister guiding spirit behind Bessette's troubles? Or was his role more akin to that of a traditional charivari go-between, the respected local figure who handled the negotiations between persecutors and victims and then collected the fine and distributed the proceeds according to the agreement? The government and its supporters, naturally unwilling to believe that popular support for the Patriots could be deep and widespread, tended towards the former explanation. In these circles it was believed that the charivari and all other similar disturbances were carried out on orders from Bardy, as well as from a local shopkeeper, Charles Mongeon, and a physician, Joseph-François Davignon. The rank and file were seduced by rhetoric, so it was said, and bribed with gifts of 'grog, whiskey,

---

37 ANQM, Affaires Criminelles, déposition de François Ouimet, 20 November 1837; ibid., déposition de Jean-Baptiste Arcand, 7 December 1837; ibid., examen volontaire de Jean-Baptiste Arcand, 28 March 1838

bread and cheese.'[38] Across the Richelieu in L'Acadie county, Dr Cyrille Côté had a similar reputation, though his activities ranged over a wider area, and accordingly he was held responsible for many more charivaris than was Eusèbe Bardy.

If Bardy and his bourgeois cohorts pulled all the strings, it does seem strange that none of the members of the charivari party ever said so, even when they fell into the hands of the authorities and had every reason to deflect blame in the direction of their social superiors. In the days of fear and demoralization that followed the defeats of 1837, many plebeian prisoners did tend to plead that they had been coerced or manipulated by middle-class Patriots. Indeed, Jean-Baptiste Arcand, lying in the Montreal jail under charges of high treason, went so far as to testify that he had resigned his militia commission because Bardy and the innkeeper Sancerre had 'threatened' him. Yet he never claimed that they had ordered him to take action against Bessette; he merely suggested that Sancerre had been 'at the head' of the charivari, whereas all the other testimony indicates that Arcand himself had been leader on the spot.[39] It is true that Bardy and Côté actually accepted the commissions extorted by means of charivaris and transmitted them to Quebec City. But who in a Lower Canadian rural parish, besides the little elite of the professions, had the education, much less the experience with bureaucracy, to deal with formalities of this sort? Notaries and members of the Assembly would have been expected to handle such business whether they had initiated the affair or not.

On the other hand, when one looks beyond this specific example at the larger pattern of charivaris, it is true that a large number occurred over a fairly extensive area during the fortnight following the St Charles meeting. This fact does suggest some supra-local coordination of a sort that the bourgeois Patriots of the region would have been best equipped to provide. There is indeed no reason to doubt that Côté, Bardy, and the rest played

38 Ibid., deposition of John Hill Roe, 1 January 1838
39 Ibid., examen volontaire de Jean-Baptiste Arcand, 28 March 1838

a vital role in communicating news of wider political developments and in giving advice to their habitant neighbours on the timing and direction of demonstrations. Thus, while the conspiracy theory that would have events entirely manipulated by a scheming middle-class clique is to be rejected, there is no use in standing the interpretation on its head and insisting that the charivari campaign was the spontaneous work of the unaided masses. Though they did not control the rank and file, the local Patriot elites certainly did channel and direct its ire. It is important to note, however, that the actions against non-resigning officers and magistrates drew on the traditions of popular culture: the maypole and other customs connected with the militia, as well as the charivari.

What about this novel political use of the old charivari custom? One more example might help to illustrate the general phenomenon. This charivari occurred up the river from St Athanase, in the parish of St Valentin, four days before the attack on Louis Bessette. Dudley Flowers, the victim, recounted his ordeal two weeks later in a judicial deposition that is so rich in detail it bears quoting in extenso.

I am a Lieutenant in the Militia. On the twenty seventh day of October last in the afternoon the following persons viz. C.H.O. Côté, Olivier Hébert, L.M. Decoigne, Julien Gagnon, Amable Lamoureux and Jacob Bouchard, came to my house and demanded my commission as such Lieutenant to which I made answer that I would give it up to none but the governor of the Province. Doctor Côté said that if I did not give up my commission I would be sorry for it – to which Gagnon added, 'Si vous ne voulez pas vivre en haine avec nous autres rendez votre commission.' Upon this they went away. About eleven o'clock in the night of the same day the same persons returned – at least I have every reason to believe that they were the same persons ... They began yelling in the most frightful manner. They threw stones at my house and broke the greatest part of my windows. A large stone passed very near one of my children and would have killed him if it had struck him. Julien Gagnon who had seen my barn full of oats when he came in the day time told me that I should not have to thresh them unless I gave up my commission and also said that my grain, my house and outhouses would be burnt. I saw one of the mob go with a firebrand to my barn with the intention as I verily believe of setting fire to it. But it was in a damp state from the recent rain and the fire would not take.

On the night of the following day (28th October last) it might be about ten o'clock a masked mob, composed of about thirty or forty persons attacked my house in a similar manner, yelling and throwing stones as at first and repeatedly threatening to take my life and burn my property if I did not give up my commission ...

On the following day (Sunday) about seven in the evening, some sixty or seventy individuals attacked my house a third time in the same manner and with the same threats as on the former occasions but if possible with much more violence, beating kettles and pans, blowing horns, calling me a rebel, saying it would be the last time they would come as they would finish me in half an hour. They had in a short time with stones and other missiles broken in part of the roof of my house and boasted that it would soon be demolished. Fearing that such must inevitably be the case, I opened the door and told them that if four or five of their party would come in and give their names I would give them up my commission. Four or five of them did come in, disguised in the most hideous manner but refused to give their names. Finding that my life was actually in danger if I refused to comply with their requests, I handed them my commission. There were about fifteen of the last mentioned mob masked ...

The same persons have declared in my presence that they were determined to compel in the same manner all persons holding commissions from her Majesty to surrender them. One of these individuals told me boastingly that they had obtained no less than sixty two commissions in one day. I firmly believe that if Doctor Côté and some of the ringleaders were taken up and punished it would have the effect of alarming the others and keeping them quiet.[40]

40 ANQ, 1837, no. 146, deposition of Dudley Flowers, 3 November 1837. For accounts of similar charivaris, see the following depositions: ibid., no. 75 (Isaac Coote, 10 February 1838), no. 109 (Louis-Marc Decoigne, 17 February 1838), no. 122 (Pierre Gamelin, 9 November 1837), no. 90 (David Vitty,

To begin at the level of forms, notice that many of the features of the 'traditional' charivari were present in this episode: the nocturnal setting, the 'hideous' disguises, the raucous serenade of blaring horns, banging pots, and shouted insults. Even the lieutenant's initial encounter with the patriot delegation recalled the negotiating process by which charivari fines were normally set: the talks were businesslike and superficially polite, but with an undertone of menace, and they were held in daylight in an atmosphere that contrasted sharply with that of the charivari itself. Flowers resisted for some time the summons to resign, but following the example of an ordinary charivari crowd faced with a stubborn old widower, his attackers simply intensified their efforts, bringing more supporters and threatening ever more ferocious punishment on each successive evening. There were differences of course, notably the stone-throwing and the overt threats of serious violence.

That the patriots should have had recourse to the charivari custom at this juncture is not surprising. A coercive practice in which the aggressors' identities were concealed had obvious attractions at a time when arrest was still a real danger. 'The method concerted to raise a mob,' reported a L'Acadie county magistrate, 'is to pass along ringing a bell, when all are to turn out with their faces blackened, to prevent detection; under these

Rickinson Outtret, Robert Boys, and Thomas Henry, 5 November 1837), no. 103 (Nelson Mott, 6 December 1837), no. 128 (C.H. Lindsay, 8 November 1837), no. 87 (Antoine Bruneau, 17 December 1837), no. 314 (Jean-Baptiste Casavant, 12 November 1837), no. 115 (François St-Denis, 7 November 1837), no. 318 (Benjamin Goulet, 20 November 1837), no. 516 (Orange Tyler, 16 November 1837), no. 3557 (W.U. Chaffers, 9 November 1837), no. 158 (Ambroise Bédard, 10 November 1837); NA, LC Civil Secretary, 524: 11 (Loop Odell, 17 November 1837). Additional information appears in *Le Populaire*, 5 November 1837; *L'Ami du Peuple*, 8 November 1837; NA, LC Adjutant General, vol. 48, James McGillvary to David McCallum, 26 November 1837; ACESJQ, H.L. Amiot to Mgr Bourget, St Cyprien, 16 November 1837.

circumstances, no one is supposed to recognize another.'[41] This anonymity probably also served an equally important psychological purpose for the participants, that of overcoming inhibitions against aggressive behaviour. Indeed, the entire ritualistic package of charivari surely had this function. After all, Dudley Flowers was apparently a long-time resident of the community and he knew his attackers personally; even though he was a political enemy, the lieutenant was also a neighbour and therefore someone with whom it was important to maintain peaceful, though not necessarily cordial, relations. To turn on him with overt hostility would be to go against ingrained habits; masks and a familiar ritual may have made easier the transformation of neighbourly Jekylls into frightening Hydes.

Alcohol, another renowned solvent of inhibitions, seems to have been used for much the same reason. Many charivari parties, including the one that attacked Louis Bessette, met in taverns, where the members fortified themselves with doses of rum before setting off on their business, (usually a feature of traditional charivaris as well). Taverns were commonly used as meeting places for all sorts of purposes, and since the St Athanase innkeeper François Macé dit Sancerre was a leading instigator of the charivaris, it was only natural that men should gather at his public house. Nevertheless, it is clear that strong drink played its part on the evening of 2 November. Indeed, a repentant participant later tried to convince the examining magistrate that 'If he had not been under the influence of intoxicating drink, he would not have done such a thing.'[42] This was a clever ploy, playing upon the authorities' comforting illusion that the turmoil of 1837 resulted from the machinations of middle-class leaders who manipulated a benighted – indeed an intoxicated – peasantry. Yet these men had not gone to the tavern without a pur-

---

41 *BPP*, 9: 107, 'Letter from a Magistrate ... dated St. Valentine, 30 October 1837'
42 ANQM, Affaires Criminelles, déposition de François Ouimet, 20 November 1837 (author's translation)

pose, and they did not gulp down tumblers full of liquor merely to slake a thirst. The inebriation, like the masks, was, paradoxically enough, a sign of serious purpose: individuals who feared arrest and who no doubt entertained ambivalent feelings about the propriety of their enterprise prepared themselves for actions that seemed to be required for the common good.

The charivari custom offered more than simply a cover for fears and uncertainties. The turning over of a sum of money was the central event of a traditional charivari and much of the pageantry was designed to extort this gift from an unwilling giver. What a perfect vehicle for forcing loyalists to resign or, more precisely, to 'turn over their commissions' as the patriot mobs usually put it. Participants in the political charivaris of this stage of the drama of 1837 were rather blunt in declaring their intention to overcome opposition to their demands, and low-level violence, consisting mainly of stone-throwing, was common. There was little or no damage in most cases, though men who, like Dudley Flowers, resisted the initial attack, were likely to have their windows broken. The charivari mounted against Louis Bessette was the most destructive of any on record. This toll of broken glass and damaged roofs, though severe by the standards of ordinary pre-Rebellion charivaris, seems quite light when seen in the context of serious political crisis. Even more striking is the complete absence of personal injuries. When one places this record against the cracked heads and burned houses that resulted from, for example, the anti-Irish riots of contemporary New England and New Brunswick – not to mention the destruction wrought by crowd action in revolutionary episodes comparable to 1837 – the restraining influence of the charivari form becomes even more apparent.[43]

---

43 Ray Billington, *The Protestant Crusade 1800–1860: A Study of the Origins of American Nativism* (New York: Macmillan 1938); Scott W. See, 'The Orange Order and Social Violence in Mid-Nineteenth Century Saint John,' *Acadiensis* 13 (Autumn 1983): 68–92. See also Sean Wilentz, *Chants Democratic: New York City and the Rise of the American Working Class, 1788–1850* (New York: Oxford UP 1984), 264–5.

Of course Dudley Flowers was not impressed with the relative mildness of the treatment he received, and 'restrained' is the last word he would have used to describe it. Flowers truly thought his life and his property were in real and immediate peril, and though he was no coward, he was frightened enough to abandon his home and flee with his family to the city shortly after the events reported in his deposition. The charivari, 'political' or otherwise, was designed to be frightening, particularly in the eyes of those who resisted its edicts. Before 1837 coffins and skull-and-crossbones designs hinted at deadly intentions, but during the Rebellion the threats were much more explicit. Crowds attacked stubborn magistrates and officers with talk of arson and murder. Who could be sure they were simply bluffing when, as was often the case, masked revellers were seen carrying guns as well as firebrands? Lieutenant Flowers felt he had had a lucky escape and that only the damp weather had saved his grain-filled barn from the patriot torches. He might have been less worried had he known how many other loyalists had been similarly threatened without a single building being fired. The fact that he did believe himself to be in serious danger shows just how well the charivari served its theatrical purposes in the autumn of 1837 when dozens of local officials capitulated to the patriot mobs.

So far, I have been discussing the way in which the charivari form was applied for wholly novel political purposes during the campaign of late October/early November. Yet beyond the surface resemblances there were also elements of continuity with the past in the basic functions of the ritual. For example, the extortion of royal commissions seems to have been more than simply a means of destroying the government presence in the countryside; it also had meaning in the context of the specific relationship between an individual and the community of which he was a member. In other words, this forced gift played a role analogous to that of the ordinary charivari fine in signifying the giver's submission to the authority of the collectivity. But now the community as a whole and the Patriot cause were identified. Accordingly, some charivari victims were forced to shout 'Vive la liberté!' or to cheer for Papineau, as further proof of recognition of the incipient new régime. In accepting the victim's commission, the crowd gave its implicit assurance (sometimes it was clearly stated) that the charivari was at an end.[44]

There was a sense in which a non-resigning officer like Dudley Flowers was treated as a sinner, a contaminating influence in a community otherwise true to new civic ideals. The charivari worked so as to force him into the position of a penitent who had to purchase his reintegration into the fold at the price of a militia commission. Thus the admonition addressed to Lieutenant Flowers by the habitant Julien Gagnon during the preliminary visit to his home: resign your position, 'if you do not wish to live in a state of hatred with us.' No one expected him to become a militant patriot overnight, but he was being offered an opportunity to make peace with his offended neighbours. It is important to emphasize that, just as conventional charivaris were aimed not against general immorality but against a specific affront to the wedding ceremony, so Flowers was targeted for a particular offence rather than some general non-conformity. No one reproached Dudley on national or religious grounds. His 'crime' was not in professing Protestantism, in speaking English, or even in believing in the queen's majesty, but was simply in retaining a commission at a time when all good citizens had a duty to resign. The atonement required of this wayward soul was just as specific and limited as the 'sin' itself. He had merely to make a gesture – that of turning over his commission – that signified a renunciation of former 'treason' and an acceptance of the author-

---

44 There may have been an exception to this rule in Dudley Flowers's case; for a man approached him a few days after he had surrendered his commission and told him he must sign a copy of the resolutions passed at the St Charles meeting, failing which he would receive another visitation that night. Understandably intimidated, the lieutenant hastily packed up his family and left the parish, so it is impossible to know whether any attack really was planned. It seems likely that his visitor was an isolated individual playing a cruel joke, since all the other charivari accounts indicate that hostilities ceased once the commission changed hands.

ity of the patriot crowd. The emphasis was on the outward act indicating a transfer of allegiance without any further surrender of personal autonomy. This was made clear to another loyalist militia officer who proclaimed to the fifty blackened faces shouting for his resignation 'that if they compelled him to give up his commissions that they could not change his principles'; that is alright, came the sarcastic reply, we do not wish to alter your religion.[45]

Once the campaign was fully under way, many militia officers and magistrates could be persuaded to resign on the mere threat of a midnight visitation. 'The request was always made politely,' according to C.H.O. Côté, the physician designated by Lieutenant Flowers as the 'ringleader' in his area, 'it was only when this met with a refusal that violence and charivari ensued.'[46] It is impossible to know exactly how many charivaris occurred and how many resignations were secured by this means. The figure related to Dudley Flowers of sixty-two commissions surrendered in a single day is doubtless an exaggeration designed to break down the lieutenant's resistance. What is clear is that the campaign was

45 NA, LC Civil Secretary, vol. 524, no. 11, deposition of Loop Odell, 17 November 1837. This point needs to be qualified in the light of one isolated but glaring counter-example. In the parish of St Valentin, a French-Canadian convert to Protestantism was visited one night in mid-October by a party that 'made ludicrous noises with horns, bells, pans and other things'; after asking him if he was a patriot, the attackers 'required that he should renounce his religion and go back to the Roman Catholic religion.' ANQ, 1837, no. 135, deposition of Eloi Babin, 13 November 1837. Though scarcely an issue in other parts of Lower Canada, religion was a source of controversy in this one locality, where a group of Protestant Swiss missionaries was active. Local habitants tended to view the mission as an instrument of the government party, since it accepted money from the Montreal merchants and refused to take part in the patriot campaigns of 1837. Worse still, it was associated with the hated seigneur, W.P. Christie (see chap. 6, fn10).
46 ANQ, 1837, no. 122, déposition de Pierre Gamelin, 9 November 1837. Cf. ibid., no. 134, deposition of Albigence Waldo Robinson, 9 November 1837; no. 516, deposition of Orange Tyler, 16 November 1837; no. 1477, deposition of Samuel Bean, 12 November 1837.

a success. 'By means of this system of terrorism and midnight marauding,' reported Governor Gosford early in November, 'they have succeeded in overawing the well-disposed.'[47] Soon only a handful of militia officers and justices of the peace still held the queen's commission in the rural counties of the District of Montreal, and these individuals were isolated and beleaguered, bravely holding out for form's sake but virtually powerless.

It began with the government's attempt to suppress 'seditious assemblies,' followed by the campaign to remove disloyal officers and magistrates. These initiatives provoked resistance that four or five months later had effectively dismantled the established system of rural law enforcement; by October there was scarcely any government presence in the western countryside of Lower Canada. At the same time, new institutions of local government were beginning to emerge in defiance of the rule of the British empire. The elective magistracy and militia never had time to establish themselves firmly, but they were marked at conception by the notions of popular sovereignty and (masculine) democracy that were characteristic of the patriot movement as a whole. Moreover, the insurgent régimes derived their specific shape from the community traditions of rural French Canada.

The crisis was then moving in unanticipated directions, impelled by the clash of various agents and forces in rapidly changing circumstances. Governor Gosford played a part in the drama; so did Louis-Joseph Papineau and the other professional men of the Patriot party; the English-speaking businessmen of Montreal helped to shape events, as did the habitants of the French-Canadian countryside. It has to be said that the habitants, along with the artisans and cottagers of the Montreal District, were playing a more significant part as time passed. At the outset of agitation in May the initiative belonged to the middle-class politicians with their rallies, boycotts, conventions, and other strategies inspired by the history of the Thirteen Colonies. The

47 *BPP*, 9: 103, Gosford to Glenelg, 6 November 1837

role assigned to the grass-roots rural patriots had then been a rather passive supporting function. By the autumn of 1837 these activities were fading, as the focus shifted to charivaris, militia elections, and the transformation of parochial government, all of which brought events closer to home for the habitants in more ways than one. The fall campaign required them to take a much more active role and to draw upon cultural traditions and political experience reaching many generations into the past.

Even at this stage, however, the habitants were hardly an independent and a self-sufficient force. Village notaries and doctors remained indispensable local leaders, and Papineau and the radical press of Montreal continued to inspire peasants to see the struggle in larger than local terms. As in the past, the patriot movement brought together diverse elements – town and country, peasant and professional – and united them in a common anti-imperial cause. To be a patriot was, ideally, to overcome personal, class, and local interests and to join with others of goodwill to win independence and democracy for Lower Canada. Yet in spite of deliberate efforts to foster unity, there were bound to be divergent tendencies within the patriot alliance; for the outlook, background, and material interests of rural plebeians and urban bourgeois were quite dissimilar. Had the revolution not been snuffed out at such an early stage, these differences might well have led to serious conflict within the patriot camp. As it was, they remained largely submerged, revealing themselves clearly only where the troublesome issue of seigneurial tenure was concerned.

9

The question of property

'The whole French population of this Province are now united against the Government,' reported General Colborne in mid-November 1837. 'The habitans in all parts of the Province refuse to pay their rents; as they have been informed by the leaders of the Revolutionists that they are to have their deeds; and that the Seigniorial rights and tithes are to be abolished. Thus they are all interested in the success of the menaced revolt.'[1] Several other observers at the time of the insurrections and in the years following concurred with this assessment: opposition to feudal exactions, ecclesiastical as well as seigneurial, played a major role in mobilizing the peasantry. A La Prairie notary, testifying before a parliamentary inquiry in the early 1840s, referred to seigneurial dues in the following terms: 'They are so prejudicial to the inhabitants, that I can say with safety that, if we have had an insurrection in this country, we may assign the seigneurial tenure as the cause of it ... I asked them [the habitants] for the reasons they had ... They answered me that it was to bring down the seigniors, who were their ruin, and that by this means they hoped to do away with the seigniorial tenure.'[2]

1 Colborne to Bond Head, 14 November 1[
  R. Sanderson (Toronto: UTP 1957), 1: 22
2 Cited in Fernand Ouellet, *Lower Canada* [
  alism (Toronto: McClelland and Stewart
  in 1839, had a similar analysis of contin[
  rule: 'They object to the payment of the

Anyone steeped in the literature of Canadian or Quebec historiography is bound to find these contemporary observations troubling, since we have hardly been taught to view the Rebellion as in any significant sense anti-feudal. How could it have been so when French-Canadian seigneurialism was an empty shell? According to one interpretation (not mine: see chap. 1), rents and other exactions were too light to have provoked any serious discontent. Fernand Ouellet, on the other hand, recognizes the reality of seigneurial exploitation and the consequent development of tense relations between seigneurs and habitants. As far as the Rebellion is concerned, however, Ouellet argues that landlord-peasant tensions never erupted into the sort of open conflict that one might expect in a revolutionary situation. Instead, the anti-feudal discontent of the habitants was neutralized or diverted into harmless channels through the efforts of the bourgeois Patriots. The latter, led by the seigneur of Petite Nation, Louis-Joseph Papineau, appear in this version as the great defenders of seigneurial tenure and all the other archaic institutions of the ancien régime. Why would peasants struggling to throw off the feudal yoke make common cause with such firmly conservative 'revolutionists'? Ouellet's response is to insist that the habitants were simply deceived, fooled into taking up arms in a patriot cause that was dedicated, in spite of its liberationist propaganda, to the greater subjection of the peasantry. Had they been more aware of where their interests lay and who their friends were, the cultivators of Lower Canada would have sided with the pro-government English-speaking business community. After all, it was the Montreal merchants and their political allies who had consistently attacked seigneurial tenure and called for its 'abolition.'[3]

to the fees to the clergy for occasional services.' ANQ, 1837, no. 3731, Weatherall to Civil Secretary, 14 November 1839. See also Brian Young, *In Its Corporate Capacity: The Seminary of Montreal as a Business Institution, 1816–1876* (Montreal: McGill-Queen's UP 1986), 239 fn31.

3 Fernand Ouellet, *Economic and Social History of Quebec 1760–1850: Structures and Conjonctures* (Toronto: Gage 1980), 440–2, 585, 589–91, 596–9, and passim; Ouellet, *Lower Canada*, 150–1, 164–5, 182, 333, and passim

Even more than in the interpretation of the Rebellion in general, this view of the land tenure question requires the habitants to have been uncommonly idiotic and the middle-class Patriots exceptionally duplicitous. It rests, moreover, on an oversimplified conception of the conflict over seigneurialism, as if contemporaries lined up along one linear scale ranging from a pro-seigneurial to an anti-seigneurial pole. In fact, there were all sorts of possible positions on the subject, and accordingly the debate was complex and constantly shifting. Contemporaries naturally differed on the questions of what seigneurial tenure was in essence and what exactly the system's rules entailed. Were seigneurs treating censitaires the way they 'ought to'? If not, would it be possible to rectify the situation by 'reforming' the law (whatever that might imply) or by improving regulatory enforcement? Or should seigneurialism be done away with? And, if so, what property régime would replace it and how exactly would the transition be arranged? Would seigneurs be compensated for their lost privileges? By whom? Even when they did not say so explicitly, people in the 1830s knew perfectly well that there would be winners and losers in any alteration of the land law, depending on what changes were made and how they were implemented.

THE DEBATE OVER SEIGNEURIAL TENURE

The different classes of Lower Canadian society tended, as one might expect, to develop divergent positions on the land question. If we begin with those most directly concerned – the habitants – we find virtually no pronouncements, positive or negative, on 'the seigneurial system' or 'feudal tenure' as such. While abstractions of this sort provoked endless debates within the 'educated classes,' the peasants were interested in more concrete realities: rents, monopolies, tithes, and the priests and seigneurs who exacted them. The distinction may sound obvious, but it deserves to be stressed. Habitant-censitaires naturally wanted to keep feudal dues low and seigneurial prerogatives limited. They were also keenly aware that the seigneurs' interests in these matters were diametrically opposed to their own.

Certainly the habitants 'accepted' seigneurial tenure in a certain sense; that is to say, they were not constantly in arms against their exploiters and demanding an end to all feudal privileges. It was partly a matter of habit and custom; until the late eighteenth century, when English tenure was introduced into some parts of the province, people would have had difficulty imagining an alternative to seigneurialism. And even if they had yearned to overthrow their landlords, the Church taught them that any attempt would be immoral, and, more compellingly, common sense told them it would be futile and dangerous. Such considerations did not prevent peasants in other countries from rising up in anti-feudal jacqueries. They usually occurred in desperate circumstances, however, and there was never anything desperate about the situation of the Lower Canadian habitants. Feudal exactions, though bearing down on the peasantry with increasing weight in the early nineteenth century, had always been less burdensome than those prevalent in most parts of early modern Europe. Moreover, the government did not pile direct taxes on top of seigneurial dues. The French-Canadian habitants were indeed far less under the thumb of landlords than were their counterparts in countries like Ireland, Poland, or Mexico, but this does not mean that they were consequently grateful to be living under a comparatively mild feudal régime and happy to support their seigneurs.

The Canadian peasantry did sometimes give indications that seigneurial exactions constituted an unwelcome and not entirely legitimate imposition. On occasion, the point was made quite explicitly. When a seigneurial mill on the island of Montreal burned down in 1716, the settlers declared the accident the work of divine providence: 'Such practices [mill monopoly] were fine in France,' they announced, 'but not in a country that they had themselves conquered at the risk of their lives.' Even under the French régime, when rents were especially moderate, the record contains traces of numerous local disputes over specific grievances. Here the censitaires tore down the fences on the seigneur's pasture; there they routinely contravened a timber monopoly or contested banal restrictions. Everywhere they avoided paying rents whenever possible. When the Americans occupied Canada during the revolutionary war and temporarily eliminated the colony's judicial and administrative apparatus, habitants immediately stopped paying all rents and tithes. The government sent seigneurs to call out men for militia service against the invaders, but many rural communities responded by mounting fierce attacks on the loyalist seigneurs.[4]

In the remote seigneurie of Murray Bay a dispute over fishing rights pitted John Nairne against his censitaires in the 1790s. The seigneur found himself quite unable to overcome the resistance of habitants like Joseph Villeneuve: 'I only mentioned the subject very discretly the other day to that man but found that this was nothing to him, he roard and bellowed and set me quite at defyance ... he acknowledges no law nor government and in his own person he is not weak.'[5] Sometimes habitants sued their seigneurs, but not often, since they had few illusions about the bias of the judicial system and the likely result should they take a seigneur to court. 'They are in general too timid,' wrote a sympathetic country priest, 'and they are always afraid of losing against their seigneurs; and when they have been reduced to beggary [by legal fees], who will listen to them if they have no money to offer. "The lawyers are in cahoots with the seigneurs," they say, "and we will end up being the dupes of both." '[6]

The contretemps at Murray Bay was caused by the seigneur's

4 Louise Dechêne, *Habitants et marchands de Montréal au XVIIe siècle* (Paris and Montreal: Plon 1974), 258 (author's translation); S.D. Clark, *Movements of Political Protest in Canada, 1640–1840* (Toronto: UTP 1959), 92–102; Sylvie Dépatie, Mario Lalancette, Christian Dessureault, *Contributions à l'étude du régime seigneurial canadien* (Montreal: Hurtubise 1987), 80; Young, *In its Corporate Capacity*, 46–7

5 Mario Lalancette, 'La Malbaie et la révolution française,' in *Le Canada et la Révolution française*, ed. Pierre H. Boulle and Richard A. Lebrun (Montreal: Centre universitaire d'études européennes 1989), 48

6 Bellenger to Plessis, 23 November 1825, quoted in Jean-Claude Robert, 'L'activité économique de Barthélémy Joliette et la fondation du village d'Industrie (Joliette) 1822–1850' (MA thesis, Université de Montréal, 1971), 82–3 (author's translation)

attempt to institute new fishing regulations, and in fact most instances of censitaire complaints and resistance were a result of innovations. Like other peasantries, the habitants of French Canada would put up with customary impositions for years, but they often reacted fiercely to unprecedented burdens, even seemingly minor ones. They were in that sense 'traditionalists,' although that term implies an irrational attachment to past practice which is somewhat misleading in this context. The habitants never objected to any change that diminished the seigneurial burden, but they had perfectly sound reasons for opposing the rachet mechanism by which seigneurs tightened their grip on the peasant economy, adding new impositions without discarding old ones. Given this stance, conflict naturally boiled up in the nineteenth century as more exacting styles of estate management became increasingly popular among seigneurs (see above, chap. 2). It was at this time that the Patriot-dominated House of Assembly became known as an official body to which complaints could be addressed and from which, it was hoped, relief could be obtained.

Petitions relating to feudal tenure became particularly numerous in the 1830s.[7] Since most were probably drawn up by the local professional men who formed the core of the Patriot party, they cannot be regarded as the unmediated expressions of habitant sentiment. However, they were accompanied by long lists of signatures, and their tenor seems for the most part in keeping with peasant concerns as revealed by behaviour of the sort discussed above. Few of the petitions call for the outright extinction of seigneurial privilege; instead they demand legislation to prohibit certain specified 'abuses' and to curb allegedly 'illegal' exactions. Some modern commentators have taken this as

7 Colette Michaud, 'Les censitaires et le régime seigneurial canadien (1791–1854): étude des requêtes anti-seigneuriales' (MA thesis, University of Ottawa, 1982); Micheline Clément, 'Le discours patriote: égalitarisme agraire ou projet de démocratie de petits producteurs' (MA thesis, Université du Québec à Montréal 1984), 94–112

evidence of a strictly 'reformist' attitude that eschewed the fundamental issues.[8] Yet if we look closely at the actual 'abuses'
denounced in the petitions and the 'reforms' they call for, we
find that they are based on a very narrow conception of legitimate seigneurial privilege, one that was justified with reference
to a particular version of the history of Canadian land law and
that was radically at odds with the beliefs and practices of the
seigneurs as a class.

Consider, for instance, the complaints voiced in many petitions
about the iniquities of the banalité. They were particularly frequent in petitions from seigneuries where there was no grist mill
or where the banal mill was not in reliable working order; in
many such cases seigneurs would still not permit anyone else to
set up a rival mill in their fief. Petitioners from the Richelieu
valley therefore proposed that a law be passed exempting censitaires from all feudal dues as long as their seigneur failed to
provide a grist mill in good working order.[9] This proposal may
not have been overtly revolutionary, but had it been acted upon,
it would have transformed the banalité from a privilege to an
obligation for seigneurs.[10]

Another common grievance arose from the refusal on the part
of some nineteenth-century seigneurs to grant uncleared lands to
prospective settlers. A related complaint targeted those who
exacted an initial payment from would-be censitaires. The custom
through the seventeenth and eighteenth centuries had been for
seigneurs to grant lots under perpetual leases, but at no initial
charge, to all comers. This was a policy that corresponded to
rational self-interest at a time when a seigneur's prosperity was

8 For example, Michaud, 'Les censitaires'
9 Ibid., 181
10 Citing French-régime legislation ordering seigneurs to build grist mills on
   pain of losing their monopoly rights, some might argue that the banalité
   indeed had been an obligation for seigneurs since 1686. The fact is, however, that the rule was not enforced. Allan Greer, *Peasant, Lord, and Mer-*
   chant: Rural Society in Three Quebec Parishes, 1740–1840 (Toronto: UTP 1985),
   130

directly related to the number of rent-paying peasants settled on his estate. A royal edict of 1711, designed to stimulate the development of the colony, made it a legal requirement for seigneurs to grant lands freely, even though they seem to have been doing so anyway.[11] As far as I can tell, this rule was not enforced under the French régime (there was no need), and after the conquest the courts had doubts about its validity.[12] Nevertheless, petitioning censitaires of the 1820s and 1830s were inclined to elevate the obligation to grant lands at no initial charge into a central and time-honoured element of Canadian land law. From the point of view of many seigneurs, especially the English speakers, it was simply a matter of good estate management to withhold grants of land in the uncleared domain at a time when trends in the real estate market indicated that it could be alienated under much better terms in the future. But the habitants clearly considered this strategy unjust and illegal. Above all, it was in conflict with a fundamental right of the Canadian peasantry: 'The right and privilege of choosing a forested lot and of settling on it, was reserved exclusively and guaranteed to the inhabitants of this country, provided that they thereafter pay to the seigneur the legal rent of the country, and nothing more.'[13] For the government to permit seigneurs to keep the domain or to

11 W.B. Munro, ed., *Documents Relating to the Seigniorial Tenure in Canada, 1598–1854* (Toronto: Champlain Society 1908), 91–4. R.C. Harris points out that this provision of the Edict of Marly was quite redundant and arose from the fact that 'the king and his advisors did not altogether understand the Canadian situation.' *The Seigneurial System in Early Canada: A Geographical Study* (Madison: University of Wisconsin Press 1968), 106. Note that a subsequent document, 'Royal Instructions concerning the Enforcement of the Arrêts of Marly,' makes it clear that the French government's main aim was to ensure that lots be confiscated from censitaires who failed to reside on them and develop them. Munro, ed., *Documents*, 166–7
12 Evelyn Kolish, 'Changements dans le droit privé au Québec/Bas-Canada entre 1760 et 1840: attitudes et réactions des contemporains' (PH D thesis, Université de Montréal, 1980), chap. 5
13 Beauharnois petition, 15 December 1832, quoted in Clément, 'Le discours patriote,' 110

charge money for concessions would be 'to allow royal munificence to degenerate into land speculation.'[14]

Even more deeply entrenched among habitants was the belief that French-régime legislation had set a strict limit on the rate of seigneurial rent. A parliamentary commission in 1843, 'aware of the prevalent belief that there existed an edict fixing the rate of concession generally at a certain specific amount,' searched the records thoroughly without finding any trace of such a regulation. Sympathetic to the censitaires, the commissioners clearly wanted to find a justification for this 'prevalent belief,' but the closest they could come was in citing an article of the Edict of 1711, which empowered the Intendant of New France, in a case where a seigneur refused to grant land to a settler, to make the concession himself 'on the same conditions as were imposed on the other concession in the seigniories.'[15] Without necessarily referring to any particular legislation, post-conquest petitions tended to take for granted the notion that the rents exacted on newly granted lands could not exceed the rates established under the French régime in the oldest sections of a given seigneurie. The habitants and their spokesmen conveniently forgot – if they were ever aware of it – that rents set on new concessions had begun creeping up well before the conquest, and the government had done nothing to restrain the seigneurs.[16] They maintained that it was patently unfair for some censitaires to pay up to ten times the annual rent owed by their neighbours – for lots of the

14 'Pétition de divers censitaires possesseurs de terres en roture dans la Province, concernant la tenure en fief et seigneurie,' 1825, quoted in ibid., 106
15 'Report of the Commissioners appointed to Inquire into the State of the Laws and other Circumstances connected with the Seigniorial Tenure, as it obtains in that part of the Province of Canada heretofore Lower Canada, March 29, 1843,' in Documents, ed. Munro, 332–3
16 Louise Dechêne, 'L'évolution du régime seigneurial au Canada: le cas de Montréal aux XVIIe et XVIIIe siècles,' Recherches sociographiques 12 (May-August 1971): 152; Louis Lemoine, 'Une société seigneuriale: Longueuil: méthode, sources, orientations' (MA thesis, Université de Montréal, 1975), 72–4, 145; Greer, Peasant, Lord, and Merchant, 123

same size and quality and in the same seigneurie – simply because they had been granted a century later. This was not only inequitable, it was illegitimate, according to the habitant version of historically validated justice. Since the law courts did not recognize this position, petitioners called upon the House of Assembly to pass measures that would 'restrain the cupidity of the Seigniors.'[17]

Petitions from rural seigneuries complained of a variety of different 'abuses,' though the most common grievances concerned rents, refusal of free grants, and mill monopoly. These were, in most cases, specific complaints about particular seigneurs; rarely was seigneurial tenure criticized as a whole; and the remedies called for were expressed in the conservative language of restoration. But look at the vision of the seigneurial tenure to be 'restored': if the habitants had their way, seigneurs would have no control over the disposal of lands in their domains, nor would they be able to determine the terms of tenure under which censitaires would hold their farms. A seigneur would then be reduced to the status of a functionary, a land-agent-cum-tax-collector. He/she would not be what most seigneurs considered themselves, that is, a landlord, a person with a proprietary interest in a particular territory.

In putting forward such a denatured version of feudal tenure, the peasantry was not being 'dishonest'; it was not fabricating claims out of thin air. Rather, it was behaving as subordinate classes subject to a hegemonic relationship often do: they interpret ambiguities in custom, law, and ideology in ways that minimize their burdens and maximize their rights. In this case there was the ambiguous thrust of government policy under the French régime. Desirous of endowing an aristocracy with estates that would eventually provide revenues appropriate to its station, the state also wished to prevent the short-sighted greed of seigneurs from jeopardizing the long-term prospects for the agrarian development of the fledgling colony. The habitants dwelt entirely on

17 Petition of the censitaires of Beauharnois (1832), *JHALC*, 1832–3, 161

the second preoccupation as if the colonial régime's concern to protect censitaire interests was permanent and basic, rather than contingent on the peculiar circumstances of the period. Likewise, and more fundamentally, French-Canadian settlers consistently interpreted the ambiguous conception of proprietorship inherent in seigneurial tenure in pro-censitaire ways. Whereas we might see it as a defining feature of feudal land law that peasant and landlord share the various attributes of ownership over a given piece of territory, the habitants made it clear by their words and actions that the land belonged rightfully to those who cleared and tilled it (or to those who bought or inherited it from their original occupiers). Rents and other dues might be grudgingly allowed, but there was no recognition that seigneurs had a legitimate claim to the title of proprietor. (It might be noted in passing that this theory left no room for any concept of aboriginal title, but that is another story.) Rather, it was the habitants who owned the land they occupied and who even had a rightful claim to the unconceded forest tracts still held 'in trust' by their seigneurs.

Such a notion of habitant rights naturally clashed with the pretensions of seigneurs. Friction increased through the first half of the nineteenth century, as demographic and economic circumstances favoured more active styles of estate management and brought issues of rents and domain lands to the fore. The presence of numerous English seigneurs – just as impatient as the habitants with the ambiguities of feudal tenure, but in a very different way – only made matters worse. Conflict seemed to be coming to a head in the 1830s: seigneurs (at least some of them) were becoming more intransigent, hard-pressed peasants were experiencing unprecedented difficulty paying feudal dues and finding land for their children, and the liberationist rhetoric of the Patriot movement was encouraging a critical attitude to established inequities. The situation favoured a more global approach to the problem: habitants began to realize that local grievances stemming from the particular 'abuses' of specific seigneurs were symptoms of a more basic injustice. Alexis de Tocqueville noticed this when he visited Lower Canada in 1831: 'We have perceived in our conversations with the people of this country a deep hatred and jealousy of the seigneurs.'[18]

No doubt hatred was particularly strong in the Upper Richelieu-L'Acadie region where, as mentioned in chapter 2, rents were so high. This was also the area – no coincidence here – where charivaris were most numerous in 1837 and where the rebels placed their headquarters during the insurrection of November 1838. The radicalization of the region was not instantaneous; it proceeded by degrees, spurred on by the agitation of Doctor C.-H.-O. Côté and by the developing confrontation with local seigneurs. A crisis of sorts occurred two years before the Rebellion when De Léry and several other fiefs in the region passed by inheritance to William Plenderleath Christie. The testamentary executors of the Christie estates attempted to take stock of the properties and rationalize collection procedures. Invoking a clause common in post-conquest concessions that required censitaires to present their title deeds whenever the seigneurie changed hands, the executors tried to force each habitant to sign a notarized IOU for the total of all outstanding arrears. The peasantry of L'Acadie reacted with alarm to such a step, since the notes, unlike book debts, were subject to interest and since they would make litigation more feasible. Initially, resistance took the form of mass evasion: when the seigneur's agents went calling at farmhouses, they never found anyone at home.[19] Soon there was talk of more active measures, such as a concerted campaign of withholding rents, to be followed by armed resistance in the event of lawsuits or of court-ordered seizure of property. There is no indication that matters ever actually went so far – whether the seigneur or the censitaires relented is not clear – but there is no doubt that habitant-seigneur relations were further embittered in L'Acadie after 1835.

18 Quoted in Ouellet, *Lower Canada*, 181
19 *JHALC*, 1836, app. EEE; Françoise Noel, *The Christie Seigneuries: Estate Management and Settlement in the Upper Richelieu Valley, 1760–1854* (Montreal: McGill-Queen's UP 1992), 60

Hostility to seigneurial dues and privileges as such became pronounced, and political meetings gave unusual prominence to anti-feudal themes.[20] A shift in habitant consciousness from opposition to specific 'abuses' to a rejection of the basic tenets of seigneurial tenure was well under way in this part of Lower Canada by 1837.

If the habitants of Lower Canada were increasingly unwilling by the 1830s to bear the burden of seigneurial exactions and more and more inclined to view them as illegitimate impositions, why then did they turn a cold shoulder to those who had been campaigning for years to have the whole 'feudal system' done away with? The English-speaking business community was consistently critical of seigneurial tenure, singling it out as the most barbaric element of a generally anachronistic French system of civil law. Urban merchants and their allies in government were particularly critical of the lods et ventes which amounted to a tax on improvements, and they considered the tenure generally to be an obstacle to economic development. Their favoured solution was a wholesale conversion of all seigneurial lands to the British tenure of 'free and common soccage.' 'Free' tenure, 'free' men, and 'free' enterprise were the prime ingredients in their vision of a reformed Lower Canada.[21]

It seems strange that several of the leading critics of feudal tenure themselves were seigneurs. Indeed, the most influential exponent in the 1820s of the conversion to common soccage was Edward ('Bear') Ellice, proprietor of Beauharnois, a large and valuable fief near Montreal.[22] One of Lower Canada's greatest landlords, Ellice was also one of the most detested of seigneurs. He was notorious for jacking up rents to unprecedented heights,

20 *Vindicator*, 19 July 1836
21 See, for example, Donald Creighton, *The Empire of the St. Lawrence* (Toronto: Macmillan 1956), 114, 273
22 André LaRose, 'La seigneurie de Beauharnois, 1729–1867: les seigneurs, l'espace et l'argent' (PH D thesis, University of Ottawa, 1987), 195–246. For further information on Edward Ellice, see *DCB*, 9: 233–9.

while exacting mutation fines – which he himself denounced as odious – with exceptional vigour. Most maddening to local habitants was his refusal to grant lots in the extensive unconceded domain of Beauharnois. It was actually his agents who carried out these affronts to seigneurial custom, since Ellice was an absentee landlord who spent most of his life in Great Britain, though he did visit Canada several times. His father had amassed a huge fortune as a fur trader and land speculator in colonial New York and Montreal, leaving Beauharnois and other valuable properties in North America to Edward.

Bear Ellice established himself in London as a leading merchant specializing in colonial commerce; he was a central figure in the fur trade. A liberal Whig member of parliament, he was also a man of considerable political influence. He was regarded as the House's resident expert on British North American affairs and successive governments sought his disinterested views on the subject from the 1820s to the era of Confederation. His advice naturally tended to reflect a commercial point of view; it was decidedly unfavourable to French-Canadian nationality and nationalism. Ellice played a major role in framing a bill, the Canada Tenures Act of 1825, by which the imperial parliament made it possible for seigneurial property to be commuted to free and common soccage.[23] This legislation proved very controversial in Lower Canada, and because the commutation was so complicated and costly, few seigneurs availed themselves of the opportunity to change their tenure. Edward Ellice nevertheless set the example, and by 1832 he had converted to soccage tenure the portion of Beauharnois (about half) not yet granted to censitaires. In the rest of the seigneurie, landholders had the option of commuting their individual lots, but only on payment of a lump sum to compensate the seigneur for lost future revenues; virtual-

---

23 Arthur G. Doughty and Norah Story, eds, *Documents Relating to the Constitutional History of Canada, 1819–1828* (Ottawa: King's Printer 1935), 291–3.
Note that this bill clarified and complemented an earlier piece of legislation to the same effect also passed at Ellice's behest in 1822. See ibid., 118–19.

ly no one could raise the required capital, and so the settled half of Beauharnois remained a seigneurie.[24]

As for the liberated half of the Ellice domain, the area now under free and common soccage: in what sense was it 'free'? These lands were certainly not free and gratis to settlers. The seigneurial agent put uncleared farm lots on the market for about £100 each, double the cost of land in the Eastern Townships and far beyond the resources of local habitants.[25] Accordingly, the censitaires of Beauharnois gained no measure of freedom; for they were now deprived of the possibility of establishing succeeding generations on uncleared lands close to home where relatives could aid them in getting a start in life. The only sense in which freedom had anything to do with this commutation was in so far as it concerned Edward Ellice and his estates. Instead of being saddled with grants in perpetuity with unchangeable terms of tenure, the seigneur could now rent portions of the commuted territory under limited-term leases that would allow him to adjust rents with changing economic circumstances and evict unsatisfactory tenants. Ellice preferred the option of ridding himself of future administration costs by simply selling lots once and for all. He was perfectly free to do so, since the act of commutation released him from any lingering moral or legal obligation to make his domain lands available to settlers at limited customary rents. 'Free' tenure is a fine thing so long as you own land. What was crucial in this transformation was not so much the theoretical differences between French and English land law as the fact that the unconceded domain of Beauharnois was

24 A similar pattern emerged in the rural seigneuries of the Sulpician order between 1840 and 1859. In this case, post-Rebellion legislation permitted censitaires to take the initiative in converting their holdings to free and common soccage regardless of what the seigneurs did with their domain. The Sulpicians held the island of Montreal as a fief, and in the city large numbers of censitaires commuted. In the agrarian seigneuries of St Sulpice and Two Mountains, however, only twenty-seven lots – none of them held by habitants – were commuted. Young, *In Its Corporate Capacity*, 101

25 LaRose, 'La seigneurie de Beauharnois,' 411–15

recognized as the unrestricted property of the seigneur, not an endowment for future generations of habitants.

This was just the sort of arrangement that Bear Ellice considered right and proper, as well as being personally advantageous. His views, and the attitude behind the Canada Tenures Act, correspond exactly to those of the Constitutionalist businessmen of Montreal and Quebec City.[26] They objected to seigneurial tenure more because of the restrictions it placed on large property than because of the burdens it placed on the small property of subsistence farmers. Viewing the subject through English and commercial eyes, they naturally tended to see the seigneur as a landlord, the ultimate proprietor of all the lands in his fief. Accordingly, their plans for 'abolishing feudal tenure' meant doing away with the ambiguities of ownership inherent in seigneurialism essentially at the expense of censitaire rights. The simpler, absolute, and individual form of property they had in mind for Lower Canada was designed to facilitate commercial transactions in real estate. Given the merchants' fundamental commitment to existing property rights, they assumed that the peasantry would gain relief from rents, mutation fines, and other exactions only on compensating the seigneurs fully for all lost revenues. Commutation thus implied no economic gain for the censitaires but a serious reduction in their access to new lands.

It is no wonder that the merchants' program for tenure reform commanded no support in the French-Canadian countryside. Both habitants and businessmen may have been anti-feudal in 1837, but their positions on seigneurialism were similar only in the most superficial way. The respective interests of these two classes, as well as their different conceptions of the problem and its solution, placed them at opposite poles. Occupying something like an intermediate position – though a complex and shifting one – were the

26 Kolish, 'Changements dans le droit privé,' passim. See also the terms in which feudal tenure was criticized at the loyalist meeting at Montreal, 23 October 1837: Jean-Paul Bernard, ed., *Assemblées publiques, résolutions et déclarations de 1837–1838* (Montreal: VLB 1988), 242, 254–5.

professional men and politicians of the Patriot party. The Patriots' initial reaction to English attacks on seigneurialism was strictly nationalistic. They were infuriated by the Canada Tenures Act, not only because as an act of the imperial parliament it represented an infringement on the rights of the colonial Assembly, but also because it appeared to be part of an objectionable program of anglicization. The bill did stipulate that in areas commuted to free and common soccage English civil law generally (including mortgage, inheritance, and so on) would prevail in place of French law. Indeed, Edward Ellice and other supporters of the measure were quite explicit in their hopes that the progressive conversion of land tenure would encourage British immigration and promote the eradication of French-Canadian culture.

In reaction, the Patriots tended to adopt the stance of defenders of the seigneurial regime, an unjustly denigrated element of a national tradition under siege. The Ninety-Two Resolutions of 1834, for example, devote eight whole paragraphs to the iniquities of the Tenures Act, scarcely recognizing any problems with seigneurialism. 'The Seigniorial charges may have been found burdensome in certain cases,' they admit, while hastening to add that this situation was 'chiefly by reason of the want of adequate means of obtaining the interference of the Colonial Government and of the Courts of Law, to enforce the ancient Law of the Country in that behalf.'[27] Spokesmen for the Papineau party were on stronger ground when they counter-attacked the proponents of English tenure, pointing to the downtrodden condition of agricultural tenants in the British Isles. Of course there is a difference between tenure, the legal rules defining real property, and the actual distribution of land ownership in a given society (It was the concentration of property in a few hands that was so injurious to the tenantry of England and, above all, of Scotland and Ireland), a distinction the Patriots tended to gloss over. They did argue, however, that common soccage tended to facilitate the concentration of property. And, closer to home, they could draw attention to the record of the Eastern Townships of Lower Canada, where would-be settlers had difficulty getting access to free and common soccage land, owing to the effects of speculative holdings, government patronage grants, and crown and clergy reserves. These points made admirable grist for the mills of partisan debate, but it did not provide much in the way of material relief for the French-Canadian peasantry.

The Patriots' fondness for blistering attacks on the anglicizing and interfering British parliament may have had something to do with the fact that beyond this aspect of the issue there was little consensus within the party on what to do about feudal exactions. The politicians were well aware of the mounting tensions between seigneurs and censitaires. It was becoming impossible after 1830 to ignore the growing stream of anti-seigneurial petitions. Consequently, many bourgeois Patriots became convinced that 'reforms' were needed to suppress the 'abuses' that were bringing 'the ancient Law of the Country' into disrepute. A series of parliamentary inquiries was held, witnesses were heard, reports were issued, and remedial measures were discussed, but no concrete action resulted, largely because there was so little agreement on what was wrong and how it should be made right.

Some members of the Assembly wanted to legislate a maximum level for seigneurial rents; others wished to force seigneurs to grant concessions to all applicants on traditional terms; and some even proposed the abolition of the lods et ventes as an obstacle to economic development. These were major changes (or at least they would have been had they been put in practice), and they were quite unacceptable to the more socially conservative Patriots, including, most notably, the seigneur of Petite-Nation. It appears that the powerful influence of Papineau, who was convinced that seigneurial tenure was a fine democratic institution marred only by the avarice of a handful of English seigneurs, effectively checked the impulse to reform.[28] But Papineau was not the only obstacle to remedial action: even the more radical Patriot politicians, though anxious to relieve the burden borne by Lower Canada's censitaires, were reluctant to inflict any injury upon the seigneurs. Their bourgeois squeamishness about

28 Kolish, 'Changements dans le droit privé,' chap. 7, 9

the sacred rights of (large-scale) property would eventually separate them clearly from the habitants whose friendship they sought. For the time being, however, the latter seem to have been impressed with the concern and good will expressed by the liberal professionals of the Assembly. In some cases their faith was not misplaced.

AGRICOLA AND JEAN-PAUL

The young doctor who represented L'Acadie county in the Lower Canadian Assembly was coming around to a more clearly anti-feudal position in the years prior to the outbreak of rebellion. C.-H.-O. Côté lived in the village of Napierville, in the middle of the Christie seigneuries, the very area where habitant indignation was boiling over by 1835. Consequently, the hand-wringing that had become the Patriots' preferred response to seigneurial problems was beginning to wear thin here. In any case, Côté was not one for compromise or for mincing words, and so he did not hesitate to come down on the side of the agrarian censitaires. He mounted a virulent campaign against rents, mutation fines, and seigneurs, and just for good measure he lashed out against the tithes and priests as well. A scandalized local curé reported that Côté was touring the region delivering rabble-rousing speeches to parishioners after Sunday mass: 'What attracted the favourable attention of his listeners ... were the following words, uttered in emphatic tones: "I will work with all my strength to abolish seigneurial exactions; for, as you know, they weigh you down, they are severe and onerous." '[29] Note that the doctor spoke of doing away with 'seigneurial *exactions*,' not simply the *abuses* that exercised his more moderate Patriot colleagues. Côté took up what was essentially the peasant position and aimed his rhetorical darts squarely at seigneurial privilege as a whole.

There seems to be no doubt that C.-H.-O. Côté had a combative and anti-authoritarian personality that led him to challenge

---

29 *L'Ami du Peuple*, 2 September 1835 (author's translation)

the government, the seigneurs, the Catholic clergy, and even the Patriot elite. Yet it is just as important to recognize how much his radicalism on the land issue owed to the local situation and to the influence of his aroused constituents. Côté may have expressed, channelled, and sustained the anti-feudal sentiment of the local peasantry, but he did not create it; that work fell to the gouging seigneurs of L'Acadie. The censitaires of the region had been submitting petitions on the subject for at least two years before the young doctor moved to Napierville in 1833.[30] It is clear, moreover, that other local leaders, notably the habitant Julien Gagnon, played an important part in organizing the anti-seigneurial resistance.

Nevertheless, it was Dr Côté who injected the radical position on land tenure into public discussions at the provincial level. On the very eve of the Rebellion, between December 1836 and March 1837, he published his views in a series of letters to the editor of *La Minerve*. In so doing, Côté broke with Patriot decorum, which required such controversial issues to be debated in private so as not to 'confuse the electorate' or provide ammunition to political enemies eager to portray the Patriots as dangerous revolutionaries hostile to property and order. He softened the shock somewhat by adopting the persona of 'a poor farmer' and signing his missives with the pseudonym, 'Agricola.' But no one in the know would have been fooled; for the prose of this supposedly simple rustic was liberally sprinkled with Latin quotations and literary allusions.[31] Agricola's letters provoked several responses, both positive and negative. Among the latter was a series of critical

---

30 Gendron, 'Tenure seigneurial,' 120–34; *DCB*, 7: 208–11
31 *La Minerve*, 26 December 1836; 5 January, 12 January, 30 January, 13 February, 2 March, 9 March 1837. Although no one has ever attributed these communications to Côté, the identity of Agricola seems undeniable. Dated 'comté de Lacadie,' the letters are written in a verbose style all too familiar to anyone who has ploughed through the doctor's correspondence. What clinches the identification is the fact that the gist of Agricola's arguments corresponds exactly to Côté's testimony before a committee of the House of Assembly in March 1836. See *JHALC*, 1835–6, app. EEE. (Quotations in the pages that follow are as translated by the author.)

comments signed 'Jean-Paul,' the pseudonym of Amury Girod, pretending, like Côté, to be a simple cultivator. Of Swiss origin, Girod was a gentleman-farmer, writer, and member of the Assembly; his mission was to set out the mainstream Patriot position on seigneurial tenure.[32]

Côté begins his 'Agricola' letters with inspiring quotations from the American Revolution condemning privilege in all its forms. The time has come, he announces, to recognize the seigneurial elements of French-Canadian law as fundamentally unfair, aristocratic, and anti-democratic: 'The exclusive privileges accorded to seigneurs in this country ... are incompatible with liberty and with the natural rights of man ... These exclusive privileges can only give birth to monopoly and the oppression and degradation of the people.' This republican language, with its moral-political preoccupations, its tendency to oppose rights and liberty with monopoly and privilege, continues throughout. Côté does detail at length the economic woes of the censitaires of L'Acadie county, subjected as they were to burdensome rents, entry fees, and mutation fines. He also denounces seigneurialism in instrumental terms for being 'detrimental to the development of the commerce and the industry of the country.' Yet his primary objection to the tenure is not, as it was for merchants such as Bear Ellice, an economic one. What arouses the indignation of Agricola is rather the power that it confers on some citizens at the expense of others. (The idea that other forms of property might lend themselves to unequal political leverage seems far from Côté's thoughts.) In this discourse 'exploitation' and the shackling of enterprise are objectionable mainly because of their association with the fundamental evils: 'injustice,' 'oppression,' and 'tyranny.' For Côté, these ills flow of necessity from the seigneurial privileges built into French-Canadian civil law.

Agricola's opinions were of course rank heresy to most middle-

32 *La Minerve*, 9 February, 13 February, 27 February, 27 March, 30 March 1837. See also the unsigned letter in the issue of 12 January 1837, which was likely written by L.-J. Papineau.

class Patriots. 'You have blamed the law for a situation that results from the abuse of the law,' writes 'Jean-Paul' Girod.[33] Seigneurial tenure, as instituted in Canada before the conquest, had nothing to do with the servitude of European feudalism. Under the French régime, 'The legislator did not conceive of the seigneurs as *proprietors* ... but as executors ['dépositaires'] of territories given to them in trust and under certain conditions favouring the mass of habitants. All considered then, the seigneur in Canada is simply a public officer charged with supervising and helping the settlement of the country and who receives in virtue of this a remuneration, which has lasted rather a long time, I admit, but which, *according to the law, should be light.*'[34] In more recent times, shameless 'foreign' seigneurs have imposed heavy burdens on the habitants, and the British colonial government and law courts have done nothing to stop them, concludes Jean-Paul, nicely summing up the version of history then prevalent among the Patriots.[35]

Côté has a different conception of the French-régime origins of Canadian seigneurialism, attributing them to 'the prejudices in favour of the nobility which prevailed in France in former times.'[36] Moreover, even if feudal tenure was appropriate at an early stage of the colony's settlement, it is no longer proper now that land is in short supply. Agricola adds that it is misleading to attribute exorbitant rents solely to the misdeeds of English-speaking seigneurs, since there are also French-Canadian seigneurs notorious for their grasping ways.[37] In any case, the question for the Lower Canadian House of Assembly is what should now be done about the situation?

33 *La Minerve*, 9 February 1837
34 Ibid., 27 February 1837
35 This, by the way, is a version of the history of Canadian seigneurialism that has had lasting appeal. See, for example, Jean-Pierre Wallot, 'Le régime seigneurial et son abolition au Canada,' in *Un Québec qui bougeait: trame socio-politique au tournant du XIXe siècle* (Montreal: Boréal 1973), 225–51.
36 *La Minerve*, 5 January 1837
37 Ibid., 2 March 1837

Like most Patriots (except perhaps Papineau), Amury Girod admitted the need for remedial measures, and his 'Jean-Paul' letters adopt a tone of moderate reformism. What is called for, he argues, is legislation that would prohibit the 'abuses' that have crept into seigneurial practices since the conquest. Seigneurs would then be required to grant concessions to all would-be censitaires, and they would be allowed to charge no more than one sol per arpent, the rate of rent common in the early eighteenth century. Jean-Paul goes further, however, and proposes to allow mutation fines (lods et ventes) to be exacted only on the value of land sold by a censitaire, not, as the Custom of Paris has it, on the price of land and improvements. This is clearly a concession to the liberal critique of seigneurial tenure as inimical to enterprise and development. Bending further in the same direction, Girod even suggests that the seigneur's mill monopoly (banalité) be declared illegal.[38] If all these measures had been carried into effect, they would indeed have turned the Canadian seigneur into mere land agent, as moderate Patriots imagined he had been under the French régime.

Though expressed in the language of tinkering, Jean-Paul's proposals implied a substantial transformation of agrarian property relations. It is easy to see that the 'reformist' program of the moderate Patriots might appeal to habitants who had their own very similar ideas about how to make seigneurial tenure work as it 'ought to.' Certainly it must have looked attractive when the alternative seemed to be 'abolition' on the terms laid out in Ellice's Tenures Act of 1825. On the other hand, it is important to bear two facts in mind. First, the Patriot-controlled House of Assembly never took any steps to reform seigneurialism. Second, Jean-Paul and his colleagues had no intention of damaging the interests of the seigneurs: 'They ['abuses'] must disappear, but without it being a matter of depriving the seigneurs of just compensation for the loss of what is justly and legally due them.'[39]

38 Ibid., 27 and 30 March 1837
39 Ibid., 9 February 1837

Although there might be disagreement over what was properly due to the seigneurs, this insistence on compensation narrowed somewhat the distance between the mainstream Patriots and the anglophone merchants of the Constitutionalist party.

C.-H.-O. Côté had no time for reforms, however extensive. 'The vice is in the system itself,' writes his Agricola, 'consequently the remedy should be radical. It must strike the evil at its root and extirpate it.'[40] This rooting out of feudal tenure was anything but the sort of 'abolition' envisaged by the Canada Tenures Act: 'If the tenure of free and common soccage were simply introduced here, we would be subject to all the misfortunes which are now forcing our co-subjects to leave the United Kingdom of Great Britain. The sad effects of this tenure, praised so much by our *gentlemen* [English in original], have already been felt in our townships.'[41] Furthermore, there is no mention in the Agricola letters of any sort of compensation for the loss of seigneurial rights. Small wonder, since in Côté's view the seigneurs were 'little tyrants, made to harass the people and to suck their blood.'[42]

Yet Côté was neither a communist nor an anarchist; in his own way he revered the rights of property as much as any nineteenth-century bourgeois: 'Indeed, after life and liberty, what is there more dear and more sacred than the right of property.' One of Agricola's lines of attack against feudal tenure was to point out the way in which seigneurial reserves of wood, minerals, and mill sites infringed upon the property rights of the censitaire: 'It is odious to see, in an enlightened country such as this, a proprietor liable any day to see his property invaded by a *privileged individual* who can exploit its best resources.'[43] Of course the crucial assumption here is that the censitaire is a 'proprietor' – a proposition taken for granted by Côté – so that any exercise of a

40 Ibid., 19 January 1837
41 Ibid., 2 March 1837
42 Ibid., 9 March 1837
43 Ibid., 5 January 1837, italics in original

seigneur's rights of eminent domain is, by definition, illegitimate. Moderate Patriots also tended to recognize the censitaire as proprietor, but Agricola went further, refusing to allow any limit to peasant control of the land. Clearly what he had in mind – though this is not spelled out in so many words – was the simple extinction of seigneurial rights, a radical plan that cut through all the complicated discussions of commutation and reform. Here again, Côté's radicalism was in perfect harmony with a powerful, though largely underground, current of habitant belief.

The fact that the habitants of Lower Canada were dissatisfied with seigneurial exactions was in itself sufficient grounds for their abolition as far as Côté was concerned. Since the people of Canada had no part in framing the land laws by which they were oppressed, the latter had no legitimacy. And if 'the people' were now calling for relief, the House of Assembly had no choice but to accede to their demands. Côté's position on land law was closely related to his conception of the Patriot party as the representative of a popular movement, and, although his colleagues shared this basic idea, few were prepared to go as far as the member for L'Acadie in adopting the habitants' agenda as their own and in disregarding Papineau's feudal sensibilities.

HABITANTS AND SEIGNEURS IN 1837

The debate between Agricola and Jean-Paul came to an inconclusive end in April 1837, when news of the Russell Resolutions reached Lower Canada and all other subjects were swept from the pages of the colonial press by the storm of anti-British indignation. This left middle-class Patriots – apart from the few, such as Côté and Papineau, who had decided views on the subject – in the midst of searching re-evaluations on the seigneurial issue. Though they still harboured uncertainties that kept them from undertaking action long deemed harmful to the legal traditions of French Canada as well as to existing property relations, many could nevertheless see the political appeal of Côté's stance.

One politician expressed in his private correspondence an ambivalence that must have been widespread. Louis-Hippolyte

LaFontaine, still a young radical but already showing signs of the astute political sense that would ensure his success in later years, recognized the importance of the agrarian question in any attempt to create a potent mass movement. His approach to the tenure question and to the idea of a popular alliance that underlay it, was crassly instrumental: 'To arouse the people we cannot simply wave the banner of purely abstract questions. There must be something more substantial. We must touch the sensitive spot: the purse. As long as a question of this nature is not raised, agitation cannot be constant and lasting. In the circumstances, I see nothing better to achieve this end than the question of the abolition of seigneurial rights.'[44] At that point (February 1837), LaFontaine had in mind parliamentary measures, but in the revolutionary months that followed he advocated more direct action to stimulate the armed participation of 'les bonnets bleus du Nord.' 'We must abolish the feudal system,' he urged, 'otherwise the vassal will never wake from his lethargic slumber.'[45] It seems to have been recognized on all sides that this was the key to attracting the active support of the peasantry. To that degree, the habitants were setting the agrarian agenda of the Rebellion.

Inevitably, the land tenure issue surfaced at the anti-coercion rallies held in the summer and fall of 1837, and in the published accounts of their proceedings one finds the odd call for abolition of feudal exactions scattered among the resolutions dealing with lofty constitutional matters. A meeting at St Ignace in the Vaudreuil peninsula called for far-reaching changes to the seigneurial laws of the province.[46] Mutation fines should be done away with, it was asserted; or they should at least be exacted only on the value of land, not on improvements. Censitaires should not be prevented by the banalité from establishing mills on their

44 Quoted in Ouellet, *Lower Canada*, 245
45 Undated letter, LaFontaine to Girouard, quoted in Béatrice Chassé, 'Le notaire Girouard, patriote et rebelle' (PH D thesis, Université Laval, 1974), 366
46 *La Minerve*, 21 September 1837

property. Rents everywhere should be reduced to the rates set on the oldest concessions in a given seigneurie. Seigneurs should not be allowed to withhold land grants. And finally, seigneurial retrait, as well as hunting and fishing rights and 'a host of other harmful restrictions' must be abolished. Of the body of seigneurial privilege, it need hardly be added, these measures would leave an exceedingly gaunt skeleton. Another assembly attacked seigneurialism on political grounds as an aristocratic institution at odds with the democratic tendency to 'equalize the social conditions.'[47] Elsewhere it was seen as an obstacle to individual enterprise and economic development.[48] The L'Acadie meeting resolved simply 'That this county is of the opinion that the feudal tenure does not suit the present condition or wants of the country, and that this tenure should be replaced by one more equitable and less odious.' It went on – and clearly C.-H.-O. Côté had a hand here – to call for 'the total abolition of seigniorial rights,' making no mention of any compensation for seigneurs.[49]

At four-fifths of the protest rallies the land tenure question was never mentioned in the formal resolutions. That omission, however, does not mean it was absent from the thoughts of the habitants in the crowd. A conservative newspaper reporting on one meeting – one at which no anti-seigneurial resolutions were proposed – asserted that the organizers had assembled an audience by going house to house promising people that 'if they went to the assembly they ran a good chance of not having to pay rent to the seigneurs and of having the robes of the curés trimmed.'[50] One public meeting in the summer of 1837 was in fact devoted exclusively to seigneurial matters. It was held in early August at St François in the District of Trois-Rivières, and La Minerve published the twelve resolutions 'unanimously' approved there by the assembled electors of the county of Yamaska.[51] The drift of

47 *Vindicator*, 16 June 1837
48 Ibid., 29 September 1837
49 Ibid., 18 July 1837
50 *Le Populaire*, 16 August 1837 (author's translation)
51 *La Minerve*, 14 August 1837

the propositions, evidently drawn up in advance by local Patriot leaders, is quite legalistic; the pro-censitaire version of the history of seigneurial tenure under the French régime is evoked, with the implication that post-conquest 'abuses' like the raising of rents should be rectified. Mutation fees, on the other hand, are condemned without qualification as 'immoral and unjust.' Without breaking stride, the resolutions proceed from this critique of seigneurial infringement on individual property rights to an attack on the 'douaire coutumier' for recognizing a widow's claim to a share of a family estate. The 'père de famille' – it hardly needed to be stated explicitly – ought to be in sole possession and full control of property; wives and seigneurs should not be allowed to interfere. This was a message perfectly consistent with the liberal outlook of the doctors and notaries who framed it, yet nicely calculated to appeal to an audience of habitant men.

The circumstances surrounding the calling of this unique meeting at St François are quite illuminating as regards the different viewpoints of habitant and bourgeois patriots. Again we must turn to a Constitutionalist paper to get the full story.[52] According to Le Populaire, the assembly had originally been planned as a conventional anti-coercion rally; the main organizer, local parliamentary representative Jean-Baptiste Proulx, announced it in advance as an occasion to discuss 'public affairs in the province.' But the county of Yamaska was outside the Montreal region and somewhat shaky in its support of the Patriots. Thus, when Proulx learned that his opponents were bringing in high-powered Constitutionalist orators from Trois-Rivières for the occasion, he had reason to fear that they might sway the crowd and turn a protest meeting into a loyalist demonstration. He countered this threat with a move that the anti-Patriot newspaper considered a wily stratagem. Proulx and his supporters simply toured the county proclaiming that the St François meeting was, and always had been, for the purpose of considering seigneurial dues and dower rights. Constitutional matters were then eliminated from the

52 Le Populaire, 21 August 1837

agenda and the notables from Trois-Rivières found themselves unable to score their debating points and unwilling to oppose the land tenure resolutions.

What seems clear from this episode is that for the political elites on both sides of the great debates of 1837 the seigneurial question was a secondary issue, or even an irrelevancy. Yet, at the same time, they all recognized it as a matter of great importance to the habitant masses. Taking an anti-feudal stand was not repugnant to most bourgeois Patriots, but they pursued it with any energy only as a concession to the peasantry, and some leaders were bitter when they found that the habitants did not live up to their end of the implied bargain. The people of Yamaska itself, as it turned out, refused to take up arms at the time of the insurrection of November 1837, and a frustrated local doctor upbraided them in these terms: 'You know that we took your part where the seigneurs and the priests were concerned, and now you don't want to join the patriot side!'[53]

There are definite indications that the habitants of the Montreal District saw the Patriot cause in 1837–8 as fundamentally anti-feudal. A peasant named LeGros declared at the time of the first insurrection, 'We must get rid of the English who want to take the revenues of the province. If the Patriots win, the mutation fines and the tithes will be abolished by Papineau.'[54] Another habitant, from Doctor Côté's region, cited similar motives for supporting the Patriot cause: 'Personally he would fight to the last for it & hoped he would have an opportunity of shooting some seignior.' According to his neighbour, it was only after attending a protest rally at Napierville in late October 1837 that Alexis Boudreau dit Labonté adopted this revolutionary stance filled with resentment against 'taxes, seigniorial rent, Romish clergy's dues.'[55]

53 ANQ, 1837, no. 2831, déposition de Bazille Guigaire, 12 February 1838 (author's translation)
54 ANQ, 1837, no. 567, déposition de Casimir Tétard de Montigny, 6 February 1838
55 ANQ, 1837, no. 1341, deposition of Richard Beswick, 11 December 1838

It is no accident that, when it came to armed conflict in November–December of 1837 and again in November 1838, the insurgents occupied more than one seigneurial manor house. The manor of Beauharnois was a target during the second rising, and Edward Ellice's son and daughter-in-law were taken prisoner by local patriots. A year earlier rebels had occupied the manor houses at St Charles and St Eustache. These imposing buildings were seized primarily for reasons of military strategy, but an anti-seigneurial impulse was undoubtedly at work also. There was a special satisfaction for the habitants of the Richelieu valley in violating the residence of Pierre-Dominique Debartzch, seigneur of St Charles as well as large parts of the sprawling seigneurie of St Hyacinthe and the region's pre-eminent landlord. 'They took all the Honble. P.D. Debartzch's cattle & grain for food,' a witness reported. 'They destroyed his accounts & livre terrier [estate roll], & committed shameful havock in his house &c &c.'[56]

P.-D. Debartzch, a French Canadian of Polish ancestry, was probably the most unpopular man in Lower Canada in the autumn of 1837. Once a leading Patriot politician with his own radical newspaper, *L'Echo du Pays*, and a prominent supporter of the Ninety-Two Resolutions, Debartzch had for years provoked the province's Constitutionalists with his extreme and rhetorically violent anti-British stands. Two years before the Rebellion, however, he suddenly broke with Papineau and his other collaborators. Debartzch now preached moderation as he burrowed deeper into the bosom of the colonial administration. As of August 1837 he was on the Executive Council, and, according to the Patriots, he used his influence with Governor Gosford and

56 Toronto Public Library, Nelson Papers, George Nelson, 'A Short Account.' Cf. *L'Ami du Peuple*, 25 November 1837: 'Les livres seigneuriaux ou terriers tombèrent entre les mains de ces barbares qui les mirent en pièces ... ' Debartzch later claimed to have suffered £6,500 in damages during the patriot occupation. ANQ, 1837, no. 3973, 'Estimate of damages to the property of P.D. Debartzch,' 29 January 1839

General Colborne in the months that followed to urge harsh measures to re-establish order. It is no surprise that he faced hostile demonstrations, death threats, and a frightening charivari when he returned from Quebec City to the Richelieu. In early November he was, to all intents and purposes, under house arrest at St Charles, but middle-class Patriots eventually persuaded the local habitants to let him go; an intensely relieved Debartzch quickly loaded his family and some of his valuables onto a chartered steamboat and made his escape to Quebec.[57]

Clearly Debartzch was reviled and his property attacked mainly because of his notorious political activities, his previous anti-government position serving only to render them all the more odious in patriot eyes. Accordingly, historians have never been prepared to recognize any connection between feudal tensions and the assaults on the seigneur of St Charles. Yet the destruction of estate records in November 1837 seems to speak eloquently of specifically anti-seigneurial motives, at least on the part of local habitants if not of the radical elite who organized the armed camp. But even leaving this evidence aside, we are faced with the more important question of why Debartzch abandoned the Patriot cause on the eve of revolution and whether the answer might have something to do with his position as seigneur. If his were an isolated case, Debartzch's defection might be explained in terms of purely individual quirks, ambitions, or jealousies; but was he unique?

Debartzch's friend Clément Sabrevois de Bleury was another 'turncoat' whose change of allegiance infuriated all good patriots. A lawyer and seigneur of part of Boucherville, Sabrevois de Bleury's name reflected his ancestors' aristocratic pretensions (to

57 See the accounts in *Le Populaire*, 27 September 1837 and 20 November 1837; Robert Christie, *A History of the Late Province of Lower Canada, Parliamentary and Political, from the Commencement to the Close of its Existence as a Separate Province*, 2nd ed., 6 vols (Montreal: Richard Worthington 1866), 5: 450–4; Pierre Meunier, *L'Insurrection à Saint-Charles et le seigneur Debartzch* (Montreal: Fides 1986); Elinor Senior, *Redcoats and Patriotes: The Rebellions in Lower Canada 1837–38* (Ottawa: Canada's Wings 1985), 67.

his enemies he was known as 'Sabre-de-Bois'). Nevertheless he had been an ardent Patriot in his youth, and, as member of the Assembly for Richelieu country, he had thrown his support behind the Ninety-Two Resolutions in 1834. Like his friend, he began to favour reconciliation with Britain a year later, as events moved towards a crisis, and he too felt the full force of all the muck-raking and derision of which the Patriot press was capable. His response was that of a true gentleman: in 1836 he met two leading radicals in successive encounters on the field of honour. The polarized climate of 1837 left no room for compromise positions of the sort Sabrevois de Bleury had favoured, however, and he therefore moved firmly into the Constitutionalist camp, helping to found an anti-revolutionary newspaper, *Le Populaire*, and joining francophobic Montreal merchants in loyalist rallies.[58]

Though Debartzch and Sabrevois de Bleury were the most famous 'girouettes,' there were several other seigneurs whose anti-government nationalism changed to active support of the colonial authorities as the Rebellion approached. Amable Dionne seigneur of La Pocatière and Grande-Anse, was another supporter of the 92 Resolutions who 'rallied to the defence of order during the rebellion of 1837.'[59] Pierre-Benjamin Dumoulin, a seigneur from the Trois-Rivières region, supported the canadien party in the 1820s but later opposed the Patriots and spoke out strongly against the protest rallies of 1837.[60] François Languedoc, the notorious seigneur of St Georges in L'Acadie county too seems to have been a nationalist of sorts in the previous decade, but he distinguished himself, along with his fellow seigneur John Boston as the leading loyalist activist in C.-H.-O. Côté's region. After the quelling of the insurrection, Languedoc proved a most energetic magistrate, arresting rebels and taking the oath of allegiance from the cowed habitants.[61]

58 *DCB*, 9: 696–7; Gustave Turcotte, *Le Conseil Législatif du Québec 1774-1933* (Beauceville: L'Eclaireur 1933), 127
59 *DCB*, 8: 222–4
60 Ibid., 8: 248–9
61 Ibid., 7: 484–5; *La Minerve*, 7 August 1837

When British troops marched to attack St Charles, they were quartered on the way at 'the splendid residence of the Seignior, Colonel de Rouville, a venerable gentleman of the old school, wearing a frilled shirt and ivory miniatures in a conspicuous place. He was a model of hospitality.' This was Jean-Baptiste-René Hertel de Rouville, seigneur of Rouville and Chambly, and he did seem to personify the old French-Canadian noblesse. He had not always been 'Colonel de Rouville'; as a member of the Assembly, he opposed Governor Dalhousie in 1827 and consequently lost his militia commission for a time. Resident on his estates, in the midst of patriot territory, de Rouville tried to avoid taking an extreme position at the time of the Rebellion. Yet he knew where his duty as an officer and a gentleman lay when revolution broke out. He accepted a seat on the Legislative Council in August 1837 and worked as a magistrate taking evidence against rebels in the wake of the insurrection. A humane and paternalistic conservative, de Rouville fell afoul of some of the more ferocious Constitutionalists when he tried to protect local people from the more arbitrary forms of repression, but he remained, in his own mind, an actively loyal subject of her majesty.[62]

The Dictionary of Canadian Biography lists other seigneurs who went from campaigning against the administration in the 1820s to a stance of active loyalism in 1837–9: Marc-Pascal de Sales Laterrière, François-Xavier Malhiot, and Dominique Mondelet.[63] If we were to add to this roll-call of seigneurs who abandoned oppositional stances with the approach of revolution those of unwavering pro-government loyalty who took an active role at a local or a provincial level during the Rebellion, the list would become tediously long. It would have to include English sei-

---

62 DCB, 8: 393–4; Armand Cardinal, *Histoire de Saint-Hilaire: les seigneurs de Rouville* (Montreal: Editions du Jour 1980); NA, LC Civil Secretary, 533: 75, Hertel de Rouville to W. Rowan, 5 April 1838; ANQ, 1837, no. 1596, Lespérance to Leclerc, 6 January 1839. The quotation is from Sydney Bellingham, *Some Personal Recollections of the Rebellion of 1837 in Canada* (Dublin: Browne and Nolan, 1902), 13.
63 Ibid., 10: 431–2, 8: 605–6, 9: 559–61

gneurs like William Plenderleath Christie, who volunteered to come out of retirement to run the military administration of Lower Canada.[64] Out in the Richelieu valley his estate manager, William McGinnis, organized opposition to the patriots.[65] Notable also are the numerous French-Canadian seigneurs – from established aristocrats like Charles-Etienne Chaussegros de Léry to parvenu seigneurs like Barthélemy Joliette of Lavaltrie – who did what they could to combat Patriot influences.[66] Not to mention the various branches of the Roman Catholic Church, with their extensive seigneurial holdings and their message of obedience to the crown. No one could have been more zealous in their support for government than the Sulpicians, seigneurs of Montreal, Two Mountains, and St Sulpice, who rendered invaluable logistical support to General Colborne's forces.[67]

64 Ibid., 7: 184–5
65 Indeed McGinnis seems to have been the most active and effective Constitutionalist leader in the region; early in the hostilities, he managed to disperse a force of habitants preparing to fire on a provincial cavalry squadron at St Athanase. ANQ, 1837, no. 253, déposition de François Ouimet, 25 January 1838
66 DCB, 7: 169–70, 184–5, 446–50. Leafing through the DCB, I found mention of twenty-six seigneurs who were active on the government/Constitutionalist side. Apart from those already named in the text, they were Mathew Bell (7: 64–9), John Boston (9: 61–2), Kenelm Chandler (7: 165–7), Antoine-Gaspard Couillard (7: 212–13), Emmanuel Couillard-Desprès (8: 174–5), Ross Cuthbert (9: 187–8), Edward Ellice (9: 233–9), Léonard Godefroy de Tonnancour (9: 321–2), Louis Gugy (7: 359–60), Janvier-Domptail Lacroix (8: 480–1), Pierre Laviolette (8: 605–6), Joseph Masson (7: 592–6), Toussaint Pothier (7: 702–3), Jean-Roch Rolland (9: 682–3). See also, ANQM, Affaires Criminelles, Chandler to Young, 24 September 1839; ANQ, 1837, no. 2833, déposition de Léonard Godefroy de Tonnancour, 12 February 1838. One might add the name of François-Roch de St Ours. A seigneur of ancient noble lineage, St Ours was reviled by patriots because, as sheriff of Montreal, he was in charge of incarcerating political prisoners at the time of the Rebellion. [Azarie Couillard-Despres], Histoire de la seigneurie de St Ours, 2 vols (Montreal: Imprimerie de l'Institution des sourds-muets 1915–17), 2: 80
67 Young, In Its Corporate Capacity, 55–6

It is not hard to find loyalist seigneurs, but if you look for seigneurs on the patriot side, you will search in vain. Stretching the definition of 'seigneur,' you might include the patriot artist Joseph Légaré, who owned a fractional share of a tiny urban fief in Quebec. Questionable also is John Donegani, the businessman-seigneur of Foucault who was arrested as a patriot sympathizer in 1838. Hardly a rebel, Donegani retained his magistrate's commission in November 1837 and did his best to suppress demonstrations by the Sons of Liberty extremists in Montreal.[68] There was an active rebel named Lussier, whose habitant parents had purchased part of the seigneurie of Varennes.[69] Beyond these marginal individuals, I was able to discover only one solitary instance of a full-fledged seigneur who was also clearly on the rebel side in 1837; his name, of course, is Louis-Joseph Papineau, and he was a special case in a number of respects.

Although there are no statistics on the subject, it does seem clear that seigneurs flocked to the government standards at the time of the Rebellion and in the years preceding revolution when the Patriots were becoming increasingly radical. Of course many seigneurs, especially the English-speakers, had never been anything but pillars of the establishment. In the minds of some, combating subversion was one of the duties of a seigneur. Thus, Louis Dumont of St Eustache expressed real shame for the misdeeds of 'his' habitants during the insurrection; 'wishing to bring my censitaires back to order,' he volunteered to administer the oath of allegiance locally.[70] But even those who had once identified themselves with French-Canadian nationalism now renounced the movement that was capturing the allegiance of a majority of their male censitaires. This change of heart might be

---

68 *DCB*, 8: 494–8, 9: 207–9; Amédée Papineau, *Journal d'un Fils de la Liberté* (Montreal: Réédition-Québec 1972), 56–7

69 *La Minerve*, 21 September 1837; NA, LC Civil Secretary, 527: 2, A. Pinet to Governor, 16 December 1838

70 NA, LC Civil Secretary, 528: 91, L.C.L. Dumont to D. Daly, 8 January 1837 [sic, 1838] (author's translation)

seen as an illustration of the general tendency among those with a major proprietary stake in any existing order to recoil at the spectre of revolution. One seigneur, briefly jailed on political charges in 1838, proclaimed his innocence, citing his status as seigneur as prima facie evidence in his favour: 'The Boucherville family has never been lacking in honour. As seigneur of Boucherville and of Verchères, he would, in joining an insurrection, risk losing the estate which has come down to him from his forefathers.'[71]

The loyalism of the seigneurs can be seen, more specifically, as a reaction to developments within the Lower Canadian patriot movement. The latter was rapidly becoming more radical in the mid-1830s, moving from anti-clerical positions towards a searching critique of seigneurial privilege. This transformation, in turn, was connected to the growing influence of the 'plebeian masses,' particularly the peasantry, within the movement. Thus, it was no accident that the political trajectories of seigneurs and rent-paying habitants diverged so markedly. The defection of the seigneurs and the adherence of the habitants was a mutual and reciprocal process that helped shape the Patriot movement and determine the direction of the Rebellion. The effects of agrarian class tensions were of course mediated, wrapped up in, and expressed through struggles of a different order; consequently we do not find peasant masses storming the manor houses with anti-feudal slogans on their lips. Nevertheless, if we look a little beyond the surface, it is hard to escape the conclusion that the conflict of seigneurs and habitants played a major part in the revolutionary events of 1837–8.

71 ANQ, 1837, no. 1041, examen volontaire, Pierre de Boucherville, 10 December 1838 (author's translation). See also Senior, *Redcoats and Patriotes*, 110.

10

Unsparing force

He who uses force unsparingly, without reference to the bloodshed involved, must obtain a superiority if his adversary uses less vigour in its application.

Carl Von Clausewitz, *On War*[1]

By the beginning of November events were clearly moving – and moving rapidly – towards a violent showdown. Lower Canada had been racked by intense political agitation for six months, and the civil government had proved itself utterly incapable of stemming the tide. Attempts at repression had only expanded and intensified the opposition, an opposition increasingly directed against the colonial régime itself, not merely specific individuals, laws, or institutions. Most ominous was the development of insurgent local administrations in the rural parishes of the District of Montreal. Their very existence represented a challenge to the sovereignty of the colony's government, since it implied a rival claim to legitimate authority. This challenge was voiced quite explicitly at the St Charles meeting, and it was given practical punch in the campaign of coercive charivaris waged against agents of the queen. The result was an inherently unstable situation of 'dual power' through much of the province's country-

---

1 (London: Penguin 1968), 102

side, a condition that no state could tolerate for long. Recourse to arms became virtually unavoidable.

Many of the people involved, particularly those of a humane and non-violent disposition, were reluctant to recognize the inevitability of war. The governor, Lord Gosford, continued to cling to the hope that the Patriots could be brought to their senses without bloodshed. At the beginning of the crisis in the previous spring he had taken the precaution of summoning military reinforcements, but they were intended to intimidate the opposition, not to slaughter it. Papineau and the other Patriot leaders were not so easily cowed, however, even though they clearly had no wish to enter into a military contest with the world's number-one imperial power. Their hope had been that the moral force of a united Lower Canadian nation would be enough to repel British political aggression in the short term, while helping to prepare for a re-enactment of the American Revolution in the more distant future. But revolutions never unfold according to anyone's script.

While Gosford and Papineau fought – with weapons drawn from the politician's arsenal of rhetorical and administrative devices – to master an unfamiliar situation, others were pressing for action. Elements in the Constitutionalist camp, particularly the men of Montreal's anglophone community, had watched with growing alarm the development of French-Canadian republicanism in the 1830s. Like Ulster Unionists of a later period, they tended to channel their anxieties into aggressive paramilitary groups like the 'Doric Club.' By the autumn of 1837 the indignation of militant Constitutionalists knew no bounds. Treason, they believed, was rampant and the blame rested squarely on a pusillanimous government that refused to do its duty and send every agitator to the gallows.

The 'enormities' committed by rural patriots were appalling enough, but to make matters worse in the eyes of Constitutionalists, sedition was starting to take active forms in Montreal. Radical young men had organized, in conscious imitation of American models, as the 'Sons of Liberty.' The group began in August 1837, but it adopted a paramilitary character only in October, when weekly drills were held in a field at the edge of town. Most of the participants in these military exercises, however, seem to have come from the farming communities surrounding Montreal.[2]

The Sons of Liberty were at a real disadvantage in Montreal. Their rivals commanded support in the English-speaking community, which by now constituted a slight majority of the city's population. Moreover, wealth, power, and political influence were on the side of the Constitutionalists, and the formidable military establishment naturally tended to be sympathetic. Perhaps equally important was the fact that the Constitutionalists had taken the initiative in organizing themselves for physical force three years before the patriots followed suit. Consequently, when rival demonstrations mounted in Montreal on 6 November by the Sons of Liberty and the Doric Club degenerated into street fighting, the Constitutionalists emerged triumphant. After 6 November radicals could feel secure only in the countryside and the villages. In spite of the fact that the leadership of the Patriot party was drawn primarily from Montreal, the conflict in Lower Canada tended increasingly to take on the character of a rural/urban confrontation.[3]

This triumph did not soothe the militant loyalist party as long as the patriot revolution remained strong in the countryside. Urban Constitutionalists, as well as refugee rural loyalists like P.-D. Debartzch, stepped up their calls for blood and hangings, and they seem to have received a sympathetic hearing from the stern commander of her majesty's forces, General Sir John Colborne, who, as the man on the spot in Montreal, was increasingly setting government policy. Months earlier Colborne had taken steps to reinforce his troop strength at Montreal, bringing up men from Quebec and transferring forces from the Maritimes and from

2 NA, LC Civil Secretary, 519: 226, Maillard to Colborne, 23 October 1837
3 See Allan Greer, 'La dimension ville-campagne de l'insurrection de 1837,' in *Sociétés villageoises et rapports villes-campagnes au Québec et dans la France de l'ouest XVIIe–XXe siècles*, ed. François Lebrun and Normand Séguin (Trois-Rivières: Université du Québec à Trois-Rivières 1987), 231–8.

Upper Canada. Now he was convinced of the need to provoke an armed confrontation in order to crush the nascent revolution. Governor Gosford too had no choice but to rally to the punitive option, and he quickly authorized the formation of 'Volunteer Corps' – essentially loyal embodied militia. These units were quickly filled by members of the Doric Club, who, having anticipated and indeed requested the formation of colonial military forces, were ready for action almost immediately. About the same time, the 'Montreal Cavalry,' a sort of amateur mounted police long controlled by the well-heeled sons of the anglo-Tory establishment, was transformed into a regular, full-time, paramilitary force.[4]

One of the first tasks of the reorganized cavalry was to mount an expedition to St Jean, a strategic centre on the upper Richelieu. St Jean was in the L'Acadie region, the scene of so many recent charivaris; according to Colborne's informants, 'the country is in a dreadful state. Yesterday a number of the most respectable residents came into town, having been obliged to leave everything behind them in consequence of the riotous proceedings of several Radicals there.' Arriving on 10 November, the troopers soon found themselves surrounded by a hostile mob. The situation was grave, but before anyone was hurt, both sides drew back from the brink and tried to strengthen their respective positions. A company of British regulars came to St Jean the next day to reinforce the cavalry. Dr Côté and Lucien Gagnon assembled 2–300 men with the intention of attacking the troops. It became clear, however, that there were not nearly enough guns for an offensive operation; the patriot camp eventually broke up and the leaders fled to the United States.[5]

4 Elinor Senior, *Redcoats and Patriotes: The Rebellions in Lower Canada 1837–38* (Ottawa: Canada's Wings 1985), 28, 60–1; idem, 'The Provincial Cavalry in Lower Canada 1837–1850,' *CHR* 57 (March 1976): 1–24

5 Senior, *Redcoats and Patriotes*, 38; Jean-Paul Bernard, *Les Rébellions de 1837–1838: les patriotes du Bas-Canada dans la mémoire collective et chez les historiens* (Montreal: Boréal 1983), 105–6; *Le Populaire*, 20 November 1837; ANQ, 1837, no. 253, déposition de François Ouimet, 25 January 1838; ibid., no. 511, deposition of Honoré Lord, 13 November 1837

Meanwhile, preparations were under way in Montreal to arrest all the prominent Patriot politicians on charges of high treason. There seems to have been some hope in government circles that the turmoil might be ended if the leading 'agitators' were taken into custody. This was a strategy doomed to failure; quite apart from the fact that it was based on a fundamental misconception of the Patriot movement as something entirely orchestrated by a small clique, there was no way that the slow and rickety judicial apparatus could actually capture its chosen prey. Word leaked out of what was afoot, and by the time arrest warrants were actually issued (16 November), the Patriot chiefs of Quebec and Montreal with few exceptions had made their escape to the insurgent rural parishes.

If Papineau and his associates had possessed elaborate plans to seize control of the state, this certainly would have been the moment to put them into operation. As they slipped out of the city disguised and under cover of darkness, however, the Patriot 'leaders' presented the appearance not of determined conspirators but of bewildered fugitives. Their movements were uncoordinated, uncertain, and almost aimless.[6] While some of his colleagues headed for exile in the United States, Louis-Hippolyte LaFontaine attempted to engineer a capitulation, appealing to the governor to reconvene the provincial Assembly. Meanwhile, most of the urban Patriots were congregating in the villages of St Charles and St Denis on the Richelieu and at St Benoit in Two Mountains. Notices circulated calling for a 'convention' that was to meet on 4 December, either at St Pie or at St Charles, at which arrangements would be made to issue paper currency to finance the purchase of arms.[7] Uncertainty and improvisation were the order of the day.

6 See Amury Girod's journal for a vivid account of his own wanderings and his more-or-less chance encounters with Papineau, O'Callaghan, and others. *PACR*, 1923, 370–1
7 NA, 'Quelques notes historiques sur les événements politiques de 1837 en Canada,' 22

Following the Constitutionalist interpretation of the period, some modern historians have suggested that the Patriot elite had actually elaborated plans for a coup d'état. In support of this position Fernand Ouellet cites the warlike bluster of Dr Timothée Kimber, a radical leader in the Richelieu valley. On 25 October, the day after the meeting at St Charles, Kimber thrilled a Chambly audience with his daring predictions: 'As soon as the river is frozen we will go with 40 or 50,000 armed men to capture Montreal ... and, after Montreal, we will take Quebec.' Impatient for action, the Chambly patriots immediately collected money to purchase gunpowder for an old cannon stolen from the nearby seminary. Far from besieging cities, however, they used their armaments to fire off a twenty-two-round salute to the Federation of the Six Counties![8] There were other occasions on which rural patriots talked of attacking Montreal, but this aggressiveness was clearly morale-building bravado; no one ever made any real preparations for such a foolhardy offensive. The fact is that even in the middle of November there was nothing that could reasonably be called a Patriot strategy; all planning revolved around elementary considerations of survival in the face of the government's impending crack-down.

ARMED CAMPS AND PRELIMINARY SKIRMISHES

Whereas disarray prevailed at the 'top' of the Patriot movement, the situation was more promising in the countryside and at the 'grass-roots' level. It was, after all, in the rural parishes of the District of Montreal that the revolution had advanced the furthest; here there was at least a framework for anti-government

---

8 ANQM, Affaires Criminelles, deposition of Augustus Kuper, 17 November 1837. Without ever mentioning the harmless sequel to these brave words, Fernand Ouellet quotes Kimber's speech as though it expressed serious Patriot military plans. See 'Les insurrections de 1837–38: un phénomène social,' in Eléments d'histoire sociale du Bas-Canada (Montreal: Hurtubise 1972), 356; and Lower Canada 1791–1840: Social Change and Nationalism (Toronto: McClelland and Stewart 1980), 294.

mobilization. Active steps to prepare for resistance came in the second week of November as rumours emanated from Montreal that the Patriot elite was to be rounded up. In the parish of Vaudreuil there was a more specific report indicating that local leaders would soon be arrested. The militia turned out to protect their chiefs, and eventually, after the immediate threat to their community seemed past, the Vaudreuil militiamen crossed the Lake of Two Mountains, intending to proceed on to the patriot camp at St Benoit 'and their [sic] make a stand.'[9] At St Marc in the Richelieu, armed habitants kept a guard posted at the house of Joseph-Toussaint Drolet, the Patriot member of the Assembly.

The people of St Denis learned in the middle of the night of 10–11 November that Dr Wolfred Nelson's name was on the list of those to be arrested. Overestimating the swiftness of British justice, forty villagers immediately converged on Nelson's home vowing to protect the popular local leader at all costs. Neither cavalry nor troops appeared that night, however, and some of the men dispersed, but not before they had made arrangements to provide the doctor with a permanent armed guard. The next day Nelson's wife and children moved to a safer location, and soon 'his house resembled a barracks,' with barricaded doors and windows and a rotating garrison of habitant militiamen. George Nelson, Wolfred's brother but a staunch Constitutionalist none the less, observed developments at St Denis from his farm a few kilometres away: 'For the space of three weeks were they in that condition. Their minds wrought to the highest pitch of fury & dread. They kept urging & encouraging each other to stand to the last, and they did. Every day, every hour brought them some accounts, sometimes cherishing [sic], sometimes discouraging, but always magnified.'[10] Thus began the encampment that ten days later would be at the centre of the patriots' most celebrated military victory.[11]

9 ANQ, 1837, no. 116, deposition of William Kell, 23 November 1837
10 Toronto Public Library, Nelson Collection, George Nelson journal
11 The best first-hand accounts are to be found in ibid. and in ACESH, parish correspondence, St Denis, Demers to Lartigue, 13 December 1837.

The first blow against the government actually occurred a week before the battle of St Denis and it was entirely the work of local militiamen, operating under habitant leadership. This encounter was set off by one of the few successful arrests in the government's sweep of prominent Patriots. A party of about twenty troopers of the Montreal Cavalry, accompanied by the high constable, had managed to capture two Patriot leaders at St Jean, and on 17 November they were returning to the city with the two prisoners securely manacled and chained. They had descended on St Jean the previous night, moving swiftly and hoping to accomplish their mission before anyone in this overwhelmingly patriot region could intercept them. Such a tactic might have worked at the time of the July troubles in Two Mountains county, but not this time. Word of the cavalry's movements spread quickly, and even before they had captured their prisoners, militiamen were beginning to assemble along the route back to Montreal. The leaders in the Longueuil area, near the south-shore ferry landing, were Bonaventure Viger and Joseph Vincent; these two habitant militia officers lost no time in arranging an ambush. Up and down the concession roads went their emissaries summoning men for duty. By ten o'clock, about 150 men had assembled near the village of Longueuil; 100 of them had guns, the rest carried pitchforks and staves. Unlike the legendary 'Minutemen' of Massachusetts, these local militia units had no evocative name, but they certainly proved their effectiveness in this initial encounter.

Bonaventure Viger assumed the command. He posted his men behind rail fences on either side of the highway from St Jean, and, as the Montreal Cavalry approached, Viger stepped into the road and called on them to stop. The riders hesitated for a moment, then continued on their way. The attackers thereupon unleashed a musket volley that quickly scattered the outnumbered troopers. No one was killed, but the cavalry sustained numerous wounds. Meanwhile, Viger immobilized the high constable's carriage by cutting the throat of one of his horses with a sabre. The liberated prisoners were then conducted in triumph to the local blacksmith, who removed their irons.[12]

The Longueuil skirmish galvanized the province and encouraged the distraught Patriot leadership to coordinate rural resistance to the inevitable British attack. Thomas Storrow Brown, a Montreal merchant who had been at the head of the Sons of Liberty, was one of the few bourgeois Patriots prepared to take charge. Still convalescing from a severe beating he had received during the 6 November riot, Brown was on his way to refuge in the United States when word reached him of the liberation of the two prisoners. He and his friends immediately decided to organize a fortified camp at St Charles and assemble Richelieu valley patriots there. They happened to meet Papineau and some of his associates, who approved the scheme, and with

12 ANQ, 1837, no. 50, déposition d'Edouard Labonté, 22 November 1837; ibid., no. 51, déposition de Pierre Fontrouge, 24 November 1837; ibid., no. 54, déposition de Louis Benoît fils, 22 November 1837; ibid., no. 56, déposition d'Olivier Fournier, 20 November 1837; ibid., no. 58, affidavit de Joseph Tremblay, 21 November 1837; ibid., no. 59, déposition d'Eugène Rocque père, 21 November 1837; ibid., no. 61, déposition de François Goyet, 21 November 1837; ibid., no. 62, déposition de Jean-Marie Morin, 2 December 1837; ibid., no. 63, affidavit de Godefroy Lavigueur et al., 22 November 1837; ibid., no. 66, déposition d'Amable Patenaude, 22 November 1837; ibid., no. 68, déposition de Louis Malo, 18 November 1837; ibid., no. 70, report of Sydney Bellingham and P.-E. Leclerc, 19 November 1837. Highly coloured accounts of the Longueuil skirmish can be found in various works, including L.-O. David, Les patriotes de 1837–1838 (Montreal: Jacques Frenette 1981), 37–9. See also Senior, Redcoats and Patriotes, 54–5. This is one case where I have my doubts about the accuracy of Senior's usually reliable narrative. At one point, she describes the Longueuil patriots as acting on instructions from Papineau (54), but elsewhere she asserts that Timothée Kimber of Chambly was the mastermind (61). I find no confirmation for either assertion in the primary sources. No doubt both Papineau and Kimber would have approved of the liberation of prisoners, but all indications are that Viger and Vincent acted on their own initiative. There is no reason to suppose they took orders from anyone, although they were certainly part of an informal regional network that would have been transformed in the Tory imagination of the day into a conspiratorial command structure.

Papineau's blessing Brown set himself up as 'general.' The people of St Charles and vicinity rallied to the cause and to Brown's confident leadership. Urban and middle-class direction – in addition to Brown, Henri-Alphonse Gauvin, a young Montreal doctor, played an important role, and from time to time Papineau and O'Callaghan participated in meetings – was particularly evident in the St Charles camp.[13]

One of General Brown's first acts was to seize Debartzch's seigneurial manor, converting it into a military barracks and command centre. Apparently the people of St Charles, having chased their seigneur from the region, had already laid hands on his house and some of its contents.[14] The evidence on this point is not clear, although it does seem certain that local residents destroyed the seigneurial records, either before or after Brown arrived on the scene. Within a few days a low wall of logs and earth had been built around the perimeter of the manor. Debartzch's ample stores were expropriated to feed the hundreds of volunteers who came to man the St Charles camp. The patriots also took over a shop owned by a merchant-protegé of the seigneur and used its contents for the same purpose; likewise, two schooners laden with grain for export were commandeered. In every case, according to Brown's retrospective account, receipts were issued so that the victims of such seizures could later claim compensation from the revolutionary régime. Although there was no shortage of provisions, armaments were a different matter. Until the very eve of the battle of St Charles, the camp contained only about fifty hunting rifles, though powder was in plentiful supply and, once the lead pipes of Debartzch's distillery had been melted down, so was shot. 'Hundreds were coming in to defend their country's rights,' Brown lamented, 'and thousands were in readiness, but I had no arms to put into their hands.'[15]

13 The best eyewitness accounts are NA, T.S. Brown Papers, Brown to L.-O. David, 8 May 1873, and ANQ, 1837, no. 356, interrogation of Henri-Alphonse Gauvin, 27 January 1838.
14 See ANQ, 1837, no. 356, interrogation of H.-A. Gauvin, 27 January 1838.
15 NA, Brown journal, 6

Meanwhile, just down the Richelieu, St Denis was also militarizing rapidly, though never to the same degree as St Charles. Here, too, guns were lacking. Two blacksmiths did their best to respond to the emergency, labouring full time to repair hunting muskets. Other volunteers melted lead and made balls, in some cases employing hollowed-out potatoes as molds.[16] Public meetings were in session almost constantly throughout the crisis in the 'salle des habitants' of the local rectory. At an early stage the people of St Denis decided to use parish vestry funds to purchase arms, but the curé had taken the precaution of hiding the vestry strongbox; when the patriots finally located it, there was no time to put the funds to use before the parish was attacked. Still, the dispute with the priest as well as the stormy meetings in the habitants' hall must have been familiar scenes for St Denis parishioners, even if pew rentals and supplies of sacramental wine were no longer the points at issue.

The insurgent Richelieu region, effectively self-governing since late October, was now assuming additional attributes of a sovereign state as it girded for war. Not only was property subject to expropriation, additional measures were taken to ensure security under emergency conditions. In order to keep the authorities in Montreal as much in the dark as possible, the patriots restricted movement into and out of the region. 'They allowed no communication with the other parts of the country without a *Permit*, a Passport was necessary to go out or come in,' a disgusted George Nelson noted, and he added, with considerable exaggeration, 'The rod of terror was showed over the heads of all the surrounding parishes. Country merchants travelling on business to Montreal, if only suspected, were considered traitors & rifled of their property.'[17] As a further security measure, several prominent Constitutionalists in the region, including Debartzch's seigneurial agent, were arrested and confined in the patriots' headquarters.

16 J.-B.-A. Allaire, *Histoire de la paroisse de Saint-Denis-sur-Richelieu* (Saint-Hyacinthe: Le Courrier 1905), 375
17 Toronto Public Library, Nelson Collection, George Nelson journal

Although St Charles was the main concentration of patriot strength, by 20 November there were a number of other 'camps' where insurgent militiamen maintained some sort of organized presence: at Pointe-à-la-Mule and St Denis in the Richelieu, as well as at nearby St Césaire; north of Montreal there were ephemeral camps at Terrebonne and Vaudreuil and more substantial gatherings at St Benoit and St Eustache. The establishment of such military cantonments had long been a standard procedure in French Canada during wartime. As recently as the War of 1812–14, camps of embodied militia were scattered through the province – particularly in the area south of Montreal – and many middle-aged patriots like Wolfred Nelson had experienced them at first hand. There were even precedents, dating back to the turmoil accompanying the American invasion of 1775, of camps formed for the purpose of resisting agents of government. Like the charivari and the community meeting in the rectory, the military camp formed part of the cultural heritage of French Canada; it seems only natural that the embattled peasants and villagers of 1837 would draw upon their historical experience in this way.

What purpose was served by this localized mobilization of forces? Certainly there is no indication that anyone seriously regarded the dispersed camps as staging areas for a mass assault on Montreal or any other British stronghold. Neither can one see the geographic disposition of camps as corresponding to any other strategic logic; taken together, they did not interrupt the enemy's communications, nor did they protect lines of contact with potential allies in the United States. In the end, the primary function of the scattered and basically independent camps was to ensure the success of the opposing forces, which were able to defeat them one at a time. From a strictly military viewpoint, it would of course have made far more sense for the amateur soldiers of the patriot movement to have engaged in guerilla raids. If they were going dig in for defensive warfare, the patriots should at least have concentrated their forces in one or two strategically significant locations.

The establishment of rural camps should be understood in

the first instance as a reflection of the desperation of the patriot position. Initially, the habitants mobilized simply for the purpose of protecting Patriot leaders from arrest. They must have been aware that, if the government could incarcerate radicals at will, the nascent revolution was as good as dead. At the same time, some habitants were no doubt taken in by the morale-building propaganda of middle-class Patriots assuring them that all the troops were supporters of Papineau and that victory would be easy; at least that is what rank-and-file insurgents tended to tell the magistrates after they had been defeated and imprisoned. Actual behaviour in November 1837, however, suggests that few were so utterly deluded. In setting up their little village strongholds, the patriots, both bourgeois and ple-beian, acted like men who were aware that their chances of victory were slim, but the only alternative to resistance was a surrender that they would surely have considered cowardly and dishonourable. Jean-Baptiste Roy of Terrebonne phrased it this way, when his village was in turmoil over rumours – which proved groundless – of an impending attack by armed 'bureaucrats': 'We must defend ourselves. It is better to kill the devil than to let him kill you.'[18]

That armed camps should spring up in scattered locations and in defiance of any strategic logic was also a reflection of the revolutionary process under way in the District of Montreal. It was at the parish level, after all, that the insurgent institutions of government had developed a month earlier. Small wonder that the populace should organize on an essentially local footing. To be sure, 'national' leaders from Montreal played a part in setting up the camps, most notably in the case of St Charles, but they chose this community because of the strength of anti-government sentiment there. Whether or not these 'outsiders' took a hand, the disposal of patriot forces reflected the political geography of Lower Canada, not any centrally planned strategy. The mobilization of November 1837 reveals the limited horizons of the habitants as well as their

18 ANQ, 1837, no. 1114, déposition de Joseph Beauchamp, 15 November 1837

aspirations towards political change on a national scale. In some parishes on the fringes of the patriot heartland people took up arms for local defence in politically ambiguous ways. Their language sometimes recalled the 'Great Fear' of 1789: people spoke of resisting 'brigandage' without its ever being clear who it was they thought was menacing them.[19] The patriot mobilization in the county of Two Mountains, while politically quite well defined, also had a strictly local dimension corresponding to long-standing suspicions and rivalries within the region. Yet the patriot movement tended to function, as it always had, as the link connecting the habitant drive for local self-government with larger national conflicts. The people of the Richelieu valley were not simply protecting their hearths and homes; they were clearly determined to defend Papineau and the Lower Canadian movement he personified.

The odds against them were nothing short of overwhelming. Civilians, even when they have a substantial advantage in numbers, cannot be expected to hold their own in any sort of 'war of position' against trained soldiers led by professional officers. And the patriots faced troops who were among the best in the world: trained, experienced, and well equipped. Moreover, the latter were 'foreigners' in Lower Canada and therefore unlikely to fraternize with the insurgents, as soldiers often did in non-colonial revolutions (Paris in 1789, for example, or Petrograd in February 1917).

To make matters worse, the rural patriots were pathetically short of arms. There were hunting fusils hanging in many an habitant cabin, but they tended to be old and unreliable, and in any case there were only enough for a small proportion of the insurgents. Only as of the middle of November did the

---

19 ANQM, Affaires Criminelles, vol. 48, déposition d'Amable Gabouriaux fils, 5 December 1837; ibid., no. 195, déposition de Michel Valois, 5 April 1838; ibid., no. 197, déposition de Jean Giguère, 5 April 1838. Cf. Georges Lefebvre, *The Great Fear of 1789: Rural Panic in Revolutionary France*, trans. Joan White (Princeton: Princeton UP 1973).

patriots endeavour seriously to procure guns, and even then their efforts proved quite inadequate. After their abortive attempt to attack the soldiers at St Jean (11 November), Dr Côté and his associates had sent across the line to the United States for 500 muskets and 500 bayonets, urging haste, 'as they did not know how soon they would be attacked by the British troops.' But since the request was not backed by hard cash, no guns were forthcoming.[20] In many localities, collections were taken to finance arms purchases; (in one parish patriots even donated money to buy manuals of military training!) But of course money was scarce, and even when funds could be raised, it was difficult to smuggle the guns across the border from the States or out of Montreal to the countryside.[21] Faut de mieux, blacksmiths did their best to fashion swords and pike blades out of scythes and sickles; one middle-class Patriot provided a pattern based on his study of Roman spears and battleaxes.[22] Thousands of guns were needed, but it seems unlikely that more than a few dozen were procured in the lead-up to the battle of St Denis.

ST DENIS AND ST CHARLES

Needing to move quickly before the St Lawrence froze and the rebels solidified their positions, General Colborne gave orders on 22 November for a two-pronged assault on the patriot camps of the Richelieu valley. The troops already at Fort Chambly were to proceed north that night in order to attack St Charles the following morning. They were to be aided by a second force, which would travel to Sorel by steamboat and then march south along the Richelieu, carrying St Denis on its way before converging on St Charles. The plan made good sense, and if only the weather had been more favourable, it might have succeeded. As it was,

20 ANQ, 1837, no. 124, deposition of Allen Clark, 14 November 1837
21 Ibid., no. 799, déposition de J.-Bte Chaulette dit Laviolette, 17 January 1838; ibid., no. 131, déposition de Louis Fréchette, 12 December 1837
22 Ibid., no. 116, deposition of William Kell, 23 November 1837

conditions for the overnight march could not have been worse. The soldiers were buffeted by rain and then by snow, while underfoot they found themselves mired in mud in some parts of the road and stumbling over frozen ruts in other places. Consequently, the southern detachment was unable to reach St Charles on the assigned date and had to rest for a day at the seigneurial manor at St Hilaire. Meanwhile, the troops coming from Sorel managed to reach St Denis by the morning of the twenty-third, but after a gruelling all-night march they were cold, hungry, and utterly exhausted. 'At long last,' wrote George Nelson, 'they came in sight of the place where they were to breakfast, and where they did breakfast on Powder and ball!'[23]

The patriots at St Denis had been warned of the attack the night before; indeed they had already taken one prisoner in the form of a British officer who inadvertently had strayed into the camp well in advance of his unit. All night messengers scoured the neighbouring countryside calling out militiamen to come to the defence of St Denis. At the same time, local patriots were hastily preparing defensive positions in a massive stone house and some smaller buildings at the north end of the village (until then, attack had been expected from the south). By morning there may have been 800 men at St Denis, though only 200 of them had firearms; further reinforcements arrived throughout the day as the battle raged. Arrayed against them were about 300 soldiers, mostly British regular infantrymen, along with some members of the Montreal Cavalry as well as a party of Royal Artillery with their twelve-pounder howitzer.

There was skirmishing at the approaches to the village, but fighting began in earnest just before 9 a.m. when the British cannon began firing at the patriot positions. Just then, a cart carrying three militiamen and the captured British officer, Lieutenant George Weir, was passing through the village on its way to a more secure place of captivity. Weir spoke no French, and even though he had been kindly treated at St Denis, he seemed to be

23 Toronto Public Library, Nelson Collection, George Nelson journal

convinced that the rebels were taking him away only in order to shoot him in some deserted spot; no reassurances could persuade him otherwise. The tension in the place must have been palpable: church bells were ringing furiously and incessantly, families were hurriedly packing valuables and preparing their children for evacuation, while men with guns, scythes, and clubs streamed in from the surrounding districts. And now the boom of artillery was echoing through this peaceful little village that had not seen war for sixty-two years. Suddenly Weir jumped up in the cart and bolted out the back, running in the direction of the gunfire. The guards sprang to pursue him and soon brought him down with blows from the side of a sabre. By now a crowd of villagers had surrounded the fugitive; they were almost as terrified as he was, yet strangely excited and infuriated too. Weapons lashed out at the struggling figure, and before long he was mangled and bleeding, scarcely alive. A militia officer put the lieutenant out of his misery with a shot from his musket; the body was then thrown in a nearby creek bed and covered with stones.[24]

As this grisly scene unfolded at one end of St Denis, patriot snipers were coming under cannon fire in their stone house at the opposite end of the village. One of the very first shots pierced a weak spot in the walls and destroyed four men in an instant. Modeste Roy, a young blacksmith who had been standing nearby, was seized with terror; he ran down to the basement and remained there for the rest of the day. Wolfred Nelson managed to rally his forces after this unlucky beginning, however, and with well-aimed musket fire they soon forced the artillerymen to move their howitzer to a less commanding position. For six hours shots were exchanged with no decisive effect. At one point the attackers did attempt an encircling movement to the left, which might have given them a significant advantage; but they were beaten back by St Antoine militiamen who had

---

24 Most of the secondary accounts of this incident are quite distorted. Elinor Senior, *Redcoats and Patriotes*, 83, is an exception. See also the numerous depositions in NA, Rebellion Records, vol. 1, as well as A.R.C., *Procès politique; La Reine vs. Jalbert, accusé du meurtre du lieutenant Weir du 32e Régiment de sa Majesté* (Montreal: F. Cinq-Mars 1839).

hidden themselves in anticipation of such a tactic. At about three o'clock in the afternoon, the British commander, noting that the patriot forces were continuing to build and that his own men were in no state to continue the fight, ordered a withdrawal.

First the ambush at Longueuil and now a small but very real battle at St Denis, and in both cases the patriots had scored clear victories. Few could seriously have predicted such an outcome in an encounter between poorly armed peasants and professional soldiers. But the British were by no means routed. Casualties at St Denis were, as Elinor Senior rightly observes, quite light for such a long engagement: she puts the figures at six dead, ten wounded, and six missing on the British side, with twelve deaths and seven wounded on the patriot side.[25] Yet the attackers were turned back and the insurgents even managed to capture their cannon, symbolic of triumph.

Louis-Joseph Papineau was nowhere to be seen when the patriots celebrated their victory. He had been at St Denis, staying in Wolfred Nelson's house, when the British first struck that morning, but he and his close associate E.B. O'Callaghan disguised themselves as habitants and rode off to safety soon after the fighting began. Ever since that day, this unheroic exit has provided wonderful material for the polemics of Papineau's enemies. A politician, not a soldier, Papineau was certainly not famous for his physical courage; but if we simply condemn him for cowardice and leave it at that, we lose an opportunity to understand his withdrawal in any but crudely moral terms. It does seem to be part of a larger pattern of hesitant, uncertain, and ineffectual behaviour that was evident several weeks prior to 23 November and would continue long after his flight from the battle. Papineau was present in the region, scuttling between St Charles and St Denis through most of the period the camps were in existence, but clearly he was not in command; the initiative belonged to Nelson, Brown, and the younger Patriots. Could

25 Senior, *Redcoats and Patriotes*, 87. Other sources provide casualty figures slightly at variance with this account.

it be that the seigneur of Petite Nation was, not simply out of his element, but also quite ambivalent about the popular, anti-feudal, and genuinely revolutionary directions the struggle with Britain was taking?

The victors of St Denis had little time to celebrate, since they expected an attack on St Charles at any moment. Indeed, two days after the initial clash on the Richelieu the troops sent north from Chambly arrived before the insurgent stronghold. It was a larger force – made up of 406 regulars, together with twenty colonial cavalry and two cannon – than the one defeated at St Denis; moreover, the men were rested and well fed and the weather was clear and bright. These factors greatly favoured the attackers, as did the disorganization that quickly became apparent in the patriot camp. Brown had made comparatively elaborate defensive arrangements, featuring a low wall forming a perimeter around the Debartzch manor as well as a series of pickets who were to harass the troops from prepared positions along the road. But the 'general' had not managed to establish any effective command structure. Consequently, he himself was constantly dashing back and forth dealing with every detail, large and small; it was altogether typical that, when the British first reached St Charles, Brown was in the village attending to the baking of bread.

The pickets guarding the approaches to the fort slowed the advance only slightly before retiring behind the walls. Hard on their heels came the soldiers, who quickly took possession of the fields surrounding St Charles. Arriving in columns, the troops were redeployed in long lines for the attack. The patriots would have been able to hear the sergeants shouting orders, the men wheeling and marching, the whole ominous spectacle as this ponderous military machine slowly and deliberately prepared itself for action. Soon the two field pieces were sending cannonballs and shrapnel into their midst. The effect must have been unnerving for the habitant-militiamen, and almost immediately scores began making their escape. Flight in the face of battle is of course the most natural behaviour in the world. In fact the central purpose of military training and discipline has always been to counteract this basic human reaction.[26] The imbalance in training and discipline in this case was far more important than the shortage of arms on the patriot side in sealing the outcome of this affray. In the days leading up to the battle there had been as many as 1,500 to 2,000 men at St Charles; fewer were present when the troops arrived, and with the defections that followed, Brown claimed that only 200 to 250 remained to fight; of these few, many were more or less unarmed.[27]

While the two sides exchanged volleys of musket fire, Brown rode to the rear and attempted to stem the flow of fugitives and rally his forces. Failing in this endeavour, he himself eventually joined the flight and made his way north to St Denis. Before going, he ordered his second-in-command, the Montreal physician H.-A. Gauvin, to escort the Constitutionalist prisoners to safety in St Hyacinthe. This move, undertaken no doubt in order to avert a repetition of the massacre of Lieutenant Weir, suggests that Brown did not trust the local militiamen. Moreover, it had the effect, coupled with the general's own desertion, of removing all members of the Montreal Patriot elite who had originally organized the militarization of St Charles. Only the region's own men now remained to face the wrath of the British.

After about an hour of heavy musket and artillery fire, the troops were ordered to fix bayonets and charge the low wall from which the patriots were firing. The assault was devastatingly effective. All we know about what happened next comes from the point of view of the victors; the most vivid account was penned later in life by Sir George Bell, a young officer in the Royals in 1837:

On entering the town there was little quarter; almost every man was put to death; in fact, they fought too long before thinking of flight. Many

26 John Keegan, *The Face of Battle* (London: Penguin 1976), 70–2
27 ANQ, 1837, no. 356, examen volontaire d'Henri-Alphonse Gauvin, 27 January 1838; NA, T.S. Brown memoirs. The general's figures should be treated with some scepticism, since he had good motives for exaggerating the extent of desertion and for understating the size of the force left to defend the fortifications.

were burned alive in the barns and houses, which were fired, as they would not surrender. Gun-barrels and powder flasks were exploding all night in the burning houses, and the picture that presented itself the following morning to my eyes was terrible. A number of swine got loose, and were eating the roasted bodies of the enemy who were burned in the barns and killed in the streets: those brutes were afterwards shot. The loss of the rebels was great; their position was strong, and they defended it with desperation; but they were totally routed, and received a lesson that they are not likely ever to forget. We took twenty-eight prisoners, destroyed a great quantity of arms and ammunition, spiked their two guns, and sunk them in the river, burned every house from whence a shot was fired, turned the priest's house into an hospital, and the church into a barrack.[28]

This 'old soldier' does tend to embellish his account, making much of the 'arms and ammunition,' which cannot have been plentiful, and of the 'two guns' which hardly needed spiking, since to all intents and purposes they had been inoperative from the start. Similarly, Bell probably exaggerates the more macabre aspects of the carnage. The fact remains that the loss of life was considerable. Parish burial records are of little use in establishing the exact number because many bodies were burned beyond recognition; others drowned trying to swim to safety across the Richelieu; and a large number were buried in a mass grave in unconsecrated ground, owing to the bishop's condemnation of rebellion. Figures quoted in official reports ranged from fifty-six to 152 deaths on the insurgent side. The British lost three men.[29] There is one point on which all the accounts, save that of Thomas Storrow Brown, agree with George Bell: 'The Canadians fought like devils at St. Charles.'[30]

28 Sir George Bell, *Rough Notes by an Old Soldier* (London: Day & Son 1867), 50–1
29 Senior, *Redcoats and Patriotes*, 98
30 These are the words of a British officer as quoted in ibid., 98. See also Sydney Bellingham, *Some Personal Recollections of the Rebellion of 1837 in Canada* (Dublin: Browne & Nolan 1901), 19: 'The enemy fought bravely, but fired too high.'

After their victory the British might have been expected to continue north and attempt to capture St Denis, but resistance was still lively in the Richelieu, and, hearing reports of armed patriot activity all along the river, Wetherall decided to return to Chambly. His men faced some sniper fire and harassment on the march south, but they had no trouble dispersing the largest concentration of militia at Pointe Olivier. At the end of November the troops reappeared in Montreal and paraded their prisoners, as well as the liberty pole consecrated at the meeting of the Six Counties, before the cheering Tory crowds. Meanwhile, news of the St Charles disaster spread throughout the Richelieu with the result that patriot resistance melted utterly and a military expedition was therefore able to occupy St Denis and the rest of the region in early December without encountering any opposition.

ST EUSTACHE

The southern campaign concluded, the patriots still remained in control of the county of Two Mountains. Here, just north of Montreal, deeper and more bitter conflicts developed in the first two weeks of December, reflecting partly the more serious political and ethnic divisions that had long been evident in the region and partly the more desperate position of northern patriots after the defeat at St Charles.

The patriot mobilization had begun in Deux-Montagnes about the same time and in much the same way that it took shape in the south.[31] News of impending arrests led to mass turnouts

31 The events in Two Mountains have been admirably covered not only in Senior's book, but also in an old but still very useful monograph, Emile Dubois, *Le feu de la rivière du Chêne: étude historique sur le mouvement insurrectionnel de 1837 au nord de Montréal* (Saint-Jérôme: Imprimerie Labelle 1937). There are also two excellent narratives written by first-hand observers: Amury Girod's journal, published in English translation in *PACR*, 1923, 370–80; and the account, published anonymously but clearly the work of one of the two priests of St Eustache parish: *Journal historique*

aimed at protecting local leaders; soon after, Patriot politicians fleeing the city came seeking asylum. Chief among the latter was Amury Girod, actually a gentleman-farmer from Varennes, but in most other respects a representative figure of the urban bourgeois Patriot elite. Similar to Thomas Storrow Brown in his energetic self-confidence, Girod soon secured his election as 'general' of the 'Patriot Army of the North.' He did his best to organize the military resources of the region in ways that he judged most useful to the insurgent cause as a whole, but, it must be said, the general could impose his will only when it coincided with that of his supposed subordinates, and frequently his designs were frustrated by the refusal of locals to follow his orders. The latter were particularly resistant to Girod's proposals to attack Montreal, insisting instead on a strictly defensive posture.

The villages of St Benoit and St Eustache (actually a small town) were the main rallying points for the region's patriots. St Eustache, it will be recalled, was a divided community with a substantial French-Canadian loyalist faction (see above, 160–1) that was especially strong in the parish's urban nucleus. It was partly for this reason, presumably, that insurgent activity centred on the back-country village of St Benoit through most of the second half of November. A more important consideration, however, was the fact that St Benoit seemed more exposed to attack. Two Mountains patriots felt that the immediate threat came from their old political enemies, the anglophones of St Andrews and the other settlements to the north, rather than from the British troops stationed in and around Montreal. Their fears were only intensified when the immigrant settlers, understandably nervous themselves, fielded a well-armed Volunteer force. Thus it was that militiamen converged on St Benoit around the time of the

des événements arrivés à Saint-Eustache pendant la Rébellion du comté du Lac des Deux-Montagnes (Montreal: John Jones 1838), reprinted in *La Rébellion de 1837 à Saint-Eustache, Maximilien Globensky,* ed. Hubert Aquin (Montreal: Editions du Jour 1974), 43–80. I have relied on these works in addition to the depositions of prisoners and informers.

Battle of St Denis and began erecting barricades on the roads leading into the parish from the north. Girod and his associates, annoyed with the way men came and left the camp as they pleased, tried for a time to institute a regular system of formal enlistments. Men signed up, as they understood it, 'pour la liberté.' More specifically, they were told that 'it was to guard against the people from the north that these enlistments were made.'[32]

On 24 November highly coloured reports of the previous day's victory at St Denis reached Two Mountains, encouraging local patriots, thought not to the point where they would consider any diversionary attack to relieve the pressure on their southern comrades. From that point on, however, the insurgents' own security measures (among other things they arrested the mail courier) had the effect of cutting the region off from the rest of the province. It was only after eight days, in fact, that definite news of the Battle of St Charles reached St Eustache, and even then bourgeois leaders did their best to keep the rank and file from knowing the full extent of the disaster. Meanwhile, rumours naturally filled the air, alarms followed one another, and tensions rose to a higher and higher pitch. Under these adverse and nerve-wracking conditions, the solidarity of the patriot leadership began to fracture, and before long die-hards and realists were openly in conflict.

The bulk of the patriot forces moved from St Benoit to the village of St Eustache on 29 November. Their motives are not entirely clear, but most likely they determined that in the absence of any sign of hostile action in the north an attack from the south was now more to be dreaded. At this point the insurgent bands seem to have been composed mainly of habitants from the parishes of St Benoit and Ste Scholastique. But they might as well have been Huns, Goths, or Scythians as far as the loyalist burgers of St Eustache were concerned. As the militiamen made their

---

32 ANQ, 1837, no. 645, examen volontaire de Damase Dehêtres, 12 May 1838 (author's translation)

straggling way down the Rivière Du Chêne that day, panic-stricken messengers spread the word through the southern parish, and dozens of families packed their belongings and fled to Montreal. There the men among them soon organized themselves into a Volunteer Corps in time to join in the British assault on their home village. Unlike the other engagements of the Rebellion, the conflict at St Eustache had some of the characteristics of a local civil war.

While a modest camp remained in existence at St Benoit, St Eustache was the main patriot military centre through the first half of December. The garrison was housed in the seigneurial manor house, the rectory, and a newly constructed convent, all clustered, along with the church, on a little square in the middle of the village. Over the course of the fortnight the strength of the insurgent force fluctuated widely, though normally it hovered around 700. For a time there were over 1,500 men in the camp according to Abbé Paquin, the local priest, an unwilling witness who was kept under house arrest by the insurgents.[33] On 2–3 December, on the other hand, the force dwindled almost to oblivion when respected local chiefs made an impassioned plea to the men, urging them to disperse as the only way to avert disaster. Vague reports of prisoners from the Richelieu being paraded through the streets of Montreal 'in fetters two and two tied together like felons' heightened the effect of these speeches: to the familiar physical risks of war they added the spectre of public degradation.[34] In the face of these warnings, the St Eustache doctor Jean-Olivier Chénier maintained a hard line. Initially he lost the debate, but he nevertheless managed to resurrect the camp by bringing in reinforcements from back-country parishes like Ste Scholastique and St Jérôme.

These were the redoubtable 'bonnets bleus' of the north, and they descended on St Eustache by the hundreds on 4 December,

33 Ibid., no. 715, examen volontaire de Richard Hubert, 27 January 1838; *Journal historique*, 51
34 ANQ, 1837, no. 813, deposition of Moyse Ollier, 19 February 1838

picking up more men, through persuasion or threats, from the settlements along the way. Some of the new recruits, such as Jérôme Longpré (the leader a few weeks earlier of the raid on Paisley), had a Bacchanalian image of revolution. 'Come along with us,' he urged a neighbour. 'You are well armed. We'll have fun; it's like a wedding, there's drinking, eating, violin playing, and dancing. We're free, you can do what you want. Anyone who needs leather can have it to make shoes.'[35] Such expectations of food, drink, and shoe leather did not necessarily accord with a complete respect for the sanctity of private property. Curé Paquin paints an unflattering portrait of the northern militiamen:

General Girod's efforts to establish discipline among his newly minted soldiers had little effect. These men would recognize no rules and believed themselves masters to do anything they pleased. This is how they conceived of the freedom of patriotism. Often they could be seen passing through the village in small groups of five or six, carrying rusty old guns on their shoulders, in their mouths the black and sooty old stub of a pipe, belching enormous puffs of tobacco smoke. Usually they wore great leather mittens and clothes made from homespun linen. They walked with a heavy step and often stumbled drunkenly.[36]

The pillaging or confiscation of property (there is no neutral term for this sort of thing) was much more extensive in Two Mountains than in any other area affected by the Rebellion. This is partly because so many men were mobilized and in need of provisions for a relatively long time; it is also because after 4 December most of the militiamen were some distance from their homes and in the midst of a rather unfriendly populace. In addition, one can detect at this stage indications that the incipient class conflict within the Patriot movement was becoming manifest as peasants began to challenge the bourgeois norms of their leaders where property was concerned. To some degree, the

35 Ibid., no. 640, déposition de Joseph Léveillé, 1 February 1838
36 *Journal historique*, 52 (author's translation)

revolution at St Eustache evolved into a struggle pitting poor against rich.

The first seizures of property occurred in the second half of November, and in many cases they were carried out on orders from Amury Girod and other middle-class Patriot officers. Sometimes they were punitive measures, essentially fines. For instance, a Constitutionalist doctor was accused of perpetrating a hoax that convinced everyone that the British were about to attack, spreading confusion in patriot ranks: 'He was arrested and sentenced by a Court martial to furnish a Gun and a Barrell of Powder.'[37] As happened at St Charles, leaders also occupied buildings in St Eustache and requisitioned arms, provisions and horses for military and security purposes. They did so in what they considered an 'orderly' fashion, as befitted a legitimate sovereign authority facing an acute emergency. Among the many actions aimed at securing munitions and neutralizing potential enemies, the largest in scale was the 1 December expedition against the Hudson's Bay Company post and Indian settlement at Oka.

Hoping to obtain cannon, small arms, and ammunition in significant quantities, several hundred patriots from St Eustache and St Benoit converged on Oka. They managed to secure only one cannon and some lead at the Hudson's Bay Company store before proceeding to the native village, where a mixed population of Mohawk, Algonquin, and others had been established under the auspices of Sulpician missionaries for over a century. Here Amury Girod entered into talks with an unnamed local chief. At first he tried to persuade the Indians to throw in their lot with the rebels, and when it became obvious that this was out of the question, he asked them to declare their neutrality in the coming conflict and to sell the patriots the two cannon they reportedly possessed. The chief replied diplomatically and somewhat enigmatically, as might be expected under the circumstances, but he firmly declined to turn over his armaments. Unwilling to risk open conflict, Girod and his men left the village

37 *PACR*, 1923, Girod journal, 374

with nothing more than the disappointing booty they had found at the trading post. As he congratulated himself on thus securing 'the good will of these Sons of nature,' it apparently never occurred to the general that the Indians might consider 250 armed men invading their settlement without warning a rather unfriendly act, even if they did depart peacefully. The next day the Oka chiefs sent their cannon to the loyalist Volunteers of St Andrews.[38]

Meanwhile, the farmers and townsfolk of St Eustache were subjected to a series of forcible requisitions, starting from the moment the village was occupied on 29 November: 'The said body of armed men on their way to and at the said village of St Eustache took from all the Loyal Inhabitants that they met with in their route their fire arms, provisions and ammunition which they carried away.'[39] In the days that followed, bands of militiamen made regular tours up and down the concession roads, stopping at each farmhouse to order the men to report for duty at the camp or suffer the consequences. If they met with refusal or, as was more often the case, if the man of the house had already taken refuge in the woods, they took away potatoes, wheat, or, most commonly, cattle and other livestock. The pillaging was not indiscriminate, nor was it by any means unrestricted. Although the raiders occasionally demanded a small sum of money or an item such as a tobacco box, usually they limited their seizures to a few specified animals.[40] I suspect that the amount taken was roughly proportional to the apparent wealth of the victim in each case, although I have no real proof beyond a remark by curé Paquin that the 'rich' especially suffered.[41] All indications are that these confiscations would have inflicted real economic injury without actually depriving a family of the means

38 Ibid., 375–8; Senior, *Redcoats and Patriotes*, 118–20
39 ANQ, 1837, no. 652, deposition of James Gentle, 6 December 1837. This, it should be noted, is not a first-hand report. The deponent, a St Eustache merchant, had fled the village before the patriot militiamen arrived.
40 See, among other depositions describing specific visitations, ibid., no. 625, déposition de Pierre Charbonneau, 6 January 1838.
41 *Journal historique*, 54

of maintaining itself. In this respect they differed from the all-out looting and burning soon to be visited upon the rebels of Two Mountains by the triumphant loyalists. A Ste Scholastique habitant named Augustin Sanche dit L'Espagnol was in charge of most of the recorded expeditions. When later arrested, he naturally claimed to have been acting against his own inclination under orders from General Girod, but all the sources indicate that he entered into the task with a zest and an enthusiasm that could not have been forced.[42]

Meanwhile, depredations of a different sort were proceeding in the village, where a number of stores, as well as the homes of comparatively prosperous residents, had been abandoned by their owners. Some of the rough 'bonnets bleus' apparently felt entitled to help themselves to the goods belonging to 'deserters' and political enemies. An employee left alone to guard the shop of Hubert Globensky watched, powerless to prevent a gang from carrying off three barrels of wine, a barrel of whiskey, and a keg of peppermint.[43] In this and many other cases straight forward theft was carried out by unruly elements in a situation where traditional restraints had disappeared. The resulting drunkenness of course only increased the disorder, much to the dismay of Amury Girod.

The general's candid personal diary makes it clear that he was appalled by the looting; though convinced that it was the work of a small minority, he feared 'it would stamp us with the character of Robbers.' Far from supporting Augustin Sanche's plea that he acted under orders, Girod's journal contains the following entry for 29 November: 'Depredations had been committed under the pretense of punishing the Loyalists. – Some individuals plundered Arms, Cattle and furniture. – I proposed to the Committee to take measures, to put a stop, to these depredations.' He did indeed issue a proclamation to that effect, posted guards at points in the village where looting had been reported, and imprisoned three looters. Even the unsympathetic curé Paquin

42 ANQ, 1837, no. 628, examen volontaire d'Augustin Sanche, 27 January 1838
43 Ibid., no. 786, déposition de Théodore Girard, 1 January 1838

observed that the commander assembled his troops to condemn plundering in the strongest terms. The audience was evidently not convinced, and Girod was forced to explain the difference between casual theft and his own requisitions, which were, he argued, exclusively for the needs of the service; moreover, they were officially sanctioned by virtue of his authority as general; finally, they were subject to later repayment by the provisional government.[44]

The habitant-militiamen seem to have had a different view of the moral issues involved. Some of course were simply delighted to get drunk on someone else's whiskey without giving the matter any further thought. For others, however, the act of taking another's pigs, grain, or cattle, whether ordered by an insurgent general or not, posed serious questions of conscience. One group, discussing such topics over dinner, decided that 'there is no sin in taking things from a neighbour in order to survive.'[45] This 'ethic of subsistence' does seem to have played a role in much of the pillaging that went on prior to the battle of St Eustache. At a time when many men from St Jérôme were away at the rebel camp, the parish's most substantial merchant, a French-Canadian loyalist, was threatened by a party of insurgents and ordered to provide food for ('faire vivre') the families of men serving at St Eustache. There were overtones of economic redistribution in another incident, when half a minot of flour was taken from a St Eustache farmer 'to give to a poor man who was going to join the rebels.'[46]

In the final days of the St Eustache camp the transfer of goods from rich to poor began on a substantial scale. At least three men

---

44 *PACR*, 1923, Girod journal, 375, 379, 380; ANQ, 1837, no. 721, examen volontaire de Jacques Dubeau, 31 January 1838; *Journal historique*, 51–2. Note that victims of official patriot requisitioning were indeed given receipts signed on behalf of the 'provisional government.' See ANQ, 1837, no. 779, déposition de Jean-Auguste Cloutier, 7 December 1837.

45 ANQ, 1837, no. 682, déposition de Jean-Baptiste Jubenville, 30 December 1837

46 Ibid., no. 567, déposition de Casimir Tétard de Montigny, 6 February 1838; ibid., no. 656, déposition de Pierre Touchette, 20 December 1837

with sleighs were kept busy transporting potatoes from the cellars of a village merchant, firewood from the seigneur's domain, and beef from the patriot butchering operation; all these goods were delivered in specified quantities to local 'poor people.' Not only militiamen and their families were supplied; among the beneficiaries was the widow Lanthier, who received one minot of potatoes.[47]

Evidently private property – whether in the form of seigneurial estates or movable goods – was not an absolute value for the embattled rural plebeians of Lower Canada. Neither was it totally taboo for the middle-class leaders of the Patriot movement. Like anyone else claiming sovereign power, the latter reserved the right to punish criminals and traitors with confiscation; they also believed themselves justified in requisitioning supplies, subject to later compensation, in a military emergency. The habitants seem to have accepted the propriety of economic conscription and punitive confiscation, but they were unconcerned about formalities and (note the parallel with their attitude to seigneurial privileges) disinclined even to promise future compensation. Instead they invoked, by implication at least, a standard of substantive justice. Those who refused to defend their country, they apparently believed, should not enjoy any surplus when others were doing their patriotic duty at the cost of their own and their families' subsistence. Following this logic, it would be legitimate to take some, but not all, the animals and grain stocks from uncooperative habitants. The less restrained looting of village shops presumably reflects a peasant belief that merchants were by definition wealthy and above any worries about subsistence.

Nevertheless, plebeian patriots were not starvelings hostile to

47 NA, LC Civil Secretary, 531: 150, déposition d'Antoine Giroux, 25 February 1838; ibid., 531: 157, déposition d'André Thibault, 29 January 1838; NA, LC Adjutant General, vol. 50, Deux Montagnes, déposition de Marguerite Girouard, 2 July 1839; ibid., déposition d'Alexis Danis, 2 July 1839. For evidence of a similar distribution of provisions to 'poor families' a year later in the vicinity of the patriot camp at Napierville, see ANQ, 1837, no. 2431, examen volontaire de Jean Baptiste Dozois, 16 November 1838.

all forms of property and bent on appropriating all wealth for the benefit of the needy. For the most part they themselves were peasant property holders, and research shows that active insurgents enjoyed an average level of wealth at least as high as the mean in their respective communities. Under normal circumstances few habitants would have dreamed of taking anything that did not belong to them. The point is that under the very unusual conditions prevailing in November-December 1837 they acted on a particular conception of the limits of private property rights. Their theory and their practice in this regard tended to highlight a certain divergence between the bourgeois and the peasant elements in the patriot movement, much to the chagrin of leaders like Amury Girod. As it was for Papineau at St Denis, the general must have faced the prospect of a British attack with some misgivings about the men nominally under his command and the sort of revolution they seem to have had in mind.

Girod and his men had to wait until 14 December to face the enemy. After the debacle at St Denis, Colborne was compelled to treat the rebels with greater respect, all the more so since the reports of fugitive loyalists had greatly exaggerated the strength of the insurgents assembled at St Eustache and St Benoit. Consequently, the British commander waited until the bulk of his troops had returned from the Richelieu and an additional regiment from Quebec had arrived at Montreal before launching his northern expedition. Such was the pathetic state of patriot intelligence that the onslaught took Girod and everyone else in Two Mountains completely by surprise both in its timing and in its scale and ferocity.

The alarm sounded shortly after 11 a.m. when a party of Volunteers was sighted across the river from St Eustache. Thinking this was the entire force arrayed against them and confident of victory, 300 patriots set out across the ice to skirmish with their attackers. No sooner had they engaged than they were assailed by a burst of grapeshot coming from their left. Looking up, the insurgents gazed in astonishment at the enemy's main force snaking its way along the St Eustache side of the river and bearing down on the village from the east. Colborne had succeeded in surprising his opponents by taking a circuitous approach and by sending on a small detachment as a diversionary ruse. His two-mile-long column was composed of 1,280 British regulars and 220 Lower Canadian Volunteers, together with five field pieces and even some rockets. As the patriots fled back to their stronghold, the attackers slowly and methodically made their way around the village in a great arc. The purpose of this movement was of course to cut off all avenues of retreat, but before the circle closed completely, the majority of the patriots, including Amury Girod and most of the other leaders, had made their escape. (Cornered by bounty-hunters several days later, Girod blew his own brains out.) Earlier that morning, St Eustache had been defended by about 8–900 men, but only 200–250 remained to face the final siege. They took refuge in the stone buildings surrounding the central square; fifty or sixty under the command of Dr Chénier placed themselves around the balcony of the church, demolishing the stairway behind them. For four hours they managed to fend off the vastly superior force arrayed against them. Colborne began with an extended artillery barrage; eventually he ordered an infantry assault on the rebel positions. Sir George Bell takes up the story at this point:

From the priest's house they kept up a brisk fire upon our men. The guns came up to a corner of the main street, and riddled the church door. The Royals then were ordered to storm it [the rectory], which they did in most gallant style, firing the adjoining house, which burned out the rebels there. Under the great column of smoke that issued from this building, many of the enemy escaped from the church, and crossed the river on the ice; but they met the Volunteers who were waiting for them in the wood, and were slaughtered. The flames soon communicated to the church. There was but one choice left – to bolt out and be shot, or burned alive. There was no escape, and they died as they fought, regardless of life. Chenier, the only chief who stood by them to the last, was killed in the churchyard ...

The wounded were most severely riddled; many of them bled to death for want of surgical aid. I found one poor fellow with his arm shattered above the elbow with a grape shot. Some soldiers were just going to dispatch him, when I came up. He was crying for mercy, and the blood was pouring from the wound most rapidly. I took off one of my mocassin strings, and bound his arm tight, which stopped the effusion of blood. It was amputated the same night, and I believe he recovered. I had some difficulty in saving a few other prisoners from the soldiers, who were much excited. I walked about the most part of the night, not being in a sufficiently composed state to lie down. The town was in flames. The cries of the wounded were piercing, many of them being roasted alive. The heat of the fire melted the snow, and the street was in a puddle. The soldiers were cutting down houses, to prevent the fire reaching the hospital, and altogether the scene was too terrible to permit me, fagged as I was, to retire to my humble billet.[48]

There is no way of knowing how many patriots died at St Eustache. Elinor Senior's estimate is seventy, whereas she puts the figure for British losses at three. The village was burned to the ground, though not before the soldiers and Volunteers had carried off everything of value. Martial law having been declared a week earlier, almost anyone without the most impeccable loyalist credentials was subject to arrest. No one therefore could safely gather up the dead, and when a magistrate was sent from Montreal four days after the encounter, he was horrified to find bodies still lying in the streets.[49] Among the insurgent casualties was Eustache Lantier of St Jérôme. His wife, Marianne, later recounted that Lantier had been one of a group of reinforcements summoned to the camp on the very eve of the battle. Some thirty men had met at the Lantier house that day, and there had been heated discussion as to whether they should heed the call to arms. Eustache himself was reluctant to go, but he bowed to the will of the majority: 'My friends, either we all march, or we all stay home.' The others wanted to go, and so, with five or six guns between them, they set off for St Eustache. Marianne never

48 Bell, *Rough Notes by an Old Soldier*, 55–6
49 Senior, *Redcoats and Patriotes*, 213; McCord Museum, de Rocheblave Collection, De Rocheblave to Bouthillier, 21 December 1837; Bibliothèque Nationale, Montreal, Romuald Trudeau journal, 12: 91

saw her husband again. No body was recovered, but she heard he had been among the defenders of the church of St Eustache and that he had been killed during the artillery barrage. Jérôme Longpré, on the other hand, escaped unscathed. This was the man who had done so much to encourage the recruitment of St Jérôme militiamen with tales of drinking and dancing at the camp. He had taken part in the initial foray against the Volunteer detachment across the ice; on catching sight of the main attacking force, he took flight, along with many of his comrades, and did not stop until he reached home.[50]

General Colborne's troops moved on to St Benoit on the day after the battle. There, by prearrangement, they met a large force of Volunteers who had come down from the English-speaking settlements to the north, pillaging and burning selected farmhouses as they went. The St Benoit patriots sent advance word that they were surrendering, and they had all their weapons grounded by the time the soldiers arrived. Nevertheless, the unresisting village was looted and burned just as thoroughly as St Eustache had been. The military authorities had ordered only three houses put to the torch, and they blamed overzealous Volunteers for the conflagration. Any nice allocation of responsibility is impossible and beside the point: firebrands were deployed in a concentrated cluster of wooden buildings, and the results were altogether predictable. On this glorious note ended the military campaigns of 1837.

The Lower Canadian fighting had not been on a gigantic scale, and any comparison with the wars of Napoleon, Grant, or Hitler would certainly make them appear paltry and inconsequential. Yet in the context of the history of this small colony it was a painful and costly episode with decisive and lasting results. The loss of life at both St Charles and St Eustache had been heavy enough that General Colborne felt a need to defend his troops against charges of excessive cruelty when he reported to the

---

50 ANQ, 1837, no. 636, déposition de Marianne Valiquette, 1 February 1838; ibid., no. 702, examen volontaire de Jérôme Longpré, 14 February 1838

colonial secretary. The problem, he pointed out, was that the rebels refused to surrender even when they were beaten: 'I heard, however, that so determined and excited were many of these deluded men, under the command of Chenier, they continued firing at our troops, even after the houses had been forced open and entered.' The general had a comforting explanation for this behaviour: 'Such instances of obstinacy and desperate conduct can only be accounted for by their having been kept constantly in a state of intoxication, and from the dread of their leaders that should they be made prisoners they would be tried and condemned.'[51]

If the patriot rank and file were often under the influence of alcohol, there is every reason to suspect that Colborne's men also were. Referring to the British at Waterloo, the distinguished military historian John Keegan writes, 'Many of the soldiers had drunk spirits before the battle, and continued to drink while it was in progress'; and the same observation could be made of almost every military engagement since the Middle Ages.[52] No doubt it is also true that the habitant militiamen were afraid of being captured and punished for treason. Indeed, the memoirs of patriots imprisoned in the wake of the insurrection reveal that they suffered greatly, not only from the loss of freedom, but also from the disgrace of being treated as criminals.[53] But these anxieties could be invoked to account for quite contradictory behaviour: surely this is why some insurgents ran away from the battles as well as why others fought to the end. In fact, so many Patriot leaders may have deserted their troops precisely because they knew they were more likely to be hanged if they fell into the hands of the enemy.

How then do we explain the determination of Eustache Lantier and all the other habitants and craftsmen who sacrificed their lives at St Denis, St Charles, and St Eustache? If we take at face

51 BPP, 9: 209, Colborne to Glenelg, 30 March 1838
52 Keegan, Face of Battle, 183, 333
53 Allan Greer, 'Rebels and Prisoners: The Canadian Insurrections of 1837–38,' Acadiensis 14 (Autumn 1984): 144

value the testimony of patriot prisoners arrested following the defeats of November and December and facing charges of high treason, all were coerced or fooled into taking up arms by the threats and promises of Papineau, Brown, Girod, and other leaders. But could so few have compelled so many had the latter truly been unwilling? Bishop Lartigue did not think so, and he forbade the curé of St Denis to accept this excuse from rebels trying to avoid ecclesiastical sanctions. 'Those who were threatened had only to unite and make common cause against those threatening them,' he pointed out.[54] Lartigue was well aware that support for the patriot cause was overwhelming, indeed virtually universal, in St Denis and many other rural parishes in the District of Montreal. Coercion, ranging from the peer pressure that persuaded Eustache Lantier to accompany his friends to the patriot camp, to the punitive plundering of habitants who failed to report to St Eustache and Wolfred Nelson's threat to cut the throat of anyone who deserted his position at St Denis, was primarily a matter of internal discipline. Compulsion is an inseparable part of 'civilized warfare' (to use an oxymoron favoured by military historians to distinguish the clash of disciplined bodies of men from the 'savage' style of combat that depends on the courage of individual warriors), given the natural human impulse to avoid danger, regardless of principled commitments. Certainly the troops serving under General Colborne were subject to it (imagine the fate of any soldier who dropped his musket and ran from the field of St Denis!), and so were the militiamen who were subject to the much less effective authority claimed by the Patriot movement.

What Sir John Colborne failed to grasp – and it is a point that has tended to elude the more sophisticated historical minds since his time – is the genuine popularity of the patriots and their revolution. The idea of resistance to British rule and the formation of an independent Lower Canadian republic did not orig-

---

54 Lartigue to Demers, 19 December 1837, quoted in Allaire, *Histoire de Saint-Denis*, 419 (author's translation)

inate within the French-Canadian peasantry. Yet the male habitants did become involved in the political/constitutional struggles of 1837. The revolutionary process as it unfolded – with its arbitrators, its charivaris, its local elections – increasingly bore the imprint of the rural lower classes, their habits, attitudes, and aspirations. By November an anti-feudal and masculine-democratic thrust was unmistakable. Without ever overthrowing the hegemony of the professional middle class, the habitants were making this revolution their own.

11

Repression, resurgence, and final defeat

Men fight and lose the battle, and the thing they fought for comes about
in spite of their defeat, and when it comes turns out not to be what they
meant, and other men have to fight for what they meant under another
name.

William Morris, 'The Dream of John Ball'

REPRESSION

By the beginning of 1838 Lower Canada was no longer a colony
governed by British law; it was enemy territory occupied by
military force. The constitution had been suspended, the elected
Assembly replaced by a 'Special Council' packed with loyalists,
and General Colborne himself now occupied the governor's
palace. In the District of Montreal a régime of martial law prevailed as of 5 December 1837, and habeas corpus was no longer
in effect. Even more draconian legal restrictions followed the
insurrection of November 1838. Jean-Marie Fecteau is right to
draw our attention to the extraordinary character of this collection of authoritarian measures.[1] Such wholesale abandonment of
trial by jury, protection of the accused, and all the cherished

1 Jean-Marie Fecteau, 'Mesures d'exception et règle de droit: les conditions
  d'application de la loi martiale au Québec lors des rébellions de 1837–1838,'
  McGill Law Journal 32 (July 1987): 464–95

principles of British justice was unheard of in the mother country, although there were precedents in the history of Ireland and of some other colonies. In the eyes of the government and its supporters, of course, all was justified by the 'unsettled state' of the province. The authorities actually had no need of special legal weapons to defeat the patriots on the field of battle, but they knew that, as long as juries decided guilt and innocence, there would be few convictions for political offences. Thus the setting aside of civil liberties was testimony to the continuing alienation of the majority from a colonial régime that had not yet converted military triumph into political victory. It might also be regarded as one further gauge of the truly revolutionary nature of the Lower Canadian crisis, since recourse to such means constituted an implicit admission on the part of the conquerors that their rule rested on naked force.

From the moment the smoke cleared, it was open season on 'rebels': anyone could be arrested and imprisoned, their property seized or destroyed, with no trace of formalities, due process, or appeal. Of course the same conditions applied in the places where the patriots had held sway at the time of the armed camps, but their little punitive gestures were utterly eclipsed by the repression later visited upon the rebellious sections of the province.[2] To take one example among many, the wife of a

2 This point should be qualified in the light of two grisly episodes, both of which occurred in the Richelieu region in November 1837. One was the murder of Lieutenant Weir during the Battle of St Denis (see above, 309–10). The other was a bizarre 'execution' carried out a week later near the town of St Jean and involving, it seems, a mixture of personal and political motives. A 'chouayen' stonemason named Chartrand fell afoul of a small group of patriot militiamen; they arrested him, went through the motions of a treason trial, then tied him to a tree and shot him dead. See ANQ, 1837, nos 382–419; *Procès politique: la reine vs. Nicolas et al: accusés d'avoir mis à mort, le 27 novembre 1837, pendant l'insurrection, le nommé Joseph Armand, dit Chartrand, l'un des volontaires au service de Sa majesté, stationnés à St Jean, cités pour répondre à cette accusation devant le tribunal ayant juridiction dans ce district, le 6 août 1838, et acquittés par le jury, le 7 août 1838* (Montreal: F. Lemaître 1838); *BPP*, 10: 174–80; F. Murray Greenwood, 'The Chartrand Murder Trial: Rebellion and Repression in Lower Canada, 1837–1839,' *Criminal Justice History* 5 (1984): 129–59.

patriot merchant who had taken refuge in the United States reported that a party led by a local justice of the peace had come to the store one day and confiscated the entire stock. Not only did they ignore her request to show by what authority the seizure was undertaken, but they forced her to provide boxes to pack their loot; she could not even persuade them to leave her a few turnips and cabbages for winter provisions.[3]

More significant than the burning and looting, however, were the arrests. The two jails in Montreal were packed with over 500 political prisoners, some of them rebels taken, arms in hand, at one of the battles, most the victims of anonymous denunciation or simple bad luck. A Constitutionalist magistrate from Montreal found that matters were out of hand in St Eustache in the days following the battle there: 'I put a stop to the arrests which were increasing ad infinitum. Everyone wishing to demonstrate his zeal by the number of prisoners that he made, there was a fine opportunity to satisfy feelings of envy, jealousy or hatred that one might harbour against one's neighbour.' Several individual cases from various parts of the province indicate that this sort of 'zeal' was quite widespread. One concerned Jean-Baptiste Vallée, who must have considered himself exempt from danger because he lived at Kildare, some distance from any fighting or serious revolutionary activity. A party of Volunteers was nevertheless quartered at his house one night in December, and Vallée sat up late drinking with his guests. All went well until they started bragging about how one Englishman or a Scot could frighten several French Canadians; Vallée erupted in anger and a shouting match ensued. There was no violence, but all the same, the Volunteers took the habitant into custody next day and packed him off to prison. Whereas Vallée's hot temper got him into trouble, Louis Dérigé dit Laplante owed his punishment more to cowardice. This St Constant habitant claimed to have taken no part whatsoever in the Rebellion, but when Volunteers came to his home on 2 February, he took fright and hid in the cellar. Some

3 ANQ, 1837, no. 536, deposition of Adelaide Bureau, 4 January 1838

well-placed jabs with a bayonet flushed him out, and he was led away, bleeding from chest wounds, his guilt proved conclusively by his attempt to escape detection.[4]

From one viewpoint, this semi-indiscriminate repression was justified; for in many parts of the District of Montreal almost every man had been implicated to some degree in the patriot movement. The authorities were looking for evidence not only of violent revolutionary activity; even attendance at the meeting of the Confederation of the Six Counties was deemed in retrospect an act of treason. Together with the suspension of civil liberties, this broad definition of political crime gave wide scope for the sort of passions mentioned above by the Montreal magistrate, particularly on the part of Constitutionalist Volunteers who had previously been persecuted by the patriots. In and around the parish of La Présentation, a JP named Simon Talon dit Lespérance instituted a particularly oppressive régime that even fellow loyalists compared to the despotism of the Bey of Algiers. A country merchant, Lespérance had been held for several days at the St Charles camp, while local patriots had helped themselves to the wares on display in his shop. At the time of the battle, he was evacuated from the camp, and on the road from St Charles he managed to overpower his guards and take them prisoner.[5] Captive became captor and, within days, scourge of the region. Lespérance had grounds for sending dozens of men to jail, and when evidence was lacking, he would arrest an innocent individual and threaten him with prison unless he swore a deposition incriminating the intended victim. He and his bailiff harassed the wives of political prisoners in a variety of petty ways, sending them on long and ultimately pointless journeys, for example, or

4 McCord Museum, de Rocheblave Collection, Rocheblave to Bouthillier, 21 December 1837 (author's translation); ANQ, 1837, no. 1092, examen volontaire de Jean-Baptiste Vallée, 12 February 1838; ANQM, Affaires Criminelles, examen volontaire de Louis Dérigé dit Laplante, 19 February 1838
5 ANQ, 1837, no. 291, déposition de Simon Talon Lespérance, 26 November 1837

repeatedly requisitioning their horses. They also committed more serious offences: Félicité Giasson testified that Lespérance lured her into a back room with promises of news of her imprisoned husband and then began fondling her 'shameful parts' until she managed to break away. Two other women complained of the same treatment.[6] Men were blackmailed into paying inflated 'debts' and performing errands and other services gratis.[7]

Few Constitutionalists were as unprincipled or as cruel as Simon Talon Lespérance, but most joined him in calling for the execution of at least a substantial proportion of the vanquished rebels. Since hanging was the recognized punishment for high treason, those taken into custody (not to mention their families) must have suffered mortal anguish. Louis Fréchette of St Jean remembered of his arrest: 'The armed Volunteers, who were keeping guard over me, appeared to take a brutal pleasure in frightening me, and talked in a free and easy way of shooting me.'[8] But in the end no one was shot or hanged in the wake of the 1837 insurrection. Men were released through the course of the following spring, and in June Lord Durham, the new gov-

---

6 Ibid., no. 289, déposition de Félicité Giasson, 12 February 1838; ANQM, Affaires Criminelles, vol. 51, requête d'Amable Rousseau, 12 February 1838

7 See, in addition to the materials cited above, ANQ, 1837, no. 282, déposition d'Amable Rousseau, 18 February 1838; NA, LC Civil Secretary, 532: 100, Hertel de Rouville to Colborne, 20 March 1838; ibid., 532: 124, déposition de François Gagnon, 23 March 1838; ibid., 533: 78, déposition de François Chapdelaine dt Larivière, 3 April 1838; ibid., 533: 117, déclaration de François Guillemet and François Nadeau, 9 April 1838; ANQM, Affaires Criminelles, vol. 48, déposition de Louise Roberge, 15 December 1838; ibid., déposition de Charles Gauthier, 15 December 1838. The seigneur Hertel de Rouville, who had been so helpful to the British forces on their way to attack St Charles, assembled evidence of Lespérance's tyranny and tried to get the government to stop it. The latter dismissed all the testimony, however, since it came from politically suspect witnesses and the merchant/magistrate was in effect exonerated. NA, LC Civil Secretary, 533: 150, Leclère to Ogden, 6 April 1838

8 Translated affidavit of Louis Fréchette published in [B.C.A. Gugy], *Some Incidents related by Credible Witnesses, in the Life of a Provincial* (Quebec 1861), 7–8

ernor-general, issued his famous amnesty order, which freed all the remaining prisoners except for eight of the most prominent leaders, who were exiled to Bermuda. This might be considered an act of clemency, but it was also a matter of expediency, since it obviated the need for potentially embarrassing trials and avoided creating martyrs. In Upper Canada, where the insurgent movement had been much weaker, two rebels were hanged; the absence of executions in the lower province could be seen in fact as a reflection of the continuing strength of revolutionary sentiment and the consequent need on the government's part to proceed carefully. Moreover, even as we recognize that the repression could have been more severe (think of the savage bloodlettings that followed the defeat of so many popular revolts known to history), it is well to remember that it was real enough and must have had devastating and lasting effects on Félicité Giasson, Jean-Baptiste Vallée, and hundreds of others. Thousands more were affected by the fear of punishment.

How else can we explain the huge number of signatures on 'loyal addresses' and the massive swearing of the oath of allegiance in the early part of 1838? As part of its ad hoc campaign of pacification, the government nominated commissioners to administer the oath in different parts of the province, leaving it to the commissioners to impose the oath as they saw fit. Most people complied when the consequences of refusal became clear. Magistrates examining a St Ours carpenter in the Montreal jail on 13 February learned that he had been arrested two months earlier, 'because I hesitated to take the oath of allegiance to the queen.' In Boucherville, a young man declined the oath in spite of explicit threats of imprisonment, but he advised his friends to conform for the sake of their families: 'As for me, since I was a bachelor and no one would suffer as a result of my detention, I preferred prison to taking the oath of fidelity.'[9] In some com-

---

9 ANQ, 1837, no. 274, examen volontaire de Denis Peloquin dit Félix, 13 February 1838; ibid., no. 1933, examen volontaire d'Adolphe Dugas, 12 May 1838 (author's translation)

munities people took the oath, assuring themselves that it was not binding because it had been sworn under compulsion. But a surprising number resisted in spite of the dire consequences. Refusal was particularly common in areas that had not been in the forefront of the patriot cause in the previous year. At St Paul de Lavaltrie, the commissioner and his assistant encountered stubborn resistance, and, when they tried to arrest the ringleader, the crowd successfully fought them off. Refusal was a massive phenomenon also in the Irish parish of St Columban north of Montreal, in English-speaking Stanstead county, and in the Quebec region at Lotbinière and St Jean Deschaillons.[10]

THE HUNTERS' CONSPIRACY

Even in these dark days, rural patriots were not without hope. The knowledge that many leaders had escaped to the United States, together with the belief that the latter might secure foreign assistance to renew the fight, helped to sustain morale. Travellers talked of great armies of Americans that would be led by Papineau, Mackenzie, and even 'Bonaparte's cousin'; they would capture Quebec, burn Montreal, and destroy everyone 'under the Crown.' 'The upheaval is not over yet; we have only seen one little leaf fall from the tree,' declared Joseph Bonin in a church-front conversation. 'Mr Papineau is going to come with a great quantity of men.'[11] The reports, embellished with fanciful details

10 Ibid., no. 586, déposition de Charles Gougé, 15 January 1838; NA, LC Civil Secretary, 531: 112, [illegible] to Griffin, 8 February 1838; ibid., 530: 251, Ritchie to Walcott, 27 January 1838; ibid., 530: 151, Legendre to Walcott, 15 January 1838. For further evidence of refusal of the oath, see ANQ, 1837, no. 176, déposition d'Etienne Filteau et Charles Bazinet, 11 December 1837; ibid., no. 589, Mandat d'arrestation pour Pierre-Denis Normand, 10 January 1838; ibid., no. 621, déposition de Jacob Martins, 18 January 1838; ibid., no. 1095, deposition of William Berczy, 15 January 1838; ibid., no. 1096, déposition d'Alexis Landry, 22 December 1837; ibid., no. 1789, déposition de Frederick Hart, 13 January 1838.
11 ANQ, 1837, no. 1055, déposition de Charles et Eustache Belair, 18 January 1838; ibid., no. 322, déposition d'Augustin Berthiaume, 5 January 1838 (author's translation)

though they often were, accurately reflected the essential facts. Across the northern states, from Maine to Michigan, refugees from Upper and Lower Canada were at work with American sympathizers in an effort to salvage the revolution and extend the struggle against Great Britain and its Canadian partisans.

It would not be Louis-Joseph Papineau, however, who would lead any liberating invasion of Lower Canada. Even in the fall of 1837 Papineau had evinced growing discomfort with the developing rural revolution; by the early months of 1838 he was a rather isolated and marginal figure among the Canadian exiles. He ended up on the losing side of some acrimonious disputes that divided the refugees over points of strategy and matters of principle. By all accounts, it was the agrarian question that formed a major focus of contention. C.-H.-O. Côté, along with Robert Nelson, was at the head of a radical faction determined to pursue a thoroughly republican political program featuring, among other things, the complete liquidation of seigneurial tenure. The 'Declaration of Independence' they issued in February 1838 called for the abolition of 'the feudal or seigniorial tenure ... as if it had never existed in this country.' Other Patriots, most notably Papineau himself, could not support such a position. His personal copy of the 'Declaration' has survived; on it the phrases dealing with feudal tenure have been angrily struck out, and a note in the margin states, 'It is not legal, nor is it just to rob a seigneur any more than another man.'[12] Meanwhile, the sometime rebel leader held aloof from all revolutionary activities. 'Papineau has abandoned us,' wrote a bitter Robert Nelson, 'and this through selfish and family motives regarding the seigniories, and inveterate love of the old French bad laws.'[13]

---

12 Fernand Ouellet, ed., *Papineau: textes choisis* (Quebec: Presses de l'Université Laval 1970), 83
13 *BPP*, 10: 101, Nelson to Ryan, 25 February 1838. Cf. *Report of the State Trials, Before a General Court Martial Held at Montreal in 1838–1839: Exhibiting a Complete History of the Late Rebellion in Lower Canada*, 2 vols (Montreal: Armour and Ramsay 1839), vol. II, app. 13.

Papineau's defection, foreshadowed in his flight from the battle of St Denis, should be seen as part of a larger process: the political polarization of seigneurs and censitaires. Like Pierre-Dominique Debartzch two years earlier, this seigneur had no stomach for a movement that threatened to upset agrarian class relations; it just took him longer to recognize the direction of events. Through 1837 he managed to overcome his misgivings in hopes of securing neat and pure political independence for Lower Canada, but as it became clear that a serious commitment to the expropriation of the seigneurs was the price of maintaining popular support, Papineau could go no further and leadership passed to the Patriot left wing.[14] More than land tenure was at stake in his conflict with Côté and Nelson; behind that issue lay the whole question of the role of the peasantry in the patriot revolution. The radicals were willing to go much further than Papineau was in embracing the habitants and the revolution they had done so much to shape in the fall of 1837. They made it their business, therefore, to give clear and explicit voice in the campaign of 1838 to the democratic and anti-feudal aspirations of the patriot rank and file. Accordingly, their Declaration of Independence called for a 'Republican form of Government,' universal manhood suffrage, the secret ballot, as well as the abolition of seigneurial tenure.

Though this radical program might consolidate popular support for revolution within Lower Canada, what the Patriot leaders stood more in need of was arms and military assistance from outside the province to counter the continuing British troop build-up. Three infantry regiments completed the overland march from the maritime provinces at the end of December 1837, and two more came from overseas in the following May. In June two cavalry regiments arrived, giving Colborne a total of over 5,000 British regulars as well as thousands more Lower Canadian Volunteers by mid-summer.[15] Under the circumstances, the

14 Fernand Ouellet, *Lower Canada 1791–1840: Social Change and Nationalism* (Toronto: McClelland and Stewart 1980), 312
15 Elinor Senior, *Redcoats and Patriotes: The Rebellions in Lower Canada 1837–38* (Ottawa: Canada's Wings 1985), 159

patriots' best hope lay in provoking war between Britain and the United States. With this goal in mind, Nelson and Côté led an incursion north from Vermont in late February, intending to capture a piece of Lower Canada, declare it an independent republic, and then appeal for American assistance as well as Canadian insurrection. The plan was foiled by vigilant anglo-Canadian militiamen, however, and the retreating patriots were arrested by the U.S. army. Evidently, the American government was not willing to risk war with Britain, however much the people of the border states sympathized with the Canadian revolutionaries.

Facing repressive measures on both sides of the international boundary, Patriot leaders eventually turned to clandestine organization. A secret society, the 'Frères chasseurs' ('Hunters' Lodges'), was formed, with branches in Lower Canada and the northern states. The rituals were basically masonic, with passwords and secret hand signs, all reminiscent of the Italian *carbonari* and other revolutionary conspiracies of the reactionary post-Napoleonic years in Europe.[16] Canadian motifs were much in evidence among the Hunters: for example, officers were called 'castors' (beavers), while non-commissioned officers were 'raquettes' (snowshoes). Moreover, habitant members often referred to the lodges as 'confréries,' unconsciously assimilating the revolutionary brotherhood with the devotional confraternities that played such an important part in French-Canadian religious life.[17]

Though established and commanded by middle-class Patriots based in Montreal and in the border towns of the northern states, the Hunters' Lodges quickly attracted a mass following, particularly among the habitants of the District of Montreal. In this respect they differed from the *carbonari*-style conspiracies of

16 See E.J. Hobsbawm, *The Age of Revolution 1789–1848* (New York: Signet 1962), 144–5.
17 See, for example, ANQ, 1837, no. 1664, déposition de Louis Favreau, 27 November 1838.

Europe which remained small and elitist. Through the summer of 1838, men (the chasseurs seem to have been exclusively male) took the oath by the thousands. Each recruit was taken blindfolded to a darkened room where he swore a blood-chilling oath promising not to reveal the society's secrets on pain of having his throat cut 'to the bone.' Plebeian chasseurs who were later arrested generally acknowledged that the purpose of the society was to 'overthrow the government of the province and have a republic in its place.'[18] Some seem to have seen their adherence to the Hunters as an act analogous to taking the government's oath of allegiance; one man spoke of having 'taken the oath of allegiance to the new order.'[19] And many claimed to have joined the organization for the same reason that they swore fidelity to her majesty the previous winter: to avoid punishment. Antoine Grégoire told the examining magistrates after the defeat of the Hunters' conspiracy that he had joined because a neighbour had warned him 'that all those who were not part of this association their lives and their properties were in peril.'[20] Given the circumstances of Grégoire's testimony, this seems a suspiciously convenient excuse, but it is quite likely that fear of retribution was one of the motives – in some cases perhaps the major motive – leading men to take the chasseur oath.

With such large numbers involved (there is no precise count), it was impossible to keep the secret conspiracy entirely secret. The curé of Napierville was writing to his bishop in August about the processions of carriages making the twenty-five-kilo-

18 Ibid., no. 2433, examen volontaire de Joseph-Armand Hébert, 7 December 1838. Another man spoke of 'overthrowing the government of the queen in order to join the Americans of the United States.' Ibid., no. 1487, déposition de Joseph Archambault, 28 November 1838. More common was the idea of having a government *like* that of the United States, rather than actually joining the American union.

19 Ibid., no. 2433, examen volontaire de Joseph-Armand Hébert, 7 December 1838 (author's translation)

20 Ibid., no. 1389, déposition d'Antoine Grégoire, 26 November 1838 (author's translation)

metre trek to Champlain, New York, every Sunday to take 'mass' (i.e., the Hunters' oath) from Dr Côté. In and around Chateauguay, 250 men were sworn in on a single day.[21] A patriot turned government spy gave a clear warning that the essential aims of the organization commanded popular support.

Having resided in the country all summer, I must say that the people are, for the most part, ripe for revolution, and that the indecision and want of firmness and courage, which they have shewn under certain circumstances, are only to be attributed to a sense of inferiority in discipline and military organization in arms. The counties of L'Acadie, Rouville, Laprairie, Terrebonne, Vaudreuil, and Two Mountains, and a good number in the town and county of Montreal, are disposed for a radical change in the Government, and nothing has made them more so than the affairs of St. Charles and St. Eustache. The destruction of life and property, far from suppressing the fire of rebellion, has only heightened it.[22]

The authorities were well aware by the fall that something sinister was in the offing, but no one knew its exact nature until the very eve of the Hunters' attack.

Though repression had been severe in the immediate wake of the 1837 fighting, the colonial government could hardly be considered a police state. Indeed, mechanisms of surveillance and control were quite ineffective by modern standards, particularly in the countryside. The corps of provincial magistrates had at least been purged of patriots, but even 'loyal' JPs such as Simon Talon dit Lespérance were not exactly reliable instruments of the state. Scattered detachments of troops were useful for deterring only the most overt forms of revolt. Sir John Colborne's main source of information was a group of sixteen army officers who

21 Amiot to Lartigue, 20 August 1838, quoted in Pierre Brault, *Histoire de L'Acadie du Haut Richelieu* (St-Jean-sur-Richelieu: Editions Mille Roches 1982), 192; NA, Durham Papers, 21: 953, Grey to Durham, 19 December 1838
22 *Report of the State Trials*, 2: 556, testimony of an unnamed prisoner, November 1838

arrived from Britain in March 1838 and stationed themselves in various villages and small towns of Lower Canada.[23] Patriots considered them 'spies,' but of course they could collect only the most rudimentary sort of intelligence, reporting on public sentiment and activities that were common knowledge in their localities. It might seem strange to characterize the régime as 'repressive' when it had such limited ability to observe the populace, but in fact the heavy-handed and rather indiscriminate punishment visited on the rebellious regions was partly the result of this very weakness. Deficiencies in this area also explain the government's failure to root out the Hunters' Lodges until after they had made their move in an ill-fated coup d'état in the autumn of 1838.

THE RISING OF NOVEMBER 1838

The night of 3–4 November was eventually settled upon for a rising of patriot chasseurs within Lower Canada, with a simultaneous invasion from the south led by Nelson and Côté. The complicated details of this botched enterprise can best be followed in Elinor Senior's *Redcoats and Patriotes*. For our purposes, a brief summary of the main events will suffice. Nelson and Côté managed to establish a substantial armed camp at Napierville and maintain it for about a week. Meanwhile, patriots at Beauharnois attacked and occupied Bear Ellice's seigneurial manor, capturing the seigneur's son and his agent. Several hundred men also assembled at various points along the Richelieu, though they dispersed without undertaking any attacks on the military forts of the region. Another major mobilization occurred in the Châteauguay area; anxious to secure their position, the patriots here set out to disarm local loyalists and to neutralize the Iroquois of Sault St Louis. There was some fighting at Beauharnois, where the insurgents carried the day, but bloodier encounters followed a few days later when the insurgents fought to keep open the lines of communication between Napierville and the U.S.

23 Senior, *Redcoats and Patriotes*, 154

border. In engagements at Lacolle and Odelltown, the patriots were defeated by loyalist militia with about seventy casualties in all.

Some 1,500 men assembled at Napierville, most of them habitants summoned from the surrounding parishes. A large flag flew from the local militia captain's pole, its two blue stars representing the twin republics of Upper and Lower Canada. Robert Nelson and C.-H.-O. Côté presided at the camp, struggling to preserve order while they vainly awaited the cannon and small arms needed to begin offensive operations. Meanwhile, there were speeches, in which anti-feudal themes were prominent. 'Doctor Côté harangued the patriots and told them that they would be free and independent and would pay no more rents to the seigneurs or tithes to the priests,' recalled one listener.[24] All indications are that Nelson and Côté gained enormous credit among the habitants as a result of their clear stand on the land-tenure question, enough perhaps to make up for the fact that they lacked the support of L.-J. Papineau's prestige and charisma. Rank-and-file insurgents made no secret of their anti-feudal aspirations. The prisoners they held at Beauharnois reported that the main object of the embattled peasants was to abolish rents, lods et ventes, and tithes.[25]

Hostility to English-speakers and to native Indians was also more in evidence in 1838 than it had been during the crisis of the previous year. In the vicinity of La Prairie and Châteauguay bands of Hunters systematically called on the homes of 'inhabitants of British origin,' confiscating firearms and in many cases taking the men captive.[26] To some extent this was a matter of neutralizing active Volunteers who had proved themselves to be

24 ANQ, 1837, no. 1231, déposition d'Isaac Lecuier, 11 November 1838 (author's translation). See also ibid., no. 2437, examen volontaire de Jacques David Hébert, 7 December 1838.
25 *Report of the State Trials*, 1: 314, 1: 318, 2: 162, testimony of David Norman, Robert Orr Wilson, and David M'Clennaghan
26 Ibid., 1: 25–30, testimony of John M'Donald and passim.

dangerous enemies in 1837, but it does appear that people were targeted purely on the basis of ethnic origin. Blood was spilt in one ugly incident at La Tortue. Here three men gathered their families together in David Vitty's farmhouse and foolishly attempted to resist the patriot forces. Vitty fired on the intruders as they smashed through the door and in the ensuing gun battle he was wounded in four places and his neighbour Aaron Walker was shot dead.[27]

On that same night of 3–4 November a potentially more serious confrontation was taking place at the Iroquois village of Sault St Louis (now called Kahnawake). Most of the inhabitants of this community were Mohawk, and their relations with their French-Canadian neighbours were not good. Since the seventeenth century, when both French and Iroquois had first established settlements in the area, their relations had been marked by mutual mistrust. Land was the focus of much discord. Habitants from La Prairie, Chateauguay, and St Constant over the years had occupied large stretches of territory that the natives believed were theirs.[28] There were no violent incidents in this gradual encroachment; instead, ill-defined boundaries and the connivance of the Jesuit seigneurs of Sault St Louis allowed the settlers to nibble away at the edges of the Iroquois reserve. Resentment simmered for generations and, since occasions for friendly contact between natives and French Canadians were quite limited, nothing counteracted its effects. Though no more prejudiced against natives than other North American settlers of European origin, the habitants of the region seem to have disdained close contact with their 'sauvage' neighbours. Not surprisingly, long-standing tensions and underlying conflict bubbled to the surface during the disturbed years of rebellion.

The troubles of November 1837 had caused alarm in Kahna-

27 Ibid., 1: 227–92
28 Denys Delâge, 'Les Iroquois chrétiens des "réductions," 1667–1770: I – Migration et rapports avec les Français,' *Recherches amérindiennes au Québec* 21 (1991): 66–8

wake, but there was no actual fighting. Rumours had circulated to the effect that men from the surrounding parishes were planning to attack the reserve, kill all the Indians, and take their lands.[29] There is of course no way of knowing where the report originated, but it is easy to see why the Iroquois would take it seriously. In fact, the local patriots, even if they did harbour evil schemes, would have been insane to pick a fight with the Mohawks just when armed conflict with Great Britain seemed imminent. The missionary priest at Sault St Louis believed that the patriots were simply trying to frighten the Indians into staying out of the impending civil war, and, if indeed they were the source of these threats (which is by no means certain), this seems the most plausible explanation. The Christian Indians of the St Lawrence valley had long had a special relationship with the colonial government. Under France and later under England, men from Oka and Sault St Louis had played a prominent military role in the North American wars of empire, and the successive imperial regimes made every effort to foster their loyalty through grants of economic assistance in peacetime. The patriots then had good reason to fear that the Indians in their midst might be employed against them as military auxiliaries of the crown.

Yet the people of Kahnawake, like the natives at Oka and in other parts of the province, were not as firmly attached to the government at this time as they had been in the past. An increasingly parsimonious Indian department was cutting back on the quantity and quality of presents and medical aid, and the resulting complaints were loud and bitter.[30] The Patriots accordingly had a golden opportunity to neutralize the Indians as a military threat, or even to enlist their active support, by taking up native grievances and welcoming Indians into the anti-government

29 ACESJQ, 3A/187, Marcoux to Lartigue, 13 November 1837; NA, LC Civil Secretary, 524: 91, Marcoux to Napier, 17 November 1837
30 Rainer Baehre, ' "Melting Like Snow before the Sun": Canadian Indians and the Cholera Epidemics, 1832–34,' unpublished paper presented to the Canadian Historical Association, May 1990, 4–8

movement. To be fair, there do seem to have been some Patriot efforts in this direction. They were effective enough that at St Regis (Akwesasne), on the border of Upper and Lower Canada, one party in that deeply divided Iroquois community rallied to the cause of Papineau.[31] For the people of Oka and Kahnawake, however, the overtures came too late for anyone to be convinced of their sincerity. As a parliamentary party, the pre-1837 Patriots had shown little interest in the fate of Lower Canada's Indian population.

Thus it was in an atmosphere of the deepest distrust that the Indians and French Canadians of the south shore confronted one another in the middle of November 1837. With many of their men away on winter hunting expeditions, the Iroquois naturally felt exposed and vulnerable when they heard of the threatened invasion. They responded with menaces of their own, combined with conciliatory messages. The Indians would stay neutral in any civil war, they assured the Patriot chiefs of La Prairie, but, if they were attacked, they would call on 'les nations d'en haut' to lay waste the surrounding countryside. The patriots replied that they had no aggressive intentions, and for the moment peace was maintained here even when fighting broke out in other parts of the province. The atmosphere of mutual misunderstanding remained, however, now truly poisoned with deadly suspicions. The men of Kahnawake determined to stay close to home in the future, and the stage was set for more serious confrontations when insurrection erupted once more in November 1838.

Frères chasseurs were exceptionally thick on the ground in Châteauguay, the parish next to Sault St Louis, and they assembled in large numbers on the night when the rising began. One of their first acts was to send a large detachment to Kahnawake. 'We understood that the Indians were coming against us, so we wished to get their arms,' testified one of the habitants involved.[32] The raid was a disastrous failure. The

31 NA, Colborne Papers, 11: 2952–5, Phillpotts to Colborne, 17 November 1837
32 *Report of the State Trials*, 1: 42

Mohawks had enough warning to take to the woods at the approach of the intruders and, under cover of darkness, surrounded them completely before the patriots knew what was happening. The insurgent leader tried to talk his way out of the predicament by explaining that his men had no intention of harming the natives, but to no avail. Without a shot being fired, the intimidated militiamen were soon convinced to lay down their arms, and before most of Lower Canada knew that an insurrection was under way, sixty-four of them were bound up and on their way to prison in Montreal.[33] This was not the first episode of white-Indian conflict in the Kahnawake/Châteauguay area, nor would it be the last.

The encounter at Sault St Louis was a terrible set-back for the patriot cause, and it set the tone for the 1838 rising generally. Though it succeeded in taking General Colborne and his administration by surprise, the Hunters' offensive quickly began to unravel through a combination of bad luck, poor coordination, and the surprisingly effective efforts of the loyalist militia in stopping supplies from bases across the border. Colborne had more than enough troops at his disposal – and they could be reinforced at a moment's notice with Glengarry Highlanders from eastern Upper Canada – to deal with the insurgents. The patriots at Napierville melted away as these forces came bearing down upon them. The British soldiers were therefore able to occupy all the rebel positions south of the St Lawrence without a fight and turn their attention to the business of chastising and pacifying the insurgent countryside.

The patriot military failure of 1838 was even more dismal than that of the previous year. In 1837 the mobilization and fighting had been an impromptu affair: fragmented, localized, and defensive. The second rising was quite different: an offensive operation featuring clearly defined political goals and an elaborate military strategy. This in turn entailed authority, hierarchy, a command structure inevitably dominated by middle-class elements, and

33 Senior, *Redcoats and Patriotes*, 127, 170

therefore a less conspicuous role for the parish republics of the countryside. The habitant grass-roots were not organically implicated in the insurrectionary developments of 1838 to anything like the degree they had been in 1837; yet this was by no means a socially isolated coup d'état. Côté and Nelson required the active and voluntary participation of the peasantry, and their radically democratic and anti-feudal program demonstrates their commitment to maintain the patriots as a truly popular movement. All indications are that support for the insurrection was high in rural French Canada, though it evaporated quickly when it became apparent that the plot had misfired. And why did the plans go so badly awry? In large measure because they were overly elaborate and therefore excessively dependent on the successful coordination of several elements (movement of men and supplies over the border, rapid capture of several forts, cutting of communications along the St Lawrence). Defeated in 1837 partly through a lack of central direction, the patriots suffered from the opposite problem in 1838.

While it is important to recognize the specific circumstances leading to British victories in the two major episodes of fighting, it is fair to say that the overall defeat of the patriots was also determined by some basic factors present throughout the 1837-8 period. The revolutionary movement was weakened by the fact that it tended to alienate major elements of the Lower Canadian population, including women, natives, and English speakers. Moreover, for a variety of reasons the patriots were weak (though not necessarily unpopular) in the province's cities. Finally, and perhaps most decisively, the fight for an independent Lower Canada took place in the most unfavourable international circumstances. Britain was close to the peak of its power and well able, given the absence of major wars at the time, to devote whatever military resources were needed to keep Canada within its empire. Only with significant help from external allies, therefore, could the patriots have hoped to prevail. Given the relative weakness of the radical element in Upper Canada, this meant in practice that assistance from the United States was crucial. The American government's determination to preserve peace with

Great Britain consequently sealed the fate of revolution in Canada.

AFTERMATH

Though significant armed conflict ended with the British victory of November 1838, intense anti-government sentiments remained widespread, particularly in the rural District of Montreal. It continued in the face of repression that made the punitive measures following the earlier round of fighting seem mild in comparison. Houses were once again put to the torch: eighty homes were destroyed at Napierville, twenty at Chateauguay, and Beauharnois was 'completely gutted.' One British officer found these reprisals a 'most painful duty. I cannot bear to see the poor wretches of women and children when their husbands are dragged away by the Volunteers and in many cases the houses of these unfortunate people generally burnt by the Volunteers whom it is quite impossible to prevent retaliating for the fright they have been in.'[34] More significant was the extensive pillaging carried on by regulars and loyalist Volunteers in the actively rebellious area west of the Richelieu and south of the St Lawrence. Most notorious were the Scots of the Glengarry regiment of Upper Canada, who apparently stole 800 horses in the space of a few days: 'On their march from Beauharnois towards the major rebel encampment at Napierville, the Glengarries boasted that they left a trail six miles wide as they came along "burning and pillaging." ' In the words of an anti-patriot Montrealer, 'The Glengarries made war like Cosacks.'[35]

There were also arrests, on a larger scale and with less dis-

34 Colonel Charles Grey, quoted in Elinor Senior, 'Dragooning the Disaffected' (unpublished paper kindly provided by the author)
35 Elinor Senior, 'Suppressing Rebellion in Lower Canada: British Military Policy and Practice, 1837–1838,' Canadian Defence Quarterly 17 (Spring 1988): 54, 53; McCord Museum, de Rocheblave Collection, Bouthillier to de Rocheblave, 24 November 1838

crimination than in 1837. The official records show 851 political prisoners committed to the Montreal jail after 4 November 1838, but it seems that many more were taken into unrecorded custody for days or weeks in other parts of the region.[36] Olivier Gagnez, for example, an habitant living in the predominantly anglophone seigneurie of Lacolle, tried to join the local loyalist Volunteer corps at the earliest stage of the Rebellion. His services were rejected, however, because he did not understand English; instead, he was locked in jail for two days on the grounds that, 'as a [French] Canadian, he might be forced to march with the patriots.'[37] Arrests were truly indiscriminate in some localities. On Sunday morning, 11 November, Volunteers took away all the men leaving church at St Valentin.[38] Elsewhere, troops and Volunteers arrested anyone – or at least any French Canadian – they encountered in the road. Thus, one man who claimed to be going to his father-in-law's barn to thresh grain and another on his way to fetch a doctor for his sick wife were taken into custody. They were in prison for four weeks and six weeks, respectively, before they were given an opportunity to explain themselves to a magistrate.[39] An agricultural labourer picked up under similar circumstances – 'under suspicion' because he was abroad after dark – was shot dead when he tried to run away.[40]

As in the previous year, the majority of prisoners were released without charges or trial after periods of incarceration

---

36 ANQ, 1837, no. 3101, 'List of the names of the State Prisoners ... '
37 Ibid., no. 1145, examen volontaire d'Olivier Gagnez, 22 November 1838 (author's translation). Other instances of arbitrary arrest strictly on the grounds of French-Canadian nationality are even more striking. See ibid., no. 1780, examen volontaire de Pierre Héroux, 8 December 1838.
38 Statement of Curé Théberge, in Gugy, *Incidents in the Life of a Provincial*, 16; ANQM, Affaires Criminelles, examen volontaire de Jean-Baptiste St Amand, 21 December 1838
39 ANQ, 1837, no. 1224, examen volontaire de Germain Choinard, 22 December 1838; ANQM, Affaires Criminelles, voluntary examination of Pierre Massé, 4 December 1838
40 ACESJQ, 17A/36, Moll to bishop, 20 November 1838

ranging from a few weeks to a few months. This time, however, the government was determined and confident enough (confident, that is, that it could carry out the death penalty without provoking dangerous reactions) to place some of the more seriously implicated on 'trial. Needless to say, juries, together with most of the other inconvenient legal safeguards that the accused normally counted on under the British system of justice, were out of the question. Instead, the authorities had recourse to the extraordinary device of a court martial to try civilians. During the first half of 1839, 111 men faced charges of high treason and, of these, twelve were eventually hanged and another fifty-eight transported to Australia.[41]

The less publicly visible, but far more widespread, forms of punishment – the plunder, destruction, and arrests visited upon the rural District of Montreal – were, as always, directed by a mixture of private and official motives. There can be no doubt, however, that the government and military command intended to terrorize the population into submission. Lieutenant-Colonel George Cathcart, in command of her majesty's forces at Chambly received clear orders to cow the local populace in the wake of the insurrection by conducting needless house searches and other harassing devices.[42] By the beginning of 1839 the punitive measures were subsiding, indicating that the authorities felt confident that the immediate threat had passed, although large numbers of troops remained in the disaffected areas. Quartered as they were among a sullenly hostile rural population, the soldiers were bound to commit a certain number of outrages. Among the recorded incidents can be found a gang-rape by soldiers of the 71st Regiment, as well as the repeated stabbing of an unarmed and unresisting prisoner. In a third case a dragoon sergeant entered an habitant's house, and 'without any manner of provocation he discharged a pistol at the owner and

41 Senior, *Redcoats and Patriotes*, 201–2
42 Michael Mann, *A Particular Duty: The Canadian Rebellions 1837–1839*
   (Salisbury: Michael Russell 1986), 129–30

subsequently laid the man's cheek open with a blow of that weapon.'[43] Under the circumstances, it is unremarkable that thousands left the province for the United States, and that those who remained were intimidated but not thoroughly 'pacified' (to employ the counter-insurgency vocabulary of the Vietnam era).

In order to reduce the irritation and random oppression inseparable from a purely military occupation and, more generally, to bolster the government's claim to legitimacy and authority, a mounted police force was organized in early 1839 for service in the rural District of Montreal.[44] With between 200 and 300 constables, supervised by professional stipendiary magistrates, the Rural Police had an explicitly political function. Of course they pursued robbers and arrested murderers as required; even if crime of this sort was extremely rare in the French-Canadian countryside, such activity did demonstrate the general utility of the law and the equity of the police. More important, the police troopers seemed able to take political suspects into custody without the energetic application of bayonets. Above all, they were charged with keeping a close watch on political activity and preventing the church-porch oratory that had played such a central part in forging an anti-government movement in recent years. When contemplating a reduction in the size of the force, the commissioner of the Rural Police warned that 'The first consequence of such a measure would be to ensure impunity to certain popular orators and apostles of sedition who are now restrained by the police.'[45]

The stipendiary magistrates and policemen had enough sophistication to realize that there was more to the patriot movement

43 NA, LC Stipendiary Magistrates, vol. 2, Quesnel to Goldie, 1 January 1839; ibid., Gugy to Coffin, 17 January 1839; ibid., Gugy to Goldie, 25 March 1839. All these incidents occurred in 1839, it should be noted, long after the heat of battle had subsided.
44 For more on the police, see Allan Greer, 'The Birth of the Police in Canada,' in Colonial Leviathan: State Formation in Mid-Nineteenth-Century Canada, ed. Allan Greer and Ian Radforth (Toronto: UTP 1992), 17–49.
45 NA, LC Stipendiary Magistrates vol. 3, Gugy to Murdoch, 4 November 1839

than middle-class rabble-rousing however. They set out to regulate not only overtly political meetings, but gatherings of almost any sort, demonstrating in the process that they were aware of the role of community life and habitant popular culture in sustaining the revolutionary challenge to colonial rule. At La Prairie the stipendiary magistrate banned the annual festival of the parish's patron saint, while a vigilant police sergeant flushed out equally dangerous activities late one night at St Césaire. 'I found in the residence of Bats. Bellere,' he reported, 'a large assembly of people of the worst description who had a drum, triangle, and two fidelles playing.' The police also seem to have done their best to break up the Sunday afternoon socializing that brought together normally scattered habitants after the celebration of mass. At least one country priest expressed his appreciation for these repressive efforts: 'Previous to their coming the people collected in large numbers, before, and after church, the public houses filled on Sundays, which has not occurred since.' The new magistrates were particularly inclined to target taverns, reducing the number of licensed establishments and cracking down on licensing infractions. There were political, as well as moral, grounds for regulating these 'hotbeds of idleness, immorality and disaffection': 'Independent of the dissipation engendered by this practice, Sunday, from the occupations of the habitants, is the only day upon which they can meet in any numbers, and their meeting under such circumstances, cannot but be productive of evil.'[46]

The first, but not the last, mounted police force in Canadian history to take on the job of containing political disaffection, the Lower Canadian Rural Police discharged this duty from 1839 to 1842. They met with little or no active opposition during that time, but they were supported by the immense deterrent effect of the British military forces, still at peak strength. Knowing they

46 ANQ, 1837, no. 3725, Weatherall to Goldie, 10 September 1839; ANQM, Affaires Criminelles, vol. 50, Brown to Chaffers, 22 May 1839; ibid., Hanson to Coffin, 19 March 1839; ANQ, 1837, no. 3575, Coffin to Goldie, 23 August 1839

could call on the soldiery in case of need, the police were supposed to present a firm but comparatively benign face to the populace. Urging stipendiary magistrates to offer advice and assistance to the habitants, over-optimistic officials hoped the former might be successful in 'gaining the confidence of the people, and in destroying the pernicious influence which produced the disturbances of 1837 and 1838.' Indeed, there were no more serious attacks against the colonial régime once the Rural Police began operations, but it is clear that this was not because the new institution had really won over 'hearts and minds.' A sensible stipendiary magistrate wrote a year after the 1838 insurrection:

I cannot however report that the tranquillity which exists is the result of any alteration of the political opinions of the People. On the contrary, I believe that, in addition to the existence of the feeling which has shown itself in open rebellion, they are now labouring under a sense of sullen disappointment and of disgrace at the failure of their illegal proceedings which would break into open resistance to the Government if a favourable opportunity offered. ... I attribute the present tranquillity of the district entirely to the presence of the Rural Police; to the fact that no illegal meeting can be held without their knowledge ... and to the immediate assistance of a military force if required.[47]

This depressed and alienated 'tranquillity' continued into the early 1840s, and in the absence of further active resistance, the authorities were able to disband the rural police in 1842 and reduce the British military presence in the province.

RESULTS

Meanwhile, the authoritarian régime of the Special Council (1838–41) had a free hand to govern Lower Canada without

47 *Rules for the government of the Rural Police* (Montreal: James Starke 1839), 5; ANQ, 1837, no. 3731, Weatherall to Civil Secretary, 14 November 1839. See also ibid., no. 3554, Coleman to Assistant Civil Secretary, 21 March 1839.

regard to the views of the population. Though restrained in many respects, the government-appointed legislature did not play the role of a neutral caretaker. Instead, it enacted far-reaching programs of political, legal, and institutional reform, with changes (e.g., to town councils and to land tenure on the island of Montreal) that favoured the interests of the urban business community.[48]

Lord Durham's 'Report on the Affairs of British North America' appeared in 1839, calling for the unification of Lower Canada with the predominantly English Upper Canada in order to end 'racial' conflict by anglicizing the French Canadians. The Act of Union did amalgamate the two provinces in 1841 and its thrust was unmistakable. In framing the act British parliamenarians did cheat a little on Durham's strictly liberal plan; for example, they weighted representation in the legislature of the new 'Province of Canada' in favour of voters in the former Upper Canada. Clearly the aim was not only to institute linguistic uniformity and political harmony in the long run, but also, in the short run, to marginalize the French Canadians politically. Regardless of how exactly it was implemented, the union was immensely unpopular, and certainly it would not have gone ahead had it required the approval of any Lower Canadian representative body like the pre-Rebellion Assembly. In this respect, among others, the counter-revolutionary settlement of the early 1840s has had a significant and lasting effect on the course of Canadian history. Over the dead body of democratic republicanism Lower Canada was locked into a larger, predominantly anglophone unit, and ever since the relationship has been a source of discomfort, trouble, and periodic crises.

The grand sweep of French-Canadian history and Canada's modern constitutional problems lie outside the scope of this book, which began with a focus on rural Lower Canada, scene of

48 Brian Young, 'Positive Law, Positive State: Class Realignment and the Transformation of Lower Canada, 1815–1866,' in *Colonial Leviathan* ed. Greer and Radforth, 50–63

the major episodes of the drama of 1837–8. How did life in the countryside change after the defeat of the patriots? To begin with, habitants had to contend with a more energetic and intrusive state. The advent of the Rural Police heralded this change in a dramatic, though temporary, fashion. Later, municipal institutions and public school facilities would increasingly place communities under state tutelage to a degree unknown in the past. Expanded and strengthened in the mid-century decades, the colonial state was scarcely opened to women in the wake of the Rebellion. The ideology of female domesticity and of an exclusively male 'public sphere,' though championed with pioneering energy by the Patriots, survived their downfall and flourished in the 1840s and 1850s.

The Catholic Church, another major winner in the post-Rebellion settlement, also grew in power, influence, and institutional elaboration. Rural areas increasingly felt the presence not only of a reinforced corps of parish priests, but also of newly established colleges and convents, as well as cleric-dominated temperance associations, charities, missionary organizations, and so on, all determined to bring about the spiritual and moral rebirth of the peasantry.[49] Almost a quasi-state, and at the same time an influential partner of the state, the French-Canadian Church of the mid-nineteenth century did its part in subjecting rural society to outside supervision. Something of this sort occurred in other

49 See, among other works, Louis Rousseau, 'Les missions populaires de 1840–42: acteurs principaux et conséquences,' Société canadienne d'histoire de l'Eglise catholique, *Sessions d'Etudes*, 1986, 7–21. It should be noted that the Church, unlike the state and the political parties, did have a place for women. The Catholic Church as a whole was of course still run by men and dedicated to an ideology stressing the maternal and nurturing role of women. Nevertheless, there was still room for female activity outside the strictly domestic sphere; particularly in the realms of charity, education, and medical care, the numerous religious orders offered significant outlets for ambitious girls. See Marta Danylewycz, *Taking the Veil: An Alternative to Marriage, Motherhood, and Spinsterhood in Quebec, 1840–1920* (Toronto: McClelland and Stewart 1987).

Catholic countries in the nineteenth century, but in Lower Canada/Quebec the forces of democratic secularism had been badly weakened (which was not the case in, e.g., Third-Republic France or Mexico under Juarez), and they were consequently unable to offset the pervasive conservative influence of the clergy.[50]

Would developments really have been all that different, as far as the autonomy of rural communities is concerned, had the middle-class Patriots succeeded in overthrowing the British colonial régime and setting up their own independent republic? If the history of the French Revolution is any guide, one can well imagine a triumphant patriot régime thrusting the 'civilizing' and regulating tentacles of a bourgeois state out into the French-Canadian countryside just as surely as any bishop or imperial administrator. Indeed such a scenario seems to accord well with the elitist inclinations of chiefs like Louis-Joseph Papineau or Amury Girod. But once we embark on the path of counter-factual speculation, we cannot stop simply because we have identified the orientation of the leaders; we must also consider whether they would still have been leaders in the event of a patriot victory. In the case of Papineau and Girod, there is every reason to doubt it. The patriots clearly derived their strength, such as it was in 1837–8, mainly from the voluntary adhesion of the habitants, and this fact bolstered the position within the movement of bourgeois radicals, such as C.-H.-O. Côté, who were committed to a genuinely popular and democratic revolution. More to the point, it greatly enhanced the power and influence of the peasantry in the

50 Certainly the *Rouge* party, along with cultural organizations like the Institut canadien, struggled to maintain a liberal and anti-clerical presence in the generations that followed the defeat of the Rebellion. See, particularly, Jean-Paul Bernard, *Les Rouges* (Montreal: Presses de l'Université du Québec 1971). However, the radicalism of the *rouges* had much less purchase than did that of the Patriots outside the middle class. And its struggle against the entrenched clerical and monied elites of the second half of the nineteenth century was, of necessity, defensive and limited in its practical objectives.

patriot revolution. After mobilizing the political and military potential of the habitants, the politicians of the professional middle class could hardly have imposed an iron rule on their former allies. It seems most likely, therefore, that any new patriot state would have had a large place for the rural plebeians, their needs, and aspirations.

One can speculate endlessly on what might have been. All we know for sure is that the 'other side' prevailed: in the wake of the Rebellion, it was the colonial administrators, the Catholic clerics, and the various Constitutionalist elements, rather than the patriots, who enjoyed the ascendancy. These groups had never mobilized the habitant majority, and consequently they owed them nothing – indeed, less than nothing. It is little wonder that their forays into the countryside were strictly authoritarian, and that the subsequent modernization of rural French Canada took place under conservative auspices. After 1840 the efforts of virtually all 'educated' outsiders were directed towards neutralizing the peasantry's political potential, rather than encouraging the development of its democratic and progressive potential.

Meanwhile, the men of the professional middle class who had provided the parliamentary leadership of the patriot movement rapidly abandoned their democratic populism. Chastened by defeat and imprisonment, those who had not been permanently exiled or otherwise marginalized tended to make their peace with the prevailing order. Many, such as Louis-Hippolyte LaFontaine and George-Etienne Cartier, resumed their political careers and moved further and further into the conservative camp of urban business and Catholic hierarchy. The habitants and villagers were thus left with no significant allies among the educated and the influential who were prepared to lead them in democratic directions. Does this mean that rural folk settled into a life of obedience and harmony, as their 'betters' hoped they would once the rabble-rousers had stopped preaching sedition? Not at all! Lower Canada (or Canada East as it was then called) became a much more violent place in the 1840s and 1850s than it had been in the 1830s.

A typical disorder was the 'guerre des éteignoirs' (candle-snufı fers' war) that shook the southern District of Trois-Rivières from 1849 to 1851.[51] The attempt to impose school taxes in this region led to massive resistance in the form of mob violence and arson. This was almost entirely the work of habitants, rallying around traditional notions of local independence. Though they had the sympathy of some of the region's 'notables,' the rioters were opposed by an alliance – unthinkable fifteen years earlier – of government officials, priests, and professional men. Wendie Nelson, the historian of the candle-snuffers' war, argues that the éteignoirs were not as retrograde as they seem; rather than fighting to extinguish the flame of learning as the sobriquet implies, they were simply defending their right to organize schooling without central government interference. This may be true; yet the contrast is striking between the aims and procedures of the candle-snuffers and those of the habitant activists operating in cooperation with middle-class radicals in the summer and autumn of 1837. The desperate anti-statism of the éteignoirs took the form of physical force and arson (as opposed to threats) almost from the outset. More important, they had nothing to propose as an alternative to the hated school law, no positive program of any sort and no apparent interest in issues and principles that went beyond their own communities. The patriot-habitants of 1837, on the other hand, despite all their uncertainties, misunderstandings, and unfamiliarity with formal political philosophy, had begun to connect their own grievances, their own rather narrow aspirations for 'freedom' and 'independence,' to larger political problems.

We see the same pattern of political aimlessness and increasing violence in the post-Rebellion history of the charivari. René Hardy's study of the Trois-Rivières region, 1850–80, indicates that charivari was no longer linked exclusively to marriage and the

51 Wendie Nelson, 'The "Guerre des éteignoirs"': Popular Resistance to School Reform in Lower Canada during the 1840s' (MA thesis, Simon Fraser University, 1989)

sanctity of the wedding rites.[52] Rural Lower Canadians, displaying an intolerant streak not so evident in earlier times, had by
then turned the charivari into an all-purpose weapon for chastising moral transgressions and punishing non-conformists. Sexual
deviants, drunkards, and converts to Protestantism now joined
mismatched couples as common targets of noisy demonstrations.
Moreover, the attacks were much more vicious than they had
been during the insurrection and earlier. Barns were burned and
men were stripped, beaten, and thrown in the river. No longer
did a victim have to resist for a crowd to be provoked into violence: the first notice one villager had of his charivari came in the
form of a whip lashing across his face. There was less emphasis
than in the past on monetary exaction; for many mobs sought,
not a token of surrender, but the expulsion from the community
of an offensive neighbour. In the changed circumstances of the
post-Rebellion era, the charivari form was deployed in radically
new and decidedly more cruel ways.

The consequences of the Rebellion were not entirely negative.
The habitants emerged from this painful crisis with fewer illusions about power and privilege. Certainly any lingering mystique associated with seigneurs and seigneurial tenure was gone
for good. The clamour for an end to feudal exactions became
deafening in the 1840s, and law-makers wisely took heed. Parliamentary complications delayed the passage of remedial legislation for several years, but finally a bill was passed in 1854 to
eliminate seigneurial dues. The 'abolition' settlement was a compromise between Edward Ellice's pro-seigneur approach and the
pure-and-simple extinction proposed by 'Agricola' Côté: the
seigneurs were to be compensated fully for lost revenues, but the
government and the former censitaires would share the costs of
compensation. Certainly the seigneurs would not have fared so
well had the patriots won in 1837–8; on the other hand, the

---

52 René Hardy, 'Le charivari dans la sociabilité rurale québécoise au XIXe
siècle,' in De la sociabilité: Spécificité et mutations (Montreal: Boréal 1990),
59–72

habitants probably would not have gained even the modest benefits allowed them by the law of 1854 had they not given graphic proof of their ability to make serious trouble. In the resolution of the land tenure problem, as in the post-1838 settlement generally, the conservative triumph was less than absolute.

The habitants were indeed defeated. Yet there is something impressive about their performance in the revolutionary drama of 1837–8. A seemingly incoherent mass of 'quiet and obedient subjects,' the peasantry of the District of Montreal mounted a remarkably effective challenge to British imperial rule in Canada. They did so in spite of the institutional poverty of rural French Canada and of its 'individualistic' pattern of family farming. Below this unpromising surface lay a rich and complex community life of ritual, sociability, and discipline, developed over the centuries by the habitants themselves. In every parish webs of interconnection bound together the diverse elements of the peasantry, and a collective spirit, hardened in many cases through fierce disputes with the clergy or the seigneurs, provided the habitants with unsuspected political strength when the revolutionary crisis erupted in 1837. Obviously they were not strong enough to stand for long against the British military onslaught, but they did succeed in putting their own distinctive stamp on the course of the Rebellion.

Picture Credits

Metropolitan Toronto Reference Library, Baldwin Room: Riviere-du-Loup (T16677); National Archives of Canada: Nelson (C133484); British troops (C394); Battle of St Charles (C393); St Denis (C2060); Viger (C18414); Battle of St Eustache (C896, C41981); Girouard (C119981); rebels carried to Montreal (C3613); Papineau (C5462); St Benoit (C133473); patriot militiamen (C13392)

Index